Storyville

Photograph by Ernest Bellocq

THE UNIVERSITY OF ALABAMA PRESS

Al Rose

STORYVILLE, NEW ORLEANS

Being an Authentic, Illustrated Account

of the Notorious Red-Light District

UNIVERSITY, ALABAMA

Permission to quote copyrighted material is gratefully acknowledged to publishers and authors as follows:

Passages from *Hear Me Talkin' to Ya,* edited by Nat Shapiro and Nat Hentoff. Copyright © 1955 by Nat Shapiro and Nat Hentoff. Reprinted by permission of Holt, Rinehart & Winston, Inc.

Passages from *Gumbo Ya Ya* by Lyle Saxon. Copyright © renewed 1973 by the Louisiana State Library. Reprinted by permission of Houghton Mifflin Company.

Passages from *Mister Jelly Roll* by Alan Lomax reprinted by permission of Hawthorn Books, Inc. Copyright © 1950, 1973 by Alan Lomax. All rights reserved.

Passages from *True* magazine, November, 1947. Copyright © 1947.

Photographs by David E. Scherman. Copyright © 1941 by Time, Inc.

Dedicated respectfully to
William Russell

Contents

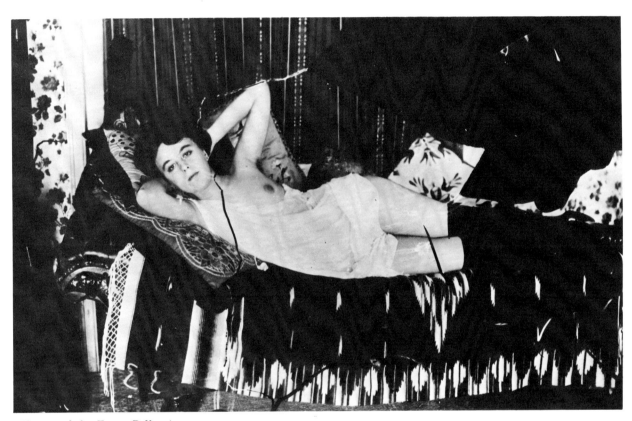

(Photograph by Ernest Bellocq)

Preface

Florence Mantley's

The Latest Octoroons,

215 N. Basin St.

"Storyville," New Orleans' legally established red-light district, existed from January 1, 1898, to the fall of 1917, when it was closed by the United States Department of the Navy, the federal government having decreed, in effect, that only illegal prostitution was to be practiced in the vicinity of its military installations.

I was born in New Orleans just a year before this tyrannical exercise of federal power. The area that had been Storyville was off-limits to me as a child, but I did catch occasional glimpses of its surviving structures. I suppose I was eight or nine years of age before I understood what prostitution was and, with my strict Roman Catholic education, I was sure it was something very nasty. Nevertheless I couldn't fail to notice that many of the adults around me seemed to recall Storyville, "the District," with a certain nostalgia. It became for me a legend of mystery and better times.

In later years, when I sought to learn more about Storyville and its contribution, if any, to the development of early jazz music, it didn't take me long to discover why nobody had ever written a history of the area. The public library's files of newspapers and periodicals had been vandalized, with countless issues carefully clipped, very likely by persons who had a stake in suppressing the information in them. The relevant pages in the real estate plat books in the City Hall had been ripped out. In 1938, the *Times-Picayune* threw out its files of photographs. And during the early 1940s the city fathers went so far in their continuing embarrassment as to change the names of some of Storyville's streets. Thus Basin Street became North Saratoga, Franklin Street became Crozat.

By 1945 the city's boosters at last came to recognize that the jazz myth and the legend of Basin Street's association with it could be promoted as a tourist attraction, whereupon the name Basin Street was formally restored in a ceremony sponsored by the city, the National Jazz Foundation, and *Esquire* magazine. But the most serious damage could not be undone: virtually all of Storyville's buildings had already been demolished to make room for a low-cost housing project. And so it was that the city was deprived of a tourist attraction that would have made millions every year—enough to finance ten or a hundred housing projects.

In recent years, all sorts of people have exhibited a keen interest in the legends and the realities of "the District." I have been queried about the subject by sociologists, psychologists, ethnologists, jazz fans, criminologists, the city councils of two major cities, folklorists, musicologists, artists. A book on the District seems to be needed.

In Herbert Asbury's *The French Quarter: An Informal History of the New Orleans Underworld,* a seductively well-written but often misleading work, Storyville is introduced almost as an afterthought, being covered in only thirty-eight pages out of a total of four hundred sixty-two. Moreover, some of what Asbury wrote about Storyville in those few pages, though he doubt-

less had the best of intentions, is simply untrue. We read for instance, that "On July 17, 1917 the City Council adopted an ordinance establishing a special district for Negro prostitutes in the area bounded by the upper side of Perdido Street, the lower side of Gravier, the river side of South Franklin, and lower side of Locust Street. This act was to have become effective on August 15, but no effort was ever made to enforce it, for segregated vice in New Orleans had already been doomed by America's entrance into the World War."

In point of fact, the ordinance was adopted on February 6, not July 17, and attempts to enforce it were not only made but even went so far as the arrest, trial, and conviction of one of

Storyville's most prominent and popular madams, Countess Willie Piazza. Some of her octoroons were similarly tried and convicted. Many additional errors in Asbury's Storyville chapter could be cited (most notably his belief that all or part of Storyville was in the French Quarter), but little would be accomplished by so doing. The principal value of his book is in the extensive, highly readable coverage of the pre-Storyville centuries, in which factual inaccuracies are by no means lacking but do not seriously detract from his evocation of the period.

In preparing to undertake my own work, in which the principal emphasis would be on Storyville per se, I set about systematically to gather all the information I could to supplement my already fairly extensive but unsystematic fund of knowledge on the subject. Collecting the additional documentary material, conducting the interviews (hundreds of them, over the years), and processing the thousands of photographs took many years and cost a great deal of money. When I had found what I thought was every scrap of knowledge that *could* be found at this late date—every faded print, every yellowed document—I began to put the book together. To my knowledge, not a single additional authentic item has turned up in the past ten years.

Faced with the problem of organizing this mass of data, I became convinced that it should not be presented in conventional narrative form but should be set forth in a way that would make it attractive, interesting, and informative for both general readers and specialists. I wanted readers to be able to start at almost any page and find something of interest.

The publishing house with which I originally contracted for publication of the work did not agree with this concept. They objected, for example, to my inclusion of so much (actually comparatively little) pre-Storyville background material and, as I would later discover, to the no-holds-barred interview material. I felt that without some knowledge of the early history of prostitution in New Orleans readers might not fully understand the significance of Storyville. I finally had to withdraw the manuscript when the publisher insisted, without even consulting me, on "revising" the utterances of some of my interviewees with the apparent intention of changing their meaning and deferring to the censorious.

My next step was to put the manuscript in

the hands of a prominent New York agent, who diligently turned up several lucrative offers, all of which entailed my making radical changes in the form and emphasis of the work. These publishers seemed especially interested in developing the book for greater appeal to the readers' prurient interests. I had to refuse these offers —though I have nothing against anyone's prurient interests—and again took possession of the material.

In 1967, I contracted with yet another publishing house, one seemingly eager to add *Storyville, New Orleans* to its list, but month after month went by without anything being done to further the work. Investigation revealed that a principal in the firm was closely related to a person who figured in the book in a decidedly unheroic role. I had to retain an attorney to retrieve my manuscript and documents from this house, which apparently never really intended to publish the work.

Now, what sort of manuscript was it, that it should suffer such tribulations? It was neatly typed, and the author was at all times sympathetic to the suggestions and proposed revisions of copyeditors, so long as the integrity of quoted material was respected. The various specialist readers consulted by the several publishers all agreed that there was much of great value in the work and that it should be published (although they invariably objected to all that space being given to aspects of the subject that didn't touch their own specialties). At one point the author even agreed, albeit with some misgivings, to permit the manuscript to be rewritten as narrative history by a person of the publisher's own choice—a Pulitzer Prize winner, by the way. The result was a disaster, from the author's standpoint, and even the rewrite man agreed that his labors had not improved things.

This work is not, and was never intended to be, a narrative history of Storyville! It is, rather, an attempt to evoke something of the "feel" of the place—not in poetic or mythic terms, but in the light of facts that have been affirmed, confirmed, and reconfirmed by thousands of documents of various kinds and by personal testimonies (some hundreds of them, mostly unpublished). In the weighing and sifting of this material, a great deal of interesting and colorful detail has been omitted because it could not be substantiated and added nothing essentially new to the picture. If rumors and legends

have been included here and there (that concerning the Countess Piazza's face-lift, for example), they have been identified as such and the reader may believe or disbelieve, as he or she chooses. Here and there, differing accounts of particular events have been juxtaposed so as to allow the reader to weigh the one against the other.

Nor is this book a brief for or against legalization of prostitution or other "victimless crimes" such as exhibition or possession of pornographic materials by adults, possession and use of marihuana by adults, homosexuality among consent-

Miss B. Golden,

213 N. BASIN STREET,
Doing a Large Business on a Small Scale.

ing adults, etc., although the author has strong views on these matters and has even been called as an expert witness in hearings concerning the legalization of some such "crimes." The facts of New Orleans' experiment with legalized prostitution are quite clear, and if one extrapolates from the Storyville experience to the present day, and takes into account the greatly improved anti-V.D. measures, sanitation facilities, etc. of today, one may be led to certain conclusions.

The debatable question of whether prostitution was indeed "legal" in Storyville, or was merely tolerated, is considered in a brief introduction. Readers not interested in this aspect of the subject may safely skip both the introduction and the extensive appendices in which ordinances, legal briefs, and court decisions are reproduced for the delectation of legal specialists. (It should be noted, however, that the *Piazza* case has a present-day interest and "relevance" that transcends the fate of the "Countess.")

Nor is this book a history of "Storyville jazz," and still less of "New Orleans jazz" (which I consider to be the only form of music to which the much-abused term *jazz* may properly be applied). I have sought to give only the highlights, set against a background of the generality. Readers interested in tracing the careers of any

The most popular hard liquor in Storyville was Raleigh Rye. Striped stockings were expensive and could be afforded only by the high-priced bawds of Basin Street. Opera length, the hose were sold by traveling salesmen who, with a tricky demonstration, made them seem run-proof. They cost six dollars a pair and lasted through one or two washings. (Photograph by Ernest Bellocq)

or all of the two hundred or so jazz musicians who played in Storyville at one time or another will find a list of these musicians in an appendix. Accounts of the careers of many can be found in *New Orleans Jazz: A Family Album,* by the present author and the late Dr. Edmond Souchon (Louisiana State University Press, 1967) and in a number of the works mentioned in the bibliographical note elsewhere in this volume. Readers having no interest in the music of Storyville—I assume, and I regret, that there must be such people—may simply skip the music chapter.

Having found it uncongenial to approach this work with the chronological narrative bias of the historian or the novelist, I saw it, rather, as a painter sees a huge mural—yet a mural that could be admired not only from a distance but also with a magnifying glass, should the reader's special interests so motivate him. This approach entails a certain amount of duplication from one chapter to the next, as the same or similar things are viewed several times but from different vantage points. It is not the most "efficient" approach to the subject, perhaps, but it is one to which the richness of the material seems to lend itself, and one that encourages the reader to discover for himself factual relationships and associations that are not set forth explicitly in the way that they would be in a straightforward narrative. You may see this as a disorderly book about disorderly houses—and so it may be. But I doubt whether you will find it dull.

And so, after a dozen years I have found my publisher at last and am gratified to be able to offer this work very much in the form I sought for it when I began.

NEW ORLEANS, LOUISIANA   AL ROSE

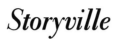

Storyville

Introduction

"Sin"—the deacon's word for sex out of legal wedlock—has always had its large and loyal following. According to recent advices it continues to flourish everywhere despite police, pulpit, and politics. Being so highly valued by so many, it has always been a marketable commodity, with hosts of willing sellers and eager buyers.

At the turn of the present century in America, much of this commerce was being conducted in some hundreds of red-light districts, ranging in size from a discreet "house" or two in or near small towns and cities to block after bawdy block of brothels and worse in larger cities such as Chicago and San Francisco. This book is about the most famous of the large districts, that in the city of New Orleans. Its purpose is to give the reader a reasonably true-to-life impression of "the District"—its people, its music, its press, its rise and decline, its "ways."

The New Orleans red-light district, "Storyville," in the period from January 1, 1898, through November 12, 1917, inclusive, was unique among them all in being the *only* one that was legally established as a district. That is, it was not simply a "house" or two or an area of the city within which prostitution and associated vice flourished because politicians and police "turned their heads" (often in return for illegal financial considerations). It was an area, carefully defined by law, *outside* of which prostitutes and other lewd and abandoned women were not permitted to live or work. The intended effect of the law setting up this District, and its actual effect, was to legalize prostitution inside the District insofar as it was possible to do this within the larger contexts of state and federal law and precedent.

That this was indeed the intention of the lawmakers requires a word of explanation, since the several ordinances passed in the course of establishing the "segregated district" each included words to the effect that nothing in the ordinance was to be construed as legalizing prostitution, etc. in *any* section of the city. The inclusion of this phraseology in all these ordinances has led some writers to conclude that the ordinances did not actually legalize prostitution in the District. This conclusion, though technically correct, is misleading. Paradoxical as it may seem, it was precisely the fact that the final Storyville ordinance, as written, did not positively legalize prostitution in Storyville that in the end made it possible for the courts to find the ordinance, and thus in effect Storyville, "legal."

In enacting the ordinances in question, the city council was mindful of a long history of past efforts to suppress, regulate, or otherwise control prostitution in their city. All such efforts had been largely unsuccessful, for one reason or another, but principally because measures that might have been effective administratively, if enforced, had failed to pass constitutional muster in the appellate courts. What was needed, obviously, was a regulatory ordinance that would be not only effective in controlling vice during the period of time during which the ordinance was in force but one that the appellate courts would permit to remain in force. That is, it was recognized that the most efficient ordinance in the world would be of little value if it were declared to be unconstitutional within six months or a year of its passage.

The city's lawmakers knew from past experience that an ordinance that positively sanctioned or granted license to vice would almost certainly be overturned by the appellate courts on any of several grounds. They were mindful, for instance, of the dictim laid down in Black's *Constitutional Law,* a work widely respected by jurists, beginning: "No person can have any right to engage in the business of gambling, prostitution, or any other avocation which is contra bonos mores. . . ." Their problem was, then, how to draft an ordinance establishing an area within which prostitution would be permitted *de facto,* and thus could be regulated and controlled, without actually stipulating, in so many words, that prostitution would be legal within this area.

That such an analysis of what was required was correct would be proved later by the Supreme Court ruling in the decisive legal test of the Storyville ordinance, the *L'Hote* case. "It is urged [by the plaintiffs]," the court's decision declared, that "the ordinance is a license for vice, and, hence, illegal. . . . Undoubtedly, the Court should refuse its aid to any ordinance, if of the character asserted by [this] argument." However, the court concluded, the ordinance did not sanction or grant a license to vice. It was merely regulatory in nature and so fell within the "competence" of the municipal government. (*L'Hote* vs. *City of New Orleans*, 51 Ann. 93.)

Thus, the argument that the ordinance sanctioned vice could be rejected by the Supreme Court because the ordinance, in addition to specifying the area(s) outside of which prostitutes could not live or work, added that nothing in the ordinance was to be "so construed as to authorize any lewd woman to occupy a house, room or closet in any portion of the city." So far as the wording of the ordinance stipulated, then, prostitution was definitely illegal outside Storyville but was neither legal nor illegal within it. But its existence there being a fact, obviously the city had a right to regulate the terms of its existence.

That the foregoing interpretation of the City Council's intentions is correct is confirmed, in the author's judgment, by the fact that during the course of Storyville's legal existence, before it was closed down by the federal government during the hysteria of World War I, literally everyone in New Orleans concerned with law enforcement and kindred disciplines, including both proponents and opponents of Storyville, seems to have acted on the premise that prostitution as such was legal inside the District and illegal outside it. Some of the prostitutes operating inside the District were arrested from time to time, but not for prostitution; they were arrested on charges of disorderly conduct, theft, and the usual run of misdemeanors and felonies having no necessary connection with their professional activities. Prostitutes found to be working outside the District, however—except for those in a small "District-to-be" delimited in the July 8, 1897, ordinance but postponed for a time (actually until early 1917, but carefully watched by police in the interim)—were put out of business in very short order indeed. *De facto,* prostitutes working within the District were considered to be engaged in legal enterprises so long as they confined themselves to prostitution and to such associated activities as dispensing food and drink to their customers.

If the legal stratagems of the New Orleans city council seem a bit devious, it must be remembered that its members acted out of a sense of, if not desperation, at least frustration, after decades of attempting to deal rationally with a serious social problem only to see their best efforts undone by the appellate courts. Prostitution, as we shall see in the pages to come, had been a problem in New Orleans from the city's earliest days, a problem that had worsened over the years and become a veritable plague in the late 1880s and early 1890s. To understand something of how the problem looked to New Orleanians one has to consider its origins and evolution.

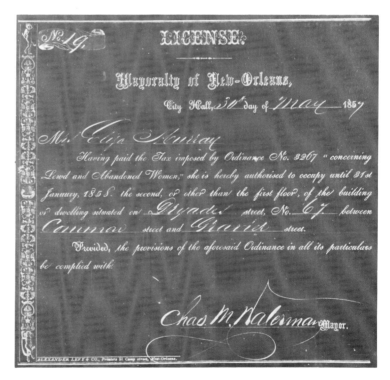

License to operate a brothel, issued May 30, 1857, to Eliza Murray at 67 Dryades Street between Common and Gravier. She paid her fee but got her money back later when ordinance No. 8267 "concerning lewd and abandoned women" was found to be unconstitutional.

ONE

Basin Street Open for Business

Prostitution was a favorite avocation, and for many the profession, of an extraordinarily large proportion of the earliest female residents of New Orleans. These women came to the New World under royal auspices, for it was the French kings Louis XIV and, after 1715, "the Well-Beloved" Louis XV (through his regent, the duke of Orléans), who were, in a manner of speaking, the city's first procurers. As such, they were responsible for transporting to the new French colony of Louisiana many dozens, and indeed hundreds, of prostitutes and other disreputable women—including, it is said, the real-life Manon Lescaut, the prostitute-heroine of Abbé Prevost's celebrated novel.

And if the kings (or in the case of Louis XV, the regent) were procurers, the Mississippi Company of that notorious scoundrel John Law was a white-slave gang—and not merely in a manner of speaking. It was common knowledge that this company, in furtherance of its land promotions, kidnapped innumerable "gypsies" and other "women of bad repute" and shipped them off to the New World as "colonists." Among the kidnapped there were, of course, a number of hitherto respectable people of both sexes, who were herded away to Louisiana, along with prostitutes, thieves, vagabonds, and every other kind of wretch.

Charles Gayarré relates, for example, in his *History of Louisiana* (1847), that on January 3, 1721, "a ship of the company [that is, of the Mississippi Company] arrived . . . and in February eighty girls who had been taken from a house of correction in Paris called La Salpêtrière were landed in Louisiana." These women, according to Jean Baptiste le Moyne, Sieur de Bienville, then governor of the colony, "had not been well selected." Intended to serve as wives to male colonists who had been shunted to Louisiana from Canada, where they had evi-

5

dently acquired a taste for Indian women, most of the "correction girls," as they would be called by historians willing to admit to their existence, "could not be restrained" no matter what "vigilance [was] exercised upon them." "It would seem," Gayarré noted, "that dissolute women were not looked upon as being included in [a] recent royal edict which prohibited the transportation to Louisiana of . . . persons of bad morals; or it may be that this edict, as it is frequently with such things, had been issued merely to stand on paper for some particular purpose, but not to be executed."

At all events, with the apparent blessings of French kings and dukes and their lackeys, seeds had been sown whose fruits would be a long succession of New Orleans red-light districts. And this state of affairs quite suited the tastes of many of the early inhabitants, who had been chacterized by an earlier governor, Antoine de la Mothe Cadillac, in 1714, as "no better than the ["wretched"] country; they are the very scum and refuse of Canada, ruffians who have thus far cheated the gibbet of its due, vagabonds who are without subordination to the laws, without any respect for religion or for the government, graceless profligates, who are so steeped in vice that they prefer the Indian females to the French women!" Importuned by pious missionaries to expel "loose women" from Louisiana, Cadillac declared that if he did this "there would be no females left, and this would not suit the views of the [French] government."

The Spanish government, to which New Orleans was ceded by the French in 1762, had somewhat different views. The Spanish governor Esteban Rodríguez Miró made it clear, for example, that he had no taste for the fruits of the French kings' planting. In his *Bando de buen gobierno* (June 2, 1786), a proclamation issued upon his assuming office and summarized in François Xavier Martin's *History of Louisiana* (1827): "He declares his intention to proceed with severity against all persons living in concubinage. He observes that the idleness of free negro, mulatto, and quarteroon [sic] women, resulting in their dependence for a livelihood, on incontinence and libertinism, will not be tolerated. He recommends them to renounce their mode of living, and to betake themselves to honest labor; and declares his determination to have those who neglect his recommendation, sent out of the province, warning them that he will consider their excessive attention to dress, as an evidence of misconduct."

Louis XV's edict against transporting women of loose morals to the colonies, alluded to earlier, had not actually prevented such transportation. Similarly, it is doubtful that Miró's stated policies had much effect on the incidence of prostitution in New Orleans. Prostitution was accepted as a fact of life in both France and Spain, and the Latinate governors in the New World, unlike their New England counterparts, were not, by and large, religious zealots. (Governor Miró, indeed, is credited with having risked his own neck to thwart an attempt by certain Spanish clerical interests to impose the Holy Inquisition on Louisiana. As Gayarré commented: "Considering the dread in which the holy tribunal of the Inquisition had always been held in Spain, the energy with which Miró acted on this occasion cannot be too much admired.")

During all these years prostitution, and still more commonly, concubinage (much of it interracial) existed to a seemly degree and was practiced, for the most part, with some discretion and, among the propertied classes, with some regard for good manners. And, even taking into account places catering to men off the river and the other "lower" elements, there sim-

6

ply wasn't all that much of it, relative to the total population. It was only after the American accession to power in 1803, only after the introduction of "puritan" morality, that prostitution burst forth out of all previous bounds within the decade.

The infusion of puritan hypocrisy into Old New Orleans was not the sole factor, of course. For one thing, Mississippi River commerce increased enormously, bringing to New Orleans riotous crews of rough and ready rivermen—fresh off their boats, eager for whiskey and women, and with money in their pockets. Increasing numbers of prostitutes, gamblers, and other tenderloin types gravitated to the city where the money was. Finally, toward the end of the War in 1812, Andrew Jackson led his ill-assorted thousands to New Orleans to battle the British. This horde, sometimes called the "dirtiest troops who ever defended freedom," made the trip without too much grumbling on the promise they would be paid off, including accrued back pay, in the Crescent City. This promise and the troop movement were not secret, and the convergence of prostitutes on New Orleans soon became a scarlet migration without precedent. Loose ladies who followed the dollar sniffed a savory air and came from all over the country.

The city was situated then, as it is now, on sea-level delta land. Generations of Creole inhabitants had been going just "back-o-town"—a few blocks from the French Quarter—for landfill with which to build up home and business sites. The most convenient place from which to obtain this earth gradually became larger and deeper and soon filled with water to form a sizeable pond or "basin."

New Orleans' self-styled solid citizens, unwilling to accept the regiments of whores into Creole society, barred them from living or doing business in the city itself. At this time, the entire city was what later could be called the "French Quarter" (or *Vieux Carré*), and the "basin" was still well outside. The loose ladies retreated to the latter. With their own hands, and with a bit of help from levee loungers and members of General Jackson's forces, they dug a drainage ditch, erected shacks and shanties for themselves, and hung out their red lanterns. "Basin Street" was open for business.

With the presence of the army and with constantly increasing river traffic, the bawds prospered and managed, for the most part, to survive the yellow fever epidemics of the early 1830s (during which, it is said, they performed heroically as nurses). They even paid liberally to improve sanitation in the area, and fared well without interruption until 1849, when the California gold rush turned the area into a ghost town in a few months. As suddenly as they had arrived, most of these mobile "ladies of the evening" left to seek better fortune among the prospectors. Those who remained struggled along for a half-dozen years, invading all parts of the burgeoning metropolis, including the uptown "American Section" (what is now called the Garden District and the Irish Channel).

The first of the tenderloin districts of New Orleans to attain special notoriety was the "Swamp," an area bounded by South Liberty and South Robertson streets, and by Girod and Julia streets. It was an incredible jumble of cheap dance halls, brothels, saloons and gaming rooms, cockfighting pits, and rooming houses. A one-story shantytown jammed into a half-dozen teeming blocks, the Swamp was the scene of some eight-hundred known murders between 1820 and 1850. Into this fearsome hell

7

the city's police feared to go and indeed did not go.

Construction was primitive indeed, most of the lumber being timbers from old disassembled flatboats and crude cypress planks. Every proprietor had to be ready to defend his life and property at all times. Deceptive signs like "House of Rest For Weary Boatmen" (which all too frequently meant *permanent* rest) were crudely painted on the fronts of these shacks and lighted by red lanterns. In the dense fogs that are so common in New Orleans the area looked at night as if it were being consumed by a huge conflagration—as indeed many New Orleanians prayed it would be.

The ordinances that the city fathers put on the books to control the situation proved to be ludicrously inadequate. The first, passed in 1817, provided for a twenty-five dollar fine or thirty-days imprisonment of any woman deemed "notoriously abandoned to lewdness" who "shall occasion scandals or disturb the tranquillity of the neighborhood," plus certain other punishments for furnishing lodging to such a woman. By 1837 any three "respectable citizens" could by signing a petition empower the mayor to order eviction of prostitutes from any premises named in the complaint. In 1839 harlots were proscribed from inhabiting the ground floors of surrounding alleys and walks of any building in the city. By 1845 all coffee houses and places of entertainment where alcoholic beverages were sold were declared legally off-limits to prostitutes.

Such laws were unenforced because they were unenforceable. Throughout the entire period, while the city fathers passed ordinances, the rough, tough "ladies of the evening" were attracting hundreds of flatboatmen, "Kaintucks," and the assorted underworld types with which port cities have always been well stocked and

were "processing" them with assembly-line precision and then turning them out penniless into the dawn. The arsenal of weapons used to extract the loot ranged from cajolery to cold steel, through an inventory of pistols, "knockout drops," and blunt, heavy objects, to the standard flow of whiskey dispensed over crude bars. A man could wander into the Swamp and for the going rate of a picayune (about six cents) obtain a bed for the night, a drink of whiskey, and a woman. So long as he carried no other money he was eager to defend, he had a better than average chance of leaving in the morning under his own power and without further economic loss.

By 1856 property owners and religious groups had found so much occasion to complain about the social and economic effects of prostitution in the city that a serious attempt was made to regulate it legislatively. Accordingly, the Common Council, in 1857, passed New Orleans' first ordinance designed to acknowledge the existence of prostitution by requiring licensing and thereby making this particular profession taxable. No such effort had ever been made in America before.

This legislation could have made the Swamp relatively safe and, at the same time, been a strong factor in controlling the city's oldest profession, which by now had spread into every neighborhood. But, alas, the ordinance was not to survive its first legal test.

On May 22, 1857, a Mrs. Emma Pickett applied for a license to operate a bagnio at 25 St. John Street, between Gravier and Perdido streets, but she paid her license fee, as required by the new ordinance, under protest, and immediately filed suit to recover the fee. The case dragged on through 1858 into the spring of 1859,

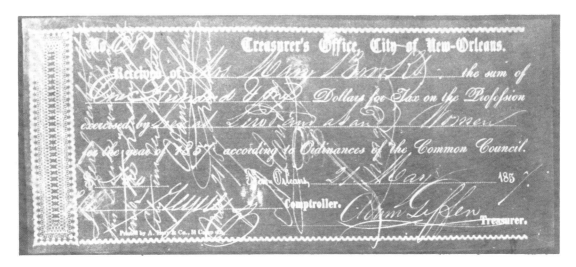

A license receipt issued to Mrs. Mary Brooks on May 21, 1857. It cost her a hundred and one dollars, which she paid, according to her hand-written notation, under protest.

when the appellate courts declared the law to be unconstitutional.

The jubilant bawds and their protectors flaunted their sins even more openly. Mrs. Pickett's victory was hailed by carriage-borne groups of hundreds of painted hussies variously constumed, rolling along Canal Street and through the French Quarter, gesturing obscenely, displaying themselves, insulting shocked house-wives, and otherwise calling attention to the triumph of the sin industry.

During the late 1850s and early 1860s the Swamp declined for purely geographical rea-sons, as its inhabitants drifted downtown into Gallatin Street behind the French Market, a lo-cation even more convenient, now that pretense of legal control had been demolished, and where the pedestrian traffic was heavier.

Gallatin Street, just two blocks long, was a true "port of missing men," along which police were constantly on the lookout for missing per-sons from all over the world. Frequently, these were to be found among the bartenders, cut-throats, dance-house operators, fight promoters, thieves, thugs, and pimps who made up the permanent male population of the street.

Mortality among law enforcement officers was high, and the police soon learned to tackle the Gallatin Street beat only in groups. The street was the center of narcotics traffic, as well as the home of dealers in stolen goods. Fugitives from every nation's laws found shelter here.

Mike Haden, who had so thoroughly ventilated his brother with a razor; America Williams, "the world's strongest whore"; Mary Schwartz, who had permanently blinded a customer in a row over her fifty-cent fee; Red-Light Liz, the one-eyed paramour of Joe the Whipper, who made a good living administering beatings to masochistic harlots, using whips, switches, steel rods, razor straps, or canes, according to the lady's preference—such as these were typical of those who found safe haven on Gallatin Street.

There was music to be heard in the area's "dance houses" from dusk to dawn. These were staffed with women, unpaid by the manage-ments, who were there to solicit customers. Nightly, a visitor might find base amusements in any one of these places where men danced with naked women on crowded floors to the raucous sounds of improvised musical groups of random instrumentation.

A reporter for the New Orleans *Daily Picayune* (July 31, 1869) described a typical dance house as ". . . filthy and unclean to a degree . . . [that] beggars description . . . a piano and two or three trombones for an orchestra . . . dances so abandoned and reckless that the can-can in comparison seemed maidenly and re-spectable." He noted, in particular, "a state of awful nudity."

Among the most notorious of the so-called dance houses was the one operated by Dan

O'Neil from 1860 to 1869. Its demise was hastened by his act of vengeance against an erring harlot who had been close to his heart but whom he drugged, stripped, and threw into an alley where she was raped and otherwise maltreated by a group of savage and intoxicated hoodlums. For his part in the affair, O'Neil was arrested and his place of business, the Amsterdam, was padlocked. Powerful friends in city hall arranged for his release and acquittal, but after a couple of further openings and closings, the premises were shuttered for good. Considering the normal run of activity in Gallatin Street, these events would not seem to have been serious enough to cause a place to be closed down. In a letter to one of the city's newspapers (July 31, 1869), O'Neil theorized on the reasons for his difficulties with the authorities:

> To the reporter of the N.O. Times—About the Amsterdam Dance House—there ain't much in it, as you have written, as appeared in your evening's edition, that's true. As for leaving there I paid, during the past five months, to the Captain of Police, $80 for each of three months, and $40 for each of two. In other words, I paid the police during that time, $320 for keeping the place open. I believe if there had been no trouble about paying up regular I would have been allowed to stay there still.
>
> DAN'L O'NEIL

Meanwhile, the part of Basin Street that was destined to become the main stem of Storyville continued its rise as a vice center. The *Daily Southern Star* (January 26, 1866) proclaimed it a "public calamity," complaining that although it had "natural attractions and advantages," not the least of which were "avenues of beautiful trees" along the center of the street, it was "occupied by the low classes of immodest and impure women." The paper, advocating reform, also complained that so beautiful a street, which might well serve for a first-class residential area, was "synonymous with crime and degradation."

A little enviously, it reported that "the only improvement there recently consisted in the erection of a spacious and elegant house, costing from thirty to fifty thousand dollars, to be occupied when completed by a . . . class which created for Basin Street a name not creditable to the city or the locality." This presumably refers to the house of Hattie Hamilton at 21 South Basin Street. The *Tagliche Deutsche Zeitung*, the city's German daily, would later report (September 22, 1870) that citizens living in and around South Basin Street were seeking an injunction to stop its operation.

During the 1870s and until 1885, possibly the lowest element ever to practice prostitution in New Orleans was crowded into a single block of Burgundy Street between Conti and Bienville streets, known to the press and citizenry of the era as "Smoky Row."

Its contentious inhabitants, numbering nearly a hundred female blacks who ranged in age from prepuberty to the seventies and engaged actively, one and all, in the game of commercial sex, would line the banquette (sidewalk), seated on curbs or in wicker rocking chairs, dipping snuff, chewing cigars and tobacco, smoking pipes, and drinking beer and whiskey. The more notorious among them—Gallus Lu, Kidney-Foot Jenny, Fightin' Mary, and Sister Sal (who became known as One-Eye Sal after an altercation with Fightin' Mary)—were known to the police and press as the most dangerous and indeed murderous women in town.

It must be assumed that some of the men who took their pleasure along Smoky Row did so of their own choice, but this collection of sluts in low-cut, filthy Mother Hubbards must have been of the most limited seductiveness. This is probably why at least a portion of the Row's income depended on the women's literally dragging men in off the street, spitting tobacco juice in their eyes to blind them, slugging them over the head with baseball bats, robbing them, and tossing them unconscious back into Burgundy Street.

Increasing public pressure inspired the police to make a decisive move against Smoky Row and its inhabitants in July, 1885. Gallus Lu, One-Eyed Sal, and their cohorts in the block were successfully encouraged to leave. The officers made an attempt to unearth the many bodies that were said to be buried in the patios and courtyards of the buildings, but they found none. They did find several score bloodstained wallets (empty) and a mound of miscellaneous items of male apparel.

While Gallatin Street and Smoky Row catered to the more primitive elements, the "flower of evil" was achieving a handsome full bloom in the high-class establishments of South Basin Street. Here were such celebrated courtesans as Minnie Ha Ha, Kate Townsend, and Hattie Hamilton. These early queens of the un-

MISS HATTIE C. HAMILTON.

Hattie Hamilton was the first of the big-time Basin Street madams. Her enterprising paramour David Jackson guided her from bankruptcy to a fortune, but the state concubinage laws kept him from sharing in her estate.

MR. DAVID JACKSON.

derworld, all of pre-Storyville days, were far more gracious practitioners of the purple arts than their more professional sisters who would flourish later in Storyville.

Orleanians today continue to recall them and their era, as well as some of the men who were part of that showy scene, with a touch of affectionate nostalgia.

Hattie Hamilton, probably the first of the influential whore-queens, was the mistress of Senator James Beares, with whose help she rebuilt the palace at 21 South Basin Street, known as the Twenty-One. A New Orleans *Daily Picayune* reporter "reviewed" the premises on February 7, 1869:

> The entrance was through a passageway adorned with a couple of statues representing some obscure divinities of light, and in whose hands were held lighted flambeaux. Beyond this lay the drawing-room, peopled with a few figures in glittering attire, and who, from their costumes and manners, might have been visitants from the Mountains of the Moon. Neither did the decorations of the rooms, in the pictures that hung on the walls, the plated mirrors, the delicately tinted furniture, appear to be altogether of a sub-lunar character, though evidently intended to embody a sybarite's dream—luxury and repose. The grotesque and bizarre aspect of everything —splendor without comfort, glitter and sparkle suggestive of death and decay—gave rise to singular reflections.

In May of 1870 the senator was shot to death at his home, where Hattie was living with him. As the butler hurried in, Hattie was still holding the smoking pistol in her hand, but she was released without questioning by the police. The Twenty-One's popularity waned thereafter, for lack of the "high-class" patronage that the senator had directed to Hattie's at fifty dollars per.

Hattie's successor as queen bee of the pre-Storyville demimonde was the celebrated and notorious Kate Townsend, of 40 South Basin Street, whose melodramatic career ended in abrupt violence on November 3, 1883, at the hands of her ne'er-do-well Creole lover, Troisville Sykes. This was the most widely publicized sex murder in New Orleans history.

Sykes pleaded not guilty. He was able to establish the fact that he had stabbed Kate with a bowie knife only in self-defense and was acquitted. He then proceeded to offer her will for probate. She had wished, this document attested, to leave all her worldly goods—slightly over ninety thousand dollars—to him. After five years of courtroom nonsense, most of it center-

ing around the concubinage law, Sykes emerged
with a grant of about thirty dollars.

It has been asserted by many observers that
with Kate Townsend prostitution in New Orleans reached its pinnacle of luxury. The *Daily Picayune,* in its account of her demise (November 4, 1883), described her room:

In the left-hand corner was a magnificent *etagere,*
upon which were statuettes, the work of renowned artists, and small articles of verdu, betraying great taste both in selection and
arrangement. A finely carved though small table
stood next, while adjoining this was a splendid
glass door *armoire,* on the shelves of which were
stored a plethora of the finest linen wear and
bed clothing. Next to the *armoire* was a rep and
damask sofa and over the mantel was a French
mirror with a gilt frame. A large sideboard stood
in the corner next to a window on the other side
of the chimney, and in this was stored a large
quantity of silverware. Another *armoire* similar
to the one described, a table and the bed completed the furnishings in the room. Saving the
armchairs, of which there were a number, covered

Troisville Sykes killed his affluent mistress, Kate Townsend, in self-defense, but the papers tried to hang him anyway.

KATE MEETS HER HUSBAND IN LIVERPOOL.

MISS MOLLY JOHNSON THE PRINCIPAL WITNESS

THE VICTIM

KATE TOWNSEND.

TROISVILLE SYKES

KATE BIDDING ADIEU TO HER CHILDREN

OYSTERS

KATES FIRST APPEARANCE IN A PUBLIC HAREM IN NEW ORLEANS.

RETRIBUTION. Mᶜ LERN AS WAITER IN TEXAS.

→ The TOWNSEND → TRAGEDY. ←

with the finest rep and damask, with tete-a-tetes to match. The hangings of the bed, even the mosquito bar, were of lace, and an exquisite basket of flowers hung suspended from the tester of the bed. Around the walls were suspended chaste and costly oil paintings. The bloodstained carpet was of the finest velvet.

In the economically deflated eighties, champagne at fifteen to fifty dollars a quart and a fee for sexual services fixed at a hundred a night made Kate Townsend's the flossiest brothel in the hemisphere. Catering strictly to the carriage trade, at these prices, the madams required evening dress of their patrons, ball gowns of their girls—downstairs. Most of the accepted rules of etiquette applied and the young Cyprians were carefully schooled in good manners and tasteful grooming.

La Townsend permitted, in fact encouraged, charge accounts, and once a man had established his credit, he was treated like a king. Her investigative facilities are said to have been as efficient as today's major credit bureaus, though she operated through channels less conventional than theirs.

Contemporary with Kate Townsend and Hattie Hamilton was the remarkable Minnie Ha Ha, another of the early Basin Street madams, who preferred that Orleanians take her to be an Indian rather than a Negro. In the late 1860s hers was one of the most elaborate mansions in the city. She was descended, she asserted, from Mr. and Mrs. Hiawatha, and an oil painting of these forebears graced her wall as documentation.

In 1903, the police patrol wagons were still horse-drawn. This one careens up South Basin Street past what had been the Kate Townsend mansion but by the time of this photograph had become the Elks Home. In the distance on the right, the cupola of the Arlington is clearly visible.

13

These were among the more orthodox entrepreneurs of the red light. Others were less conventional. Perhaps the most colorful adventuress ever to keep a house of assignation in New Orleans was Fanny Sweet—thief, lesbian, Confederate spy, poisoner, procuress, and brawler—whose affairs were, in part, guided by the ubiquitous "queen of the voodoos," Marie Laveau, and her "staff."

In 1860 Fanny enlisted the aid of the voodoo queen to turn up an "angel" to finance a new brothel venture. She was convinced that it was the "Laveau power" that was responsible for the entry into her life of the patron who provided her with the house at the corner of South Basin and Gasquet streets and stocked it with imported potables and the best domestic help. Here, unknown to her generous "john," she mulcted old men of thousands upon thousands of dollars by a judicious combination of the procurement of innocent young girls and subsequent blackmail. Fanny's confidence in the "black arts" became public knowledge later the same year when she was one of those rounded up in a police raid on a voodoo ceremony. The next year, when Fanny was accused of poisoning a lover, the police went through her place and turned up all manner of gris-gris and voodoo paraphernalia, including a lock of human hair—bloodstained. The magic seems to have served her well: Fanny Sweet never did time for any of her innumerable misdeeds. She operated her house for two uninterrupted decades before her final retirement in 1889. She died in Pensacola, Florida, in 1895, at the age of about sixty-five.

Josephine Clare, said to be the District's most "frigid" tart, was Madame Gertie Livingston's prime attraction. Various prizes were advertised for the Lochinvar who could bring her to life but, so far as is known, the widely known "Josephine Icebox" was never defrosted.

Happy Charley was an entertainer who amused patrons of saloons in the tenderloin by playing a tin whistle through his nose while singing, somehow, some lines that the *Lantern* for May 14, 1887, would preserve under the title "Der Nue Orleans Tuff":

I am a man dat most of yer know,
I'm known as a knocker wherever I go.
My fame it is fightin'; I kan't get enuff,
All over de town dey call me a tuff;
Yes, I'm a man dat de people all dread,
And when I gets rowdy I paints de town red.

There was a standing reward for any man who could "defrost" Josephine—but never a winner.

MISS JOSEPHINE ICEBOX.

14

I know all de cops; I stan' in wid de roughs,
Yer kin bet yer sweet life I'm er Nu'Leens tuff.

On one occasion, the record shows, Charley sang this blustering number to the wrong man. The ensuing challenge to his claims of fistic prowess left him with a broken nose that affected his musical virtuosity adversely. In 1895 he was managing a Franklin Street bar and no longer "performing."

In Archie Murphy's Gallatin Street dance hall were such characters as Lizzie Collins, who developed a compulsion to steal all the buttons from her customers' trousers, an eccentricity that led eventually to her being banished from the premises.

Bricktop Jackson, with knife and slingshot, fought her way through dozens of brawls, killing at least four men and committing mayhem on many another. She wielded a fifteen-inch knife with a silver handle in the middle and lethal steel protruding from either end. Her lover, John Miller, wore a chain and an iron ball in place of a left arm. In combat, this apparatus, coupled with a long-handled knife in his right hand, was formidable indeed, but not enough so to protect him from the rages of his pugnacious mistress, who did him in on December 7, 1861. At this time the New Orleans *Daily Crescent* took note of Bricktop's "bestial habits and ferocious manners." On another occasion, in company with two other bawds, Ellen Collins and six-foot America Williams, Bricktop stood trial for a murder that they had committed before many witnesses but of which, for reasons still untold, all three were acquitted.

America Williams was called the "Heavyweight Champion of Gallatin Street," her gender notwithstanding. She defended her title successfully for many years against inebriated challengers of both sexes, but by Gallatin Street rather than Marquis of Queensberry rules.

One-Legged Duffy (née Mary Rich) did not fare so well. Her boy friend not only stabbed her but bashed out her brains with her own wooden leg. The mid-nineteenth-century New Orleans underworld was not distinguished for gallantry.

Bridget Fury (née Della Swift) became a prostitute at twelve in Cleveland, Ohio, but came to New Orleans at an early age, achieved wide notoriety for her ruggedness and skill in hand-to-hand combat, and ended up in jail for murder.

In the course of the century, prostitution spread into every part of New Orleans. In retrospect the era may seem colorful, rather stimulating to the imagination. It must have seemed quite different to many of those living through it. Tenderloin life was costly, dirty, dangerous, and exploitative in the extreme. Brothels were stocked with young girls arriving as volunteers, dupes, slaves, or abductees. Planters came to town renting their nubile, octoroon slave girls. Runaways made their ways to the bagnios of the Crescent City. The demand for recruits made a big business of procuring.

As early as 1845 Mary Thompson was using her cigar store as a cover for her traffic in teenage virgins. From her Royal Street shop she sold the sweet young things for between two hundred and five hundred dollars each. The situation came to public attention when one such piece of merchandise, Mary Fozatte, escaped as she was being delivered to an assignation house. The girl ran home but soon found herself being arrested on the charges of having stolen her own person, representing an estimated value of three hundred and fifty dollars (the price for which she had just been sold to an impatiently waiting old man). Procuress Thompson, filled with righteous indignation, pressed the charge, but the court, to its eternal credit, dismissed the case. The Fozatte girl then brought suit against Mary Thompson for character injuries and was awarded fifty dollars.

By the late 1860s the price for virgins had gone up to eight hundred dollars each. A school teacher, Louisa Murphy, was getting that price peddling her little pupils. Later, however, in the late 1880s, what with increasing competition, virgins were being procured for as little as a hundred dollars.

A Miss Carol of Baronne Street procured young boys for male homosexuals and established a house of assignation for this type of clientele on Lafayette Street. The staff of this specialized house of sin included such males as Lady Richard, Lady Fresh, Chicago Belle, Lady Beulah Toto, Mammy George, La Sylvester, and the burly "madam," Miss Big Nellie. The place was known for large scale, noisy, interracial social functions that frequently attracted the attention and wrath of neighbors and police.

Other notorious procuresses of the pre-Storyville period were Nellie Haley, frequently referred to in the press as "Queen of the Procuresses"; Mother Mansfield of Bienville Street;

and Emma Johnson, who would later become the proprietress of the Studio on Basin Street but was operating in these days on Gasquet (now Cleveland) Street.

In business ostensibly as an employment agency at 98 Burgundy Street, Agnes Herrick, better known to the underworld and to the police as "Spanish Agnes," was probably the most successful procuress in New Orleans: she remained in business for over forty years, during which time, though frequently caught in the act, she never spent a second behind bars or paid a fine. Obviously, her "protection" had its source in extremely high places.

An article in the *Mascot* (November 22, 1890) covered one of Spanish Agnes' operations in some detail:

Sinning for Silk
Young Girls Sacrifice Humble Virtue for Dazzling Dishonor
A HORRIBLE STATE OF AFFAIRS PERMITTED TO
GO ON UNINTERRUPTED BY THE
AUTHORITIES

Why such things should exist or at least be permitted to exist in a city which boasts of its high moral standing and importance in all else that characterizes civilization is a question beyond the comprehension of all. Notwithstanding this, the fact is plainly visible that a horrible state of things exist here, and the narration of the case to be herein treated will no doubt convince all good people that something should be done to check the evil. Some time ago the assistance of the police was invoked in the search for two young girls aged seventeen and eighteen, respectively, and named Lillie Richards and Kate ———, who had disappeared from their homes in the vicinity of the St. Mary Market. The matter was placed in the hands of Detective Grabert, who soon learned that the two young girls answering very minutely the description given him were seen in the neighborhood of Burgundy and St. Louis Streets. The result of the detective's researches were that the two young girls did enter the place No. 98 Burgundy Street, kept by Mrs. Herrick, or Spanish Agnes by which cognomen she is better known, and later trunks were seen taken into the same house. The information given was that a hack drove up to the door the day after this, and both girls were driven off in it. The detective had gained enough information to guide his future action in the premises and the chief of police was communicated with. The information received by the authorities in Galveston was to the effect that the two young girls had left New Orleans (giving date and description) and were directed to a woman keeping a place of ill-repute. The case was given to Detective Williamson of the Island City force, and he set out to locate the girls. His search proved fruitful before he had traversed many miles of Galveston

for he apprehended the two damsels in the house of one, Abbie Allen, situated at the corner of 26th and Post Office Streets. When accosted by the detective, the girls demurred, but their pleading was of no avail as they were taken to headquarters and detained to await advice from New Orleans. Upon receipt of the request, the detective was instructed to accompany the girls to the Crescent City and there to safely deliver them to the police authorities. Detective Williamson arrived in the city a few days ago and delivered the fair but wayward females over to acting Chief of Police Journee, who sent for the complainant, Johnson, the man convicted of ship-burning some years ago, and who was pardoned. Johnson claimed to be the brother-in-law of the girl, Katie———. He took the pair home, they accompanying him home with reluctant motion.

The information of this escapade of the two New Orleans females having reached the Mascot from Galveston, a commissioner was detailed to ascertain the facts. An investigation was set on foot and the fact disclosed that one Leona Smith, a performer on the piano, had in some strange way become acquainted with the girls, and her conversation on the subject of a sporting life and its pleasures had completely turned their heads. So infatuated were they and so anxious, too, to quit their humble sphere and take up their abode in fairyland as pictured by Miss Smith that they asked her to help them up the golden stairs. Of course, Miss Smith lost no time in consenting to the proposition as she knew of Mrs. Herrick being ready at all times to pay commission for pretty girls, being pressed with orders from landladies in other cities. Miss Smith was to receive ten dollars apiece as her commission. The bargain was closed and the girls shipped over the Southern Pacific Road that evening to Abbie Allen, a woman well-known to the evil inclined citizens of Galveston.

The Mascot, with a view to learning something about the modus operandi of Mrs. Herrick's nefarious trade, called on that woman at her place at No. 98 Burgundy Street. Knowing her to be a pretty shrewd operator and a woman of extended experience in this world, the reporter approached her in a very careful manner. She was extremely indisposed and refused to allow anyone to enter her chamber. This would not work, however, as she soon weakened when she was informed that the matter of sending the two girls to Galveston would be revived, and, as a statement had been made against her, she would be accorded the privilege of placing herself right before the public. She yielded after some persistency on the part of the reporter, and in apparent distress, made the following statement:

"I frequently receive orders from the keepers of fashionable places, you know the kind? These ladies ask me to send them girls, or women, for that matter. I always prefer to have experienced women than virtuous girls, because there is less fear of trouble. I am in correspondence with women like Mollie Waters and Abbie Allen of

Galveston. These women very often write to me for the girls. Some time ago I received an order from Miss Abbie Allen to send her some girls, and soon after Miss Leona Smith, who plays the piano, informed me that she could secure two nice, young girls. She brought the two of whom you speak—Lillie Richards and Katie ———, and I paid her ten dollars commission. I questioned the girls about their past life and both assured me that they were experienced in wickedness, one of them claiming to be the mother of an illegitimate child. I believed them all right and at liberty to do just what they pleased, and I procured railroad tickets and sent them off to the depot in a hack. The girls looked so brazen to me that I could not doubt their declaration of being cast-outs, so I took them. Another thing that struck me was the fact that they could bring trunks with them in broad daylight. Shortly after this occurrence, a Mr. Johnson, whom I learned from the detectives keeps a grocery corner of Tchopitoulas and Delord, came here and raised a fuss about the girls. He represented to me that he was the brother-in-law of the girl Katie ———, ah, pshaw, I've forgotten the other name, and I told him to be quiet and that I would give him all the information concerning their whereabouts. This I did."

"Well, is procuring girls for keepers of places of ill-fame a regular business followed by you, and if so, why do you send innocent girls into such a sphere of unholiness?" asked the reporter.

"I do not, sir, like to have anything to do with innocent girls," replied Mrs. Herrick, and continuing, she said, "Why, perhaps you would be surprised if I told you that not a very long time ago a mother brought her three daughters to me and offered them for sale. Two, she said, were bad and the youngest still unacquainted with vice and wickedness of the world. She demanded twenty-five dollars for the girls, and expressed the belief that she ought to get more for the guileless maiden. I never had this trouble before."

At this juncture, Mrs. Herrick became weak and dispatched someone for a doctor.

The above are plain cold facts, narrated as obtained, and are without any exaggerated sentiment; now it remains to be seen if the nefarious practice of trading in female innocence will be permitted to go further. It is certainly somebody's duty to stop it, and let there be no delay in the crushing out of this monstrous evil.

Lest Spanish Agnes' account of the avaricious mother be judged apocryphal, consider the following reports published in the *Mascot:*

An Inhuman Mother
Who Allows Her Daughter To Lead a Life of Shame

. . . it seems incredible that any mother should . . . be a party to the sale of her own flesh and blood, yet, to the shame of the human race, such unnatural mothers do exist.

Unregulated "employment agencies" channeled innocent children into careers of sin. The sign advertises "500 young hands wanted for Texas. High prices paid." It turned out, the Mascot *alleged in 1894, that "hands" were not quite what was wanted.*

At 91 Conti Street, upon the second floor, Mrs. King and her two daughters reside. One daughter named Kitty is aged sixteen years, the other is a child of ten. For some months past, Kitty has led an immoral life, her mother being her aide and abettor therein . . .

A few days since the girl was seen through the window in nature's garb misbehaving herself with three young men similarly attired . . . if she is not taken away from her mother and placed in a reformatory, she will be ruined forever, body and soul.   [*Mascot*, August 1, 1891]

Disgusting Depravity

Sometime ago the Mascot stated that acting recorder Wiltz had made a grievous error in discharging from custody the thirteen-year-old girl Marie Rodrigues whom the police had arrested in a vile den of infamy at No. 135 Rampart Street where she was consorting with the worst characters—male and female—in the city and where she was with the consent and approval of her father, a vile old scoundrel who appeared to be living off the profits of her sins. When she was discharged, the girl promised that she would lead a better life and her father averred that he would see that she did.

It turned out, subsequently, that the girl on leaving the court returned immediately to her vile life, her father taking her there and securing apartments for her in the same place. The aunt of the girl, hearing of her return to such a life, called upon the mayor and he very promptly issued orders for her arrest and Judge Guy Dreaux committed her to the House of the Good Shepherd. The girl has been punished, the father should now get a dose of the police jail as a dangerous vagrant.

And as further evidence of the fact that the girl's father is determined that she shall pursue her evil ways it might be stated that she was yesterday released from custody by Judge Marr on the application of her father for a writ of habeas corpus. It might now be well for the police to give their attention to the old man.
          [*Mascot*, November 16, 1889]

It was to be expected that some of the girls who fell into these evil ways were volunteers.

Hettie and Emma Lascar, daughters of Ferdinand Lascar, who once owned a drugstore near Poydras Market and one at Washington and Magazine Streets, became homesick for the Crescent City after the elder Lascar moved the family to New York. During his absence from home the girls "obtained some of his wealth" and took a train to New Orleans. Lascar, discovering their flight and destination, wired Chief of Police Hennessey, and he arrested them on arrival, but they were released for lack of specific charges. The *Mascot* detailed the case histories of these girls on December 29, 1888:

These girls came to this city with their father and mother some six or seven years ago, and though quite young, soon became acquainted and attracted considerable attention by the cut of their attire and the general breeziness, but not at all vulgarity, of their behavior. [There follows a description of the charms and talents of the pair.] Finally, in an evil hour Hettie listened to the voice of the tempter, and as many a woman before her had done, she fell and soon flaunted her shame in the face of the world by taking up her abode in the house of one, Anna Casey, on Customhouse Street near Robertson. Her father, unable to bear the weight of his disgrace, sold out his business and returned to New York.

Yet another source of new "recruits" for the tenderloin was exposed in the January 5, 1889, issue of the *Mascot:*

How Children are Ruined

We present this week on the rear page, two cartoons representing some of the temptations to which young boys and girls, mere children, who are employed by different millinery and messenger agents are subjected. To the pernicious effects so imbibed in early life, may be attributed the evil consequences that follow in the shape of an easy fall and subsequent existence of women in palaces of sin or low hovels of vice and the total corruption of boys making them inmates of prisons or accomplished scoundrels. Every milliner or dressmaker, instead of hiring some colored porter or person of mature age, employ small children, whom they utilize to carry to their customers the dresses, bonnets, etc. ordered by them. The patrons of these milliners and dressmakers embrace all classes, their best patrons, however in the majority of cases, being the members of the demi-monde or females of questionable character. To the houses of these creatures are these frail innocent little things forced to go and while there are not infrequently encountered by half or totally intoxicated men or women, who enact before them such scenes as would make any hardened character blush. The women seldom, if ever, notice the little thing, but their behavior is carefully noted and creates a lasting impression in the susceptible minds of the young one. Generally of poor and innocent parents, these children envy the sinful elegance displayed before them and hanker after the pleasure enjoyed by their possession.

It takes little to make bloom the seeds of lustful desire so sown, and at the least encouragement it springs into a growing plant and the little one becomes a member of the grand army of sinners. Frequently, the girl, if she is of any age, is petted and coaxed, treated to wine . . . and, well, the least said of what follows, the better. It is on record, however, and there are now fallen women, who have been led astray while employed by milliners and dressmakers who make a speciality of just such a class of customers. There is hardly a single dressmaker or milliner in New Orleans who do not pursue such practices. If there are, we would take pleasure in printing their names. We make no exceptions in this matter and mention no names particularly, because every one of them is included in this generality. They are not alone responsible for this; it is the parents of these little girls who should be held to account for permitting their offspring to visit the places above mentioned. Were they to do their full duty in the premises, the number of girls so ruined would be rapidly reduced.

With reference to the messenger boys, it might be said that they are treated to just such similar scenes, the agencies that employ them making the bulk of their profits from the employment of little boys to escort frail women to different places at night to avoid arrest under the city ordinance regulating their behavior. They are constantly running on calls from either gambling houses or maisons de joie, where they are brought into the presence of vice in its very worst forms. Acquaintances thus made have become lasting, and we see now many young men of soiled reputation who are outcasts of society, who were tainted with vice while wearing the uniform of some licensed messenger service corporation.

There are no societies for the suppression of cruelty to children in New Orleans, but there might be some organized for just such a purpose. It would be a laudable one and could be made effective.

Of environs so described by the *Mascot*, it should come as no surprise that we may read, in 1886, of "Mrs. Parker and her daughters keeping an assignation house at 361 Gravier Street," or in July, 1891, that "Addie Peterson, a girl fifteen years of age . . . the orgies and dissipated life which she had witnessed in Customhouse Street had corrupted the girl . . . we are glad to see that the Chief [Chief of Police Gaster] is putting a stop to the practice of keeping minors in houses of ill-fame," and in August of the same year of a hushed-up affair whose details were not made available by the police, since very rich and powerful madams were involved, but which are known to have concerned brothel keeper Irma Rose and the granddaughter of the notorious Basin Street "landlady," Julia Dean.

"Basin street . . . land of dreams . . ."

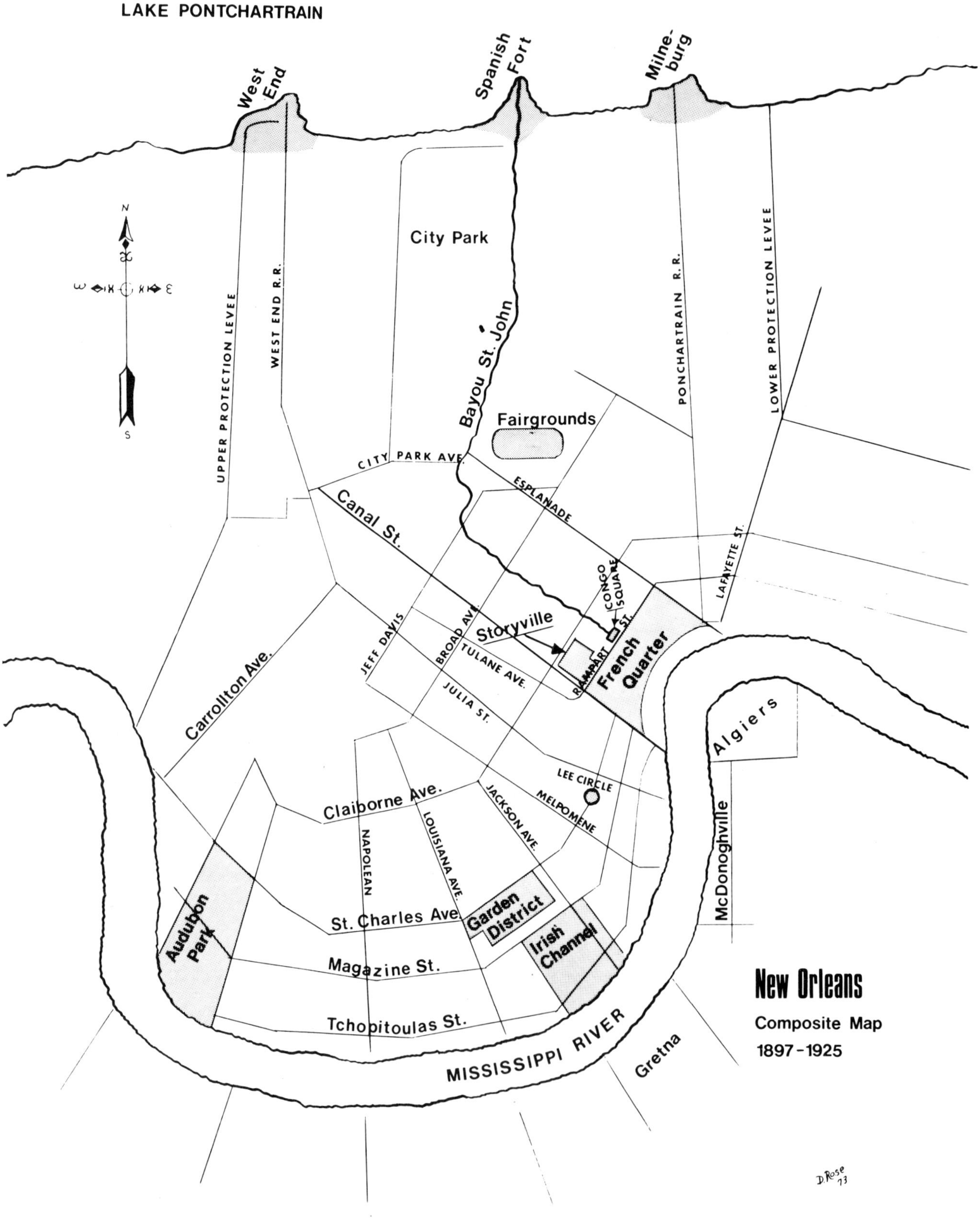

LAKE PONTCHARTRAIN

West End

Spanish Fort

Milne-burg

N

W E

S

City Park

UPPER PROTECTION LEVEE

WEST END R.R.

Bayou St. John

PONCHARTRAIN R.R.

LOWER PROTECTION LEVEE

Fairgrounds

CITY PARK AVE.

ESPLANADE

Canal St.

LAFAYETTE ST.

CONGO SQUARE

JEFF DAVIS

BROAD AVE.

Storyville

RAMPART ST.

French Quarter

Carrollton Ave.

TULANE AVE.

JULIA ST.

Algiers

LEE CIRCLE

Claiborne Ave.

JACKSON AVE.

MELPOMENE

McDonoghville

NAPOLEAN

LOUISIANA AVE.

Audubon Park

St. Charles Ave.

Garden District

Magazine St.

Irish Channel

Tchopitoulas St.

MISSISSIPPI RIVER

Gretna

New Orleans

Composite Map
1897-1925

D Rose
73

TWO

Scarlet Carnival

In the course of the nineteenth century, and especially during the 1880s and 1890s, prostitution spread throughout New Orleans with cancerous persistence, as more and more bawds succeeded in establishing themselves and their entourages in the city's hitherto "respectable" districts.

These women, with few exceptions, made little or no effort to conduct their affairs discreetly or to exhibit a decent respect for the sensibilities of their respectable neighbors. Quite to the contrary, they seemed to take a certain pleasure in flaunting their viciousness. The public visibility of prostitution and associated vice was further heightened by the appearance, early in the 1880s, of a weekly newspaper, the *Mascot*, that drew attention, in lurid, muckraking style, both to the existence of widespread vice and to its deleterious effects on real estate values and other bourgeois concerns. To judge by the *Mascot*'s columns (and by the police blotters), no neighborhood, no institution, was safe—not even Mardi Gras, that favorite of all of New Orleans celebrations since early colonial times.

As celebrated in "Catholic" New Orleans, the pre-Lenten Carnival, culminating on Mardi Gras ("Fat Tuesday"), was a great time for the demimonde and other persons professionally devoted to carnality on a year-round basis. Carnival was great for business, of course, and was thus a fit time for celebration whether or not one had personal ties to Christianity. Just as New Orleans' respectable citizens developed Mardi Gras traditions—street parades, masked balls, etc., sponsored by a host of social and secret organizations—so the denizens of the demimonde developed theirs. Thus the notorious "Ball of the Two Well Known Gentlemen," first held in 1882, became the focal point of

Mardi Gras for the pimps, procurers, prostitutes, petty politicians, and police.

Shortly after Christmas, 1884, this advertisement appeared in the weekly *Mascot*:

Grand Fancy Dress and Masquerade Ball

TO BE GIVEN BY
Two Well Known Gentlemen
New Years Eve, December 31, 1883
AT ODD FELLOWS HALL   CAMP STREET

Notice: This ball will be given under the management of the two well known gentlemen who gave previously the Mardi Gras Ball at the French Opera House.
Admission $2. . . . . Ladies Free
—Ladies invitations can be had at Leon Lamothe's Restaurant, 23 Charles Street near Common.

The "Two Well Known Gentlemen" were not, however, without competition. Rival groups such as the C.C.C. Club and the Red Light Social Club made their bids for the bawdy trade. By 1900 the two gentlemen and the C.C.C.'s had reached an armed truce and were both having carnival balls—the former on Mardi Gras night, the latter on the preceding Saturday. On this basis, both were well attended and prosperous.

The Red Lights, under the paternal arm of the chief of police, David Hennessey, were strong in membership but weak in public relations. When Hennessey was assassinated by the Mafia in 1890, the club lost its influence among the fallen set. Its final function, in 1891, was drowned in the jeering cry "Who Killa Da Chief?"—an epithet normally hurled in these times, and for years later, at all Italians, indiscriminately—a fighting phrase with loaded connotations.

In February, 1889, the *Mascot* questioned the propriety of the Red Lights' forthcoming Mardi Gras Ball:

Should This be Permitted?

Some two years since the announcement was made that a number of well-known young men, generally interested in sporting matters had formed an organization, styled the Red Light Club. At different times the club has been heard of in various ways, and in various cases, though at all times the location of its apartments and the names of its officers were as much a mystery as the day it was first organized. Upon the appointment of Chief David G. Hennessey the club sprang into prominence by the presentation to Mr. Hennessey of the magnificent badge. Follow-

Mardi Gras came to Storyville, too. The annual balls took place at Odd Fellows Hall under the auspices of "the Two Well known Gentlemen," Tom Anderson and

22

FUN! FUN!! FUN!!

DON'T MISS THE

French Balls

GIVEN BY THE
C. C. C. Club and
Two Well-Known Gentlemen

ODD FELLOWS' HALL
SATURDAY NIGHT BE-
FORE MADRI GRAS AND
MADRI GRAS NIGHT

⊄ The Balls have
been famous for
years, so if you
are out for a
good time don't
miss them.
Tickets for sale
at TOM ANDER-
SON'S SALOONS,
and LAMOTHE'S
RESTAURANT,
716 Gravier St.

Frank Lamothe. These advertisements appeared in the
Blue Book *in 1898 (left) and 1905.*

ing this affair came the announcement of some other doings of the Red Lights, in which the name of Chief Hennessey figured, the most recent being the presentation to Officer Pollock of a pair of pistols by the Chief at the rooms of the organization, wherever they may be.

Now all these things are all proper and correct and the Red Lights would not now be made mention of in this paper, but for the fact that the club has made arrangements for a mask-ball which it proposes to give shortly at the Odd Fellows Hall. It is the ball and the invitations issued to it, that objections are raised to. The ball is for the special benefit of the demi-monde and the class that support them and who are expected to bear the expenses and other burdens of the affair. Invitations have been sent out to the proprietresses of different houses of prostitution and assignation with requests that they send into the committee the names of the inmates of the establishment in order that the "ladies" might be provided with invitations to the ball. In addition to this, it is said that the members of the club are constantly visiting bagnios and gently hinting that it will be for their benefit that they attend the ball in preference to attending the affairs given under the auspices of so called well-known gentlemen, who just now, are divided as to former relations, between them.

With reference to the "Red Light" Club the *Mascot* has made an investigation and finds that the majority of its members while holding good positions—many of them being persons of wealth —are nevertheless generally recognized, to use an expression of the day, as the lovers of women notoriously lewd and abandoned.

The name of the Chief of Police is more than frequently mentioned in connection with the club, which, from all accounts, he appears to be a member of. Now with all due respect for Mr. Hennessey and for Mayor Shakespeare, we have no hesitancy in saying that it ill-becomes the head of the police force to be so mixed up with an organization framed for God-only-knows-what purpose and the members of which expect to and do profit by their connection with the public women of the town. The ball should not be allowed to take place under any considerations, and we assure our readers that if it is, we will see that a representative of the paper is on hand and that the name of every man attending the same is given publicity in these columns.

In its closing threat, the *Mascot* drew the most potent weapon in its arsenal (a watchword in the underworld was: "The *Mascot* will tell your name if you don't watch out!"), but in this particular case the indignation of the paper bore no fruit, since it never did get around to naming names. The following week, in a final note on the planned social function, the paper reported anticlimactically, in its regular column "Lorenzo Says":

The Red Lights are not so happy, as they were last Saturday (before the *Mascot* so boldly "exposed" them) and will not be joyful again for some time. [Lorenzo didn't say why. Presumably it was because their wrists had been slapped.]

Their ball will take place, however, as promised, and may be attended by men the names of whom we will publish as also the names of their female companions. The Ball is disreputable and will be attended only by disreputable females and the men whom they support.

It will also be attended by policemen who curry favor with the head of the force and who consider such things as a part of the police manual.

What were the advantages of being a member of the Red Light Social Club? It was strongly hinted, obviously, that in these prelegal days police protection for bagnios was much to be desired by the madams and that the annual shakedown was an inexpensive way to stay on the right side of the law. This was a source of profit to the "young men generally interested in sporting matters." It appears also to have been good business for some "legitimate" businessmen to give their support.

"Bridget Magee's" *Mascot* column spilled the beans on this phase of New Orleans life:

So I see that old Jew Myers, the clothier, has been awarded the contract for putting some decent togs on Chief Shakespeare's greasy police. Do any of you know how he came to get the job in spite of Godcheaux bidding lower than Myers? I tell you, Myers belongs to the Red Light Social Club, do you see? And so does the chief of the alleged police force. The chief told Shakespeare that as Mardi Gras was coming in, the men ought to have a fine fit and Godcheaux would not give it, so the old fraud, Shakespeare, said, "Well, then, let's give it to Myers." Now do you know what the Red Light Social Club is? Of course, you don't. It's a band of fellows that have immorality and indecency for their objects and unless you have the affection of or borrow a tip from the landlady of some bagnios you can't join it.

The social life of the tenderloin bawds was not generally marked by extremes of gentility. Confined to their own company as they were, the girls found frequent need to blow off steam. Necessarily they became targets for each other's wrath with the result that Crescent City police were constantly being called upon to break up differences of opinion that ranged from simple screaming to advanced forms of mayhem.

The girls at Julia Dean's and Gertie Livings-

ton's houses seemed to have been more of a burden than most on the *gendarmerie*. A report of December 8, 1894, related the "free fight" between the Misses Cecile Torrence and Josephine Vinton.

"However," said the *Mascot* man, "the fight was in Cecile's favor, as she knocked her opponent out by biting off one of the fingers of her right hand. . . ."

At the trial, Queen Gertie, in whose mansion (15 Burgundy Street) the fracas took place, was dressed "in a most becoming tailor-made gown trimmed with green. On her maidenly breast she wore Gloria de Dijon and Marshal Neil roses. The regal diamonds were in her shell-like ears. Her lovely hands were encased in immaculate white gloves, the emblem of her own purity. Her glorious hair was most becomingly arranged, and the sun playing upon it showed its golden hues in a most entrancing way."

The reporter's infatuation with la Livingston left room for an appreciation of the defendant. "Miss Cecile Torrence was dressed to kill in a brown silk dress. Her dainty little hat was surmounted by an aigrette of black ostrich feathers. Her blonde hair was elegantly dressed, and her hands were covered with white gloves. No one would imagine this fair creature would try to devour a sister's hand. . . ."

". . . Miss Josephine Vinton (the victim), who is certainly the most beautiful woman that has graced Gertie's bagnio, looked like, and was dressed like, a lady."

Helen Frank, who would later have her own problem with the good Queen Gertie, was the star witness, but she ran into difficulties when the judge refused to hear her testimony in her native Dutch.

The following month, the aforementioned Miss Frank figured in a lawsuit that raised an interesting and unusual legal point. She left the Livingston house for another on Customhouse Street, neglecting to make satisfactory financial settlement with Gertie. As a result, the "queen" held the Dutch lass's trunk. Miss Frank saw her attorney, D. C. Hollander, Esq., who promptly obtained an injunction to sequester her property, which contained about $60 worth of clothing: ". . . any amount of chemises, drawers of the latest and most approved pattern, warranted not to hold water. Among other things in the box are four dozen towels, which Helen does not think Gertie has any right to withhold, as they come under the [legal] act

MISS BRIDGET MAGEE'S SOCIETY NOTES.

"WHAT'S yer rale honist opinion av Alderman Booth, widout jokin'? sed I to me frind "Bottle-Nosed Bill av the Priss," the other day. "Do yez ramimber that Æsop's fable about the frog an' the ox?" he raploied. "Av coorse," sed I. "Will, that frog, who was so full av wind an' vanity that it burst, is himsilf intoirely. Yez will ramimber," he continued, "that two divil's own spalpeens av frogs, in the ould toimes were indulgin' in a conversation about their personal appearance, whin Misther Æsop came along be the swamp where they were an' listened to it. There was also an ox takin' in the situation." "Who was Æsop, anyway?" I inquired. "Will," he raploied, afther takin' a pull at the bottle, "he was a loive newspaper man av that pariod, who worked up little personal items loike yersilf, an' this was a case that enabled him to git the bulge in the nixt issue av his journal on a pompous, windy ould humbug loike Booth. The mornin' afther the interistin' matinee av the frogs, the follow' stirrin' idatorial appeared in Æsop's Oye Opener: 'At last a gleam av hope comes to this banoighted community. Alderman Blatherskite expired by spontaneous combustion at the City Hall, last noight. Durin' the avenin' he had indulged in callin' his collagues in the council chamber be such dagradin' titles that the aujience nivir ixpicted that he wud be allowed to lave the primises aloive, but the pore witches had bin bulldozed be him so long that they were thoroughly subdued, an' quietly submitted as usual. At last he attacked the mayor, raspictin' his inability to conduct the affairs av the city, whin that official, wid his customary placidity av manner, raquisted the loan av a pockit dictionary to enable him to dishcover the drift av the spaker's remarks. This so enraged Blatherskite that he howled at the top av his voice. 'Ah! oh, a toime will come whin yez must acknowledge that I'm a bigger man than ould Crasis himsilf wid all his spondulix!' an' he sat down on a nail that had bin judiciously inserted in the chair which racaved him. A frightful aroma filled the air, the loights wint out; the windows av the chambers were shatthered; an' whin ordher was rastored all that ramained to ramoind the astonished states-min av the missin' Blatherskite was a bad smell an' a grasy shute av clothes.'" "Bully for Misther Æsop! But, Bill," I axed, "did Blatherskite come to the office av the Oye Opener the nixt day an' damand the author av the article; or did he try the Van Benthuysen & Son rackit on the publishers? fur that sounds loike some av our own little effusions." "No, indade, fur iditor Æsop, I am tould, was the John L. Sullivan av thim diggin's an' cud have knocked all the councilmin out in liss than tour rounds widout turnin' a hair; so Blatherskite contined himsilf be sayin' the Oye Opener was a scurrilous shate, an' its iditor was too low to notice."

"Will, Misther Lagan," sed I, to me frind, the council-man, the other day "I'm ashamed av yez! To think that me pit city official should be afther dishgracin' himsilf be visitin' low dives loike the Park theayter at 11 o'clock at noight, where all thim scandilous famales go about widout any clothes worth mintionin'. Oh, whirra, whirra! what have ye got to say about it?" sed I, gittin' mad on account av the way me ancient admoirer was takin' me tongue-lashin'. "Shure, Miss Magee," he calmly raploied, "I only visited the place in me official capacity," an' he luked as innocint as an antaque chimney ornamint. "Oh, the dacate av the ould divil!" I thought, but I only sed: "An' now, what official bisniss tuk yez to such a place near midnight?" "Just to examine the stairs, mam," he answered. "Is it a born ijiot yez take me fur, Misther Lagan?" I damanded, as I got a good grip on me umbriller. "No, indade, but yez see we want some new hoind av steps in the Charity Hospital, to prevint the patients from falin' down stairs an' brakin'

Stay in that company a little longer, an' I'll offer yez an engagemint fur a licturin' tour durin' which ye will daliver noightly in vicious cities throughout the counthry a stir-rin' dishcourse, entitled: "Mountin' the Golden Stairs; or, a Raformed Alderman's Road to Glory."

I mit Misther Charles Whitney, the graceful romancer av the Times-Dimocrat, on Tuesday, on Canal strate. Afther listenin' to his complimints about me promenadin' costhume, I sed: "Begorra, Charles, that was a good fake yez got up on thim Chinase last wake." "Ralely, now, yer viry koind, but that affair actually tuk place; the indigna-tion matin' av the washermin to danounce the Frinch nation was wan av the avints av the sason," he raploied. "In yer moind," sed I, "but if yer so intimate wid the hay-thins, take me up to their shebang, an' maybe we can wurk another paragraph or two out av thim." "I shall be dalighted, I'm shure," returned Misther Whitney, as we started up Camp strate. "We will visit the istablishmint av Misther Soong Lee, who is wan av the wealthiest an' most intelligent cilistials here; quite civilized an' up to the toimes, I assure yez," continued Misther Whitney. "Some toime ago he was troied fur poisonin' a man here; but havin' studied our manners an' customs thoroughly he worked the machine 'allee same as Melican man,' as he gleefully remarked whin acquitted," an' Misther Whitney gazed inquoiringly at me to ascertain if I thoroughly ap-praciated his knowledge av Chinase history an' his palat-able mithod av dishin' up news. "We found Misther Lee prasidin' over a commodious istablishmint a little hoigher up on Camp strate than Lafayette Square. He is a bin-ivolint lookin' snoozer, an' quite good-lukin' fur a Chinee. At the toime av our visit he was arrayed in a pair av spictakles, a pig tail an' a blue slop. Afther Charles had wurked him fur the "Chang Shee Shing" rackit, which he published as a cablegram from Hong Kong on Wednes-day, I tackled him on the polițikil situation. "What do yez think av the State Cintral Committee bisniss, John?" I inquoired. "Daml robbee allee same Tweedism;

the haythen, owin' to opium or some other stimulint, was gittin' frisky. "No; his goosee is cookee. Muchee mon-ey in New Yorkee, daml little here. Fitz no gettee his finger on it. Tweed stealee millions keepee "de gang" solid. Walshee kickee; Boothee talkee too muchee; givee snap away; Fitz no get his workee in; Mealey gittee mad; lose him grip. All go to hellee; ring bustee!" croied Mis-ther Lee, as he polished his spicktkles wid the tail av his ga-bradine. "Begorra, Charles," sed I, as we dapartad, "the haythin undherstands the situation thoroughly; it's a moigh-ty grate pity the Ogden-Nicholls party did not know as much whin they took up Fitz." "Ogden-Nicholls," laugh-ed the ould chap as he followed us to the door. "Too much blowee; no workee; bustee!"

A case has jist bin brought to me notice which illus-thrates viry clearly the loose idays av morality av some av our high-toned shociety peple. James W. Godberry, Esq., a wealthy planter av St. James parish, is the pro-itictor av Mrs. Ada Fairchild, nee Pierce, who residas at 53 N. Rampart strate. He bought her furniture, an' furnishes all the money that is raquoired whin the other patrons av the istablishmint do not come to toime. Whin the fair crachur wishes to take an airin' an' have the com-pany av her Godberry, an obligin' young man from the cushtomhouse is procured to do eshcort duty. Godberry follows afther thim, an' avintually arroives at the place av matin' where he foots the bills fur the rafrishmints or da-varsion as the occasion may damand. He is a patron av whom any dizzy desolate crachur moight be proud; he niver gits on his ear whin the dalightful participator in the profits av the sugar bisniss looks sour, or the sticky enamil fram her countinance gits on his clothes; nor is he jilous av the other boarders. No, indade, on the other hand, he is so modist an' raiirin' that ginirally whin a loud ring is heard at the door he hides himsilf in the armoir

till the coast is clear wanst more. Now there is rarely nothin' much in all this; it is a common occurrence amongst the ancient an' ilivated gintlemin in this com-munity to indulge in little ixcintricities av this koind. James I. Day, Esq., the ixparienced an' accomplished un-derwriter, has the honor to provide for a ravishin' crachur an' her istablishmint, dirictly opposite Mrs. Fairchild's risidince; but there are other circumstances attached to the Godberry warren that rinder it worthy av notice. Saml. L. Boyd, Esq., that worthy an' austere dry goods merchant, who introduced the immaculate Talmage here some toime ago, an' who is invariably conspicious at iviry religious matin' where any Baptist or Mithodist light is trotted out to shine for this banoighted community, has a shute av rooms in the Godberry-Fairchild mansion. Per-haps Misther Boyd is in that naborhood to raform Messrs. Godberry, Day & Co.; or does he anticipate the toime whin the waiter visells will be dasarted be the somewhat tough an' rusty Day an' the bashful Godberry, an' hops to lade thim into the fold? Some peple may say this is no subject fur a journal wid a large public circulation. My answer to this is: the English spakin' portion av New

Her Majesty, Queen Gertie.

Her majesty, Queen Gertie, was dressed in a most becoming, tailor-made gown, trimmed with green. On her maidenly breast she wore Glorie de Dijon and Marshal Neil roses. The regal diamonds were in her shell-like ears. Her lovely hands were encased in immaculate white gloves, the emblem of her own purity. Her glorious hair was most becomingly arranged, and the sun playing upon it showed its golden hues in a most entrancing way.

Gertie Livingston seemed to breed trouble. She and her girls were familiar faces in recorder's court—the text's references to her "maidenly breast," "immaculate white gloves," and "purity" notwithstanding.

that provides that a workman's tools cannot be retained."

Many of the stories have happy endings, though. The *Mascot's* society columns noted that the "lovely Miss Josephine Vinton is now residing at 191 Customhouse Street. Miss Vinton still suffers considerably from her mutilated finger, but she harbors no resentment against Cecile Torrence." As for Helen Frank, she got her towels back.

Queen Gertie Livingston's doings were logged in some detail by the press, possibly because she seemed to be involved in more internecine difficulties than your average madam. She antagonized her competitors by "stealing" their best talent, and she was given to towering rages and vindictive actions on the rare occasions when she herself was the "victim" of one of these "raids." The *Mascot* noted (January 12, 1895) that "it is rumored that the plump and captivating Annie Dechard, 190 Customhouse Street, is quite indignant at her royal majesty Queen Gertie having captured Annie's star boarder, 'Lady Florence.' Nor is the Lady Florence the only recent acquisition to the fair queen's court, as a bevy of young maids of honor have recently graced the court, which now presents a most animated appearance. The lovely Cecile still receives the homage of her many admirers, her having proved herself an adept at biting has only enhanced her qualities."

Julia Dean was frequently in the spotlight over unsettled conditions on her premises. The *Mascot* headline for August 27, 1892, read:

FREE AND EASY HOPS.

AT THE BALL.   AFTER THE BALL.

Mascot artist Bildstein seems to have felt that organized social functions in the tenderloin were a bit too boisterous.

A Most Infamous Dive
*16 Basin Street and Its Notorious Inmates
Again Raise Hell*

On the occasion of yet another brawl, the paper proposed that if this fighting continues, "Julia Dean will have to move her establishment to the first recorder's court."

Not all of the brawling, however, could be blamed on the pettishness of the bawds alone. The roisterers who frequented the palaces of pleasure frequently contributed their share to the breaches of peace common to the area. Many were the young men who caused frequent embarrassment to prominent New Orleans families by indiscreet behavior. Thus the *Mascot* reported in August, 1894:

Toney Hoodlums
A Quintette of Them Deservedly Arrested
For Blackguard Conduct

*Bob Musgrove Prefers Charges Against Officers
Kenny and Coleman*

A few nights ago there was an election at the Young Men's Gymnastic Club. After the election several young men started out to have a real good old time. Their names are Victor and William Demornelle, R. G. Tricou, J. M. Fernare and R. E. Musgrove. The quintette went to the palace of her most gracious majesty, Queen Gertrude Livingston, situated at No. 15 Burgundy Street. A row took place at the house and Vic Demornelle used language not fitting for the scion of an old Creole family. He said that all the women in the house were bastards.

Now the women might not object to being mothers of bastards and themselves prostitutes, but they couldn't bear the idea of their mothers being prostitutes and themselves bastards.

Queen Gertie called to her assistance her faithful officers Kenny and Coleman, they ordered the men to move on, then Vic Demornelle told the officer that he was a horse's ——. The officer was not pleased at being termed that part of a horse's anatomy that is under his tail. But Vic did not give the policeman time to say anything when he said, "do you know who I am? I'm a police commissioner's son." Then to the honor of the police officers they marched the rowdy quintette to the police station.

On Tuesday the accused were arraigned in the second recorder's court and all were discharged excepting Vic Demornelle who was fined $15 or 30 days. Judge de Labretonne remarked when sentencing Demornelle that the court would not be run by police commissioners. R. E. Musgrove has preferred charges before the police board against Officers Kenny and Coleman for making an illegal arrest. It is to be hoped that when the case comes before the police board, Commissioner Demornelle may compliment both officers for fearlessly doing their duty.

Usually, in these cases, when the law was handing out fines it would let the men go free, but the girls paid and paid. This *Mascot* report of June 24, 1893, is headlined:

Six Fair Dames From Kitty Reed's Arrested

On Tuesday evening, a little after six o'clock, there was the devil to pay at 41 Basin Street, the well-known house kept by Kitty Reed.

Louis Ingham, John Sullivan and Lawrence Jackson, alias "Chip" got on a big tear and visited Kitty's house and in a short time there was a regular Donnybrook inside. The neighborhood was in a state of wild excitement. Word was sent to police headquarters and Corporals Duffy and O'Neill and Patrolmen Vijers, Lux, Lewis and Brown arrested the men . . . Kitty Reed, the proprietress of the house, and five of her nymphs, Alice Costlew, Lillian Aspinwall, Josie Raines, Agnes Miles and Alice Corcoran were also arrested and charged with being lewd women . . . Judge Whitaker fined each of the women $5 for being lewd and abandoned.

And so was carried on the tradition that had reached a peak in the days of Gallatin Street during the 1850s when America Williams and Bricktop had held sway, along with the likes of Bridget Fury and One-Legged Duffy—all irrepressible bawds ready to fight for supremacy of one kind or another, and who did so with as little inhibition as they brought to their professional pursuits.

Incongruous though it might seem, in the light of such rough-and-tumble goings-on in the tenderloin, the madams collaborated in the organization of a social club, the Society of Venus and Bacchus, whose meetings were faithfully reported in the *Mascot*. As the paper revealed on October 27, 1894, even the irrepressible Julia Dean was persuaded to host a meeting of the society:

The meeting of the Society of Venus and Bacchus took place at Julia Dean's. Nanon, The Western Beauty, was elected secretary.

Nanon took the floor and said "Last year Miss Gertie Livingston assumed the title of Queen of the Demi-Monde. This year Nellie Dorsey comes here from New York and tells that she has enjoyed the title of Queen in Gotham and does not intend to renounce that title in favor of any woman who used to be a chambermaid. Gertie's perusal of novels has made her very chic, but the only one who ever announced his allegiance to her was Baby Lou, and he renounced his allegiance when her majesty had him arrested for stealing her ring." Nanon then said, "In a Democracy like ours we should have no queen, we are all queens and earn our money by being such. It is our duty to uphold the democracy, and I propose that any man who frequents nigger dives be boycotted by us. In fact, I would go as far as to ask my dear sisters not to recognize any of those mangy sugar planters."

Nanon's speech was loudly applauded and then Miss Julia Dean stated that she had been informed that a Japanese house had been opened on Customhouse Street at Annie Merrit's old stand, and that it should be discountenanced as much as possible. Miss Wilcox said that she was sure the Japs were niggers dressed up.

A letter was read from Miss E. Ford of 16 Howard Street, in which she told that she discovered an excellent plan for landing suckers. It is that of writing letters to strangers claiming acquaintance with them and asking them to call. The general sentiment of the ladies was that Miss Ford's methods should be condemned.

The meeting was adjourned.

A couple of additional reports of the society, both from 1894, serve to confirm the impression that its doings, like everything else in the tenderloin, were animated by commercial motives:

The regular meeting of the Society of Venus and Bacchus was not held for the past two weeks, as an objection was made by several of the ladies to have the meeting held at the residence of Madame Nellie Haley. Quite a scandal has been caused by the little disruption among the ladies and it is said Madame Haley has consulted with her legal adviser in order that a suit may be instituted against the persons who said she did not keep a respectable house. It is to be hoped that the ladies of the V and B will not permit the harmony that has always existed among its members to be disturbed by the Haley controversy.

A very large meeting of the ladies of the Independent Society of Venus and Bacchus was held last Wednesday afternoon in the drawing room of the Mansion House, Customhouse Street. Miss [Annie] Deckert received the members with the grace for which she is proverbial. Refreshments having been liberally partaken of the ladies settled down to business. By acclamation the charming hostess was voted to the chair. Upon taking the chair, she, in most choice language invited all to fill their glasses and to drink to the success of the Winter campaign. The toast was drank with three times three and no heel taps. Miss Deckert then acquainted the ladies with a piece of information, she told that she had learned from a most reliable source that a number of young would-be bloods who are members of a certain club, had organized a joint stock company to run an uptown fairy palace in opposition to the down town bowers of bliss. The bloods have secured as presiding goddess of the bower a well-known Customhouse Street woman, well up in the business. Miss Deckert then said

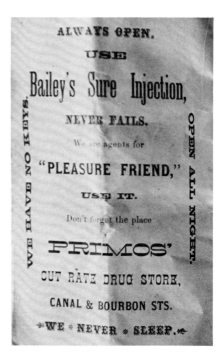

It must have comforted the afflicted to know they could depend on a quick cure at any hour of the day or night. Later editions of the Blue Book *dropped ads for venereal disease remedies, it having occurred to the editor, no doubt, that the mention of V.D. might make brothel patrons uneasy and perhaps work a particular hardship on the ladies listed on facing pages.*

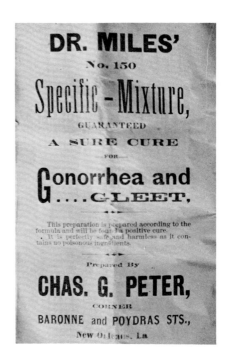

Dr. Miles went on to the Alka-Seltzer business, but back in 1898, in the first Blue Book, *he was offering a sure cure for gonorrhea and "gleet," the latter a colloquialism for the prime symptom of the former.*

she would never think of opposing legitimate business, but she did not think that this move could be termed such. All the fairies are to be imported. The new concern will undoubtedly injure downtown trade, as Military George and the other stockholders will not only have free entree, but will also go to the clubs, hotels and barrooms to drum up business. The matter will be considered at a future meeting.

It may be that the world's oldest profession, as practiced by the demimondaines in other countries, has been or is artful, subtle, and glamorous—constituting, besides its being a way of earning a living, a means of personal and cultural expression. It is probably true that the Hetaerae of ancient Hellas were, as history teaches, a creative element in Greek society. In Japan even now, despite the pernicious influence of the American Occupation Forces, women raised in the authentic geisha tradition receive a professional training in sexual arts and achieve an exquisite virtuosity. We may also infer from the *Kama Sutra* and the *Perfumed Garden* that elsewhere in the Orient efforts were made by some to raise harlotry to the level of artistry—or at least craft of a high order.

The man who walked Basin Street before the turn of the century hoping to find the American equivalents of the Hetaerae or the geishas—that man lost his illusions in the wink of an eye.

More naked than the "circus" performers, who specialized in public display of explicit sexual acts, was the overwhelming greed that visibly poisoned the atmosphere and reduced even relatively innocent acts, let alone sexual ones, to dirty interludes in dirty places. The crudity of leering hags accosting passers-by with mechanical clichés—"Wanna good time, Papa?" "Whatcha know tall, dark and handsome?" "C'mere, Baby, I wanna tell ya sumpn'"—would seem to have been crass enough to chill even the neediest men and boys. Hoarse whispers from the doorways of cribs—"Half a dolluh, half a dolluh, half a dolluh, anythin' ya want fo' half a dolluh, mistuh"—would surely make many a man decide he wanted nothing so much as his privacy. And yet the crib girls did do quite well financially much of the time.

The visitor was never permitted to forget, even for an instant, that he was in a place that sold sex for money, gave as little as it could for the most money, and had no real interest in his enjoyment or satisfaction. The mechanics

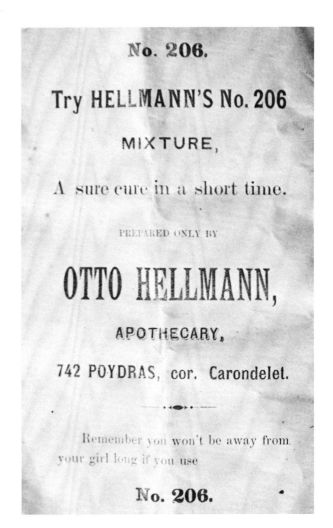

of orgasm were deemed suitable evidence of services rendered.

Behind each prostitute was a small army of avaricious leeches living off her degradation, pressuring for more "production," and fighting off any possible social change that might remove the need for this blight. There was the pimp, functioning as salesman and publicity agent, who sought to direct men to his own string of whores. There was the madam who operated the house and charged high rentals or "cuts" in return for managerial duties. There was the policeman, then as now at the lowest level of cupidity of all, willing to overlook anything, if the price was right. There was the landlord, ever on the scene, his grasping hand outstretched as he turned a face of sober dignity to the "respectable" world. (The landlord could be an uptown Creole aristocrat, who sneered at the madam's demands that the leaky roof be fixed because the rugs were being ruined, or that

This lifelike framed print, beautifully colored, hung on a boudoir wall in Mahogany Hall. It was a salesman's premium gift to facilitate a shoe sale to the room's occupant. In tiny print at the bottom of the figure is the line "copyright 1903 by Friedman Bros. Shoe Company, St. Louis, U. S. A."

a rat catcher should be employed two or three times a year to keep the vermin under control. Or he might be a Rampart Street furniture dealer who felt justified in charging the lowest class of whore thirty times more rent than the property could normally bring.) There were the conscienceless doctors with fake venereal disease cures who grew rich off these poor creatures (and their customers). There were the lawyers who waxed fat off the estates of big-time madams—shysters in and out of city government who clutched tenaciously at the negotiable remains of such as Kate Townsend and Hattie Hamilton, hoping to grab a handful of their tainted loot.

There were the obsequious representatives of out-of-town clothing and shoe firms who paid the madams for the privilege of displaying their wares to the inmates of the bordellos, to whom they grandly gave away tawdry little gifts as premiums for the purchase of enormously overpriced merchandise. There were the newsboys who hung about the entranceways of the houses hoping for a tip to fall from anywhere— from a whore for running an errand, from a man for giving directions, or from a gambler for carrying cocaine to a game. There were the pitiful music-makers of questionable talents who demeaned themselves on red-lighted doorsteps, begging for coins tossed from bagnio windows. There were the unscrupulous druggists and laundrymen who supplied all and sundry with opium, cocaine, or any other drug at inflated prices.

In sum, a very large part of the New Orleans public was, directly or indirectly, a huge collective whore. Many who were involved found Pilate-like rationalizations for themselves, believing their guilt would wash away if they refrained from actual physical contact with the women. Contact with their *money* apparently cost them little or no loss of sleep.

Of course, the prosperity that the red lights brought to the Crescent City could not but affect every inhabitant of the town—but it is shocking to contemplate the hypocrisy of the numbers of so-called "respectable" persons who were directly involved in profiteering off the sins of the women who functioned as the labor force of the sin industry.

The total annual take in the years immediately before and after legalization is not hard to estimate, simply on the basis of striking averages on the numbers of people involved. These figures are general but logical, and will serve to produce a rough approximation of financial matters in the District.

Approximately two thousand prostitutes were working regularly, averaging about seventy dollars a week for tricks alone, totaling somewhere in the neighborhood of one hundred forty thousand dollars a week. Enough information is available to indicate that the forty leading parlor houses each bought an average of three hundred fifty dollars' worth of alcoholic beverages a week, which they sold for approximately four hundred per cent profit, or one thousand four hundred dollars a week each. The entire remainder of the Distrist equaled this amount; so one hundred twelve thousand dollars a week came into the till from sales of liquor, beer and wine. About seventy professional gamblers relieved the suckers of something over fifteen thousand dollars a week. These figures include good weeks and bad, carnival season and Lent. Among the piano players, some thirty of them were taking in several thousand dollars a week in tips.

In all, over a quarter of a million dollars a week, well over ten million dollars a year, probably closer to fifteen million, found its way into the stockings of the prostitutes, the cassocks of the clergymen who owned whorehouse property, the pockets of the politicians and policemen, and the swelling bank accounts of the landlords.

This was a big pie to slice. It could have been much bigger, of course, had the degenerative lust for money not had all of prostitution's dependents clutching at short-term gains. They could have brought a little taste to its decors by bringing in competent professional help. They could have used the simple cosmetics of chambers of commerce and leagues of civic betterment. They could have kept themselves and their places at least visibly clean. All of these measures could have contributed to an increase in customer acceptance and expenditure. As it was, the vice areas remained disgusting, festering sores on the face of New Orleans, rodent and insect ridden, santitation free.

The gutters were open sewers, filled with the contents of chamberpots and garbage cans, dead domestic animals, all the debris of a crowded and careless community in a day when inside plumbing was rare and knowledge of the relationship between dirt and disease was not yet widespread. Not a word of protest was

The Mascot *viewed most businesses as corrupters of the young, but attacked dressmaking and millinery establishments in particular. The reason: they used underage boys to deliver to the houses of ill-repute. Note the very young girl "rushing" a pitcher of beer and a decanter of wine.*

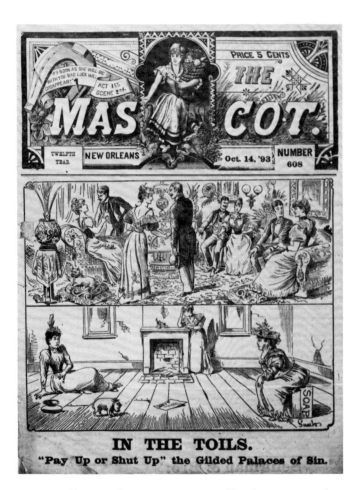

IN THE TOILS.
"Pay Up or Shut Up" the Gilded Palaces of Sin.

THE ASSESSMENT OF PROSTITUTES.
Which Compares Unfavorably With That of Poor Men.

Many madams were irresponsible about paying their bills. In 1893, many furniture dealers were suing for delinquent accounts. The story in the Mascot *surmised that "unless some friends intervene the sheffff [sic] will take a hand in the pie."*

With leading citizens and politicians so heavily invested financially or morally compromised in the bordellos, the property tax assessments on the ladies of the evening were predictably low. Some—Lulu White, for one— seem to have paid few if any property taxes.

raised by the city's inhabitants or civic health groups. Only the strongest-stomached and most lustful of males could have found its products attractive. When newspapers referred to the area as a pesthole, they referred to more than vice alone.

The women seem to have been unanimous in imagining that the trappings of elegance overcame all the repulsive characteristics mentioned. These women would, rather than wash away body odors, douse themselves with perfume and display fancy furniture to distract the eye from filth. Ornate tapestries seemed to be the best method of treating cracks in the walls where the roaches and silverfish lived.

The madams liked expensive things because they believed that showing them off helped business. But they hated to pay out good money for anything. Many a local merchant who had lost heavily by extending credit to the prostitute got himself involved in actually setting up the bawdiest of houses. These "respected" Orleanians, no less than the whores, would do anything for a profit. Consider the case of Mr. Grant and Miss Norton, for example, as reported in the *Mascot* (December 1, 1889). The situation described was typical of many merchant/prostitute relationships. The case raises an interesting point of law, but it was actually settled out of court, presumably to avoid a court ruling that might have provided a precedent by which the losses suffered by Crescent City businessmen could have been astronomical. (The case also represents at least three similar ones involving Miss Kittie Norton, who appeared to take for granted that it was unreasonable for anyone to expect a whore to pay for anything.)

> . . . March 2, 1889, Mr. James G. Grant the furniture dealer of Baronne Street between Common and Gravier . . . filed suit against Miss Kittie Norton . . . [of] Bienville Street claiming the sum of $3,423 less certain credits and claiming a vendor's lien and privilege on the furniture of the house to enforce payment of which, the suit was brought. . . . She admitted the purchase of the furniture and that the same was for fitting up the house . . . , as a place of lovers' rendezvous and so on, to be carried on by the defendant contrary to good morals, etc. The furniture was to be paid for out of immoral business and that all this was known and agreed to by the Plaintiff, Mr. Grant, and also fully understood by him. It further alleged in defense that the house was furnished for its immoral purpose by Mr. Grant, and also ordered by him, that he loaned her money, was surety on her lease and paid several months rent for her to

SECRET SESSION OF THE CITY COUNCIL.
The Necessity of Another Belt Rail Road Amply Demonstrated.

With the new courthouse situated right in the heart of the tenderloin, most public business could be conducted in Hattie Hamilton's parlor. The bottom line reads: "The necessity of another belt railroad amply demonstrated."

Removing Lewd Women From Moon's District.

These Can Be Hustled Out Easily;　　BUT　　Can These Be, Is The Question?

REMOVING LEWD WOMEN FROM MOON'S DISTRICT.

THE ordinance offered by Mr. Moon and adopted by the Council, providing for the forced removal of all lewd women from Tulane Avenue and cross streets opening into it, has been promulgated and the Chief of Police has been ordered by the Mayor to enforce its provisions.

This is a sample of the altogether unnecessary and wholly impracticable ordinances with which our Councilmen seek to acquire a reputation among their constituents, and which crowd our statute books. The region covered by the ordinance and from which it is sought to drive all these unfortunate daughters of sin, has been for the past thirty-five years abandoned to houses of prostitution and debauchery, and all the ordinances that the Council may pass will never remove the stigma that now rests on the locality, nor erase the stain that will always render the habitations contained within its boundaries tenantless save by abandoned women.

Suppose the police would turn out of doors by force all the inmates of the "spotted houses" from Poydras to Canal and from Rampart to Claiborne streets, numbering nothing short of two hundred fallen women, black and white, we venture to ask whither would they be driven? Into more respectable localities, or into less respectable to pack the over-crowded huts and hovels that now cry out for police regulations? The residents of respectable localities would oppose the advent of the hapless creatures in their midst by every power within their reach; and they would be justified in doing so.

The proper remedy is to specify a certain district within the boundaries enumerated, outside of which it will be unlawful for prostitution to be carried on, and see that the ordinance regulating the matter be rigidly enforced by the police. It will work no more hardship to the respectable inhabitants now living within these lines than they have suffered, from the fact that they are already living there, and are accustomed to the annoyances, if any exists.

We fear, too, the ordinance as passed would not be enforced impartially. Within the prescribed limits there are numbers of gilded palaces owned by the occupants where high officials and men of influence while away the merry hours, and it is preposterous to suppose that the inmates of these houses would be driven out or dragged to jail for not obeying the mandates of the Superintendent. On the contrary, it is very likely his official "nibs" would be scoffed at and his minions kicked out, as shown in the accompanying cartoon, did they dare to attempt such. Of course the poor obscure negro or white inmate of the shanty or dive would be racked off in a jiffy, but we ask, would this be impartially executing the law?

Mr. Moon may not like the idea of having so many fallen sinners for constituents, but we fear he must bear the infliction, for a while longer any way. There is no place to put them if removed, and it is better to leave them where they are.

This article, published in the Mascot *on March 26, 1887, was the first to specifically advocate a restricted red-light district. Both illustrations and text predicted that enforcement would be easier to carry out on cribs and low-class houses than in the gaudy mansions of South Basin Street.*

help her along in her business. She alleges that she finally became ruined in her business and being unable to pay, seizure followed. She wound up by asking for a dismissal of the suit on the grounds that the sale having been made for immoral and illegal purposes that the same was defiance of the law and that the purchase price could not be collected.

The case was tried last Thursday and . . . Mr. Grant testified that he went to the house and opened champagne, that he visited there and knew the character of the place . . . the decision hangs not upon whether the money is legally and rightfully owed to Mr. Grant, but whether in the face of the law he can recover.

Kittie Norton's place was considered the most elegant of its kind in New Orleans and was frequented by some of the best known men. . . .

Carrie Freeman, Mattie Marshall, May O'Brien, Nellie Williams, and Sally Levy, all madams in Customhouse Street, were, in common, indebted to a William B. Ringrose for a total of $7,493.07. Bringing suit against these prominent hussies in October of 1892, the late store-keeper's estate guarded against fraudulent conversion by posting sentries at the entrances to the palaces of the two heaviest debtors, Miss Marshall ($4,786.92) and Carrie Freeman ($1,301.65). There is no record of any of the merchandise ever having been paid for, but it is known that in the following year there no longer was a W. B. Ringrose Furniture Emporium.

The venality of police and public officials was not merely whispered at but was taken for granted as a fact of big-city life, with a tolerance that even our contemporary society couldn't have stomached. The *Mascot* asked, reasonably:

> Can the dignity and peace of a commonwealth be maintained when entrusted to a police force absolutely owned and controlled by the demimonde? When police officials place themselves under obligation to prostitutes for entertainment, etc. can decent people expect that order will be preserved and these creatures kept within their bounds? It is not likely. It is a well-known fact that patrolmen have received their orders from commanding officers regarding certain landladies and places of ill-repute.

If the paper sounds a trifle plaintive, it must be recalled that its voice was hoarse after a decade of screaming.

In 1892 the *Mascot* undertook to make a survey of the tax assessments levied on the brothels of Customhouse Street. Its purpose was to demonstrate the effects of the influence of these madams over the town's politicians. Madge Leigh, evidently not in the good graces of the city inspectors and assessors, was hit with an impost of twelve hundred dollars while a much more valuable and larger house belonging to Mamie Christine and another directly opposite, belonging to Lulu White, were both estimated at three hundred dollars, though they contained single items of furniture that alone were worth two thousand dollars or more. Other strumpet queens—Frankie Belmont, Fanny Decker, Annie Deckert and Annie Merritt—escaped assessment altogether and, so far as is known, never paid a penny in tax until the Story ordinance became effective.

The *Mascot* drew the obvious inference from the available facts, pointing out clearly the ties between prostitutes, politicians, and the leaders of New Orleans high society. Nor did the paper fail to report on the petty graft that had prostitutes paying off police at the rate of twenty-

A PLAGUE OF PROSTITUTES.

When all the moralistic cant was cleared away, the issue came down to simple matters of real estate. A man buying a home for his family couldn't be sure that a bordello wouldn't move in next door. This fact, more than any other, aroused the public indignation that brought about the demand for a restricted district.

five cents a day per girl and three dollars a week per madam. The procedure was for the housemaid to make the daily collection inside the brothel in which she was employed and to save it all until Sunday night, at which time she would leave the week's graft on the doorstep.

It is recalled by one former policeman that his Monday morning take filled a large United States Mail sack and was so heavy that it took the combined efforts of two officers to lift it. Of course, after paying his superiors a total of eighty-five percent (average) of his collection, his own cut was more moderate than it originally appeared. One case is reported in which the policeman on the beat made a deal with the higher-ups by which the entire weekly collection belonged to him. He merely paid three hundred seventy-five dollars a week to the powers as a flat fee in return for a Basin Street assignment.

By late in the nineteenth century it was evident to almost everyone that prostitution and all its accompanying evils had created such an intolerable situation in New Orleans that some action—if only a compromise—had to be taken. This was the practical viewpoint and also the knowledgeable one, for prostitution had become too intimate a part of the city's anatomy to be removed with one swift operation. If there could be no immediate cure, there could be at least some semblance of control.

The financial stability and social welfare of the city were seriously threatened by the wide dispersal of harlotry. Specifically, real estate values were seriously disrupted by the unpredictability of the "moral" development of neighborhoods. A man might purchase a home for his family on a quiet street today and find himself neighbor to a brothel tomorrow.

As the nineties dawned, organized voices began to make their demands heard. The *Mascot* carried on a lurid but effective agitational program, exposing the spread of various vices and pointed accusing fingers, sometimes recklessly, at prominent residents.

A Society for the Prevention of Cruelty to Children was formed. Its president, the Reverend Alfred E. Clay, filled his reformer's role tirelessly, turning up case after case of seduction and child prostitution. On August 20, 1892, there is a record of his having had one child prostitute, Leontine Fargoe, age fifteen, taken from a Basin Street bordello to the House of the Good Shepherd. A week later, we read, he had

Alderman Sidney Story. He hated jazz, loved Johann Strauss. It was his ordinance that provided for a restricted red-light district. The fact that it came to be known as "Storyville" in his "honor" was a bitter pill for him.

36

fifteen-year-old Celice Anderson, of 416 Howard Street, remanded after having secured her arrest at 36 Basin Street.

The situation was clearly set forth in a *Mascot* editorial of June, 1892, in which the desirability of a restricted district was considered in positive terms:

> . . . Like gambling, it [prostitution] is ineradicable, yet—if handled properly, it can be curtailed. Against houses of ill-fame as such, the *Mascot* makes no crusade, so long as they are conducted in a decorous manner and are not located in respectable neighborhoods, for they are a necessary evil. The subject is a delicate one to handle, but it must be admitted that such places are necessary in ministering to the passions of men who otherwise would be tempted to seduce young ladies of their acquaintance. But whatever good they may unconsciously effect . . . would be offset were they allowed to flourish in every part of the city. It is a notorious fact that of late such establishments have sprung up in many neighborhoods hitherto free from them, thus obtruding the evil under the eyes of growing girls of respectable family.
>
> Besides, under the present system, many of the demi-monde are diseased, yet ply their trade just the same. The consequence is that growing boys and young men contract contagious diseases which can be suppressed, but which remain in the blood. . . . The evil consequences spread further, for when they marry those affections of the blood are transmitted to their children. . . .
>
> Young men can no more be made continent by legislation than gamblers can be forced to cease gambling, yet the evil results of their intercourse with fallen women can be minimized by State regulation. . . . [There follows a description, at length, of such regulations to control disease by regular examination and put such places in predetermined areas as carried out in certain European countries.]
>
> Why should not such a system be adopted in New Orleans? The social evil is rampant in our midst. . . . Houses of assignation and ill-fame . . . are springing up all over the city. . . . Many a man has purchased a house and lot on a quiet street . . . but has woke up some morning to find the house next door occupied by disreputable people who carouse, receive visitors, hammer the piano all night, use obscene language and convert his paradise into a hell. . . . The council is powerless to interfere as long as the obnoxious people own their house or the landlord of it refuses to eject them. . . .

Opposition to legal controls came mainly from church groups, with their predictable and irrelevant objection that "sin" would be "dignified" if its existence were legally acknowledged. It was no secret that many of the landlords who owned property leased by houses of ill-fame all over town, and who did not relish the idea of losing their tenants to a downtown restricted district from which other landlords would derive the revenue, were pillars of the church for whom any flimsy rationalization would do, so long as the status quo was preserved.

The medical profession balked at the idea of police-supervised medical examinations for prostitutes under a district plan. The town was quack-ridden, with a veritable army of "doctors" who advertised quick venereal disease "cures" in the press; the prospect of any reduction in the incidence of such disease was hardly pleasing to them. Legitimate medical men—who in fairness to the profession must be judged the majority—were opposed on principle to "political interference in medical matters" and thus found the idea of police inspection obnoxious.

A police ordinance (No. 7325), requiring the lower-class bawds to leave the ground floors of Bienville, Burgundy, Customhouse, Conti, Dauphine, and St. Louis streets, had the effect of moving most of them into the areas that would later be part of Storyville. Even so, elaborate vice establishments continued to prosper noisily in the Garden District and the French Quarter. The public and the press clamored for control efforts and then proceeded to reject reasonable proposals that the city fathers offered. Thus an 1892 proposal requiring compulsory medical examination of prostitutes was denounced in a mass meeting of New Orleans matrons as an affront to Southern womanhood. An effort similar in intent to the later Story ordinance, but lacking the legal characteristics that would have made its provisions stand up under appellate scrutiny, failed to pass the combined legislative chambers of New Orleans.

But the stage was now being set for a comprehensive and fool-proof law that would free the city from the spreading anarchy of vice and contain the "evil" within acceptable limits. Such a law needed to be constitutional, enforceable, and acceptable to the city fathers on the basis of morality and equity—and economics.

Thus, when the carefully prepared legislation of Alderman Sidney Story came up for consideration, it met with only token opposition. The legal principle involved had already been articulated by the *Mascot* ten years earlier (March 26, 1887): "The proper remedy is to specify a certain district outside of which it will be unlawful for prostitution to be carried on, and

Storyville, 1906. This is the earliest aerial view of the District. The railroad passenger shed that would extend through Basin Street was still on the drawing board.

see that the ordinance . . . be strictly enforced."

Alderman Story, a respectable citizen and businessman who had made an extended study of the problem during his travels in Europe (with the aid of the prominent New Orleans attorney Thomas McCaleb Hyman, who did the legal research), came up with the finished ordinance at the beginning of 1897. The city council passed it on January 29, 1897, limiting prostitution to the area between North Robertson and North Basin streets, and from Customhouse (Iberville) to St. Louis streets. (See Appendix C.) On February 8 an attempt was made in the council to extend these limits to include certain areas on the uptown side of Canal Street, but protests from Third District property owners quashed the effort.

On July 6, the ordinance was reenacted in an amended form to set up two separate restricted areas, one downtown and one uptown. (See Appendix D.) The uptown section was to have been bounded by the upper side of Perdido Street to the lower side of Gravier Street, and from the river side of Franklin Street to the lower side of Locust Street. The council determined, however, to hold formal establishment of this uptown district in abeyance for a time.

For the next two decades, until March 1, 1917, an uptown red-light district would operate on an informal basis, catering largely to a Negro clientele, having no actual legal recognition, but subject only to minor harassment by the police. This area, thus, was not a part of the area that we think of as Storyville. On February 7, 1917, however, the city commissioners would finally act to set up an uptown district. This ordinance stipulated that "from and after" March 1, 1917, lewd women of "the colored or black race" could not live or work "without" the limits of this uptown district and redefined the downtown district (Storyville) in terms of "the Caucasian or white race." (See Appendix E.)

Alderman Story was mortified when the press proceeded to name the downtown red-light district after him. He protested indignantly and vehemently, but "Storyville" it became and will doubtless remain in history, forever. The press and the historians aside, however, for many and perhaps most ordinary folk it was "the District." As the musician-memoirist Danny Barker put it: ". . . the people I knew called [Storyville] 'the District' . . . I never heard it called 'Storyville' . . . It was never 'Storyville' to me. It was always 'The District'—the red-light district."

And so on New Year's Day, 1898, the century-old epoch of uncontrolled vice came to an abrupt end and a new and unique legal experiment made its debut. It would survive for almost twenty years and demonstrate beyond reasonable doubt that legal recognition of the "evils" incorporated therein could reduce both their incidence and their virulence to the point at which sensible city officials could keep them from becoming a moral and financial drain on the community.

The last gasp of the anti-Storyville forces began on September 22, 1897. George L'Hote, a home-owner whose domicile stood a half block from the limits of the new district, and the Church Extension Society of the Methodist Episcopal Church, established on Bienville Street within the District, jointly brought suit against the city of New Orleans to have the Story ordinance set aside on a variety of legal grounds.

In essence, these grounds summarized all the anti-District arguments that had been brought out through the entire legislative and legal history of the attempt to control vice. The plain-

tiffs dragged the case through every mandamus and injunction proceeding their resourceful lawyers could think of until the matter finally was brought before the United States Supreme Court during the October term of 1899. The court affirmed the constitutionality of the Story ordinance. (See Appendix A for the arguments and counterarguments offered in this important case.)

As New Year's Day of 1898 dawned, the final attempt to set aside the Story ordinance was viewed in most quarters as purely academic. Storyville had begun its legal existence the previous midnight. But since the area had already been thoroughly populated with prostitutes for nearly a century there was neither a dramatic physical change nor any noteworthy celebration. Establishments within the boundaries specified by law simply carried on business as usual. But a number of New Orleans' most notorious bagnios, situated in otherwise quiet and respectable neighborhoods, went dark from one day to the next, inspiring fervent expressions of relief on the part of their erstwhile neighbors.

The entire city looked forward to an era of improvement and stability as a result of the new law. Among the initial effects was an extensive emigration of some of the more aggressive harlots, who self-righteously decried the law's abridgement of their personal liberty and loudly proclaimed the virtues of laissez-faire free enterprise. One such, who went to Galveston, returned three months later as the grapevine carried tidings of a better life for magdalenes under the new regime. Reminiscing in an interview with the author, she recalled:

> I thought the District was gonna be like a big house of correction, where the "peelers" would be like stir guards—you know—you'd be all the time under their thumb—who wants that—so I got out—you know—to Galveston where the cops lay off, but the tricks is cheap—sailors and roustabouts—Anyhow, I begin to hear how great it is for workin' girls, and after a while I figured after all it's home—so I come back and rented a crib on Conti Street for three dollars a day . . . I think from Maestri . . . but maybe it was later I rented off Maestri . . . I started off charging a buck and I remember the first week I took in over a hundred dollars—which was the most I ever made in my life up to that time.

THREE

The People
Within

The administrative entity known as Storyville can be defined and described in terms of buildings, city ordinances, administrative and police procedures, court decisions, and the like. But to look at Storyville in this way is to miss most of the picture. Storyville was, first and last, people—and a colorful lot they were.

Lulu White

Perhaps the most colorful, and certainly the most notorious of all Storyville madams and prostitutes was surely the short and dumpy *café au lait* mistress of Mahogany Hall, Lulu White. Born on a farm near Selma, Alabama, she arrived on the New Orleans scene in the 1880s, accompanied by a very dark Negro who was said to be her stepfather, and immediately embarked on a career of vice. In pre-Storyville days she was arrested innumerable times on charges of prostitution, disorderly conduct, white slavery, and a wide variety of misdemeanors. "Bringing Lulu in" became an almost weekly event. She apparently became familiar enough with certain police and politicians that by the early 1890s her house on Customhouse Street, a rather elaborate mansion, was assessed so low as to be tax exempt.

Making up in showmanship what she lacked in beauty, Lulu was able to attract a successful oil man, a railroad baron, and a department store magnate, in that order, all of whom contributed to the stockpile of cash that eventually financed Mahogany Hall. Vivid is the recollection, still alive in certain aging heads, of Lulu descending the "hall's" swirling staircase, decked out in her gaudy display of diamonds, smiling her celebrated diamond-studded smile, and singing her favorite song, *Where the Moon Shines*. Attired in a bright red wig and an elaborate formal gown, she wore diamond rings on all her fingers (including thumbs), bracelets up both arms, a diamond necklace, a tiara, an emerald alligator brooch on her chest—the works! She was indeed a vision of rococo splendor. The "grand manner" assumed by Mae West in her great film *The Belle of the Nineties* is said to have been based in part on that of Lulu White, except that Mae's "belle" was really white. As originally conceived under the title "The Belle of New Orleans," the film was to have been more explicit in its allusion to Lulu's public image, but title and other changes were made owing to the producer's concern about the racial factor.

Like most prostitutes, Lulu White had her "fancy man," one George Killshaw. Slim, handsome, oozing charm, George led a life with Lulu that lasted a quarter of a century and then ended, as so many such affairs do, when an opportunity presented itself for the long-time pimp to make a big "score" by disappearing with most of Lulu's available cash.

In 1906, glutted with profits from the sin trade and anxious to diversify, Lulu turned her eyes westward to Hollywood, California, in a shrewd and prophetic appraisal of the future of the film industry in those parts. Making the trip in a private railroad car stuffed with servants and her man Killshaw, Lulu arrived in the manner of an oriental satrap. Her plan was to purchase real estate and production facilities that would have made her the proprietress of what could well have become one of the largest studios in town. While she never said so, it may be supposed that Lulu aspired to appear as a star in a production or two of her own. In any event, she was delighted with the prospects and returned to New Orleans to let the details set in her mind before deciding what she wanted to do.

In January, 1907, she sent Killshaw to California to consummate a comprehensive and carefully itemized deal for land and equipment. Unfortunately, she made the mistake of entrusting him with all of the necessary funds in cash. Something like one hundred and fifty thousand dollars was involved in this proposed transaction—an enormous sum for those days. That was the last she saw of Killshaw, and the last we know of this little man. She made no effort to find him, it seems, either because of her attitude toward the police or because of her emotional state. It is supposed that Killshaw, who was recognized in New Orleans as a

Lulu White, 1904. This is her only known photograph. A portrait photograph shown in her Mahogany Hall promotional booklet was, in fact, not Lulu but one of her girls.

41

"black" only because he chose to be, since his color and features were quite Caucasoid, decided to take this opportunity to vanish with his windfall into a new life in the white world.

In 1908, with a view to eventual retirement, Lulu built a saloon at the corner of Basin and Bienville streets, next to Mahogany Hall. This is one of the few Storyville structures that remains standing at this writing.

Mahogany Hall continued in operation under Lulu's aegis until 1917, when the District was closed by federal order. It is not clear what became of her after that. Rumors there are aplenty, but little reliable testimony. As late as 1941 she was seen alive and apparently well by a teller in the Whitney National Bank of New Orleans, where she was making a withdrawal. The most dramatic (but probably apocryphal) tale of her demise has her expiring on a folding cot in the baggage car of a train on which she was returning to her birthplace, Selma, to die. There is no record of her dying in Louisiana.

Lulu claimed to be a West Indian and fondly believed that all that separated her from white society was the fact that she chose not to deny her black ancestry. However, the many persons interviewed by the author were unanimous in the belief that she could not possibly have "passed" for white. Her early attempts to pass failed, as this bit of 1894 *Mascot* gossip shows:

> Fair Lillian (Lulu) White, the diamond queen, says that she doesn't intend to go to the races anymore unless she is allowed on the grand stand. She says that some people take her to be colored, but she says that there is not a drop of Negro blood in her veins. She says that she is a West Indian, and she was born in the West Indies. When a child, she was taken to New York by her father who was a Wall Street broker, and after his death she fell heir to 166 Customhouse Street.

Those who remember Lulu usually speak first of her diamonds, which were like the "lights of the St. Louis Exposition," just as reported in her promotional booklet. They recall also that she was quite fat. Some of the more sensitive mention her harsh and strident speaking voice, and her obsequiousness with customers.

Tom Anderson

On November 22, 1858, a year after the city of New Orleans first passed an ordinance designed to set up a geographically segregated red-light district, there was born in the home of a poor Irish Channel family an infant boy who would grow up to be the veritable tsar of just such a district—the first one that would work. The parents, Anderson by name, christened the child Thomas Christopher, and they doubtless had fond hopes for him. But they could offer him little by way of material endowment and so, like many another youngster so handicapped, he entered upon a business career as a hawker of the *Daily Picayune*.

Bright-eyed and alert, he first came to police attention by pointing out the hiding place of a petty thief and appearing at the courthouse as a witness. For this he received a small honorarium, and afterward he kept his baby blue eyes open as he pitched his papers through the uptown blocks of old Basin Street. He found frequent occasion to let the police know the things they needed to know. By the age of twelve he was already on a friendly basis with the law—as a stool pigeon.

Tom Anderson, the "Mayor of Storyville," combined the functions of super-pimp and Louisiana state legislator openly and simultaneously.

42

For a time, young Tom added to his newspaper earnings by delivering cocaine and opium, picking up the goods at local drug stores and taking them to Kate Townsend's and Hattie Hamilton's bagnios. He abandoned this lucrative sideline on being informed by friendly policemen that, although the drugs were readily available in the city, they *were* illegal, and he might get into trouble having them in his possession, since he was a minor.

Though only sketchily educated (at the Paulding School), Tom had a quick head with figures and was able to secure a position with the Louisiana Lottery Company as a bookkeeper. By the time he had reached his majority he was ready to be married and to make the first moves toward going into business for himself. In 1880 he married Emma Schwartz of New Orleans, and soon became the father of a baby girl, Irene. In 1892, in partnership with one David Heller, Anderson opened a restaurant and bar strategically located at 12 North Rampart Street, and was immediately blessed with the patronage of his old police and political pals, all eager to see their young friend make good.

The elaborate eating place was an immediate success. Anderson had laid it out with private booths and rooms ideal for confidential conferences. Bigwigs left important messages with him and entrusted him with important secrets. Openhanded and close-mouthed, he became a kind of neutral ground upon which politicos and criminals could reach agreements and treaties. In lesser matters he was at times called in to arbitrate negotiations concerning "cuts" and "pay-offs."

Together with Billy Struve, a young police reporter for the New Orleans *Daily Item* with whom he first came in contact in 1895, Anderson opened the Astoria Club on South Rampart Street, which quickly became the focal point for vice in the Negro area.

By this time, Tom was already financially interested in the establishment of a young lady named Josie Arlington, who operated a brothel at 172 Customhouse Street. He had long since separated from his innocent wife and become a frequent escort of the notorious Josie.

Armed with prior knowledge and the trustworthy, though crude, executive talents of young Struve, Anderson acquired the Fair Play Saloon on the corner of Basin and Customhouse streets early in 1897—just before Storyville became a legal entity. He rebuilt it and it opened for

As head of a profitable oil refining enterprise, in addition to his other roles, "Mayor" Anderson of Storyville thought nothing of using company stationery to complain to Mayor Behrman of New Orleans about reformers' allegations concerning the activities of procurers in the District. The two mayors were on cozy terms. In an earlier note (November 8, 1907), Anderson told Behrman: ". . . I intend building myself a home on Canal and St. Patrick and if any chance to have contractors for the water works plant to extend line in that direction as soon as possible same will be appreciated." The note transformed a possibility into a certainty. (City Archives Department, New Orleans Public Library) business in 1901. Later, in 1905, he rechristened it the Arlington Annex, in honor of his scarlet consort.

As Storyville debuted, Tom Anderson's public personality seemed to resolve itself. Forty-years-old, solidly built, of more than average height, his reddish-blonde hair beginning to silver, and sporting a luxuriant mustache, blue-eyed Tom Anderson was Storyville's own version of the turn-of-the-century political boss. An expert in delegating authority and responsibility, he was the picture of relaxed, confident leadership. He always had plenty of time for sober conversation with the hordes of strangers who visited the Annex and is remembered by surviving whores as a kind and friendly gentleman. He wandered among his many establishments in and out of "Anderson County," as many called the tenderloin, with the easy manner of a prosperous monarch—which, indeed, he seems to have been.

His amours, some of them conducted on a semipublic basis, seemed to follow his business investments closely. It is not known whether he helped Hilma Burt finance her purchase of Flo Meeker's *maison de joie* next door to the Annex, but it *is* well known that Hilma became his "old lady" (as Jelly Roll Morton put it), and that this new relationship did not weaken the friendship between Tom and the redoubtable Josie. About 1911 Hilma moved out of the house and Gertrude Hoffmire moved in. Better known as Gertrude Dix, this cultured young lady, talented and attractive, managed 209 and 225 Basin Street (The Arlington) for Anderson—and also began managing Tom himself. In later years (September, 1928) they would be married. She died in 1961, a charming little old lady in her eighties, in an attractive old French Quarter house she owned on Bourbon Street between St. Ann and Dumaine streets.

Despite virtually universal public knowledge of his sordid business and private affairs, Anderson was elected to the state legislature in 1904, and served in it for sixteen years as a member of the Ways and Means Committee and of the Committee on Affairs of the City of New Orleans, while continuing to function also as political boss of the Fourth Ward. He was also profitably involved in the oil business as president, in Storyville days, of the Record Oil Refining Company, and later as founding head (1919) of the Protection Oil Company and, early in the 1920s, of the Liberty Oil Company,

Anderson's Cafes

The Best of Everything
"MY MOTTO"

T. C. Anderson
PROPRIETOR

Anderson's Arlington Annex at Basin and Iberville streets was the business and political hub of Storyville, but if you were out for fun anywhere in the tenderloin, Tom Anderson had you covered.

NEVER CLOSED

TOM ANDERSON'S
Annex
Cafe and Restaurant

NOTED THE STATES OVER *for* BEING THE
BEST CONDUCTED CAFE *in* AMERICA

Private Dining-Rooms for the Fair Sex

MUSIC NIGHTLY
BILLY STRUVE, Manager
CORNER BASIN AND IBERVILLE STREETS
PHONES: MAIN 2825 and 3511 MAIN

The House of Sports.

THE ARLINGTON
CAFÉ and
RESTAURANT,

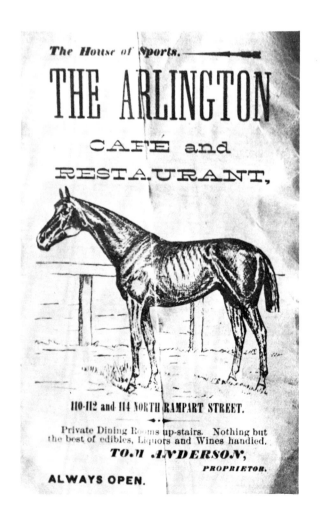

110-112 and 114 NORTH RAMPART STREET.

Private Dining Rooms up-stairs. Nothing but
the best of edibles, Liquors and Wines handled.
TOM ANDERSON,
PROPRIETOR.

ALWAYS OPEN.

which was eventually absorbed by Standard Oil.

The Anderson phenomenon was blatant enough to receive national recognition, and in a muckraking article on "The American Saloon" (*Collier's*, February 29, 1908), Will Irwin wrote about him at considerable length:

Tom Anderson overtops the restricted district; he is its law-giver and its king; one of the names for it is "Anderson County." In his shadow flourish the unblushing, street-open shape of Iberville and Bienville and Conti and St. Louis Streets; the saloons with their wide-open poker and crap games; the dives where negroes buy for fifty cents five cents' worth of cocaine. He is, too, the pad between the poor, foolish, awkward law which is written in the books and the people who dwell under his kindlier law. For example, when a woman of "Anderson County" commits robbery, and when the victim complains so loudly that she has to be arrested, Tom Anderson comes down and gets her out. He does not even have to give cash bail; a local law provides that a minor criminal, at the discretion of inspector or judge, may be released on the parole of any responsible prominent citizen.

And the "Hon." Tom Anderson represents in the Louisiana State Legislature a large and important district of New Orleans—has represented it for two terms—was nominated at the primaries last month for a third term, and will, by every probability, be elected in April. [He was.] He is a member of the Ways and Means Committee and the Committee on the Affairs of the City of New Orleans—two of the most important in the Legislature. Mr. Anderson belongs to the liberal wing of the State Legislature; he does not believe in sumptuary laws; he thinks that it degrades the citizen to take away from him the privilege of choosing for himself between right and wrong.

Briefly, here is the reason for Tom Anderson: With a little break here and there, New Orleans has been in the grip of a ring. No large city in the United States gets such poor returns for the public money expended as New Orleans. It is ill-paved, ill-policed, behind in municipal improvements; the public money is needed for a thousand and one sinecure jobs. By the same token, no other city of the country runs vice of every kind so wide open. Tom Anderson has been a great help. Highly prosperous himself, he has not failed to divide up with the power which enabled him to be prosperous; and he was helped to make the saloon-keepers, the gamblers and the brothel-keepers generous. It was his whim to go to the Legislature, and a grateful people, recognizing his services, rewarded him.[. . .]

As America prepared to enter World War I, it was widely assumed in Storyville that the empire of Tom Anderson would continue to expand, if not geographically, at least in wealth and

OUR HOUSES OF PROSTITUTION.
THEIR INMATES, PATRONS & OWNERS!

power. And so in August, 1917, when the United States Secretary of the Navy Josephus Daniels ordered the District closed down, its denizens assumed, naturally enough, that Tom Anderson would take care of everything, just as he always had. Most people simply refused to believe that Storyville could be shuttered. But Anderson, now sixty years old and slowed by wealth and good living, his notorious lusts sated by the most accomplished bawds of Basin Street, made only token resistance. As the deadline approached, he permitted his paramour, Gertrude Dix, to confront the courts with the argument that the order to close Storyville was both confiscatory and unconstitutional (as indeed it was), citing her fifteen thousand dollar investment in furnishings and equipment and a two-year home-improvement contract for six thousand dollars to which she was committed. Storyville, she maintained, was a legal entity working effectively for "the protection of public morals and public health, good order and the peace of the community." She could have spared herself the trouble.

Anderson kept the Annex open for a time, but his heart was no longer in it. He did continue some of his other enterprises, however, and one of them, a restaurant on Rampart Street, got him in trouble with the law in 1920. On February 3 of that year Anderson went on trial charged with "knowingly conducting an immoral resort within ten miles of a military camp." His Rampart Street establishment, it seems, was a place where "shady ladies" met their prospective customers and enticed them into a brothel upstairs above the restaurant. Undercover police investigators testified that forty "known prostitutes" were identified in the place on a typical night.

Anderson testified that he had been in the saloon and restaurant business on North Rampart Street for twenty-eight years (since 1892). He stated that his restaurant license was based upon an annual food business of forty-five thousand dollars and that he also paid a "large saloon license." Witness after witness paraded to the stand with damning testimony, but the big boss stuck to his claim that he had no knowledge of any illicit activities on his premises.

The case ended February 5 in a mistrial, under circumstances that the newspapers never made clear but that are not important to this narrative. The incidents of the trial did make banner headlines on all the newspapers for three days. This was the last time Tom Anderson was to be connected with prostitution, at least publicly, for the rest of his life.

Religion and repentance overcame him in 1928 when, after a frightening illness, he began to make regular visits to the church and to endow it with substantial funds. In September, 1928, now seventy-one years old and in relatively poor health, Anderson joined with Gertrude Dix in holy wedlock.

Tom Anderson died on December 10, 1931, leaving his widow a known estate of one hundred and twenty thousand dollars. However, a Mrs. Irene Delsa, widow of George Delsa, the former manager of Anderson's Rampart Street Café and Restaurant, contested the will under the state concubinage law. In a suit financed by her mother-in-law, Anna Delsa, operator of the newsstand at the corner of Rampart and Canal (close to the restaurant), Irene Delsa proved that she was the legitimate daughter of Anderson by his first wife, Emma Schwartz. The court, noting that Anderson and Gertrude Dix had actually been legally married, held that neither the concubinage law nor the precedents cited could apply. Plaintiff, however, was given a substantial share of the estate through the generosity of Mrs. Anderson, who felt that Mrs. Delsa, once proved a legitimate child, was entitled to an inheritance.

In 1931 the daily papers included very little of Tom's "colorful" background in his obituary. A few clichés, references to his devotion to the church, his personal popularity and geniality blended into an innocuous social epitaph for the one-time overlord of organized vice. Thus he closed his career in a city tolerant enough to let him die without reproach.

Josie Arlington

One of New Orleans' most prominent demimondaines from early in the 1880s until her death in 1914, Josie Arlington was born Mary Deubler in 1864 or thereabouts. At the age of about seventeen she came under the influence of an obscure "sporting man," known variously as Philip Lobrano or simply as "Schwarz," who soon had her working for him in one or another of the brothels on Basin and Customhouse streets, usually under the name Josie Alton. Their relationship continued for about nine tumultuous years, during which she supported not only Lobrano but several members of her own family whom Lobrano considered, as he put it, a "flock of vultures." He would have preferred, one supposes, to have been the sole financial beneficiary of his woman's labors.

In her early years on the turf, beginning in about 1881, Josie Alton or, as she began calling herself in 1888, Josie Lobrano (though she never actually married the man), achieved distinction as one of the most irascible bawds in the city—a considerable accomplishment, considering the competition. In 1886 one of her competitors, a Negro harlot named Beulah Ripley, tore out most of Josie's hair in the course of a ferocious encounter on Burgundy Street; Josie, for her part, bit off half of one of Beulah's ears and a good part of her lower lip, as well. When

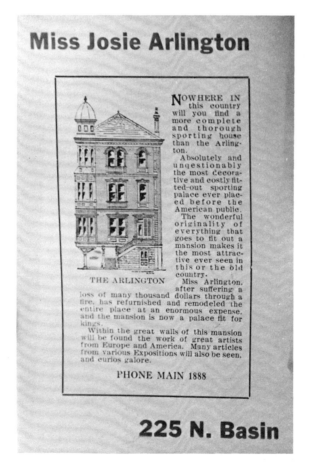

La Arlington's house as described in the third edition of the Blue Book.

Josie opened her own house at 172 Customhouse Street, in 1888 under the name Lobrano, the address was soon notorious for its choleric viragos—a type of woman seemingly of great appeal to many men, for the place prospered.

On November 2, 1890, however, on the occasion of a noisy fight involving not only Josie and her girls but virtually everyone in the building, Philip Lobrano shot one of the "vultures," Josie's brother, Peter Deubler. Lobrano was tried twice and finally acquitted but his intemperate act had cost him his meal ticket. Josie, determined, as she put it, "to turn over a new leaf," changed her name to Lobrano d'Arlington and declared that henceforth only refined gentlemen with a taste for "amiable, foreign girls" could be assured of their gracious company in her "château," a place from which all brawlers, male or female, would be forever excommunicate. It was her intention, apparently, to become the most high-toned madam not only in New Orleans but in the whole country. To the extent that such a thing can be measured, she may well have succeeded, especially after the establishment of Storyville, when she moved from Customhouse Street to Basin Street and changed the name of her establishment from Château Lobrano d'Arlington to simply the Arlington, perhaps the grandest—certainly it was the gaudiest—bordello in the District.

Josie's concept of what refined gents wanted by way of "amiable, foreign girls" is indicated by a squib published in the *Mascot* in 1895, when she was still on Customhouse Street. "Society," the announcement read, "is graced by the presence of a bona-fide baroness, direct from the court of St. Petersburg. The baroness is at present residing at the Chateau Lobrano d'Arlington, and is known as La Belle Stewart." Alas, the "baroness" was soon exposed as a "circus" specialist who had never been closer to the Russian court than the midway of the Chicago world's fair, where she had performed as a hoochy-koochy dancer. A number of Josie's other "imports" were equally fraudulent, but her customers did not seem to mind. If the girls were not "foreign," at least they were "amiable" to men with money to spend—and these proved to be legion. The château and later the Arlington were both immensely profitable.

In 1905, however, the interior of the Arlington was badly damaged by fire and Josie and her girls had to set up shop temporarily in rooms above her friend Tom Anderson's saloon while their regular quarters were being refurbished. (Anderson's would thereafter be known as the Arlington Annex, and he even had this name painted on the front of the building.) The greatest damage, however, had been to Josie's mind. Having almost died in the conflagration, she was never quite the same again. Suddenly moody and introspective, haunted by intimations of her own mortality, the one-time brawler bought an expensive burial plot in Metairie Cemetery and fitted it out with an imposing red-marble tomb. The plot alone is said to have cost her two thousand dollars, the tomb and adjacent statuary as much as eight thousand. The tomb is surmounted by two large flambeaux. There is a cross engraved on the back, while at the front, engraved in the copper door, there is a basrelief of a kneeling woman, her arms filled with flowers. A beautifully executed statue of a young girl stands at the entrance in an attitude of knocking at the door.

In earlier, happier years Josie had built for herself, at a cost of thirty-five thousand dollars, a beautiful private home on Esplanade Street. In 1909 she retired there, leasing the Arlington to Anna Casey, and lived out her life—brooding, once again noisy and violent at times, to judge by the neighbors' complaints. She died, aged fifty, on February 14, 1914, and was buried the next day. The demimonde sent flowers but did not attend the funeral, according to the New Orleans *Daily Item,* but her loyal friends Tom Anderson and John T. Brady (who were said to have advised her retirement) and a local judge, Richard Otero, were in attendance, as were the Sisters of Charity. Josie's sole companion in her last years had been a niece, whom Josie had had educated in a convent, and who married John T. Brady soon after Josie's death.

For years afterward, crowds continued to come to visit the grave, which became a kind of macabre tourists' attraction. Legend has it that the city had installed a traffic light on a corner near the cemetery and that by a trick of refraction the red light glowed upon the tomb itself. It is said to have become so great a curiosity that the remains had been moved to a different tomb. The fact is, however, that the tomb was sold and Josie's bones disposed of in an ordinary receiving vault. The tomb itself, however, still stands, albeit with a different occupant whose initials, by pure coincidence, were "J.A." The caretaker at the cemetery no longer directs the morbidly curious to the famous burial place.

The tomb of Josie Arlington in Metairie Cemetery became an object of much tourist interest. This greatly annoyed the deceased's survivors, who eventually sold the tomb and disposed of her remains elsewhere. The statuary was to symbolize Josie's boast that no girl had ever lost her virginity under the Arlington auspices. This virgin is allegedly being turned away for that reason—at least for the moment.

Emma Johnson

Long, rangy Emma Johnson was probably the most wanton of Storyville's sinners. Caring nothing for life or human emotions, a hard, masculine type who was possibly the closest approach to pure evil the crescent City ever harbored, sadistic and unprincipled, this virago was selling children of both sexes into slavery years before Storyville came into being. She then became its most sensational and unprincipled impresario, offering unbelievably lewd "shows" every night in her notorious studio on Basin Street.

Born before the Civil War of Acadian forebears in the Louisiana bayou country, this wench started life as one singularly unattractive to men. Early drawn to lesbianism, Emma exercised a strange power over many of her sex and took great pride in the fact. Long before abnormal psychology had stature as a science, Emma was consciously formulating useful generalizations that a Kraft-Ebing might have envied and discovering a host of ways to exploit sado-masochism, fetishism, and voyeurism (among other things) for monetary gain.

She became expert in ways and means for influencing countless young girls into lives of shame, and developed many an alcoholic and narcotics addict, since those so afflicted would do her bidding the more readily. She caviled neither at kidnapping nor at functioning as accessory to rape. She forced brandy down the throats of ten-year-old girls to make them amenable to sexual overtures.

Savage and full of hate, she served her own apprenticeship as a prostitute during the Reconstruction, making up for her lack of beauty with fierce energy and a daredevil willingness to engage in any form of erotic misconduct the mind of man or woman could dream up. Combined with a psychotic tendency for exhibitionism, these characteristics were so overwhelming that Emma became notorious even among the lowest classes of strumpets. She soon found that it was more profitable to perform her misdeeds in full view of an audience than merely for the fees available from individual clients. In 1880, in her house in Gasquet Street (now Cleveland Street), she frequently put on these productions, with herself as the central character. Wealthy men of the town, not in the least in-

Mme. Emma Johnson

3 3 1 AND xx 3 3 3 BASIN STREET

Better known as the "Parisian Queen of America," needs little introduction in this country.

Emma's "House of all Nations," as it is commonly called, is one place of amusement you can't very well afford to miss while in the Tenderloin District. Everything goes here. Fun is the watchword.

Business has been on such an increase at the above place of late that Mdme. Johnson had to occupy an "Annex." Emma never has less than twenty pretty women of all nations, who are clever entertainers.

Remember the name.

EMMA JOHNSON
331 and 333 BASIN STREET

EMMA JOHNSON'S

Of Emma Johnson's Studio, house pianist Jelly Roll Morton reported in Mr. Jelly Roll: "They did a lot of things there that probably couldn't be mentioned, and the irony part of it is that they always picked the youngest and most beautiful girls to do them right before the eyes of everybody. . . . A screen was put up between me and the tricks they were doing for the guests, but I cut a slit in the screen, as I had become to be a sport now, myself, and wanted to see what everybody else was seeing."

LEWD AND ABANDONED.

LEWD AND ABANDONED.

Emma Johnson, the Notorious Keeper of No.
20 Gasquet Street, is Fined Upon
the Above Charge.

In all cities where many people are congregated together, there can be found the extremes of virtue and vice. The former is the more conspicuous, for it cries from the hilltops so that all men may hear its voice. It meets in churches, whose lofty spires challenge the attention of all. Its deeds are chronicled at length by the newspapers; when it does a good deed, journeys, marries, propagates its kind or dies, the whole world is informed of the fact. It is seen by day, its inherent good qualities appearing more bright in a setting of busy streets and flowery avenues, its steps heralded by the jocund song of birds and its beauties illumined by the glad light of the sun, which it resembles; for standing in its radiance, one would hardly dream that co-existent with it is that hideous monster, Vice.

When one strolls at noon down one of the beautiful avenues of this city, the whole world appears fair. On every hand are green, well-trimmed lawns, set out with palms and other sub-tropical plants; or gardens where roses, pinks, violets, lilies, forget-me-nots, crocuses, and many other beautiful flowers blend into a variegated mass of color. Behind them rise houses in all styles of architecture, from the massive stone gothic residence of the wealthy banker to the pretty Queen Anne cottage of the newly-married clerk, which seems to exhale an atmosphere of love and content. From the shrubbery issues the music of feathered songsters; little children play upon the lawns; all is peaceful happiness.

But behind and beneath all this is the reverse of the picture. Behind the beautiful houses are the receptacles of ordure, flushed by no sewerage system, the effluvium of which mingles with the atmosphere and, on misty days, assails the olfactories of the people. Beneath the iron plates which bridge the gutters stagnates a mass of foetid putridity, which is not removed, but simply hid and ignored. In the sunlight the children romp and play; ladies gracefully perform their daily avocations or pay their calls, recking naught of evil; but from those cloaca and gutters

rise the demons of miasma, fever and ague, silent and invisible, but insidious and menacing. About some laughing child, stately dame or busy man they wreathe their misty arms; the one embraced complains of a chill. A week later, a funeral cortege passes down the avenue, and the filth-begotten Frankenstein laughs mockingly from his gutter home.

As in the material, so in the moral world. In the light of day, Virtue promenades upon the streets and raises its voice upon the highways. But night comes, and with it Vice protrudes its Medusa head from its lair, looks cautiously around, grins sardonically, and drags its serpent folds out into the dusk. Fearing the light, it loves the darkness. Its deeds are those of gloom, and necessarily so. Conscious of its own hideous aspect, it knows full well that when the sun shines full upon it, it can only repel the young and innocent. An ancient legion tells of a dragon which had daily to be appeased with a young and virtuous girl. Vice demands similar sacrifices, both of boys and girls. The girls it does not devour, but uses them to allure innocent lads, and with the money of the latter Vice dines off plate, drinks good wine, wears fine clothes and bribes the authorities.

"Why should this monster exist?" the reader will enquire. Why, indeed! Why are the gutters allowed to remain filthy? Because public sentiment has not demanded either the abolition of the monster, or the cleansing of the gutters. The moral and orderly population is responsible for part of the vice and iniquity just as it is responsible for part of the filth and garbage. A health officer tells them that their outhouses must be cleaned, they thank him and have them attended to. Newspapers rightly and fearlessly conducted are the moral health inspectors of the community. They point out the plague spots and call upon Virtue to eradicate them. If they are permitted to fester and spread, then Virtue is to blame and becomes a tacit coadjutor of Vice, and should any of its sons or daughters become the prey of the monster, Virtue can blame—not Vice—but itself.

In this city there are many gilded palaces, which are known as immoral and can be pointed out to the young. There are also dens, where sin crouches and traps the unwary. Such are to be found on Bienville, Gasquet, Gravier, Franklin and other streets in that vicinity. Behind the jalousie of such a house, sits a vile procuress. A footstep approaches, she peers through the open jalousie, sees a young man, calls him. If he enters, he finds young girls sitting in the room, who have most probably been enticed

there for the evening by the procuress who called him in. She has represented to the poor girls that they can earn money and get good clothes by deceiving their parents and visiting her. There they sit, afraid of detection, ashamed of their conduct, but dazzled by the allurements held out by the infamous woman who owns the house.

Having enticed a man, the procuress whispers to him that the girls are young and innocent, leering at him with filthy meaning. She seduces him into staying for a while. If he does, a girl loses her virtue, he stains his soul, and the procuress is enriched by the sin. Such places are hellholes; a menace to the city. Like the devilfish so graphically described by Victor Hugo, they hide in obscurity and spread forth their bloodsucking tentacles, sapping the youth and moral health of the community.

Several times in the past six months, the MASCOT has had occasion to call the attention of the authorities to a house kept by a colored woman named Emma Johnson, at No. 20 Gasquet street. On one occasion a young girl was taken from there by the police and sent to the House of the Good Shepherd. That girl was very young and said that the Johnson woman had persuaded her to go there, in order that she might make a little money. It was a sad sight to see the girl's grandmother in court when the girl was brought up. The old lady thought her granddaughter had gone to visit some friends and was griefstricken when she learned of her presence in such a den of iniquity. Last week the Johnson woman again appeared in court, charged with being lewd and abandoned.

Officer Flynn, who deserves credit for his efforts to suppress such places, testified against her. He said that on Saturday night he was passing out Gasquet street when he saw Emma Johnson sitting at her open window, thus violating the ordinance compelling such characters to keep their blinds drawn. He ordered her to close the jalousie and keep in, but she refused and abused him, calling him vile names. At that moment two drunken men at the corner raised a disturbance. He went off, placed them under arrest and returned to the house. As he approached it, he saw her call to several passing men, who entered. When he reached the window, he found her still sitting at it.

He rapped his club and again ordered her to close the blinds. She impudently asked him if he knew whom he was talking to, and told him to go and mind his own business. "I shall arrest you," said the officer. "Will you?" queried the woman. "I'll call my friend from up stairs." He ordered her to open the door, but she refused. He attempted to enter by the window, whereupon she opened the door. He entered and arrested her, at which she tried to up stairs, but he prevented her. She tried to bribe him to let her go, but he was unbribable. One of the girls got her hat and he marched her off to the station, where she was locked up. After hearing the testimony, Recorder Whittaker fined her $20 or thirty days. No comment is necessary, but the S. P. C. C. should keep a lookout upon her infamous place.

Emma Johnson was fined twenty dollars for failing to keep her blinds drawn as required by law. The Mascot *reported that her peccability extended far beyond this minor infraction.*

clined to partake of her favors, proved eager to spend their money with her for laughs, paying her more and more just to find out how depraved she could be.

In about 1883 she began to add the sale of virgins to her enterprise and became the closest thing New Orleans ever had to a jobber in girls.

On October 17, 1891, a *Mascot* reporter scouted the rumor that a virgin was for sale at Emma Johnson's, when this future Basin Street impresario was still directly in the procuring business on Gasquet Street. Posing as a prospective customer, the newsman took the girl into a bedroom. On being pressed for information, she said she had been persuaded to come to the Gasquet Street house on the promise of five dollars. When the reporter told Emma he was going to leave without "initiating" the child, but suggested he might return later, Emma was incredulous: "Why, you're foolish! You won't get another chance like it in the city in your lifetime! The girl's a virgin!"

The reporter *did* come back, almost at once, but with a policeman in tow. The girl was turned over to the House of the Good Shepherd, the home for wayward girls, and Emma was arrested. But of course she paid no fine, spent no time in jail, and got off with another "warning."

After the Story ordinance went into effect, Emma's enormous "studio" became the largest establishment in the District. It occupied the premises of 331 to 335 Basin Street, containing a huge theater-ballroom in which her "circuses" were produced.

A constant violator of the law, the woman never served time or paid a substantial fine! As widely known as she was for her impositions on minors, she nevertheless maintained an immunity that must have been based on the fact that the city fathers well knew that her place was a major factor in attracting convention business to New Orleans. (Elsewhere in this volume will be found a first-hand report of the experiences of one of Emma Johnson's performers.)

Emma was still operating at full steam when the District closed down in 1917. She was then nearly sixty years old, and had made an enormous amount of money, little of which she had spent. She seems to have left the city at once. The obituary files of the city do not contain her death notice, but she is thought to have died in St. Louis in 1927.

PHONE MAIN 9421

Willie V. Piazza

317 N. Basin St.

Countess Willie V. Piazza

In the long run, the madams with the most flare for showmanship were the ones who dominated Storyville and influenced its tone and progress. Willie Piazza was one of these prime movers, and her establishment was the setting for some of the most dramatic events ever to occur in the District.

Willie, herself, was one of the most cultured "landladies" New Orleans ever had, an octoroon fully at ease in the English, French, Spanish, Dutch, and even the Basque languages, and possibly also in Portuguese. Widely traveled, the "Countess," who of course had no hereditary claim to such a title, wore a monocle, smoked Russian cigarettes in a two-foot ivory, gold, and diamond holder, and favored a diamond choker around her slim neck. In contrast to Lulu White, Piazza could easily have "passed" for white. She was truly a fashion leader of her time, and many respectable matrons of New Orleans' first families attended the annual opening days at the Fair Grounds racetrack with their dressmakers in tow, just to copy the outfits worn by Countess Willie and her girls.

It was in Willie Piazza's house that the soldier of fortune Lee Christmas, along with Manuel Bonillas and Guy Molony (who would later become chief of police in New Orleans), hatched the Honduras revolution of 1910. It was here also that the nephew of a renowned cleric met his fate after committing an unconscionable act of sadism upon a member of Piazza's troupe. Willie herself shot the offender dead. (The incident was depicted fictionally in the Tom Sancton novel *Count Roller Skates*.)

Old-timers recall that Willie was the first of the brothel keepers to become aware of the differences in quality among the piano players who performed in the District. Early connoisseurs at times frequented her place just to hear the pioneer hot-piano greats such as Ferdinand "Jelly Roll" Morton and Tony Jackson. Her enormous white upright piano was a famed showpiece, and Jelly Roll recalled that she was the only madam in the District with sense enough to keep the instrument tuned.

Little is known about the origins of the Countess. According to an interview published by Kay Thompson in the *Record Changer,* she was still alive in 1947, living on the French Riviera with a newly acquired husband—this time a bona fide member of the nobility.

Despite her theatricality and flamboyance, Countess Willie created few antagonisms in Storyville. She is remembered as a generous and cooperative *grande dame* with an understanding heart, as being considerate of her "boarders," and as being always ready to help a colleague in distress.

In later years she was said to have avoided laughter for fear of causing her face-lift to come undone. It was also reported that she had a music box installed in her mattress. Her personal library, the best in the District, included the unexpurgated *1001 Nights, The Anatomy of Melancholy* by Robert Burton, and several works by Alphonse Daudet, who was said to be her favorite author. She was not known to have had any amatory ties during her days in the District.

Voodoo Women

The voodoo woman Julia Jackson, six feet tall, black-haired, and cross-eyed, ministered to and against the prostitutes of Storyville for years. She was last seen in the 1930s, long after the demise of the District. Among her most feared "powers" was the alleged "sealing power" which reportedly could "close up a whore so she couldn't do no business." The most dire threat one strumpet could hurl at another was that she'd pay Julia Jackson to have her enemy "closed up." She is also supposed to have been able to induce pregnancy, cause abortion, and infect people with various venereal diseases from a distance (goat testicles for gonorrhea, wasp blood for syphilis). Whenever a defective baby was born to a Storyville prostitute, it was assumed that it had no father and was a product of Julia Jackson's curse.

"Lala," another voodoo woman, told reporter Robert Tallant: "I done a lot for the women in the sportin' houses. I made 'em put red powder on one leg and green powder on the other. They got so many men they couldn't handle the business." (She also said: "Me? I is really a Catholic.")

An association of Storyville madams, which met regularly, agreed to refuse to use the services of Lala and other voodoo practitioners against each other. May Spencer, a member of this self-styled "benevolent association," established herself as a prophetess by foretelling that if the ladies kept on fighting each other with such weapons as Lala and Julia Jackson supplied, the government would one day come in and shut down the whole District. They did and it did.

Eulalie Echo, whose real name was Laura Hunter, was closely associated with the sporting women of the tenderloin until about 1905. Widely known as a "good" voodoo woman, she was constantly being consulted by madams, barkeeps, and strumpets on vital matters. Her solutions required the use of quantities of gris-gris, turtle hearts, black cat bones, and other such esoteric stock. Eulalie was the godmother of Jelly Roll Morton, who would become one of the great men of jazz, and who would attribute many of his problems late in life to his having been present when she held "séances."

Madame Papaloos was the "woman" of Aaron Harris, the most notorious of the District's "tough guys." Her powers made it possible, according to tenderloin legend, for Harris to escape legal punishment for his many misdeeds. Jelly Roll recalled that "She was supposed, from certain evidences, to tumble up Aaron's house to discourage the judge from prosecuting . . . take all the sheets off the bed, turn the mattress over, hang sheets in front of the mirrors, turn the chairs over, which was said to confuse the judge. Then she would get lamb and beef tongues from the market and stick pins and needles through them in order to tie the tongues of the prosecuting attorney and the witnesses . . . that way, Aaron Harris, the ready killer, was always successful in getting out of his troubles."

Voodoo was the true religion of Storyville—the doctrine and dogma in which most of the inmates believed at bottom, were they Catholic, Protestant, Jew, or Moslem. Part of the ritual for keeping away the evil spirits was to scrub one's doorstep with brick dust. Zozo la Brique with her loaded buckets, wearing a red bandana and a calico apron, got rich supplying such dust.

functions, and most of them were undoubtedly more interested in the Negro prostitutes who performed lascivious routines under Laveau's stern leadership than they were in voodoo as a religion.

In his book *Voodoo in New Orleans* (1946), Robert Tallant quotes a white man on the subject of Marie's orgies at Maison Blanche, a building near Lake Pontchartrain that the first Marie had built as an assignation house and that remained in the possession of the later Marie. "I'll tell you the truth," the man told Tallant,

the way I see it that place wasn't nothing but a fancy kind of whorehouse, and Marie Laveau was the madam. She had some special tricks going on out there that the young fellows used to like. You would arrange it in advance by sending somebody to her house in St. Ann Street. She would fix a date—usually a Saturday night—to have her girls out there, as many as there was fellows in the party. It cost a lot because there was plenty of food and wine and champagne. You had to give ten dollars for each girl, besides paying for the stuff. Marie Laveau didn't fool with no pikers.

The girls all danced with you naked and everybody drank lots of liquor and got higher 'n' hell. After a while, when the guys got heated up, the girls would start acting cute and running away from them. They always fought and carried on, but whatever girl you caught was yours. Marie Laveau always sat in a rocking chair in one corner, saying her beads and watching what was going on. She never fooled with anybody herself. Of course that was around 1885 and she was about sixty years old. [This "Marie" was not, of course, the original one, born in 1796.]

The drug store at the corner of Villere and Bienville Streets advertised in its window such sure fire "power" producers as "Controlling Powder", "Love Oil", "Mind Oil", "Goofer Dust", "Get-Together Drops" and "Bend-Over Oil" at twenty-five cents to a dollar the ounce. Even today, in the 1970s, shops in the French Quarter sell, as a "gag" souvenir item, a "Do-It-Yourself Voodoo Kit." Proprietors of stores that handle the package report that there are continuing repeat sales to the area's many prostitutes and "B-girls."

At the downtown end of Basin Street, in St. Louis Cemetery No. 1, rest (it is said) the mortal remains of Marie Laveau, "Queen of the Voodoos." The late Marie was actually two or more women who succeeded each other, but in the minds of true believers there was just the one Marie Laveau who was born in the year 1796. When the last Laveau died, early in the present century, most of the faithful refused to accept the fact, preferring to believe, as many *still* do, in her immortality.

The first Marie (née Glapion), a highly skilled and noted hairdresser and stylist to the fashionable ladies of early nineteenth-century New Orleans, made most of her money as a procuress and built most of her power by blackmail. Privy to the many secrets of Crescent City high society (she kept her ears open when fixing *madame's* hair), she gained such a hold on some of the leading families that nobody dared to estimate the full extent of her power. But as a supplier of attractive light-skinned Negro girls to wealthy white men, she remained on good terms with leading citizens.

Conducting open, pagan, and frequently obscene voodoo ceremonies, Marie Laveau remained a devout Roman Catholic and, strangely, was not interfered with by the local church hierarchy. More whites than blacks attended her

Tallant also relates the story of how Euphrasine Pigeon, known as "Lottie" in the Basin Street mansion where she was a star attraction, was brought to shame by her attraction for the voodoo dancer Joseph Howard, known to the insiders as Prince Basile. One day she disappeared from her home, where she had been living with a husband of her father's choosing, and lost herself in the passionate frenzy of voodoo, finally going to live with Prince Basile in his dirty one-room shack near the lakefront. When he threw her out to make room for a new mistress, she sought refuge in Storyville, where she was a great success not only as a prostitute but as a singer.

However, after many years of life in the bagnio, she was again overcome by the lure of voodoo and sought out her dark-skinned "prince." The meeting ended in a fierce argument during which Euphrasine was badly cut and beaten. Three days later she returned, after these many years, to her husband, her brain addled, and sorely in need of medical care. He credited her return to Marie Laveau's intercession with the Powers of Darkness, for which service he had paid the voodoo queen a thousand dollars.

From that time until the death of her husband some forty years later, Euphrasine remained confined to the house. After that she became a beggar in the streets of New Orleans and was to be seen as late as 1944 seeking handouts of food from back doors around St. Ann and North Rampart streets. Each morning she could be found kneeling in the aisle of Our Lady of Guadalupe Church, counting her rosary.

"And a Cast of Thousands . . ."

To Danny Barker, that extraordinary musician who has also distinguished himself as a gatherer of New Orleans and Storyville "lore," we owe the following list—a partial listing only—of individuals involved in the New Orleans demimonde: Flamin' Mamie, Crying Emma, Bucktown Bessie, Dirty Dog, Steel Arm Johnny, Mary Meathouse, Gold Tooth Gussie, Big Butt Annie, Naked Mouf Mattie, Bird Leg Nora, Bang Zang, Boxcar Shorty, Sneaky Pete, Titanic, Coke Eyed Laura, Yellow Gal, Black Sis, Boar Hog, Yard Dog, Bodiddly, Roody Doody, Big Bull Cora, Piggy, Big Piggy, Stingaree, Bull Frog Sonny, Toot Nan, Knock on the Wall, Sore Dick, Sugar Pie, Cherry Red, Buck Tooth Rena, Bad Blood, Copper Wire, Snaggle Mouf Mary, Linker-top, Topsy, Scratch, Joe the Pimp, Onery Bob, TeeTee, Tee Nome, Tee Share, Tee Boy, Raw Head, Smoke Stack, Stack O Dollars, Pupsy, Boogers, Copper Cent, Street Rabbit, BooBoo, Big BooBoo, Fast Black, Eight Ball, Lily the Crip, Tenderloin Thelma, Three Finger Annie, Charlie Bow Wow, Good Lord the Lifter, Peachanno, Cold Blooded Carrie, Miss Thing, Jack the Bear.

These might sound as though the meticulously truthful Danny had made them up, but some of the owners of these sobriquets have achieved note independent of Barker's memory. Box Car Shorty for instance is immortalized on wax in Cousin Joe's Decca record about the noted crapshooter. Boar Hog, as will be seen directly, was honored in song by Jelly Roll Morton as the assassin of Aaron Harris.

Danny also tells us of one Albertine McKay, a former sweetheart of trumpeter Lee Collins: "She marched him around with a '.38 special' loaded with dumdum bullets." And then there was Kidneyfoot Rella, who is said to have spit in Black Benny's face as he lay dead in his coffin.

The keepers of the District's saloons and "dance houses" came in for their share of notoriety. Included among them are names that will recur as this history unfolds: John "Peg" Anstedt, Eddie Groshell, Johnny Rice, Peter Ciaccio, the Parker Brothers, Billy Phillips, Johnny Lala, Sam Exnicios, and Eugene Tournier, known as "the Frenchman."

Jelly Roll Morton was a great chronicler of "sports" and "tough guys," for whom he had a not-so-secret admiration, since he longed to be considered one of them—and frequently was. His memoirs mention Willie the Pleaser, Bob Rowe (the kingpin of the District), Clark Wade, who wore diamond garters and who took over after Rowe went to California, and Chinee Morris, "the best looking guy in the District." Then there were the leading pimps: Okey Poke, the bartender, Ed Mochez, who left a hundred and ten suits when he died, Ready Money, Chicken Dick, Sheep Eye, Boar Hog, Tweedlum, and Aaron Harris. The last named Jelly considered "the toughest of them all . . . he had eleven killings to his credit . . . no doubt the most heartless man I've ever heard of or seen. . . ." For the Library of Congress folk archive Jelly sang this little blues about Aaron Harris:

Aaron Harris was a bad, bad man,
Baddest man ever was in this land.
Killed his sweet little sister and his brother-in-law
About a cup of coffee, he killed his sister and brother-in-law.
He got out of jail every time that he would make his kill,

He had a voo doo woman, all he had to do was
   pay his bill.
Aaron pawned his pistol one night to play in a
   gambling game.
He pawned his pistol one night to play in a
   gambling game.
Then old Boar Hog shot him and blotted out
   his name.

Yes, there actually was an Aaron Harris. In a recent interview, a very well-known gambler and odds-maker of Storyville days said: "Sure, I remember Aaron Harris. A big, tough guy. Used to hock his diamonds with me. He was always in hock. That's why he's so bad." But there was more to it than that.

The real Aaron Harris was born in New Orleans in 1884. He had at least two brothers, Pat and Willis, both older, and one sister, Beulah, who later worked as a prostitute under the name of Beulah Williams. On August 14, 1899, Willis Harris, then living at 2217 Valence Street, killed his brother Pat by stabbing. On August 8, 1910, the same Willis Harris, by then living at 2530 Cambronne Street, quarreled with brother Aaron over the subject of sister Beulah's immoral life. "I will send you to hell where I sent Pat," he said, and attacked Aaron with a razor. Aaron shot him, was locked up in the 9th precinct jail, entered a plea of innocent to the murder charge on the basis of self-defense, and was acquitted. The quarrel took place at the corner of Nelson and Dublin streets. Aaron was then living at 1007 Gravier. "Bad" as he was, this is the only time that Aaron Harris was arrested for murder.

In 1915 he was working full time as a cotch dealer in various chartered private clubs and residing at 333 Saratoga Street. On July 14 of that year, at 11:10 P.M., he was walking on Tulane Avenue on the lower woods side of the street nearing Franklin when he met George "Boar Hog" Robertson, a watchman for the Frisco Railroad. Both reached for pistols, but Robertson was quicker. He fired two shots and Harris collapsed. Robertson was arrested almost immediately, while standing over Harris, the pistol still smoking in his hand. Harris had a 41 Colt revolver partially pulled out of his pocket. There were several witnesses, including one who made a statement, a Porter Stokes, of 213 South Franklin Street.

Robertson stated that Harris had threatened his life, and many persons would later testify that Harris had frequently stated that he planned

Jelly Roll Morton (née Ferdinand Le Menthe). The photograph is autographed to his close friend and favorite clarinetist Omer Simeon. (Photograph courtesy of American Music Records)

*Matthew Antoine Desiré Dekemel, known as "Buglin'
Sam, the Waffle Man," the only man ever to make good
jazz music on a regulation army bugle, sold waffles and
made music here and there in the District.* (Photograph
courtesy Maurice Dekemel Collection, New Orleans Jazz
Museum)

to kill Boar Hog for his supposedly having turned him in to the police in connection with some charges of grand larceny that had been lodged against Harris a few months before. Harris' body was not claimed by anyone, and he received a common burial, at the age of thirty-one.

The members of the Razzy Dazzy Spasm Band, who serenaded all and sundry on District banquettes, were a noteworthy collection. Perhaps the most celebrated was Emile "Stalebread" Lacoume, considered by some to be the first jazz musician. He played a violin fashioned from a cigar box. One member of this troop, Harry Gregson, who sang through a section of rainspout, eventually became a captain of detectives in New Orleans. "Whiskey" was Emile Benrod, "Cajun" was the harmonica man, Willie Bussey, and his brother Frank was "Monk." One of the "musicians" went by the name Warm Gravy. The bass player, whose instrument was a homemade contraption, partially a piano

crate was Chinee. The band's utility scat-singer bore the sobriquet Family Haircut.

The boys played a sidewalk concert for Sarah Bernhardt one night as she slummed in Storyville—and one survivor recalled that she tipped "below whore scale!"

The Pensacola Kid was a professional pool player, said to be one of the greatest in history, who made his living traveling from one southern tenderloin to another taking on the local pool hustlers for high stakes in match games. Jelly Roll Morton was one of his victims.

The Waffle Man was a familiar figure in the red-light District. Actually, a long line of members of the same family filled this function. A mule-drawn wagon kept a coal fire aboard, along with a huge cast-iron waffle maker. The tender, a man named Dekemel, would make the waffle on the spot, dust it with powdered sugar, and hand it over to the purchaser. The presence of

Emile "Stalebread" Lacoume's Razzy Dazzy Spasm Band, about 1897. (Photograph courtesy the Edmond Souchon Collection, New Orleans Jazz Museum)

the waffle man in the neighborhood was loudly announced by blasts from an army bugle. a signal that proved to be a practical advertising medium. Last in the line of waffle men, Sam Dekemel, actually gained considerable fame in later years by playing genuine jazz on the same army bugle for stage, screen, radio, and television audiences. Called Buglin' Sam the Waffle Man by a generation of contemporary Orleanians, he retired as a juvenile parole officer for the city. Interviewed by the author, he gave his correct name as Matthew Desiré Antoine Dekemel and stated that he had been taught to play the bugle by his grandmother.

Many Orleanians remember the late Banjo Annie, an unkempt barfly who strummed out-of-tune solos in saloons for drinks and pennies. Many surviving District inhabitants say they do not remember any time when there was no Banjo Annie.

Dago Annie, midwife to the whores, lived on Rampart and St. Ann streets, but her ambulating figure was a familiar sight in Storyville as she hurried, with her black satchel, to deliver the "trick babies" to the laboring harlots who had been "caught." Poker-faced and agile, her record was perhaps better than that of the hospitals of the day. Her son, known as Annie's Danny, became a pimp.

General Jack Johnson was a forty-inch black midget who occasionally worked as a white-uniformed doorman for Lulu White and Willie Piazza and somehow managed to retain the loyalty of a trio of back-o'-town bawds who worked feverishly for him and gave him most of their profits. The little man was credited with having hypnotic powers, probably because Storyville's citizens couldn't imagine how else he could control these three. His name was probably derived from that of the Negro boxing champion.

Cawzi, a slim, famished-looking little man, was one of the wonders of the District. As the only male known to have performed regularly in Emma Johnson's circuses, he is said to have participated in at least ten such exhibitions a week for twelve consecutive years. Emma kept Cawzi on the regular payroll at a hundred fifty dollars a week, and he made twice that advising aging Lotharios on how to maintain their virility. On this "trade" he raised a family

and sent four children through college. For a while, he marketed his own brand of pep pills, finding ready buyers, until he was stopped by government authorities. He is alive and in good health at this writing, claiming he could still play his role, which he says anybody "who knows the trick" can perform.

Another Storyville wonder was a little man who walked like a duck and had a voice that squeaked—a grotesque hydrocephalic who just happened to have more beauty to offer the world —his world and ours today—than most of the "people within" combined (always excepting, of course, such musicians as Jelly Roll Morton and Tony Jackson).

This was Ernest J. Bellocq—called *Papá* Bellocq in allusion to his deep French accent—a commercial photographer active in New Orleans from about 1895 through the late 1930s, who was a familiar figure in Storyville during the years 1910?–?16. Only a few of his many Storyville pictures survive—eighty-nine glass plates,

A corner of the studio of Ernest Bellocq, about 1912/13. Bellocq, by appointment of their worships, the madams of the District, was the "official" photographer of Storyville. The very large painting in the center is signed "Bryson—1902." (Photograph by Ernest Bellocq)

A Bellocq photograph reconstructed from a glass negative. Note that before the negative was shattered, the subject's face had been scratched out by, it is said, Bellocq's brother, a Catholic priest, for reasons known only to himself and, presumably, his God. (Photograph by Ernest Bellocq)

some of them broken or otherwise damaged, discovered in his desk after his death. Most are portraits of prostitutes, and a good many are nudes. After Bellocq's death, many of the glass plate negatives were defaced by, it is said, the photographer's brother, a Roman Catholic priest who seemingly wished to conceal the identities of the subjects but refrained from simply destroying the plates. The logic governing Father Bellocq's curious course of action is obscure.

Dozens, perhaps hundreds, of photographers gravitated to Storyville over the years, just as they did to the red-light districts of Chicago, San Francisco, and other large cities, in search of uninhibited models. There was good money in "French pictures," and for many photographers certain personal gratifications besides. Bellocq was different. There is no evidence that he ever took a pornographic picture, and every evidence, in the pictures we possess, that he would have been temperamentally incapable of doing so, no matter the price, unless perhaps the woman herself, for her own personal reasons, insisted that he do so.

No great innovator in photographic technique, Bellocq exhibited a sensibility, a feeling for his subjects, that forbade treating them as mere objects and that elevated his photographs to the level of art. He seems to have been "accepted" by the girls as a person. Perhaps they saw him as being, like them, essentially isolated from "polite" society, as being, like them, an object of society's contempt. All this is conjecture, of course, but there is no denying the rapport that obviously existed between Bellocq and the women in his pictures, which well deserve the serious critical attention they are at last receiving. A recent publication of New York's Museum of Modern Art, *E.J. Bellocq: Storyville Portraits* (New York, 1970), edited by John Szarkowski, offers forty-four of the eighty-nine extant plates, and still others are included in the present work.

Few pictures, contrary to the Chinese adage, are worth a thousand words. For those who would know Storyville's people, Bellocq's pictures are.

FOUR

Storyville Open
for Business

Miss Martha,

1511 Customhouse St.

The completion of Tom Anderson's saloon in 1901 was by far the most significant event in the history of Storyville up to that time, and few if any later events could compare with it. This landmark, the first saloon in America to be illuminated by electricity, boasted a hundred bulbs in its ceiling plus a bright electric sign outside.

"Opening night was a thing to marvel at," Billy Struve recalled many years later *(Morning Tribune,* August 2, 1931). "More than a hundred cases of champagne were sold, the patrons outbidding each other for their favorite vintages. Before the night was over everybody was walking in champagne."

On later nights, "everybody" included the likes of New York's Tammany Hall leader Big Tim Sullivan, such entertainers and actors as George M. Cohan and Nat Goodwin, minstrel man Honey Boy Evans, actor and critic Wilton Lackage, film star William Farnum, minstrel impresario Lew Dockstader, and the vaudeville team of McIntyre and Heath; and "sports"—in every sense—such as the pugilists John L. Sullivan, Bob Fitzsimmons, and Kid McCoy, the celebrated wrestler Frank Gotch, the jockey Tod Sloan, and the baseball stars Frank Chance, Napoleon Lajoie, Babe Ruth, and Ty Cobb. In sum, many of the "beautiful people," male gender, of the time.

According to Struve, "Carrie Nation . . . came in on a Saturday night without her hatchet, jumped up on a table and began a tirade on the demon rum. She was still going at midnight. At that time," he went on, "the police were strict on the Sunday closing law and came into the saloon. They ran everyone, including Carrie Nation, out of the place."

Struve remembered many "famous wine parties" on the premises, most particularly one celebration "when state Senator Joseph Voegle's

sewerage and waterboard bill was passed. There were," he added, "quite a number of celebrated Orleanians who attended . . ."

By the time the District's operations as a legal entity were well under way and Tom Anderson's complete control over the life of Storyville was undisputed, the stature of his Mardi Gras affairs had assumed the position of tradition in Crescent City culture. The Mardi Gras edition of the *Sunday Sun* for February 25, 1906, carried the following story on its front page:

The French Balls
And the probable candidates for the Queen Title

The event of the Mardi Gras season in the four hundred social circles of which our dear girls represent a large percentage will be those warm french balls given at Odd Fellows Hall on Saturday and Tuesday night respectively. These strictly local affairs, which have long since become famous will exceed all former balls and a grand time of high revelry will be given those attending. These great events will be conducted as in the past by the two well known gentlemen which means a whole bit. The topic of conversation among landladies and leading girls of the district during the week has been relative to the queenship and much speculation has been rife among them. Among those spoken of are the Misses Josie Arlington, Margaret Bradford, Hilda Burt, Margaret Miller, Jessie Brown, Ray Owens, Florence Leslie, Flora Meeker and following all-star boarders Myrtle Burke, Eva Standford, Daisy Meritt and many others too numerous to mention.

By 1906 the price of admission had advanced from two dollars to three.

Paid publicity squibs in the *Sunday Sun* demonstrate that the Storyville madams hadn't overlooked the fact that Carnival meant an added flow of business:

Miss Gypsy Shafer, a queen among landladies of 1552 Customhouse Street entertains her patrons in true up-to-date style and those who have visited this swell establishment always return. The lady entertainers now with Miss Gypsy are of the creme de la creme stock, and as Miss Shafer herself is a fine fellow well known throughout the city it is no wonder her house is doing so well. Strangers in town for the Carnival should by all means visit this house and enjoy a swell time with the girls.

Thousands have seen her and millions have heard of her, such are the expressions of many regarding the extensive popularity of Countess Willie Piazza, who operates a swell house at No. 317 Basin Avenue. Carnival visitors should visit this establishment if they want a swell time.

Miss May O'Brien
The Irish Queen

Miss May O'Brien, proprietress of 1549 Customhouse street, popular with all, has a house full of beautiful young girls and increasing her business daily. May is the Irish Queen, and always has a sweet smile on her face. The many strangers who will come to the city during the Mardi Gras should not fail to visit this establishment. . . .

The Arlington over Anderson's Annex has been doing a fine Carnival business during the week. Miss Arlington was in hope of occupying a portion of her Mansion ere this, as was stated in this paper, but it now transpires that it will be fully fifteen days before the contractor can turn over the Mansion.

Maggie Wilson a buxom and pretty woman who lives at 1314 Customhouse street informs the Carnival visitors who are out for a good time to call on her, and she will give them a run for their money and that's no dream.

Miss Flora Meeker's
Palace of Mirth

Everybody in the sporting world knows Miss Flora Meeker and she knows everybody worth knowing. So it is unnecessary at this time to make any introductory remarks about Miss Meeker, suffice it to say she is still at her same old place where she has been for a number of years past, doing a boss business which she deserves, Miss Flora is well thought of by all and her house is patronized by the best element. Carnival visitors should not overlook this swell mansion where the cream of female loveliness will be found which is situated at No. 211 Basin avenue.

Two scarlet "sisters"—possibly a "mother-and-daughter combination," of which there were a number in Storyville's brothels—in a bit of aquatic make-believe complete with a painted backdrop. (Photograph by Ernest Bellocq)

Presumably all of these fine "landladies" could get mentioned in the *Sunday Sun* without paying, but apparently those who failed to reward the paper's solicitation with an honorarium had less influence over the published copy. For example: "Mary Smith does not expect much this Mardi Gras. No wonder she needs new material and faces." Mary would know better next year.

As may be seen in the list of candidates for Mardi Gras "queenship," racial segregation continued to be strictly enforced. The names Lulu White and Willie Piazza did not appear among the contestants in this or any other year.

The most celebrated event of the Carnival season was Josie Arlington's sensational coup at the Mardi Gras "Ball of the Two Well Known Gentlemen" in 1906.

It seems that despite the clearly unsavory character of these demimonde social functions, as judged by the "respectable" people of New Orleans, it soon became apparent to many that they offered a good deal more excitement than the more conventional affairs produced by the Krewes of Rex, Comus, Momus, *et al.* Invitations to the Ball of the Two Well Known Gentlemen began to be hard to come by. It became fashionable for the nice young ladies of the town's prominent families to plead with their menfolk to secure these billets so that they might with their own eyes—masked, of course—see intimately into the lives of these brazen creatures who so inflamed their imaginations, but whom they saw only rarely, if at all, and then only with eyes demurely averted.

The "ladies of the evening" came understandably to resent these annual slumming parties. Josie Arlington solved the problem by arranging for the police to raid the affair and to arrest any women who did not carry a card registering her as a prostitute in good standing. This stratagem caused great embarrassment to the large number of ladies of New Orleans "high society" who were summarily carted off to the police station, unmasked, and sent home. Thereafter the Ball of the Two Well Known Gentlemen took place annually without unwelcome guests.

The early days of Storyville were marked by a sharp drop in major crimes, although there was the "normal" run of arrests for disturbing the peace, assault and battery, and attempted suicide, according to the daily press. There was not even a hint of the "crime wave," or of any exceptional lawlessness, that some had feared might occur. For the first time in decades there was an atmosphere of calm in New Orleans. Vice was under control at last.

Oddly, it was in this atmosphere, when the experiment seemed to promise a high level of success, that reform groups of various kinds began to build up steam for a drive against Storyville.

There was plenty of justification, no doubt, for the Travelers Aid Society to look into charges lodged against Daisy Haines for enticing females under sixteen to an immoral house (*The Daily States*, October 16, 1908), but this case was not typical and involved, as a matter of fact, an unlawful establishment on Erato Street rather than one of the legal establishments in Storyville. Meanwhile, the Society for the Prevention of Cruelty to Children, prodded by one of its leaders Miss Jean Gordon, did yeoman duty watching for violations; very few were found.

But such groups as the so-called Progressive Union, headed in 1910 by Philip Werlein, were full of such ideas as a plan for moving the District one square away from the terminal. (This would have demolished Basin Street!) In public forums, Werlein was responsible for such statements as this: "The filthy hovels in which the negro [sic] and French [sic] women live are distasteful to the women who conduct their houses in better style and they leave the district and take up residence elsewhere in the city." "The negro woman," Werlein inveighed, "must be stamped out of the district, and with the assistance that has been promised me by District Attorney St. Claire Adams, I hope to see this realized at the next meeting of the state legislature." Such speeches were mostly ineffectual and served only to make public the deepseated prejudices of those who made them—but their publication became a rallying point for crackpots, religious fanatics, racists, and politically ambitious opportunists. At the same time the prohibitionists were actively trying to make the use of alcoholic beverages illegal. The city's more responsible citizens, basing their estimates of the situation on proven historical and sociological grounds, strongly supported the Storyville status quo and the principle behind it.

Sidney Story himself took occasion to address all kinds of groups around the country on questions related to vice control. He was very effective, for example, in addressing the Model License League Convention in Louisville, early in 1909, on the subject of the inevitable failure of prohibition in the South (*Item*, January 22, 1909).

Nevertheless, the forces of "reform," heartened by the passage of the Gay-Shattuck Law, which went into effect on New Year's Day of 1909, continued to harass the town's law enforcement agencies with trivial complaints.

This complex, unenforceable and truly absurd law had only a casual effect on the District, but it weighed heavily on such bastions of respect-

ability as the Boston and Pickwick clubs. One of its provisions was for the abolition of "automatic pianos and other nickel-in-the-slot and all other musical instruments in barrooms" (*Times-Democrat*, December 31, 1908).

Within less than a week a way of circumventing the law was found, as a headline in the *Item* for January 5, 1908, makes clear:

"Ladies' " Saloons
Converted Into
Restaurants
Clause of Gay-Shattuck Law
Evaded by Simple Plan

The Gay-Shattuck Law, specifically forbids "ladies' rooms" in connection with bar rooms, but those saloons which pander to this class of trade are eluding the law in the simplest manner imaginable. The most notorious "joints" in the city where women of questionable repute habitually congregate have been converted into "restaurants."

The first arrest made in the District under the Gay-Shattuck Law brought in one Sam Exnicios, owner of the New Waldorf saloon on Iberville Street near Villere, who was charged with the heinous offense of keeping musical instruments on the premises. He entered a not-guilty plea and was released on five hundred dollars bond, but was found guilty. He took the case through a long series of appeals and ultimately paid a fifty dollar fine. He was arrested again, under yet another clause of the law, for holding a boxing match on his premises. This cost him twenty dollars (*Item*, February 15, 1909).

Another provision of the measure called for the removal of any saloon from within three hundred feet of any church or school. It was found that the making of such measurements could be a slow process indeed. It was not without a certain cynicism that the *Item* could comment on January 8, 1909: ". . . and anyhow the old saloons are still running and will probably continue to run just about as they have done in the past."

So scarce was sensational news through the early 1900s that the newspapers seized upon even the most trivial items to offer morbid readers. The *Daily News* solemnly covered the matter of a trio of male customers stealing a "rat" from the hair of a prostitute in North Basin Street. An alleged holdup in front of Emma Johnson's, which netted the enterprising thug twenty dollars, rated its share of space, though

there was more evidence that the incident never happened than that it did.

On January 14, 1910, a respectable New Orleans physician, called professionally to Lulu White's, suddenly found himself charged with having violated the age of consent law with one Marie Gaudette, aged sixteen. The girl had been placed in the brothel by her stepfather, Edward von Bülow, a first cousin of the then chancellor of Germany. The stepfather, on being charged with concubinage, committed suicide. The doctor, fortunately, was cleared.

The topic of "white slavery" was a favorite with the circulation departments of many newspapers, and any suggestion of such activity in New Orleans was magnified beyond recognition. Thus it was that on January 4, 1909, one Sam Felix, the owner of a lunch house at 219 North Liberty, was arrested for "harboring foreign women for immoral purposes."

In banner headlines the *Item*'s front page exulted: "WHITE SLAVE TRAFFICKERS ON THE RUN." The story affirmed that "there are 240 immoral women now illegally in New Orleans and the total may reach 300, mostly from France, Italy, Russia, and Central America." It described how United States Secret Service agents, Mary E. Philbrook and her two assistants, posed as prostitutes working in cribs. As a result of their findings, the *Item* asserted, the government would attempt to "deport alien prostitutes rounded up in dragnet." The paper further hinted at a "trust" that "shuffles the girls from one city to another . . . to avoid arrests."

This yarn went through days of declining coverage until, three months later, one Fanny Rudabarger, alias Fanny Rudy, was ordered deported to Brazil, after it was proved that she was not a bona fide United States citizen. The presence of this young lady in New Orleans was the sole basis for the *Item*'s hullaballoo.

A rare arrest for maintaining an "opium den" or for finding prostitutes accused of stealing from more or less prominent customers was reported, and occasionally an item more ridiculous than anything else made "news." One such, surely, was the following: Lulu White, who was arrested frequently, customarily took a cab to the precinct station, where she would dutifully pay her little fine or be acquitted, as the situation demanded. But on February 17, 1909, according to a report in the *Item*, "Patrolman Ernest Schwartz, fourth precinct, was sentenced to loss of pay and ten days additional for allow-

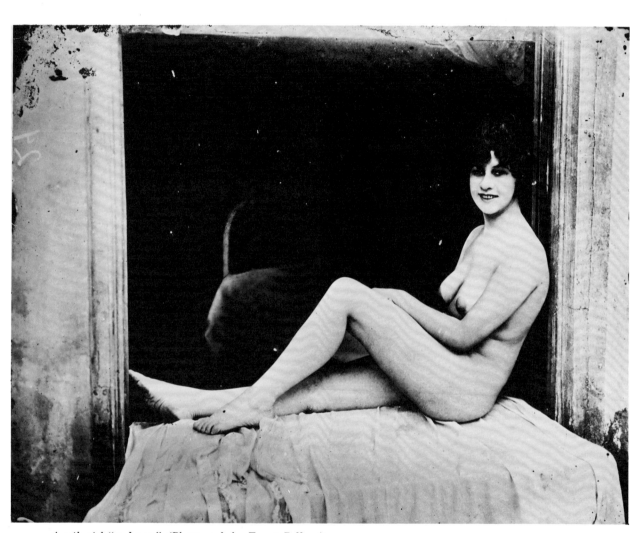

A crib girl "at home." (Photograph by Ernest Bellocq)

ing Lulu White, a notorious negress, and her escort, to ride to the station in a cab." " 'You ought to be dismissed from the force,' said Inspector O'Conor. 'You know that woman has a bad reputation and keeps a house of prostitution yet you allowed her to ride to prison in a cab. I'll dismiss you or any other man that comes before me on the charge again.' "

The history of Storyville must necessarily appear more as a series of seemingly unrelated or only slightly related incidents than as a logically progressing narrative filled with convincing causal relationships. Actually, in its twenty-year span, it did not have time to fully develop its own dialectic. Furthermore, it came to the end of its existence not by any inherent contradiction but as a result of external forces unrelated to its own purposeful destiny. This is frustrating for sociologists who would like to apply scientific criteria to its rise and fall. Its rise as it occurred has been demonstrated herein; the fall came about by federal fiat—a deus ex machina.

Nevertheless, there were straws in the wind, bits and pieces of "fact" such as might permit the sensitive observer to discern certain trends. One such trend was a developing social stratification within the District. Another was the progress of the area as a business—one might even say the decline of the area as a business.

Socially, the District fell into the pattern of racial segregation quite naturally: it was *legally* segregated, for one thing (in the sense that white and black prostitutes could not live or work in the same house and blacks were not permitted to patronize any of the mansions, even those staffed by black women, or to consort with white women in even the lowest of cribs), and such segregation had already become the "accepted" pattern for the city as well as for the whole South. Eventually, in 1917, the

segregation was carried even further and an ordinance was passed establishing a legal "uptown district" (as originally contemplated in 1897) but for blacks only, and Storyville was redefined as being for white prostitutes only. (See Appendix E.) The inevitable result was social stratification within each racial group, with the most prosperous occupying the top rungs of the ladder.

If there ever was a turning point for the worse in the history of Storyville, however, it may be said to have been an outgrowth of the antagonisms between native and outlander groups in the District, culminating in the fatal shootings that took the lives of the proprietors of two of the area's leading cabarets.

Abraham Shapiro, a New York hoodlum, came to Storyville in the early 1900s with his brother Isidore; together, they opened a saloon on the corner of Liberty and Customhouse streets, changing their names, respectively to Harry and Charles Parker. They sold this place, and in 1910 Harry opened the 101 Ranch on Franklin Street. On these premises, brother Charles got involved with a prostitute who was the mistress of John "Peg" Anstedt, a saloon keeper popular in the District.

In 1910 or 1911, hoping to improve his business at Anstedt's expense, Charles Parker tried to get Anstedt's mistress to swear out a white-slavery affidavit against him. Angered, Anstedt took a shot at Parker in Tony Battistina's saloon. Brother Parker retaliated with a shot at Anstedt in a place at Marais and Bienville. Though neither of the shots did much damage, a full-scale feud, one that would change the entire character of the District, was in the making.

In 1911, the very popular Billy Phillips, a New Orleans restaurant owner eager to do business in the District, bought into the 101 Ranch and became a partner of Harry Parker. Phillips bought Parker out in 1912, changing the name from the 101 to the 102 Ranch. Parker, in violation of his agreement with Phillips, then opened up the Tuxedo Dance Hall directly across the street from the 102. To Phillips, a friend of Peg Anstedt, this was a severe economic blow. But despite the large size of the Tuxedo and its more modern and luxurious appointments, Phillips, a native Orleanian, continued to draw more than his share of Storyville trade, and quickly became a prime object of envy for the Parker brothers.

Conscious of the low esteem in which his colleagues of the District held him and his brother, and jealous of the prestige enjoyed by Billy Phillips, Harry Parker determined to dispose of the likes of Phillips and Anstedt by methods uncommon in the Crescent City but quite current in the northern metropolises of those years. Soon thugs wanted by the New York police department began to drift into the District from Manhattan. These characters found no difficulty in obtaining employment as waiters in the Tuxedo. Among them was one Charles Harrison, a man well known to the police of the eastern seaboard by the *nom de guerre* Gyp the Blood.

It was customary in the District for waiters to be paid at the rate of a dollar a night plus tips, but when Parker imported his cohorts, he discontinued the practice of paying the dollar guarantee. Phillips, Anstedt, and the rest of the bar and dance hall operators would not stoop to so picayune a practice, and as a result much antagonism developed between regular waiters of the District and those who were working in the Tuxedo for what amounted to scab wages. Inevitably, a District-wide labor feud grew up, adding to the already existing social enmities.

At 4:00 A.M. on Easter Sunday, 1913, James Enright, a waiter employed at the 102 Ranch, accompanied by two friends, entered the Tuxedo. The group was intoxicated and Enright's two friends, after assaulting a cashier, were run off the premises by Parker. Enright was then accosted by Parker, who grabbed him by the collar and attempted to put him out. The drunken Enright resisted, but was soundly beaten and thrown into the street. During the melee, Parker is said to have made some uncomplimentary remarks about Enright's employer, and these words were later repeated to Phillips.

Phillips, who had had altercations regarding business matters with Parker on two previous occasions and who had bested the latter in fist fights, went over to the Tuxedo in his shirt sleeves. After a loud verbal quarrel, he returned to his own place and matters seemed to simmer down. Shortly thereafter, however, he decided to try to end the trouble and bring peace to the neighborhood and went back to the Tuxedo with two friends, whom he invited to have a drink with him. The moment he entered, Gyp the Blood disappeared from the premises. Phillips took out a dollar and slapped it on the bar, inviting owner Harry Parker, who was behind the bar, to have a drink with him. Phillips was unarmed.

At this point, Gyp the Blood, sans waiter's garb, re-entered the saloon, stepped up behind Phillips, placed the muzzle of his revolver to Billy's back, and fired. He then fired three more shots in rapid succession, one of which grazed Phillips' neck.

Eyewitness accounts of the events of the next thirty seconds contradict each other, but it is certain that several more shots were fired and that one or more slugs entered the persons of Phillips, Harry Parker, Gyp the Blood, Charles Parker, and a porter named Willie Henderson. The ambulance that was called to take Phillips to the hospital took Harry Parker instead, Phillips being already dead. The porter was wounded only slightly. Harry Parker died in the hospital. The other two men refused to "talk" from their hospital beds, though Charles Parker eventually accused Tony Battistina, a witness, with having slain his brother. Also arrested was Albert Morris, one of Phillips' bartenders. Both the accused were released shortly afterward for lack of evidence.

Ownership of the Tuxedo reverted to Parker's two partners, Harry Brooks and Will Harris, while the 102 Ranch became the property of Philip J. Phillips, father of the deceased young entrepreneur. As a result of these Easter Sunday events, the police closed the five dance halls in the District, and they did not reopen for a year or more.

Many, many musicians continue to refer to the big gunfight and each avers that he was "on the bandstand at the Tuxedo the night Billy Phillips was killed." (Parker's status was such that no mention is usually made of the fact that he was dispatched in the same melee.) If all the musicians who claimed to be on the bandstand on that fateful morning had actually been

The same girl, two different moods. In the interior shot, note the characteristically Bellocqian (so it seems) medallion hanging from the girl's neck and the pillow on the far right with the American flag and words from what would later become America's national anthem, This object, in wide circulation at the time, was known as "The Star Spangled Banner Pillow." (Photograph by Ernest Bellocq)

present, as reported to this author, the place would have required a dozen additional bandstands. The *Daily Picayune* of March 25, 1913, reported correctly, however, that there was neither music nor dancing that night. One musician was on the premises, but only to arrange for a job the following week. This was drummer Abby "Chinee" Foster, one of the more than fifty witnesses to the killing. Others known to have been on the scene were Josephine Brown of 1208 Bienville Street and Kittie Wilson of 1302 Customhouse Street, both prostitutes, whose names appear on the police blotter. (See Appendix H for a contemporary account of the affair.)

The closing of the dance halls had a immediate effect on the conditions of employment for some of the key musicians of the District. The regular band at the Tuxedo re-formed as the nucleus of the Original Creole Serenaders, an aggregation that included Freddie Keppard, trumpet; James Palao, violin; George Bacquet, clarinet; and Bill Johnson, bass. This group left town on a tour that took them to Chicago as the first New Orleans jazz group to appear in the North. The official climate was also responsible for the departure of Kid Ory, Papa Mutt Carey, and later the Original Dixieland Jazz Band and Tom Brown's Band from Dixieland, although neither of these groups had ever played in the District.

By 1914 the dance halls had started to open again. The women who worked in these places represented the lowest level of the District's social scale. The "check" system, forerunner of today's "B-drinking," had come into full use: each dance cost about sixty cents—two drinks at twenty-five cents each, a nickel tip for the waiter, and five cents for the band. The girl received "checks" for each drink sold to the customer; at the end of the night, she received five cents per check from the management. She was allowed to solicit for prostitution off the premises.

Occupying the highest level on the social scale was the cabaret woman. This lady was a newcomer to the Storyville scene, since the idea of the cabaret was born not out of showmanship but out of legal necessity. It was actually against the law for a woman, even a prostitute, to enter a barroom. She was permitted, however, to sing in a beer garden and thus be admitted as an "entertainer." Thus it came to pass in 1911 that the ever-ingenious Tom Anderson erected

Hospital scenes like this must have been common in those V.D.-ridden days. The standing woman may have been a nurse or, more likely, a harlot visiting a sick "sister." Evidence for the latter possibility is the medallion hanging from her neck; many of Bellocq's subjects wore this piece of jewelry and it may well have had some special meaning for him. When the Isolation Hospital at 513 N. Rampart Street opened in 1916, Dr. Paul Ehrlich's "silver bullet" against syphilis, "606," was available, and those afflicted with this disease, at least, no longer had to resort to the quack "cures" widely advertised in the city. But the quacks stayed in business anyway, treating the symptoms of gonorrhea ("the gleet"), but not the disease itself, and even continuing to treat syphilitics, to whom they promised the kind of quick, one-shot cure that did not actually become possible until decades later when penicillin treatments were developed. With their fake cures for syphilis, the quacks contributed almost as much as the harlots to the epidemic tertiary syphilis that Thomas Sancton alluded to, in the New Orleans Item, as "the debit side of the old legend that one has to balance against the color, the humor, and the power and the glory of the music that came out of it all. . . . It was a day when victims of the shadow-plague walked the streets of New Orleans and the other great cities, living corpses, eyelids dropping in early paralysis, hands and body shaking with a palsy not caused by old age. It was a day when young sports decayed and died of the 'rales.' The younger generation hardly knows the word today. But old-timers remember it well." (Photograph by Ernest Bellocq)

in the rear of his establishment a slightly raised platform on which every doxy who claimed to be an "entertainer" could sit and carry on at least *part* of her business. Other saloons soon followed suit and the cabaret business became a popular and profitable part of the Storyville scene, as well as a simple means of getting around the law against women in barrooms.

An aura of quasi-respectability was provided by the professional vaudeville performers who would frequently do their turns on these slight stages. Some were hired by music publishers to sing in the cabarets and plug the latest song "hits." As a result, many people who normally would not have felt free to visit the District for the raw pleasures for which it was instituted could rationalize that they were just going to watch the shows. The entertainer-whores who now had a chance to mingle with all elements of New Orleans society were considered to be not quite so low-down as crib and bawdy house prostitutes. Characteristically, the cabaret girls and the ordinary whores associated with each other socially and conversationally, though never without caste consciousness. But both groups looked down on the dance hall women with *grande dame* scorn.

From 1914 to the close of the District in 1917 a typical all-male "slumming" party included going into the District to watch a favorite entertainer at work in a cabaret. Then the group would take some of the "entertainers" as dates, and in a body they would descend on one of the five dance halls to do the bunny hug and other contemporary dances to the first-class music available in those days. Naturally, the girls who worked for the dance halls were treated like dirt by their high-flown sisters who were there as the consorts of customers.

Policemen were detailed to each of the dance halls but were not paid by the city. Instead, they received two and a half dollars a night from the dance hall operator. Naturally, these minions didn't maintain an objective view of law enforcement but merely served to protect the interests of the dance hall operators, whose own violations of law were ignored or quickly forgotten.

By the end of 1915 a number of factors—some subtle, some dramatic—had wrought obvious changes in the face of the District. Along Villere and Robertson streets, for example, half the cribs often stood vacant except during holiday periods. Prices were down in parlor houses and mansions alike, as their essentially pedestrian services increasingly lost their appeal for the natives. The younger generation in particular was beginning to consider it a bit declassé to have its appetites assuaged in such surroundings.

There wasn't so much sport in the sporting houses, now that their operations had become cut and dried. Everyone knew what was available and for how much, and the young men of the time found it increasingly less appealing. This was the period of suffrage agitation, equal-rights-for-women movements, and the "new freedom." Young sports found bigger and better thrills in the pursuit and conquest of "respectable" girls than in the hiring of harlots by the hour or night.

The number of prostitutes plying their trade had shrunk to about seven hundred. Even Lulu White had only eight girls working regularly in Mahogany Hall. The "ladies of the evening" had begun to drift to other cities where prostitution, as an illegal but available commodity, could command higher prices. At the Arlington in 1916 and 1917—or for that matter at any of the Basin Street mansions—a fifteen-minute session with a prostitute might be had for a dollar, a competitive "bargain" based on the sluggish prejudice that price-cutting could substitute for improving the quality of the services rendered.

The mansions had begun to run down physically. Even Willie Piazza's paint was peeling. Jessie Brown's plumbing gave up the ghost. Every available index pointed to the conclusion that in less than a decade the whole sin industry, by its own inherent failings, would have declined precipitously to perhaps half a dozen houses and only a few score women working them full time (plus a certain number of crib girls for the economy-minded)—had the federal government not intervened in 1917, bringing the experiment to an abrupt end.

The bandstand in Tom Anderson's restaurant on Rampart Street in 1922. Left to right: Paul Barbarin, Arnold Metoyer, Luis Russell, Willie Santiago, and Albert Nicholas.

1. The Terminal Saloon
2. Fewclothes' Cabaret
3. Tom Anderson's
4. Hilma Burt's
5. Diana and Norma's
6. Lizette Smith's
7. Minnie White's
8. Jessie Brown's
9. The Arlington
10. Martha Clarke's
11. Mahogany Hall
12. Lulu White's Saloon
13. Frank Toro's Saloon
14. Countess Willie V. Piazza's
15. Antonia Gonzales', Gipsy Shafer's

16. Emma Johnson's Studio
17. Firehouse
18. Willie O. Barrera's
19. The 101 Ranch
    (also known as 102 Ranch, The
    Entertainers, and Phillips' Café)
20. Frank Early's Saloon
21. Louis Miller's
22. Grace Lloyd's
23. Edna Hamilton's
24. The Big 25
25. Shoto Cabaret
26. The Pig Ankle
27. The Tuxedo
28. Anstedt's Saloon
29. The Cairo

30. Antonia Gonzales'
31. The Club
32. The Casino
33. Groshell's Dance Hall
34. The Poodle Dog Café
35. Tournier's Saloon
36. Pete Lala's
37. Rice's Café
38. Abadie's Cabaret
39. Ray Owens' Star Mansion
40. The Phoenix
41. Gipsy Shafer's
42. The Firm
43. The Frenchman's
44. Victor's Saloon

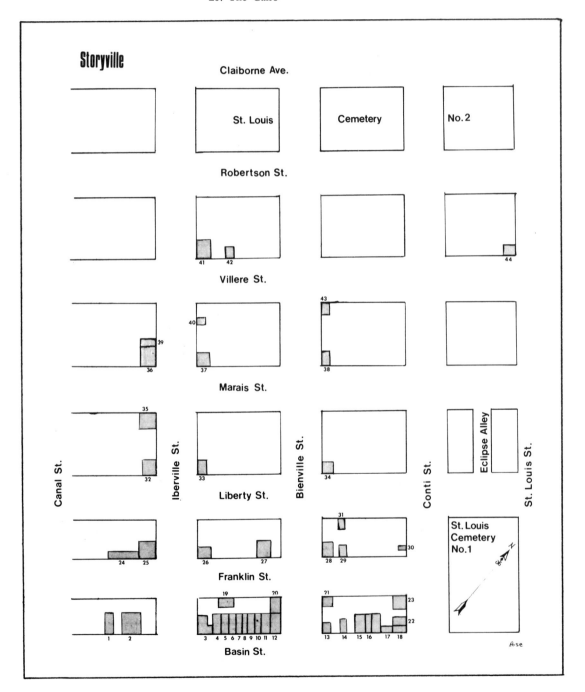

Storyville

FIVE

A Guided Tour of Storyville 1914

The gateway to Storyville was the Terminal Saloon, which ran all the way through the block from Basin Street to Franklin Street. The photograph is dated May 11, 1911. At the extreme right is Boniface Milton J. Kelly, one of the few successful entrepreneurs in the District and a friend to itinerant show folk.

By 1914 Storyville had long passed its peak as an "industry" but was perhaps more stable in its economic situation and in its personnel than it had been at any time previously or would be in later years. While the number of registered prostitutes had declined drastically from the twenty-two hundred plus of 1897/98, when the tenderloin became a legal entity, dollar-volume was steady. There were fewer brothels and many fewer prostitutes, but the slack in income was being taken up in large measure by cabarets, dance halls, and saloons operated by managers who were no longer in the novice class. Storyville had become better organized and its "points of interest" were more sharply in focus for both local customers and visitors from out of town.

The visitor to New Orleans who arrived by train at the Southern Depot could see the mansions of Basin Street from his window as the train pulled into the station. He would see elaborately bedecked females posing in the windows of these notorious houses, and some of the women would wave to him or make lascivious gestures calculated to excite his interest. Alighting from the train and out into the warm evening, he probably would be handed a copy of Tom Anderson's scarlet *Hell-o* book, a diminutive eight-page digest directory of the District. A street Arab, solicitous for his welfare, was employed to steer the city's male guests to places enjoying the favor of Mr. Anderson. Failing this opportunity the would-be guide was satisfied with a small honorarium in return for the booklet.

If interested in spending the night on the town, the man would walk straight down Basin Street with never a glance at Krauss' department store at the corner of Canal. Continuing down Basin Street toward Iberville (formerly Customhouse) Street, he might fire a few rounds at

The only known photograph of Basin Street "Up the Line" (matching the famous "Down the Line" picture, also reproduced here), shows Anderson's Saloon (lower left, with pillars), then Hilma Burt's (with awnings), Diana and Norma's "French house" (with second-floor balcony), the one-story Little Annex of Lizette Smith, a double house (Jessie Brown on the left, Minnie White on the right), Josie Arlington's (with the round cupola), the tiny place of Martha Clarke, and finally the huge Mahogany Hall. The absence of railroad sheds at the extreme right indicates that the picture was taken before 1908.

Basin Street "Down the Line," 1909, buildings in the same left-to-right order. Note the railroad passenger shed in the foreground. The first establishment on the next block, just visible at the extreme right, was Toro's Monte Carlo Café.

Charles Marcet's shooting gallery (one of two operated by Marcet in the District) and then step next door into Milton J. Kelly's Terminal Saloon for a schooner of beer. There, sipping his drink, he could study the wall of photos of the era's pugilistic heroes and the prints of English hunting scenes. Or he could plan his further movements on the basis of information in the *Hell-o* book or in the more lavishly printed *Blue Book,* which was available for purchase in Kelly's. At some point, the sound of music, coming from the building on the downtown side, would catch his ear.

Leaving a nickel for the drink, he would step out of the Terminal and into Fewclothes' Cabaret, operated by George Foucault. The name of the place was derived from its patrons' inability to pronounce the manager's name correctly. The music that had drawn the visitor had issued from the clarinet of Louis Delisle (known to later jazz enthusiasts as "Big Eye" Louis Nelson), whose band, the Golden Rule Orchestra, was able to play, according to a sign over the bar, all the "latest song hits." The visitor heard such novelties as *Sailing Down the Chesapeake Bay, Aba Daba Honeymoon, That's How I Need You,* and the enormously successful hit *Pretty Baby*—a composition of Storyville's own "Professor" Tony Jackson. The guest had heard about this lively improvised music of New Orleans—"ragtime" some called it.

Fewclothes' was the last stop before Storyville. The adjoining corner structure was devoted completely to "cribs"—single rooms, with private entrance onto the street, just wide and deep enough to accommodate a bed and a washstand —perhaps a chair. The inhabitant would stand in the doorway in what she considered her most fetching attitude and hope to entice customers by word, deed, gesture, attire (or lack of it), or any combination of these. Near this corner, at Basin and Iberville streets, crib girls could command as much as a dollar a "trick." In less desirable locations, further down Iberville, for example, the prices could drop to a dime.

Perhaps we should now draw a veil of modesty around the movements of our perambulating tourist. He might well continue along Basin Street toward the plush mansions described in the *Blue Book*—the Arlington, Mahogany Hall, and others "down the line." Or he might turn to his left down Iberville Street and its cribs. Let him continue on his sybaritic way unaccompanied, as we resume our own more sober tour in search of not pleasure but a better understanding of what Storyville was and what it would become.

In 1914 Basin Street "down the line" consisted of two blocks—the lake side of the street from Iberville to Conti. The first block, from Iberville to Bienville, consisted of nine structures, the second, from Bienville to Conti, of twelve.

The corner of Basin and Iberville was Tom Anderson's saloon, the Arlington Annex. Anderson operated a combined drinking parlor, tourist bureau, informal city hall and courthouse, with a brothel upstairs managed at various times by one or another of the boss' ladies.

The entire District was jocularly called "Anderson County," and city politicians recognized him as dictator of Storyville and dealt with the District through him. He settled internal disputes, punishing or rewarding according to his own inscrutable principles. From 1900 on, he continued to expand his Storyville holdings and by 1915 he owned, openly or as a silent partner, a dozen or more properties in the District, at least five of which were on Basin Street. These included the adjoining palace operated by wife-to-be Gertrude Dix, and the Arlington, named for a former mistress.

Tours of the District's resorts usually began at Anderson's, where the dazzling, half-block-long bar was a Storyville showpiece. A lushly carved cherrywood masterpiece with gilt bas-reliefs in neo-Empire style, its five huge, arched mirrors reflected the images of thousands of pleasure-seekers, twenty-four hours a day. Its polished brass cuspidors and brown and white tiled floors, set the tone of decor for the world's most notorious street. The ornate ceiling, studded with a hundred light bulbs, could produce a glare to compete with sunlight. This brightness is always mentioned by reminiscing survivors: "We didn't have no sunglasses in them days— but you needed 'em in Anderson's. . . . Hurt my eyes to walk *past* at night. . . . I only remember them lights and that loud, bad music." Twelve bartenders, managed by Billy Struve, poured high-quality intoxicants at moderate prices throughout the day and night.

Anderson himself, heavily mustachioed, his blonde hair parted in the middle, was the prototype of the turn-of-the-century boniface, checkered vest, gold watch chain, and all. Here he

A hundred electric bulbs in the ceiling of Tom Anderson's Annex Café and Chop House at Basin Street and Customhouse (Iberville).

played god, dispensing patronage, charity, advice. He settled quarrels, witnessed legal papers, and arranged property transfers. It was said that no transaction could take place in Storyville without a cut for Anderson.

After Anderson's, the first house "down the line," a three-story railroad-baron-style structure (No. 209–211), was Gertrude Dix's (later Mrs. Anderson, née Hoffmire). In its earlier days its four famed parlors had belonged, in turn, to Flo Meeker and Hilma Burt. It contained ornate woodwork, stained glass, mirrors, and furnishings, which included, besides countless *objets d'art* and rare books, a major collection of erotica supposedly insured for a half million 1910 dollars. (It is doubtful that it was worth a tenth of this figure, since merchants "sold high" to owners of *maisons de joie* and madams prided themselves on their willingness to "pay the price." Hilma Burt was proud to announce that she had paid five thousand dollars for the mirrors in one room.)

"These places," we are told by pianist Clarence Williams (as quoted in *Hear Me Talkin' to Ya*),

were really something to see—those sporting houses. They had the *most* beautiful parlors, with cut glass and draperies, and rugs, and expensive furniture. They were just like millionaires houses. And the girls would come down dressed

It wasn't until 1961 that this unbelievable shot turned up. A Picayune *photographer took it from a balloon probably about 1914. (The glass plate from which this print was made carries a 1922 date, but the large smokestack, bottom right, belonging to Regency Shoes, came down prior to that year.) The diagonals in the lower section are the shed roofs over the railway tracks along Basin Street. The vertical streets are, left-to-right, Iberville, Bienville, Conti, and St. Louis. The back of the District is bounded by St. Louis Cemetery No. 2. At lower right is St. Louis Cemetery No. 1. Except for the St. James Methodist Church, every building in the area was devoted to prostitution.*

76

Hilma Burt spent lots of money, but she never got out of debt. Top; the Library; left, a boudoir; bottom right, the Dutch Room.

in the finest of evening gowns, just like they were going to the opera. They were just beautiful. Their hair-dos were just so, and I'm telling you that Ziegfeld didn't have any more beautiful women than those. Some of them looked Spanish, and some were Creoles, some brownskins, some chocolate brown. But they all had to have that figure.

Places like that were for rich people, mostly white. Oh, once in a while a sailor might come, but generally only the wealthiest would come. Why do you know that a bottle of beer was a dollar? The customers would buy champagne mostly and would always insist on giving the musicians money. When the piano player would get tired, there would be a player piano that you put a quarter in and we'd make money then, too. Those houses hired nothing but the best, but only piano players, and maybe a girl to sing. And there was no loud playin' either. It was sweet, just like a hotel.

The next building (No. 213), a two-story, frame affair, housed Diana and Norma's, an establishment billed as a "French house." The term "French house" was applied to premises in which fellatio was the chief, sometimes the only, service rendered. The nature of the service reduced space needs and increased turnover, with the result that this form of activity could be, and was, priced down to the levels of more conventional practices. Diana Ray had come to New Orleans with funds said to have been derived from blackmail operations in Kansas City. Norma had been a performer in Emma Johnson's Studio. Both women were reportedly lesbians but were not, according to most educated guesses, sexually interested in each other.

Number 217, the Little Annex presided over by Lizette Smith, a one-time paramour of the ubiquitous Anderson, is described by former patrons as "the most refined house down the line" and as "just like home." The tiny, frame building, as photographed, appears to have had too little space to provide for volume business. However, knowledgeable sources state that the Little Annex was probably the most expensive emporium in the District and was used by

A prime attraction at Minnie White's place at 221 North Basin Street was Marguerite Griffin, who could not only handle the conventional duties of a Storyville tart but also knew the lyrics of countless bawdy ballads. Note the wall hangings: The pillow above her head reads "Daisies won't tell." The risque signs read, left to right, "Oh! Babe, please come," "Oh! Dearie, I give U much pleasure" (affixed to a Mardi Gras pennant dated 1910), and "Dearie, U ask for Marguerite." (Photograph by Ernest Bellocq)

its real owner, Anderson, to entertain truly important visitors in surroundings of relative privacy and luxury. Among its better known patrons were John L. Sullivan, Phineas T. Barnum, and Diamond Jim Brady. Barnum is said to have furnished a private railroad car with the effects of the Little Annex (including Lizette herself).

The four-story stone building numbered 221 and 223 held two separate places of business operated, respectively, by Minnie White and Jessie Brown. The structure was walled through the middle and had separate entrances for each number. Minnie's, at No. 221, was well known as an "entertainment" house in which a great deal of horseplay was a basic attraction. A kind of unofficial headquarters for conventioneers, the place maintained the District's largest bill for intoxicating beverages. While there were no formal shows offered, there were lots of bawdy ballads sung, occasional strip acts, and even a small dormitory where drunks could be slept off. Miss Minnie also provided a "sure-fire hang-

over cure," built around champagne and cayenne pepper, which one patient reports "made green, gooey tears come out [of] your eyes." Minnie's front parlor was the scene of many an exciting domino match and checker game. It is said that this madam made more money with fewer girls than anyone else on the street.

Next door, at No. 223, Jessie Brown kept a place catering mainly to local workingmen. At a standard rate of one dollar, the cabman from an incoming train had available what was billed as "the cleanest room in town and the undivided attention of an experienced [and not unattractive] prostitute for five minutes." According to report, the house was divided into an incredible number of rooms (some sources estimate as many as sixty-five), each equipped like a crib, with a couch and washbasin, but with framed pictures on the walls, good rugs, and tight fitting doors. Jessie also offered, in order to fill out slack hours, a one dollar "special" that included a hot breakfast (sausage

Interiors of the Arlington. When Josie died in 1914, the furnishings deteriorated quickly. At auction, they all went for less than two hundred dollars. Top left, the

Mirror and Music Hall; top right, Dining Room; bottom left, the Vienna Parlor, bottom right, American Parlor; next page left, a den; right, the Japanese Parlor.

Mahogany Hall
Souvenir Booklet
The NEW *Mahogany Hall*

A picture of which appears on the cover of this souvenir was erected specially for Miss Lulu White at a cost of $40,000. The house is built of marble and is four story; containing five parlors, all handsomely furnished, and fifteen bedrooms. Each room has a bath with hot and cold water and extension closets.

The elevator, which was built for two, is of the latest style, the entire house is steam heated and is the handsomest house of its kind. It is the only one where you can get three shots for your money—

The shot upstairs,
The shot downstairs,
And the shot in the room . . .

This famous West Indian octoroon first saw the light of day thirty-one years ago. Arriving in this country at a rather tender age, and having been fortunately gifted with a good education it did not take long for her to find out what the other sex was in search of. In describing Miss Lulu, as she is most familiarly called, it would not be amiss to say that besides possessing an elegant form she has beautiful black hair and blue eyes, which have justly gained for her the title of the "Queen of the Demi-monde."

Her establishment, which is situated in the central part of the city, is unquestionably the most

and red beans with French bread and chicory coffee) between the hours of 6:00 and 9:00 A.M., except on Mondays.

The Arlington, at 225 Basin Street, one of the District's major showplaces, was yet another Anderson enterprise. Four stories high, topped with a neo-Byzantine cupola, its madam, the notorious Josie Arlington, Anderson's former mistress, took true pride in its ostentatious splendor. Her advertisement in the *Blue Book* boasted: "absolutely and unquestionably the most decorative and costly fitted out sporting palace ever placed before the American public." Certainly it rivaled neighboring Mahogany Hall in lushness. It featured a Turkish Parlor, a Hall of Mirrors, a Japanese Parlor, a Vienna Parlor, an American Parlor, and seemingly countless luxury "dens" and "boudoirs," in times when luxury was equated with quantities of wall hangings, chandeliers, drapes, rococo furniture, afghan spreads, oriental, deep-pile rugs, and elegant, life-like paintings and sculptures.

Martha Clark's, at No. 227, was one of the tiniest houses "down the line," employing at times only the mistress herself and rarely more than two aides except during Carnival season.

Mahogany Hall, at No. 235, the most celebrated brothel in America, was built and operated by the fabled Lulu White, "the Octoroon Queen," whose all-octoroon palace was a major Crescent City showplace. The following is the

elaborately furnished house in the city of New Orleans, and without a doubt one of the most elegant places in this or any other country.

She has made a feature of boarding none but the fairest of girls—those gifted with nature's best charms, and would, under no circumstances, have any but that class in her house.

As an entertainer Miss Lulu stands foremost, having made a life-long study of music and literature. She is well read and one that can interest anybody and make a visit to her place a continued round of pleasure.

Lulu's nephew, Spencer Williams, whom she adopted at his mother's death, lived in Mahogany Hall for many years and immortalized it in an instrumental piece, much recorded by such artists as Louis Armstrong, *Mahogany Hall Stomp* (which is based on the spiritual *Bye and Bye*). Williams' background makes it all the more odd that his famous hit song *Basin Street Blues* should so misrepresent both the street and the District. Musically, the song is far more reminiscent of Tin Pan Alley than it is of New Orleans. The. lyric, indefensible as poetry,

Despite the broken glass negative, we can still see the luxury of the Mahogany Hall parlor. (Photograph by Ernest Bellocq)

is preposterous as reportage. If the dark and lights folks ever "met" on Basin Street, as the lyric says they did, it was not in any "welcome's free" spirit of camaraderie! Black customers were barred absolutely from all houses on Basin Street, including its two "octoroon" houses (Lulu White's in the 200 block and Countess Willie Piazza's in the 300 block), and it was even against the law for white and black prostitutes to occupy the same premises. According to Danny Barker, however, speaking of Storyville generally, "the big sporting houses in the District . . . were for whites. It was before my time, but they tell me that a mulatto passing for a white could get in. And there were farmers and sugar men and riverboat men all through Louisiana who were mulattoes. So if you *looked* white or Spanish, you went in . . ." (emphasis added).

Jelly Roll Morton recalled that the mirror parlor at Lulu White's cost thirty thousand dollars: "Mirrors stood at the foot and head of all the beds."

Mahogany Hall would be the last of the Basin Street pleasure palaces to be torn down to make room for the housing project that now occupies most of the area that was Storyville. The National Jazz Foundation attempted to buy the building, with a view to making it a jazz museum, but the effort failed and in 1949 the demolition took place. Jazz fans thoughout the world bought relics for their personal collections of memorabilia. The front doorknob and lock assembly and the curbstone are now displayed in the New Orleans Jazz Museum on Conti Street.

At sundown in 1922: the Arlington cupola (left) and Mahogany Hall (right).

The corner building next to Mahogany Hall was also the property of Lulu White. Known as Lulu White's Saloon, it was managed by Dan Hatch. The two-story brick structure, built in 1909, still stands, but now has only one story, owing to the ravages of Hurricane Betsy in 1965. The missing second floor once served as the business office of Billy Struve, the editor of the *Blue Book* and Tom Anderson's factotum for a quarter of a century.

All this was in the first block of Basin Street between Iberville and Bienville. The second block, from Bienville to the cemetery, was not quite so grandiose architecturally but did have its share of celebrated landmarks, most notably Toro's saloon, Countess Willie V. Piazza's mansion, and Emma Johnson's French Studio.

Frank Toro's place, on the downtown lake

The fan window over the door of Mahogany Hall is now owned by clarinetist Pete Fountain. (Photograph by Dave Scherman)

This was Lulu White's saloon at Basin and Bienville streets, with Mahogany Hall just visible at the extreme left, cribs at the far right. It later became the Broadway Cabaret. From 1909 to 1915 the Blue Book was published on the second floor. The photograph dates from 1943.

May Tuckerman's brothel at 341 Basin Street, corner of Conti. Earlier it was run by other madams, and in 1917 Willie Barrera did the honors at this address. The photograph dates from the late 1920s.

corner of Bienville and Basin, was a "low-down rough cabaret," in the words of one habitué. "But according to what things is today, you wouldn't call it rough, I guess, but just common, every day." There was a bar and a lunch counter. He sold po'boy sandwiches and pots of red beans and rice, "to go." Sometimes there was music outside on the banquette, provided by Emile "Stalebread" Lacoume and his "spasm" band, who played on homemade instruments and featured performers with such names as Warm Gravy and Chinee. Its personnel included a pan slammer named Harry Gregson who would someday become police captain of the area. This group was paid by donation only. Other than Kid Ross, these were the only white men who ever played music for money—on any basis— in Storyville during its period of legal existence.

At 317 Basin Street, the spectacular Countess Willie V. Piazza held forth with an array of a dozen octoroons who were said to be the most beautiful girls in the South. Countess Willie was one of the first to learn to appreciate the quality of the music being produced by the great New Orleans piano stars. Such performers as Jelly Roll Morton and Tony Jackson were regularly employed to play on the famous monster-sized, white upright piano.

A colorful, well-educated, and articulate woman, Madame Piazza saved her money and when the Storyville bubble burst in 1917 retired to France, where she changed her name, wed a genuine Gallic nobleman, and lived out her life in a villa on the Riviera, an honored and respected dowager.

Further down the street, at No. 335, was the huge studio of Emma Johnson. This was the District's best-known "French house" but was not limited by this characterization. Here, *every* variety of obscene performance that the fevered brain of man or woman could devise was on display in nightly sex "circuses" performed on a slightly raised stage in an enormous downstairs parlor. French Emma, as Madame Johnson was known in her earlier days at 925 Customhouse (later Iberville) Street, had built a phenomenal reputation with her "sixty-second plan." Any man who could restrain his orgasm with her for a full minute after penetration was excused from payment. Droves of economy-minded locals would jam the place confident that they could qualify for some free entertainment. According to Emma, she would permit a man to hold out now and then, so as to give heart to the others, but it was her private boast that her "secret technique" was a hundred percent effective and that she hadn't yet come across a man she couldn't "win" with. In the late 1890s, occupying only half of the double building she shared with Ella Schwartz, she was operating by herself and charging two dollars, but by 1915 the entire structure was hers and she was one of the biggest operators in New Orleans, employing as many as fifty-five girls, including many who were paid to perform only on stage and were not available to the men.

Among these talented entertainers was Olivia, the Oyster Dancer. Completely naked, she began by placing a raw oyster on her forehead and then leaned back and "shimmied" the oyster back and forth over her body without dropping it, finally causing it to run down to her instep, from which a quick kick would flip it high in the air, whereupon she would catch it on her forehead whence it started. An aged prostitute assured the author, with great solemnity, that this was now "a lost art." A retired fireman, who had been stationed for years at the engine company next door to Emma's, reports: "I guess I seen the oyster dance a hundred times. It was pretty clever—but for dirt, it wasn't nothing beside the other things they done in Emma's."

The house on the other side of the firehouse was the corner occupied by Willie O. Barrera and staff, across the street from St. Louis Cemetery No. 1. Buried there, among others, are Paul Morphy, who has been called "the father of modern chess"; Etienne DeBore who developed the first practical sugar granulating method; the historian Charles Gayarré; and Alexander Milne, the miser-philanthropist after whom the famous Milneburg resort was named (it is now Ponchartrain Beach Amusement Park). A tomb generally thought to be that of the voodoo queen Marie Laveau is also here. Distinguished neighbors, indeed, for the living inhabitants of Basin Street.

The first block of Iberville Street, between Basin and Franklin, was completely given over to cribs, except for the portion on the downtown Basin Street corner that was the side entrance of the Arlington Annex. The second block, from Franklin to Liberty, in 1914, was all cribs, except for the uptown corner of Iberville and Franklin, a building known variously as a saloon, gambling place, and restaurant. It gained much of its notoriety as the Shoto Cabaret. The opposite

The Firehouse on Basin Street, one building from the corner of Conti. Also visible: the brothels of Countess Piazza (left) and Willie Barrera (on the corner).

Upstairs at 341 Basin Street when Willie Barrera operated on this corner. (Photograph by Ernest Bellocq)

lake corner had once been the Pig Ankle Cabaret, but by 1914 it too had been converted to cribs.

On the uptown side of the Shoto, and adjoining it, with a 135 Franklin Street address and a business license issued to John T. Lala (whose name was to be seen embedded in the banquette right in front of the door sill), was the durable and famed Big 25, a hangout for Negro jazz musicians, many of whom would become world famous in future years. Here King Oliver, Freddy Keppard, Kid Ory, Bunk Johnson, and Papa Mutt Carey spent intermissions from their jobs in neighboring cabarets—hiring sidemen, talking music and jobs, drinking and smoking. Here Jelly Roll Morton "was just sitting around" hoping for his luck to change when a messenger from Hilma Burt's mansion summoned him to his Storyville debut in 1904.

The two lake corners of Iberville and Liberty were occupied by the Casino on the uptown side and Groshell's Cabaret and Dance Hall on the downtown (formerly Huntz' Cabaret and Hanan's Cabaret, respectively). These spots catered to white patrons only, but the music was supplied by blacks, including, off and on during the period at the beginning of World War I, the Keppards, Pops Foster, and Arnold Depass. There was one more saloon, Eugene Tournier's, on the uptown river corner of Iberville and Marais, but the remainder of the short block was occupied by no fewer than thirty-two cribs—and Charles Marcet's Shooting Gallery at 1404 Iberville. Ray Owen's Star Mansion occupied 1517 Iberville.

Cribs on Iberville Street between Marais and Liberty. The odd overhang on the extreme left belonged to Eddie Groshell's Dance Hall. The picture dates from 1919 or earlier.

Under the "Jax" sign is the Big 25 as it looked in 1942. The street, now named "Crozat," is Franklin Street. The corner with the barber pole was at one time the Shoto Cabaret. The building was torn down in 1957.

The uptown lake corner of Iberville and Marais, listed as the Manhattan Café (owned by Peter Ciaccio), was the real spawning ground for many of the organized bands that would bring glory to New Orleans and its music in the years to come. This place, for reasons never adequately explained, was called then, and is known now, as "Pete Lala's." There were at least two other spots in the tenderloin owned by a Lala that were *not* called "Lala's," but Ciaccio's club was. A noisy, brawling barn of a place, it featured music and dancing downstairs, heavy gambling in the back rooms, and assignations upstairs. The dancing, an unskilled but highly rhythmic activity, was vulgar and suggestive in the extreme, often resembling a kind of vertical copulation. In the book *Hear Me Talkin' to Ya* (1955) Clarence Williams is quoted to good effect on the subject of Pete Lala's place:

> Round about 4:00 A.M., the girls would get through work and meet their P.I.'s—that's what we called pimps—at the wine rooms. Pete Lala's was the headquarters, the place where all the bands would come when they got off work, and where the girls would come to meet their main man. It was a place where they would come to drink and play and have breakfast and then go home to bed.
>
> Most of the P.I.'s were gamblers and pianists. The reason so many of them were pianists was because whenever they were down on their luck, they could always get a job and be close to their girls—play while the girls worked.

Louis Armstrong, in an article in *True* magazine (November, 1947), recalled the place well, but confused it with the Big 25:

> . . . these pimps and hustlers, et cetera, would spend most of their time at The 25 until their

Though this photograph was taken in 1943, all of the buildings are originals. The "4X" sign on the left hangs on what was once Pete Lala's Café.

Pete Lala's Café. Whatever claim Storyville might have had to have been the birthplace of jazz is associated with this building, where King Oliver, Kid Ory, Freddie Keppard, and Sidney Bechet performed long ago for two or three dollars a night. The photograph dates from 1943.

One of the Iberville Street showplaces: Ray Owen's Star Mansion in its heyday. Top left, the Ball Room; right, the Dining Room; bottom left, the Colonial Room; right, the Turkish Room.

The Star Mansion (with the peaked roof) just before demolition. It once had a star set in its peak.

The uptown side of Iberville Street, as seen from the corner of Franklin. These buildings were all cribs except the one next to the corner, which was Charles Marcet's shooting gallery.

The three-story brothel with the many columns was occupied by Miss Gipsy Shafer, whom Jelly Roll Morton called "probably the most notoriety woman I ever seen." It was situated on the downtown lake corner of Villere and Iberville.

girls would finish turning tricks in their cribs. . . . They would meet them and check up on the night's take. . . . Lot of the prostitutes lived in different sections of the city and would come down to Storyville just like they had a job. . . . There were different shifts for them. . . . Sometimes—two prostitutes would share the rent in the same crib together. . . . One would work in the day and the other would beat out that night shift. . . . And business was so good in those days with the fleet of sailors and the crews from those big ships that come in the Mississippi River from all over the world—kept them very, very busy.

Rice's Café, a cabaret for white customers, stood opposite Pete Lala's, on the downtown lake corner. Another saloon, Richard Egan's on Iberville at the uptown river corner of Villere, was also a grocery store and may have been the only place in the District that sold more food than liquor. The rest of Iberville, from Liberty to St. Louis Cemetery No. 2 at Robertson Street, was mainly Negro cribs and a few white parlor houses, including that of the most flamboyant of the off-Basin Street madams, Gipsy or Gypsy Shafer. (This spelling of her surname, incidentally, is from *Soard's City Directory* of 1915. The name appears as Schaeffer or Shaffer in the *Blue Book*, Shaffer in the *Mascot*, Shaefer or Shafer in the *Sunday Sun*.) Of Gipsy, Alan Lomax quotes Jelly Roll Morton in *Mister Jelly Roll:*

Tony Jackson played at Gypsy Schaeffer's, one of the most notoriety women I have ever seen in a high-class way. She was the notoriety kind that everybody liked. She didn't mind spending her money, and her main drink was champagne, and, if you couldn't buy it, she'd buy it for you in abundance. Walk into Gypsy Schaeffer's and, right away, the bell would ring upstairs and all the girls would walk into the parlor, dressed in their fine evening gowns and ask the customer if he would care to drink wine. They would call for the "professor" and while champagne was being served all around, Tony would play a couple of numbers.

If a naked dance was desired, Tony would dig up one of his fast speed tunes and one of the girls would dance on a little narrow stage, completely nude. Yes, they danced absolutely stripped, but in New Orleans the naked dance was a real art.

Bienville Street, within the District's limits, was five blocks of almost continuous cribs, broken by a few saloons and cabarets and the well-known parlor house of May Tuckerman. On the uptown river corner of Franklin Street, Frank Early's My Place saloon stood back to back with

90

Looking down Bienville Street from Basin. On the right, with columns, was Frank Toro's saloon.

Here at the corner of Franklin (now Crozat) and Bienville streets, in what was Frank Early's My Place saloon at the turn of the century, Tony Jackson played and sang "I've got Elgin movements in my hips with twenty years' guarantee." Here, too, he wrote the all-time hit Pretty Baby. *By the early 1940s, when this picture was taken, Early's saloon had become the Little Playhouse—and much else had changed for the worse.*

Lulu White's saloon. Diagonally across the street was the bar owned by John "Peg" Anstedt, a one-legged boniface whose premises attracted young white musicians who made their headquarters here when they roamed the District listening to the outstanding black musicians employed in the area. These youngsters did not perform in the District, but it was on these premises that the Original Dixieland Band consolidated itself.

Leader Nick LaRocca gathered such men as the intellectual Eddie "Daddy" Edwards on trombone, the clarinetist Alcide "Yellow" Nunez, the drummer Tony Sbarbaro, and young, diffident but brilliant Henry Ragas, the ragtime-oriented piano man not fated to live long enough to share much of the glory to be won by this group—the first to record jazz. (Nunez was replaced by the great clarinetist Larry Shields before recording sessions took place.)

Also to be found here at Anstedt's in 1914 were Anton Lada, a drummer who in a few years would be recording, along with Nunez, for Columbia as leader of the Louisiana Five. This hangout would be host, too, to the clarinetist Nunzio Scaglione, such trombonists as Tom Brown and Ellis Stratakos, cornetists Johnny Bayersdorffer and John Dedroit, and the multiplicity of great musicians who shared the name of Brunies—Henny, Richie, Abbie, Merritt, and George. Paul Mares, who later led the New Orleans Rhythm Kings to fame and fortune, was frequently to be found here. "You come up around here," Paul said, "you *had* to be a musician."

Yet another saloon, Louis Miller's, was on the downtown river corner. Instrumental trios were usually featured at the Poodle Dog Café on the downtown lake corner of Bienville and Liberty. The river corners of Bienville and Marais were taken up with old-fashioned swinging-door saloons: on the uptown side, Noonan and Estrade's, on the downtown, Gibson J. Walker's.

Abadie's Cabaret, on the downtown lake corner, offered the legendary Sugar Johnny Smith on cornet in the band of Richard M. Jones, which also included, besides the leader on piano, Wooden Joe Nicholas on clarinet (he would later be better known as a parade trumpeter), and Ernest Rogers on drums. Jelly Roll Morton recalled:

> Those days I hung out at Eloise Blankenstein and Louis Aberdeen's place [Abadie's Café, commonly mispronounced "Aberdeen's" by New Or-

Cribs on Bienville Street between Lulu White's saloon (the brick structure at the left) and Frank Early's My Place on the corner. The photograph was taken in 1941.

A 1943 view of what was Joe Victor's saloon at the intersection of Villere and St. Louis streets, with cribs still to be seen on either side. It is at this writing (1973) one of the few original Storyville buildings still standing.

Conti Street, from Basin Street. The house on the left was May Tuckerman's. Gipsy Shafer conducted her business in the second house from the corner.

North Franklin Street, from the corner of Iberville, looking toward Bienville.

leans musicians]—the rendezvous for all the big sports like Pensacola Kid, who later came to be the champion pool shooter of the world. Bob Rowe, the man who didn't know how many suits he had, and his wife, Ready Money, were regulars, also the Suicide Queen, who used to take poison all the time. Tony Jackson also hung out there and was the cause of me not playing much piano.

Almost directly opposite was St. James Methodist Church, a Negro religious center and one of the most prosperous Protestant places of worship in Louisiana. According to a common story, the church offered first-aid services and modest hospital facilities and thus became the inspiration for the widely performed *St. James Infirmary Blues.* Unfortunately, this colorful and imaginative association is not true; indeed, the song has no connection with New Orleans whatever.

Probably the most exciting location on Bienville Street was the Frenchman's saloon on the downtown river corner of Villere. Its role and atmosphere were remembered vividly by Jelly Roll as quoted in *Mister Jelly Roll:*

> Some friends took me to "The Frenchman's" . . . which was at that time the most famous nightspot after everything was closed. It was only a back room, but it was where all the greatest pianists frequented after they got off from work in the sporting houses. About 4:00 A.M., unless plenty of money was involved on their jobs, they would go to The Frenchman's and there would be everything in the line of hilarity there.
>
> All of the girls that could get out of their houses was there. The millionaires would come to listen to their favorite piano players. There weren't any discrimination of any kind. They all sat at different tables or anywhere they felt like sitting. They all mingled together just as they wished to and everyone was just like one big happy family. People came from all over the country and most times you couldn't get in. So this place would go on at a tremendous rate of speed—plenty money, drinks of all kinds—from four o'clock in the morning until maybe twelve, one, two or three o'clock in the daytime. Then, when the great pianists would leave, the crowds would leave.

Opposite the Frenchman's, on the uptown river corner, was a drug store where cocaine was sold over the counter without the formality of prescription, and where the frequently overstocked proprietor had to put the perishable drug on "special" from time to time for purposes of inventory control. He also purveyed marihuana cigarettes at five cents each, but this price

Phillips' Café (also known at various times as the 101 Ranch, the 102 Ranch, and the Entertainers) at 206–208 N. Franklin Street. Kid Ory, Mutt Carey, and King Oliver played here.

Cribs on Franklin Street near Bienville. (Photograph courtesy of American Music Records)

94

was hardly competitive with that of the horde of tenderloin newsboys who peddled them at three for a dime.

The business of selling sex on Conti Street, unrelieved by much music or other activities, was less stimulating than on the other streets, nothwithstanding the presence of the cornetist-madam Antonia Gonzales at No. 1308, between Franklin Street and the cemetery, St. Louis No. 2. There were four saloons available to the visitor, all on uptown corners: Frederick Grau's on the lake corner of Liberty, the Berry Brothers on the river corner of Marais, and Reinhard Martin's, which was as much a grocery store as a barroom, on the lake corner of Villere. Ownership of the small bar on the lake corner of Marais, known as the Unexpected Saloon and Rifle Club, changed frequently. The rest of Conti Street, within the District, was given over to cribs.

St. Louis Street was relatively quiet, since it began at Liberty Street and functioned as part of Storyville on only one side of the street. Seven cribs were sandwiched between the two saloons in the block from Liberty to Marais— John's (Bangard) at Liberty and John McVille's at Marais. Marais to Villere was solid with cribs and houses of assignation, and with the exception of the large barroom called Victor's, on the lake corner of Villere, the cribs on this street continued unbroken from end to end.

On Franklin Street was the Big 25 and across the street, at No. 28, John the Greek's where, in pre-Storyville days, the Buddy Bolden band held forth. Franklin Street, the first street parallel to Basin, was the locale of the enterprise variously known as the 101 Ranch, the 102 Ranch, and the Entertainers. Owned by Billy Phillips until that fatal Easter Sunday in 1913 when he stopped a bullet, this place was a favorite rendezvous for the sporting crowd, especially the horse players.

Trumpeter Mutt Carey started out at the 101 Ranch: "My first job was in Billy Phillips' place. We played anything we pleased in that joint; you see, there was no class in those places. All they wanted was continuous music, and they had some rough places in Storyville in those days. A guy would see everything in those joints and it was all dirty. It was really a hell of a place to work." (*Hear Me Talkin to Ya.*)

The Tuxedo Dance Hall, and its neighbor the Villa Cabaret, had most of the best Negro jazz musicians, at one time or another. As reviewed in the *Daily Picayune*, March 25, 1913:

"Dollar cribs" on the lake side of Marais, between Conti and St. Louis streets. The building on the extreme right, with the posts, was the Unexpected Saloon and Rifle Club.

The Tuxedo, a model of the dance halls which make up a good part of the tenderloin, occupies a part of North Franklin, between Bienville and Iberville. The bar faces the street and opens, without screens, the full width of the part apportioned to it, into the street. . . . at the lower end of the hall a stand has been erected for the music, about 12 feet above the dancing floor, and is connected with it by a small, narrow stairway. Here a negro band holds forth and from about 8 o'clock at night until 4 o'clock in the morning plays varied rags, conspicuous for being the latest in popular music, interspersed with compositions by the musicians themselves. The band has a leader who grotesquely prompts the various pieces, which generally constitute several brass pieces, a violin, guitar, piccolo, and a piano.

It was from the Tuxedo that the Original Tuxedo Orchestra sprang, headed by the beloved Papa Celestin, who would perform prominently in the Crescent City for more than half a century. In the same little block between Iberville and Bienville were twenty or more cribs, all in constant operation.

On the lake side of the street from Bienville to Conti were the elaborate bordellos of May Evans and Dolly Boyd and that of Maud Hartman (the Club). Directly across the street could be seen Snooks Randella's house (the Cairo) and the pretentious establishment of Grace Lloyd at the corner. Interstices were never without occupants, since cribs could exist almost anywhere. In busy seasons, avaricious landlords even rented out the alleys between houses to prostitutes willing to turn "tricks" alfresco for fifteen cents.

Liberty and Marais streets, except for two lunch houses (John Gorce's at 209 Marais and Jerome Donatt's at No. 305), were given over to cribs, mostly inhabited by white girls.

Villere and Robertson streets, also lined with cribs, were almost exclusively used by Negro women and patronized by Negro men, though groups of white boys, usually teen-agers, could often be found taking advantage of the lower prices prevailing out of the high-rent area.

In the year 1914, Storyville was still supporting as many as seven hundred fifty women, some three hundred pimps and "macs," two hundred musicians, about five hundred domestic workers, and a hundred fifty saloon employees. Many "respectable" Orleanians from the more conservative sections of town saw modest wealth grow to large fortunes through their rental of District property. It was known as the safest, most consistent investment in the city. A single-story building that today would be considered a "double" (two-family house) could be partitioned into as many as two dozen cribs. These were rented by the night only, at an average of three dollars a night. The girl would report to the corner bartender, who usually doubled as agent for the owner, pay three dollars in advance, and pick up a key, which she would turn in at daybreak. Thus, each row of cribs brought in from forty to a hundred dollars per night. Comparable property in other parts of town was being rented for from six dollars to ten dollars per month.

In all, about twelve thousand persons lived directly off the income derived from the sin industry of Storyville. It took in as much as a million dollars a month, none of which was siphoned off to organized mobs or syndicates. By the end of the following year, however, as we have seen, a significant decline in Storyville's prosperity would clearly be evident—long before the federal government's intervention.

SIX

It Takes a Heap O' Lovin' to Make a Home a House

Certain buildings in New Orleans were notorious, apparently from earliest times, as brothels—so much so, indeed, that the fame of their "landladies" seemed to be based as much on where they were doing business as on how well they were doing it. In this chapter the most important of these structures are listed and located, where possible, in both time and space.

In a previous chapter we had the opportunity to see the District frozen, so to speak, as of 1914. However, so schematic a view will satisfy only the casual reader. There are those whose interest in Storyville goes deeper, those whose interest in each episode, character, and building of Storyville is comparable in its intensity to the interest of the Baker Street Irregulars in all matters pertaining to Sherlock Holmes and Dr. Watson. To those, to all members of the "Basin Street Irregulars," with their tattered copies of *Soard's City Directory*, this chapter is dedicated.

209–211 Basin Street

This was the original location of the Club and operated from before 1895 until 1900 under the management of Flo Meeker. (The Richard M. Jones/Paul Eduard Miller map, which appeared in the *Esquire Jazz Book* [1945] lists the name of a "Flo Mix." This was not a different "landlady" but rather a natural error caused by passing the name of Flo Meeker from oral to written testimony.) In 1900 the establishment passed to the management of Hilma Burt (variously misspelled Helma, Hilda/Burthe, Burtte) under whose supervision Jelly Roll Morton got his first real start in Storyville. During this period the building became the exclusive property of Tom Anderson. In 1911, it came under the management of Gertrude Hoffmire (Dix), who remained in charge as "hostess" until the district was closed in 1917.

213–215 Basin Street

From its very beginnings this address was a so-called "French House" and from its pre-Storyville days until the Navy Department's shut-down in 1917 was known far and wide for the occupants' practice of sitting by the windows pantomiming the act of fellatio (using their thumbs as props) for the edification of passers-by. Before 1897 this address was presided over by the octoroon Florence Mantley, who was succeeded by Yvonne LeRoy, and then by Marguerite Angell. The latter gave way three or four years later to Bertha Golden, who remained in charge until 1907, when Diana Ray and Norma took over. This pair kept it going until Storyville was disestablished, carrying on their bizarre performances at the windows for the benefit of passengers on incoming trains, who could witness the "advertising" from day-coach windows.

217 Basin Street

Antonia Gonzales—who would achieve greater fame later, when she occupied her place at Villere and Iberville, playing the cornet in duets with the pianist Tony Jackson—occupied these Basin Street premises between 1895 and 1900. She was succeeded, in order until 1917, by Gertie Sanford, Marie Denis, and Lizette Smith. Under the Smith aegis the place was known as the Little Annex and was one more harem in which Tom Anderson was involved as profit-sharer. This was the smallest house in the two blocks of Basin Street within Storyville's limits, but one of the best houses in the District, by most accounts.

221 Basin Street

In succession: Nellie McDowell in 1894–1900, Ollie Nichols in 1900–1907, and Minnie White in 1907–1917.

223 Basin Street

Up to 1900 this was the seraglio of Grace Simpson, first president of the Madam's Benevolent Society; after that Jessie Brown was overseeress for seventeen uninterrupted years.

225 Basin Street

This building was erected in 1897 by Tom Anderson for his paramour Josie (Lobrano) Arlington (née Mary Deubler of New Orleans), who brought to it the distinguished name (the Arlington) and manner under which she had been operating for some years past at 172 Customhouse Street. Done in a kind of free-style Edwardian decor, this rococo mansion was the talk of the tenderloin. As a kind of Radio City Music Hall of vice, it prospered under the combined skills of Anderson and la Arlington until her retirement in 1909, after which it continued with Anna Casey as landlady and Gertrude Dix as ex-officio administrator until "Navy day."

227–229 Basin Street

Pearl Knight kept house here up to 1900. Gabrielle Michinard was the madam until about 1904 or 1905. After that, until 1917, it belonged to Martha Clark.

235 Basin Street

Mahogany Hall was built by and for Lulu White, a lady of extravagant tastes, who maintained this garish sex emporium, as well as the saloon adjoining it (on the corner of Bienville), until the death of the District. Originally known as the Hall of Mirrors, Lulu's was the last brothel on Basin Street to succumb to the wreckers (1949).

307 Basin Street

Early period (up to 1906), Jeanette Lefebre; afterwards, Frances Gilbert, except for a very brief period in about 1915 when this address was operated by Rose Stein.

311 Basin Street

For some time before Storyville came into being, Lulu White occupied these premises, apparently while waiting for Mahogany Hall to be built. It was advertised as a "wine castle" until 1897, when Lulu moved into Mahogany Hall and Pauline Avery moved into No. 311. Ella Schwartz ran the place from about 1902 until 1914. Its final days were administered by Bertha Weinthal.

313 Basin Street

Two famous Storyville madams had their day in these premises. The first, Lottie Fisher, operated it as a "wine castle" and seraglio from pre-District days until about 1904. It then became the property of Lillian Irwin and continued under her proprietorship for its remaining thirteen years. Long before Lottie, however, well back in the 1880s, Dorothy Denning had held forth as a madam at this address. As another advertisement attests, Miss Denning also maintained a house at 132 Burgundy Street.

315 Basin Street

Erected in about 1909 on land bought from Countess Willie V. Piazza, this was the newest bordello on Basin Street. Its proprietress, May Spencer, was the only person ever to guide its affairs.

317 Basin Street

Willie V. Piazza and her crew of gorgeous octoroons inhabited this two-story house throughout the legal existence of the District. The building was being used as a brothel long before 1897, first under the direction of Caretha Lopez, and then, briefly, that of Mamie Christine.

319 Basin Street

Willie V. Piazza occupied this place until the building next door at No. 317 was completed. She was followed by Paulette Brian (up to 1905) and Camille Turner (1905–1917).

321 Basin Street

Egypt Vanita (to 1903), Violet Caddie (to 1906), and Olga Lodi, "the Italian queen" (to 1917).

325 Basin Street

Until 1906, Annie Ferris; thereafter, Vivian Bonnaville.

327 Basin Street

Rose (Rosa) Stein had something going for herself on Basin Street from the time Storyville happened. With an occasional interest in several locations, she appears to have maintained the tiny house at No. 327 as an ace in the hole throughout her and its career.

331, 333, and 335 Basin Street

This huge double building of three-and-a-half stories was, in cubic footage, the largest brothel

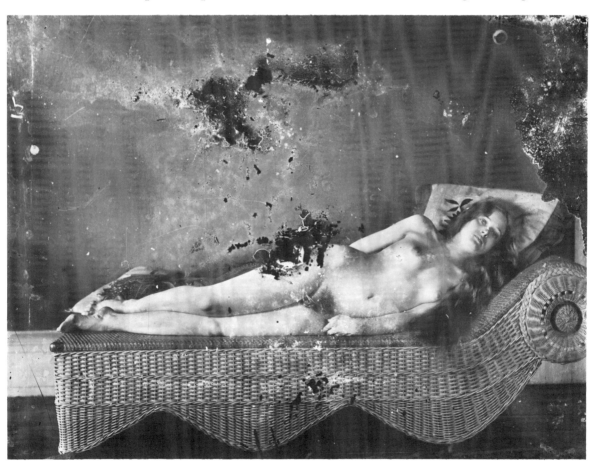

(Photograph by Ernest Bellocq)

99

in the history of New Orleans. A barnlike semi-auditorium, it achieved its widest notoriety as Emma Johnson's French Studio. As Storyville days dawned, it was considered too large to be operated by a single headmistress and was partitioned in the middle with Ella Schwartz and French Emma, herself, in the No. 331 side, Marcel Nado in No. 335. By 1905, however, shrewd impresario Emma Johnson, with her reputation for out-bawdying all others, was attracting such large crowds to her "circuses" that she was able to take over the entire building, remove the partition, and keep the place functioning as a mammoth sex carnival until she was closed down with the rest in 1917.

341 Basin Street

One of New Orlean's most popular bawds, Julia Dean, operated at No. 341 (No. 79, by the old street numbering system), a desirable corner location, until 1895. Tillie Thurman, who then ran the place until 1904, permitted a part of the place, with an entrance on Conti Street, to function as a "German house," with a German-speaking madam, Anna Blesse, in charge. Frau Blesse printed her business cards in German, giving the address as "*341 Nord Basin Str.*" and making a point of mentioning the "*Privat Eingang*" (private entrance) on Conti. Eunice Deering held sway here from 1904 until 1910, when she gave way to Willie O. Barrera, a cigar-smoking terror who seems to have remained the scourge of the neighborhood until Storyville was closed down.

172 Customhouse Street (under a new numbering system adopted in 1904 when the name of the street was changed to Iberville: 1546 Iberville)

This was the original location of the Arlington, occupied by Josie Arlington.

171 Customhouse Street (new system: 1547 Iberville)

The Phoenix, from 1893 one of the Crescent City's most notorious harems, was owned by Fannie Lambert. Half of a large double building, it was eventually absorbed by the owner of the other side, May O'Brien, "the Irish Queen," on Fannie's death in 1904.

1535 Customhouse Street

One of the most spectacular architectural specimens to be found in the District was this huge four-story house on the downtown lake corner of Customhouse and Villere streets. An ancient wooden affair with a multitude of galleries and columns, its scarlet history dated back to 1863, when the ill-fated Kate Townsend was its mistress. Years before she opened her gaudy resort at 40 Basin Street, she kept what is said to have been the finest brothel in Crescent City annals at this Customhouse Street location. Of the succession of madams who presided over No. 1535 in various periods, the most important were Antonia Gonzales, who achieved nearly as much fame for her cornet playing as for her general lewdness, and the redoubtable Gipsy Shafer, free-wheeling sponsor of the great piano playing "professors" Jelly Roll Morton and Tony Jackson.

166 Customhouse Street

This was the first location at which Lulu White did business in pre-District days. Another Basin Street fixture, Jessie Brown, also operated at this address for some years.

158 Customhouse Street

Hattie Hamilton, better known for the events associated with her operation of the bagnio at 21 South Basin Street, conducted her business at this address and at 184 Customhouse, in the late 1870s.

Other Customhouse (Iberville) Street addresses, along with the names of the madams in charge at various times:

104—Mrs. L. Mansfield	also Eva Kelly
117—Eleonora Baquie (1888)	171—Fanny Lambert
126—Tillie Stephens	172—Josie Lobrano (Arlington)— (1888)
128—Dew Drop Inn (corner Burgundy)	
	184—Hattie Hamilton
130—Mrs. E. Smithy	186—Madame Batiste
137—Lou St. Claire	227—Nellie Haley
139—Nettie Garbright	229—Marcelle Moreau
141—Annie Lee	270—Kitty Reed
155—Bon Ton Saloon	380—Mrs. Bagnetto
157—Frankie Belmont	939—Julia Dean
158—Hattie Hamilton (late 1870s)	940—Ollie Russell
	1016—Carter's
166—Lulu White	1022—Grace Simpson
167—Millie Christian (Mamie Christine)	1025—Flo Meeker
	1033—Josephine "Icebox" Claire
168—Hattie Jacobs	1208—Lou Lockwood
169—Fanny Wright,	1310—Sabena Weinblat
	1315—Emma Berger

1402—Miss Jennie	1537—Cora DeWitt
1405—Fanny Bloom	1538—Mary Smith
1407—Flossie Smith	1539—Bessie Cummings
1420—Maud Flower	1542—Jessie Brown;
1504—Bertha Golden	Miss Archie
1506—Ida Bernstein;	Clark
Florence	1545—Alice Williams
Romaine	1547—Fanny Lambert
1510—Ada Hayes;	1549—May O'Brien
Sapho (1912)	1559—Camille Lewis;
1511—Miss Martha	Nina Jackson
1517—Ray Owens	(1888);
1535—Alice Heard;	Margaret
Effie Dudley;	Bradford
Julia Elliott	1561—Hattie White
	1567—Sadie Plummer

Fannie Lambert,
"The Phoenix"
1547 CUSTOMHOUSE ST.   **New Orleans, La.**

On Customhouse Street before 1870; addresses not known:

Julia Davis	Maggie Thompson
Gentle Annie Reed	

Before 1893:

Fannie Decker	Mattie Marshall
Annie Deckert	Nellie Williams
Carrie Freeman	Sally Levy

All the above addresses and individuals were in operation prior to 1897 when Storyville was established. Shortly afterward most of them were partitioned into double houses, with the side buildings and slave quarters converted into cribs. Thus by the time of the 1910 census the (approximately) sixty addresses on Iberville Street (formerly Customhouse Street) had expanded to more than a hundred sixty, without additional structures having been added. Naturally, this caused considerable crowding and placed an even heavier load on already inadequate sanitary facilities.

It should be observed that not only was the name of Customhouse Street changed to Iberville (in 1904), but the numbering system was also changed. To estimate the approximate location, note that for the sites of the old Arlington (172 Customhouse/1546 Iberville) and for Fannie Lambert's Phoenix (171 Customhouse/1547

Iberville), both the old and new numbers are given. This should be a helpful point of reference. It must be remembered, however, that the city planners of the day had an extremely casual attitude—that is, a New Orleans attitude—toward street numbering, and it must not be assumed that all the attendant logic of their "systems" is readily to be divined.

The reader must also have noticed that some names have been listed at more than one address. This is because, obviously, the same woman occupied different premises at different times. Where possible, an approximate date of occupancy has been indicated, at least for the more prominent. All names listed for the various locations are those of madams. No attempt has been made to list the occupants, some of whom seem to have changed names, addresses, or both almost from week to week. The *Blue Books,* though admittedly incomplete and inadequate for the purpose, are the only guide to them.

The following are locations of other well-known houses of the early period, with the "landladies" listed, as nearly as possible, in chronological order:

Bienville Street

810—Fanny Gold	1404—Alice Gold
811—Lola Roig	1410—Annie West
814—Midget Ashley	1412—Mattie Soner
824—Dora Green	1418—Mrs. Anna
829—Rosie Blanchard	Howard (be-
830—(Unknown)	tween Villere
832—Lena Friedman	and Marais)
833—Laura Miller	1545—Cora Young
912—Helen Mitchell	(corner of
916—Miss Mannie	Villere)
Smith	1551—Lou Prout (be-
920—Annie Miller	tween Villere
928—(Unknown)	and Robertson)
930—Bessie	1632—Maud David
Montgomery	(opposite St.
1002—Anna Cahn	Louis Cemetery
1018—Rosie Delaire	#2)
1210—Annie Martinez	
1308—Alice Mitchell	
1318—Harriet Holland	
(corner of	
Liberty Street)	

Conti Street

50—Mrs Kronower	Gipsy Shafer
(old numbering,	(1912)
1883)	1310—Louise Dreyfus
1304—Edna Hamilton	1320—Annie Blessing
1306—Ray Owens; May	(Frau Blesse);
Evans (1906);	Mrs. Barron

(1902); May
Evans (1903);
Lou Prout
(1905); Frances
Morris (1911)
1405—Lillie O'Deall
1414—Gipsy Shafer

(August, 1917)
1418—Nina Jackson
"and Company"
1548—Garne Runiart
1550—Maud Livingston
1554—Clara Henderson
1558—Alice Thompson
1571—Sophie Shields

Villere Street

223—Florence Leslie (the Firm)

North Robertson Street

328—Aunt Cora Isaacs

South Basin Street (all prior to 1897)

6—Mary Brooks
(1857) (between
Common and
Gravier)
8—Chinese Free-
masons [sic]
16—Minnie and Emma
Griffen (1888–
1892)
18—Leila Barton
21—Hattie Strauss (to
1868; Hattie Ham-
ilton (1868 to mid-
1870s)
22—Fanny Wright
(1889); Kittie
Reed (1892)
38½—Clara's House
(1893)

40—Kate Townsend;
Mollie Johnson;
Lou Prout
45—Minnie Ha Ha (to
1868); Josephine
Lilleen (1870)
88—Gentle Annie Reed
(1868); Kitty
Johnson (1870s)
Corner of South Basin
and Gasquet—
Fanny Sweet
(1860s)
Basin Street between
Julia and Girod—
Mrs. Jackson

Burgundy Street

15—Abbie Reed;
Gertie Livingston

229—Eva Brown
508—Mattie Smith

Dauphine Street

42—Miss Emma
111—Nellie Gaspar
(1857)

336—Blanche Du-
Murrier

Gravier Street

361—Mrs. Parker and Daughters (1886)

Dryades Street (formerly Philippa)

67—Clara Fisher (1851); Eliza Murray (1857)

St. John Street

25—(between Common and Perdido)—Emma
Pickett (1857)

North Franklin Street

226—May Redmond
315—May Evans
320—Snooks Randella
(the Cairo)
324—Evelyn Carroll
327—Jean Carlton (the
Club) (1912);

Maud Hartman
(1914)
338—Grace Lloyd
Corner Franklin and
Conti—May
Tuckerman
Franklin and Bienville—
Angeline Davis

Baronne Street

187—Miss Kane

Gasquet Street (now Cleveland)

18—Mattie Smith   20—Emma Johnson

St. Louis Street

931—Lou Jackson
1424—May Tuckerman
1426—Mrs. E. Smith

Corner of St. Louis and
Burgundy—
Nettie Dean

South Franklin Street

9—Bessie LaMothe
22—McCarty's Ranch;
the Picayune House
(before 1860)

Franklin near Common
Street—Mathilda
Smith

Howard Street (formerly Delord Street)

257—Abbie Reed
(1889)

420—Alice Hastings;
Lizzie Curtis

North Liberty Street

129—Margie White
237—Josie Friedman (the Original Crescent Palace)

Valence Street

(between Dryades and South Rampart)—Mathilda
Smith

Marais Street

210—Annie Ross
226—Lizzie Springer
Corner Marais and
Canal—Estelle
Hollander
Corner Marais and Bien-
ville (uptown lake
corner)—Annie
Merritt

Corner Marais and Bien-
ville (downtown
river corner)—
Provenzano's
saloon

North Rampart Street

75—Irene Gaston
85—Alice Edwards

87—Mary Seibel

Common Street

Near Corner of Basin—Nancy Hanks Saloon

SEVEN

The Music
of Storyville

The entrepreneurs of Storyville, with few exceptions, were in the sex business, not the music business. Even so, a good deal of music, much of it excellent, was to be heard in the District.

In the dance halls and cabarets, of which there were an increasing number as the District evolved, music was of course essential—and in the dance halls it had to be danceable.

Music in the brothels, though not a necessity, served somewhat the same promotional function as wine and spirits and sex dances and exhibitions in that all helped to get men in a state of readiness for the main event upstairs. From the madam's viewpoint, one supposes, the wine and spirits must have seemed the more valuable stimulant, as compared to music, since she sold the liquor at a profit and made nothing on the music. But at least the music didn't cost her anything, since the musicians were willing to work for tips and it was a point of pride among many men out for a good time to prove their affluence by tipping them generously. Moreover, lively music undoubtedly put many a customer in a mood to buy another round of drinks, or even another bottle, which would be dispensed to him at inflated prices whose outrageousness presumably bothered him the less the more he drank.

The music varied from brothel to brothel. In many of them a mechanical piano sufficed, with the patrons expected to keep it primed with quarters. In most of the better houses the music was supplied by a live pianist, the "professor," and by a player piano only when the professor took a break. In Minnie White's establishment, however, at 221 Basin Street, many of the girls doubled as singers of bawdy ballads and song "parodies" (dirty lyrics sung to popular tunes of the day). And at Villere and Customhouse/ Iberville streets, in the brothel of Miss Antonia P. Gonzales, "the only Singer of Opera and

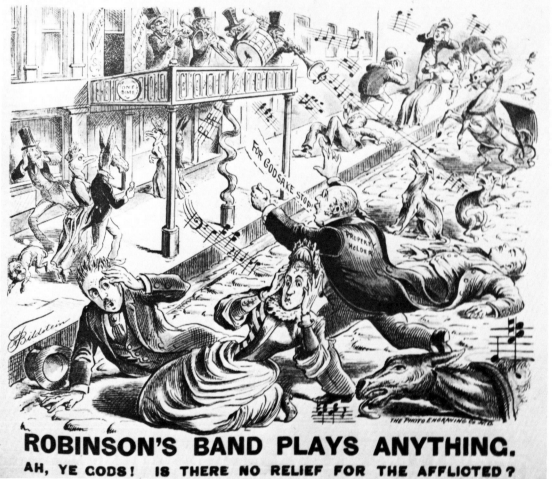

ROBINSON'S BAND PLAYS ANYTHING.

AH, YE GODS! IS THERE NO RELIEF FOR THE AFFLICTED?

The earliest known illustration of a jazz band shows musicians employed to attract customers coming out of Basin Street to Robinson's Dime Museum. The paper clearly didn't share Mr. Robinson's enthusiasm for the music: ". . . we have at last been visited by a sad affliction. . . . Several 'coons' armed with pieces of brass have banded together for what personal good we are unable to say, except that it be for two dollars a week and glue, but we are able to swear that if their object was to inflict torture upon this suffering community . . . they are doing right well. . . . If that band of windjammers have started out on a crusade against sinners —brothers and sisters, let us pray. . . . This man Robinson came here with a monkey and a blue parrot. . . . The town knew him not, but a nigger brass band betrayed him. . . . Look the picture over and you will be convinced that Robinson's balcony serenade is enough to make the dead rise from their graves. . . ."

Female Cornetist in the Tenderloin," one heard "ragtime singing"—often by the great Tony Jackson, when he was in town. Miss Antonia herself is said to have been surprisingly proficient as an instrumentalist and often joined in duets with the professor.

In some houses the professor doubled as a singer, and it was a point of pride among them to be up-to-date on the latest song hits, some of local origin but most from New York's Tin Pan Alley, plus the latest ragtime instrumentals and, actually, the gamut of popular and semi-classical music of the day, good and bad.

The type of vocal blues made famous by Ma Rainey, Bessie Smith, and countless others was not indigenous to New Orleans and was not prominent in Storyville's musical picture, but at least one such singer, Ann Cook, did perform in the District, as did the celebrated song-and-dance man Willie Jackson, who included such blues songs as *Bad, Bad Mama, She Keeps It Up All The Time,* and *Willie Jackson's Blues* in his regular cabaret routine. But most of what little of this sort of music was to be heard in the District was performed in the cabarets, dance halls, and cafés rather than in the brothels.

In a whorehouse environment it was to be expected that sex in all its permutations would be a dominant theme in the songs that came into being in or around the District. Jelly Roll Morton (of whom more later) was famous in the District for his limitless repertoire of dirty variations on such standards as *Make Me A Pallet on the Floor.* The sentimental ballad *Mamma's Baby Boy,* published by the Williams & Piron Music Publishing Company with lyrics fit for a church social, had earlier enjoyed an even greater success in Storyville. The last lines in the published version go

  . . . Someday [she] will realize
That she will have comfort, love, and joy,
With Mamma's Baby Boy.

—quite a change from the original, which went something like this, ending with the title of the tune as Storyville knew it:

She handed him this line of sass—
If you don't like my Creole ways
Kiss my fuckin' ass.

Kid Ory recorded the tune decades later under the title *Do What Ory Say,* mumbling his way

Ann Cook sang the blues in the District and was the only lady blues singer from Storyville to record. She died in 1962, 45 years after Storyville closed. Most of her later life was devoted to church work and she refused to speak of her early years.

through the crucial last line. Dr. Edmond Souchon's version ended with "kiss my ruby lips" and left it to the listener to guess the proper rhyme with "sass." Johnny Wiggs' version, also "clean," bore the title *Lillian Gaspergou*. In Storyville there were no such inhibitions, and *Kiss My Fuckin' Ass* was but one of dozens of "dirty" songs that helped to set, and at the same time reflected, the tone of the place.

Jazz music, contrary to a widely held myth, was not born in Storyville. It was already a lusty, bellowing adolescent before Sidney Story became an alderman, and some of the pioneer jazz musicians had been dead for years before Storyville came into being. Nor did jazz originate in the pre-Storyville whorehouse environment.

Jazz—as distinct from blues and ragtime, in their pure forms—first appeared as music to be played joyfully in the open air by the brass bands of New Orleans' countless fraternal organizations and by string ensembles at the parades, picnics, and "lawn parties" that have ever been focal points of New Orleans social life. It was played in the huge ballrooms where plantation folk disported themselves on festive occasions, and—more than seems to be remembered—it was played in the home and in the streets just for fun. It grew out of the whole way of life in and near the continent's most cosmopolitan city, with blacks in the forefront perhaps, but with many white musicians not far behind. The facts are that the majority of black musicians of outstanding ability in New Orleans never worked so much as a single night in Storyville, and that only one white musician, the pianist Kid Ross, is known to have worked in a Storyville bordello, cabaret, or dance hall for pay.

How is it, then, that so many people came to think of jazz as "whorehouse music"? This is not the forum in which to explore this question in detail. It is enough to note that Storyville gave employment to some scores of jazz musicians, who were thus "visible" and audible to anyone who went there, including the likes of the New Orleans *Times-Picayune* reporter quoted below, who explicitly equated jazz (or jass, as it was then spelled) with the "indecent story," "vice," and the like. It must be remembered in this connection that the syncopations, timbres, intonations, etc., of jazz (and, still earlier, of ragtime and the blues), though now commonly recognized as being, in their way, "revolutionary"—

that is, as being radically new in their musical substance—were regarded by most musicians schooled in European traditions simply as mistakes on the jazz musicians' part. They were the result, according to this view, of the jazz musician's inability, or at best his unwillingness, to play music "correctly." Even a great ragtime pianist such as James Scott, whose own playing was denigrated by some conservatory types as being simply "incorrect" according to their standards, would later denounce jazz musicians, whose playing was even further removed from the European conservatory, as "incorrect." He seems really to have believed that they played as they did, rather than as he did, because of incompetence. Jazz was disorderly music.

Quite by chance, then, the coincidence in time and space of a musical revolution and a highly visible red-light district that employed some of the revolutionists gave rise to public confusion worse confounded, such as that exhibited in the following, from the *Times-Picayune* for June 17, 1917:

"Jass and Jassism"

Why is the jass music, and, therefore, the jass band? As well ask why is the dime novel or the grease-dripping doughnut. All are manifestations of a low streak in man's tastes that has not yet come out in civilization's wash. Indeed, one might go farther, and say that jass music is the indecent story syncopated and counterpointed. Like the improper anecdote, also, in its youth, it was listened to behind closed doors and drawn curtains, but, like all vice, it grew bolder until it dared decent surroundings, and there was tolerated because of its oddity.

We usually think of people as either musical or non-musical as if there were a simple line separating two great classes. The fact is, however, that there are many mansions in the house of the muses. There is first the great assembly hall of melody—where most of us take our seat at some time in our lives—but a lesser number pass on to inner sanctuaries, where the melodic sequence, the "tune," as it most frequently is called, has infinitely less interest than the blending of notes into chords so that the combining wave-lengths will give new aesthetic sensations. This inner court of harmony is where nearly all the truly great music is enjoyed.

In the house there is, however, another apartment, properly speaking, down in the basement, a kind of servants' hall of rhythm. It is there we hear the hum of the Indian dance, the throb of the Oriental tambourines and kettledrums, the clatter of the clogs, the click of Slavic heels, the thumpty-thumpty of the Negro banjo, and, in fact, the native dances of a world. Although commonly associated with melody, and less often with harmony, rhythm is not necessarily music, and he who loves to keep time to the pulse of the orchestral performance by patting his foot upon the theater floor is not necessarily a music lover. The ultra-modernists in composition go so far as to pronounce taboo upon rhythm, and even omit the perpendicular lines on their bars of written music, so that the risk of a monotonous pulsation is done away with.

Prominently, in the basement hall of rhythm, is found rag-time, and of those most devoted to the cult of the displaced accent there has been developed a brotherhood of those who, devoid of harmonic and even of melodic instinct, love to fairly wallow in noise. On certain natures loud sound and meaningless noise has an exciting, almost an intoxicating effect, like crude colors and strong perfumes, the sight of flesh or the sadic pleasure in blood. To such as these the jass music is a delight, and a dance to the unstable bray of the sackbut gives a sensual delight more intense and quite different from the languor of a Viennese waltz or the refined sentiment and respectful emotion of an eighteenth century minuet.

In the matter of jass, New Orleans is particularly interested, since it has been widely suggested that this particular form of musical vice had its birth in this city—that it came, in fact, from doubtful surroundings in our slums. We do not recognize the honor of parenthood, but with a story in circulation it behooves us to be last to accept the atrocity in polite society, and where it has crept in we should make it a point of civic honor to suppress it. Its musical value is nil, and its possibilities of harm are great.

By the early 1960s, in the view of the same paper (by then staffed, presumably, with different people), history had absolved the revolutionists—Jelly Roll Morton, King Oliver, and all those other radicals. A November 11, 1961, editorial hailed the New Orleans Jazz Museum as "a significant addition to the cultural heritage of the city."

Though jazz was not born in Storyville, many of its early greats flourished there. That the District gave steady employment to some of them has been noted. Equally important, however, was the relatively uncritical audience that the District provided, one that permitted the musicians almost unlimited freedom to experiment and to work out stylistic qualities of their own in circumstances less demanding than those experienced by performers in other milieus.

Still more significantly, the District contributed to a breaking down of color lines among the several Negroid ethnic groups (all of which were of course lumped together as "niggers" by white adherents to racist Jim Crow dogmas) and provided a climate in which the lighter-skinned blacks (including the Creoles) and

blacker blacks were forced by circumstance to learn to play together, thereby adding greatly to the form's expressive potential. As Alan Lomax observed in his biography of Jelly Roll Morton:

> By and large these black Americans [among the musicians] were common laborers or service workers. They were not trained musicians, but won their Storyville jobs by sheer talent. Creoles [by this he means Creole Negroes in the sense sometimes still used in the North] who wanted to work in Storyville had to play in bands with them. So for the first time since reconstruction, Creoles were compelled to accept blacks as equals and this was bitter medicine. As the mulatto group had been forced down, its caste prejudice had mounted. . . . There was fear and hate on both sides; but jazz demanded cooperation.

The "Creole" attitude toward the black is revealed in an interview with violinist Paul Dominguez, quoted by Lomax:

> "See, us Downtown people . . . we didn't think so much of this rough Uptown jazz until we couldn't make a living otherwise.
> "Say, for instance, I was working with the Olympia Band, working one or two nights a week for two dollars and a half a night. The 25's [Big 25] here in Storyville pay you a dollar and a quarter and tips, but you working seven nights. Naturally, wouldn't I quit the Olympia and go to this tonk? Wouldn't I?. . . . Well . . . that's how they make a fiddler out of a violinist . . . me, I'm talking about. A fiddler is *not* a violinist, but a violinist can be a fiddler. If I wanted to make a living, I had to be rowdy like the other group. I had to jazz it or rag it or any other damn thing. . . . Bolden cause all that. . . . He cause these younger Creoles, men like Bechet and Keppard, to have a different style altogether from the old heads like Tio and Perez. . . . I don't know how they do it. . . . But goddam, they'll do it. Can't tell you what's there on the paper, but just play the hell out of it."

The bringing together of the technical achievements and knowledge of the downtown Negro and the improvisational capacity and raw power of the uptown black contributed greatly, not to the form itself, but to the quality of work produced within the form.

In addition to this cleavage between "Creole" and "black," which had important creative consequences, another division influenced the course of events, that between solo pianists and all other musicians. The guitar and banjo star Johnny St. Cyr made the distinction clear:

Storyville was closed down in 1917, the year in which these photographs were taken, but its two leading "professors" had long gone. Tony Jackson (left) was Chicago's most admired piano player, and Jelly Roll Morton (below, far right) was doing a single in vaudeville in Los Angeles. The man on the far left was impresario Shep Allen; the others cannot be identified. (Photograph courtesy of Duncan Schiedt)

... they [the piano players] made the best money. Nothing but money men come in those highclass houses and they just as soon tip you a five-dollar bill as a dollar, if they was in the mood and the music was good. So a piano player knock down . . . fifteen and eighteen dollars a night and not have to work too hard. They were lone wolves; every penny come in, *they* kept. That way they made better than us boys in the bands.

Alan Lomax elaborated in *Mr. Jelly Roll:* "Piano keys opened doors into a white world where the other boys in the bands could not follow. This bordello world gave him [Jelly Roll Morton] money and fine clothes and raised him above his brother musicians. His notoriety set him apart from the common musicians of Storyville." Commonly, band musicians were limited to cabarets and honky-tonks. Only the pianists worked steadily in mansions and parlor houses. They were a distinctive lot, but outstanding among them, by common consent, was Tony Jackson.

By now, the world has absorbed, through its various visual communications media, a mental impression of a whorehouse piano player. He is to be seen in the movies and on television, in paintings, illustrations—sometimes in advertisements. Typically, he wears a pearl gray derby, a checkered vest, a stock-tie (ascot) with diamond stickpin. His complexion is very dark. He grins readily, flashing rows of brilliant teeth. His piano is an upright and on the ledge above its keyboard stands an empty whiskey glass and a full bottle. A cigarette dangles from his lower lip. He wears spats and patent leather shoes—and arm garters, usually bejewelled or otherwise decorated. Virtually every adult now living, at least in the Western world, has been so conditioned to this complex symbol that a fleeting glance at the picture conjures up a host of mental associations.

Every detail of the costume is now a convention and any missing item *is* missed. The television producer will interrupt dress rehearsal to yell, "Somebody forgot his diamond ring! Let's get on the ball!" The public knows exactly how it wants its "professor" to look. It does not ask, "Why can't the vest be striped?," or "Why can't the derby be black or brown?" But if it did, we could safely state, in clear and confident tones, "Because, folks! Because Tony Jackson wore *checkered* vests and *pearl gray* derbies" —not always, as the rare photographs reproduced in this volume prove, but often enough for him to be identified with such garb.

Tony Jackson

Tony Jackson, so far as music went, was the undisputed King of Storyville. In the unequivocal words of Jelly Roll Morton, a man not quick to praise other pianists, unless they *really* had something, Tony Jackson was "the World's Greatest Single-Handed Entertainer":

All these men [the pianists who foregathered after hours at the Frenchman's] were hard to beat, but when Tony Jackson walked in, any one of them would get up from the piano stool. If he didn't, somebody was liable to say, "Get up from that piano. You hurting its feelings. Let Tony play." Tony was real dark, and not a bit good-looking, but he had a beautiful disposition. He was the outstanding favorite of New Orleans and I have never known any pianists to come from any section of the world that could leave New Orleans victorious. . . . There was no tune that come up from any opera or any show of any kind or anything that was wrote on paper that Tony couldn't play. He had such a beautiful voice and a marvelous range. His voice on an opera tune was exactly as an opera singer. His range on a blues would be just exactly like a blues singer . . . Tony happened to be one of those gentlemens that a lot of people call them a lady or sissy . . . and that was the cause of him going to Chicago about 1906. He liked the freedom there. . . . Tony was the favorite of all who knew him, but the poor fellow drank himself to death.

Jelly Roll reported further, as quoted in *Mister Jelly Roll*, that he bested Tony in a competitive "battle of music" in Chicago, but confessed: "I never thought the prize was given to the right party; I thought Tony should have the emblem," and he later confided to Roy Carew that he had won by deliberately upsetting Tony by leaning close and whispering in his ear, "Tony, you can't sing now. You can't sing now."

Johnny St. Cyr: "Really the best pianist we had [in New Orleans] was Tony Jackson, but, with the exception of Tony Jackson, Jelly Roll was the man."

Pianist-composer Clarence Williams told cartoonist E. Simms Campbell, in a published interview, that Tony Jackson was probably the greatest blues pianist that ever lived: "He was great because he was original in all of his improvisations—a creator, a supreme stylist." As quoted in *Hear Me Talkin' to Ya*, Williams recalled that "at that time, everybody followed the great Tony Jackson. We all copied him. He was *so* original and a great instrumentalist. I know I copied Tony . . . Yes, Tony Jackson was certainly the greatest piano player and singer in New Orleans . . . About Tony, you know he was an effeminate man—you know . . . He was of a brown complexion, with very thick lips . . . Tony played all the best places in the District . . ."

A laconic Bunk Johnson said: "Tony was dicty."

The giant among New Orleans drummers, Baby Dodds, in his autobiography, reflected his awe: "I also knew . . . the great pianist, Tony Jackson . . . In those days a beginner wasn't allowed to be with a bunch of men that played such high class music. They wouldn't have anything to do with us."

The popular blues singer Alberta Hunter reminisced, in *Hear Me Talking to Ya:*

> Everybody would go to hear Tony Jackson after hours. Tony was just marvelous—a fine musician, spectacular, but still soft. He could write a song in two minutes and was one of the greatest accompanists I've ever listened to. . . . He had mixed hair and always had a drink on the piano—always! . . . Yes, Tony Jackson was a prince of a fellow, and he would always pack them in. There would be so many people around the piano trying to learn his style that sometimes he could hardly move his hands—and he never played any song the same way twice.

Such testimonials—a few of the many that could be cited—we must accept in lieu of recorded evidence of the Jackson talent. They seem to establish that Tony was widely copied and imitated. An axiom among the old-time pianists, according to the late bass and trumpet player Richard Alexis was: "If you can't play like Tony Jackson, *look* like him." And so our image of the Storyville "professor" is the image supplied by Tony Jackson, a name known to but few people nowadays.

"Sure, I remember him," recalled Alexis. "Happy-go-lucky! Not a care in the world!" Oh, to be an epileptic, alcoholic, homosexual Negro genius in the Deep South of the United States of America! How could you have a care? Anyone would be happy, naturally, being among the piano virtuosi of his era, permitted to play only in saloons and whorehouses, for pimps and prostitutes and their customers. How could he be anything but "happy-go-lucky"?

Tony Jackson discovered early in life that a young man of such beginnings as his, such "advantages," had to try to please everybody simply to survive. If one played music, one learned to play *every* style, *every* melody. That meant operatic arias, folk songs, coon songs, rags, symphonic strains, novelty tunes, pop tunes, and dirty old blues.

Learn the tunes. Learn the words. Play 'em better, sing 'em better, than anybody alive. "What's the man gonna think he comes in here slaps a twenty on the box and says 'Poets and Peasants Overture' I got to tell him I can't *play* it? Hell, I *learn* all them things, mister! *All* of 'em!"

Tony learned them and remembered. From childhood he spent nearly every waking hour either performing or practicing. Plenty of time for it, too, in a life destined to be lived alone. He was born a twin, but his heavier, healthier, and larger brother died in infancy. From the day June 5, 1876, that he bawled his first note in the small frame house on Amelia Street in New Orleans to his whispered coda of April 20, 1921, on Wabash Avenue in Chicago, music shielded him from monotony and loneliness.

Antonio Jackson, Jr., was the son of a South Carolina fisherman and a Richmond, Virginia, domestic servant. At the age of three he was the sole surviving male in the family. Surrounded

PROF. TONEY JACKSON

The above cut is a good likeness of Prof. Toney Jackson, Pianist at Russell and Dago.

Mr. Jackson is one of the best entertainers in the city, and is well liked. He is a good card.

Tony Jackson was a favorite in Chicago's tenderloin, too. This photograph is from a rare red-light promotional throwaway circulated in that city circa 1919 or 1920.

110

by a quartet of older sisters and a possessive mother, he wasn't allowed in the streets because the neighborhood was "rough." He spent most of his childhood virtually imprisoned, without companionship, in his own backyard on Amelia Street near Tchopitoulas. There being no music making device in the family, he contrived, at the age of seven, a mammoth, ludicrous contraption, much like a crude oversized harpsichord, which he could tune and play. His mother and sisters were invited to the yard to hear his debut as he played his first complete melody, the hymn *How Sweet To Have a Home in Heaven.*

Based on an agreement with a neighbor involving his doing dishwashing chores, Tony was permitted to practice on this family's ancient reed organ. Later, at the age of thirteen, an arrangement was made whereby he could, for the first time, come in contact with a real piano. This was in a saloon on the corner of his block next to a barber shop owned by Adam Olivier, leader of an early New Orleans orchestra. Olivier made it possible for Tony to use the piano mornings, before the saloon opened for business.

There seems to have been no transitional phase in Jackson's musical life. Just like that, suddenly, at the advanced age of fifteen, he was the acknowledged king of the tenderloin when it came to piano playing. We know that first he played for a short while with Mr. Olivier's band. (Bunk Johnson, too, was in that group.) It is possible that Olivier, impressed by the youngster's piano wizardry, brought him to one of the madams in what would later be Storyville. Certainly there was no struggle for recognition—no rivalries. Old-timer Manuel Manetta recalled: "Tony was in charge from the day he went to work. We *all* listened to him. Nobody could match him. He played *anything!* Blues, opera—anything!"

The clarinetist George Baquet recalled: "He'd start playin' a Cakewalk, then he'd kick over the piano stool and *dance* a Cakewalk—and never stop playin' the piano—and *playin'*, man! Nobody played like him!"

"Sing, man—like a bird," the drummer Paul Barbarin remembered. "He's what you call an entertainer! *That's* what he was known for. But don't let nobody tell you anybody could plain *play* like Tony Jackson. He's *it, man!* The greatest!"

Tony Jackson composed a great many tunes but sold most of them for five or ten dollars to individuals who published them as their own work—a common practice in those days. Only in later years did he tend to hold on to his tunes and retain ownership, though from time to time he would share credit in return for other publishing considerations. His most successful ditty *Pretty Baby*, remains a popular standard to this day.

This famous tune, though not published until 1916, and then only with revised lyrics (by Gus Kahn) suitable to the "little girl" image of Fanny Brice, who was to feature the song in Schubert's *Passing Show*, was an early Jackson number from his Storyville years. In those days, he would improvise new and generally bawdy lyrics and "parodies," somewhat in the manner of Calypso singers, changing the words according to which of his acquaintances and regular customers happened by his place of employment that night—Gipsy Shafer's, Hilma Burt's, Lulu White's, Countess Willie Piazza's, Antonia Gonzales' (the "female cornetist" whom he accompanied on many an occasion), or later, in 1911/12, Frank Early's.

Roy Carew, friend and confidante to both Tony Jackson and, in later years, Jelly Roll Morton, evoked the Storyville scene, and the very first time he heard Tony play, in a wonderful reminiscence published in the *Record Changer* magazine (February, 1948):

> In the early days of the present century, there stood, at the downtown corner of Villere and Iberville Streets, in that part of New Orleans known as Storyville, a frame dwelling of the type descriptively called "Camel-Back." This name was applied to houses which had single story in front but were of two stories in back. The house rested on a brick foundation a few feet high, and four or five wooden steps led up to the front door which faced on Iberville Street. On the glass portion of the door was painted the inscription, "Gonzales, FEMALE CORNETIST." There was no yard in front, nor at the side, and the brick banquettes extended right up the side of the house, but few passengers got on or off in that neighborhood; the dance halls and flashy places were two or three blocks toward the river, nearer Basin Street.
>
> One evening during the winter of 1904–05, I was strolling aimlessly about downtown New Orleans, and in the course of time I found myself approaching the corner I have described. As I neared the front of the Gonzales establishment, I could hear the sound of piano playing with someone singing, which my ears told me was coming from the Villere side of the house. Always very fond of popular music, I immediately walked to the side of the house and got as close

Hilma Burt's Mirror Ballroom at 209 N. Basin Street, with Jelly Roll Morton playing his first piano job in the District, was the center of the action in 1904. Its grandeur faded quickly, however, and by 1919, sans paint and glory, but still boasting the Burt monogram on the door, the house was for sale or rent.

to the music as possible; with the banquette going right up to the side of the house, I found myself standing under one of the windows of what probably was Madame Gonzales' parlor, listening to the "professor" playing and singing. It was the most remarkable playing and singing I had ever heard; the songs were just some of the popular songs of that day and time, but the beat of the bass and the embellished treble of the piano told me at once that there was something new to me in playing. And the singing was just as distinctive. It was a man's voice that had at times a sort of wild earnestness to it. High notes, low notes, fast or slow, the singer executed them all perfectly, blending them into a perfect performance with the remarkable piano style. As I stood there, I noticed another listener standing on the edge of the sidewalk a little ways away. I did not know who he was, but afterwards found out that he was another local piano player, Kid Ross, I think. I never got to know the man, but I will never forget our short conversation.

"Who in the world is that?" I asked, indicating the unseen player as I stepped over to him. "Tony Jackson," he replied. "He knows a thousand songs."

Jelly Roll Morton

Because Jelly Roll was lavish in his praise of Tony Jackson and even acknowledged Jackson's influence on his own playing, latter-day students of jazz history have often tried to compare or even equate them. The task of comparison is difficult because Jelly Roll left a recorded legacy and Tony did not. Most of Jelly Roll's musical admirers find it hard even to imagine anyone being a better creative artist. His superiority to Tony in jazz band organization and performance was well established in the memories of their contemporaries, but neither man did much band work in New Orleans. Tony's stint in Freddie Keppard's band in Chicago was well remembered but never acclaimed, whereas Jelly Roll's Red Hot Peppers group has always been considered one of the highest peaks of recorded jazz band excellence. However, such comparisons are not especially instructive.

The fact is that Jelly Roll stands up very well on his own, with scores of extraordinary recordings and an even lengthier list of outstanding compositions to his credit: *King Porter Stomp, Wolverine Blues, The Pearls*—and some two hundred more of like quality. His recorded autobiography, made for the Library of Congress, fills a dozen twelve-inch LPs and is quite possibly the single most important jazz document extant. This material and the great biography by Alan Lomax, much of which is in Jelly's own words, afford us a remarkable overview of the Maestro's entire career. The following first-hand recollections of Storyville (quoted from *Mister Jelly Roll*), recounted in the rich but easy language it evoked, are wonderfully revealing of both the music of Storyville and the place of musicians in its scheme of things:

. . . You see, my young friends had brought me into the tenderloin district at a very young age, even before we were in long pants. In fact, we used to steal long pants from our fathers and brothers and uncles and slip on in. When the policemens caught us they would slip us on in jail. One of them, I remember, was named Fast Mail Burwell. He was known to be Fast Mail because he had two legs and feet that couldn't be beat, and he would take the straps on the ends of his club and cut our legs to ribbons. We kids were very much frightened of him and, at times would climb those high board fences to escape. In those days we had curfew in New Orleans and, when the curfew bell rang at nine, all the kids was supposed to be at home. Of course, it was our ambition to show that we were tough and could stay out after curfew. . . . This is the story of how I got my first job in music. . . . I had leave to stay out at night on Saturday and Sunday until 11 P.M., so when some boys enticed me to go to the tenderloin district, I finally accepted the invitation. I liked the freedom of standing at a saloon bar, passing along the streets crowded with men of all nationalities and descriptions. There were women standing in their cribs with their chippies on—a crib is a room about seven feet wide and a chippie is a dress that women wore, knee length and very easy to disrobe.

One Saturday night whilst on one of the wild jaunts, we heard that one of the houses was stuck for a pianist. My friends encouraged me to go for the job, but my fear was so great that the only way I would go was if my friends would go with me. I felt sure it was a plot to kidnap me, since I had had a narrow escape when I was younger on Melpomene and Willow Streets. So they finally agreed to take the other upstarts along and put them into a rear room where I could see them but their guests could not.

I was so frightened when I first touched the piano, the girls decided to let me go immediately. One of my friends spoke up, 'Go ahead and show these people you can play.' That encouraged me greatly and I pulled myself together and started playing with the confidence of being in my own circle. 'That boy is marvelous'—this was the remarks of the inmates. Money was plentiful and they tipped me about $20 which I did not want to accept, because I was not taught that way.

They wanted to give me the job of regular professor, but I could not see the idea. I was making about $15 legitimately, and furthermore, I knew that if my folks ever found out I had even passed through the tenderloin they would deal with me drastically. I asked what salary they would pay.

"One dollar a night is the regular salary," was the landlady's answer. I flatly refused.

Then my friends showed me how I had made $20 on tips in maybe an hour's playing. "You see, the $1 is a guarantee in case there happens to be some kind of a bad night so you will be sure of some salary," the landlady explained. "But I will guarantee you $5 a night a night if you don't make it in tips." . . . Anyhow I thought, whatever happens in a family, all you have to do is take some money home and everything is all right. I then accepted the job, but would not stay the night. I reported the next night promptly at the given time, nine o'clock.

The streets were crowded with men. Police were always in sight, never less than two together, which guaranteed the safety of all concerned. Lights of all color were glittering and glaring. Music was pouring into the streets from every house. Women were standing in the doorways, singing or chanting some kind of blues —some very happy, some very sad, some with the desire to end it all by poison, some planning a big outing, a dance or some other kind of enjoyment. Some were real ladies, in spite of their downfall, and some were habitual drunkards and some were dope fiends as follows, opium, heroin, cocaine, laudanum, morphine, et cetera. I was

This is Jelly Roll Morton in Harlem, 1938, shortly after his superb recording sessions for the Library of Congress. Behind him is trumpeter Wingy Carpenter. (Photograph by Danny Barker)

personally sent to Chinatown many times with a sealed note and a small amount of money and would bring back several cards of hop. There was no slipping and dodging. All you had to do was walk in to be served.

The girls liked their young professor and they worked the customers for big tips for me. I began to make more money than I had ever heard of in my life. I bought a new suit and a hat with the emblem Stetson in it and a pair of St. Louis Flats that turned up, I'm telling you the truth, nearly to my ankles . . .

There follows much fascinating narrative having to do with family relationships, working on the Gulf Coast, voodoo, and then a job once again in the District at Hilma Burt's mansion, next door to Tom Anderson's saloon. The house is the one that some years later would belong to Gertrude Dix.

. . . you never saw such a well man as I was that night when I sat down at the grand piano in Hilma Burt's mansion. Right away Miss Burt liked my style of music and she told me, "If you think you can come steady, I will be glad to have you." In a week I had plenty money . . .

Hilma Burt's was on the corner of Customhouse and Basin streets, next door to Tom Anderson's saloon—Tom Anderson was the king of the district and ran the Louisiana legislature and Hilma Burt was supposed to be his old lady [mistress]. Hers was no doubt one of the best paying places in the city and I thought I had a very bad night when I made under a hundred dollars. Very often a man would come into the house and hand you a twenty- or forty- or a fifty-dollar note, just like a match. Beer sold for a dollar a bottle. Wine from five to ten, depending on the kind you bought. Wine flowed much more than water—the kind of wine I'm speaking about I don't mean sauterne or nothing like that, I mean champagne, such as Cliquot and Mumm's Extra Dry. . . .

I'm telling you this tenderloin district was like something that nobody has ever seen before or since. The doors were taken off the saloons from one year to the next. . . .

They had everything in the District from the highest class to the lowest—creep joints where they'd put the feelers on a guy's clothes, cribs that rented for about five dollars a day and had just about room enough for a bed, small-time houses where the price was from fifty cents to a dollar and they put on naked dances, circuses and jive.

The attitude of other musicians toward Jelly Roll was much influenced by the fact that as a piano player he was in a higher economic class than most of them. It was further influenced by his well-known reluctance to accept his status as a "Negro." "Big Eye" Louis Nelson, however, had only musical comments to make to Lomax:

When Jelly Roll came around the district he knew note music—that's the way he started— started by messing around with piano scores. Course, he wasn't no real reader . . . Jelly Roll was just a *speller*. But he wasn't dumb like some of those fellows. He could pick up fast by ear . . . Years later he come to be a real good piano player. I'll give him this; he was a *busy* soul, a hustler. Stay a couple of weeks one place and he was ready to go. Not like us fellows. We made ourselves satisfied and let well enough alone.

Bunk Johnson commented:

Those fellows you been talking to didn't know Jelly . . . see, Jelly played only in white houses in those days. *They* couldn't play there. But him and Tony Jackson did. They'd have Tony one night and Jelly the next . . . All of them boys always wore fine clothes, had plenty money and plenty diamond rings. Jelly was one of the best in 1902 and after that noted more so than Tony Jackson and Albert Cahill [Carroll] because he played the music the whores liked. Jelly would sit there and play that barrelhouse all night— blues and such as that. *I know* because I played with him in Hattie Rogers sporting house in 1903. She had a whole lot of light colored women in there, best-looking women you ever want to see, strictly for white.

By 1902 Jelly Roll Morton had acquired the nickname Winding Boy. "Winding Boy," Johnny St. Cyr reluctantly explained to Lomax, "is a bit on the vulgar side. Let's see . . . how could I put it—[it] means a fellow that makes good jazz with the women. See Jelly lived a pretty fast life. In fact, most of those fellows around the District did. They were all half-way pimps anyway."

Jelly Roll remembered this with undisguised nostalgia:

All the highest class landladies had me for "the professor" if they could get me—Willie Piazza, Josie Arlington, Lulu White, Antonia Gonzales, Hilma Burt and Gypsy Schaeffer, the biggest spending landlady. Their houses were all in the same block on Basin Street, stone mansions with from three to seven parlors and from fifteen to twenty-five women all clad in evening gowns and diamonds galore. The minute the button was pushed, that meant a new customer was in and the girls came in the parlor looking like queens. "Why, hello, boy. Where you from?" Then I would hit the piano and when I'd played a couple of my tunes—"Got some money for the professor?" If the guests didn't come up with a dollar tip apiece, they were told, "This is a

high class place. We don't want no poor johns here." Matter of fact, no poor men could even get in these mansions. The girls charged high and made from twenty dollars to a hundred a night.

During much of his lifetime the Winding Boy's social and artistic status was unsettled, and it may be that it was during his Storyville years that he felt most secure, even though he admitted that there were ragtime players (Sammy Davis, Tony Jackson) who "manipulated" better than he—who had greater digital facility. Even so, these years were, to judge by the tone of his reminiscences, the happiest of his life. Worldwide recognition, which came later, was never complete enough to overcome the humiliations of race prejudice, of which Jelly Roll was to become more conscious as they revealed their economic aspects in full. He almost always chose the most ineffectual ways of lashing back at his detractors, and in his declining years he was widely considered to be little more than an out-of-date crank.

Today, however, his stature as a jazz immortal is secure. He is acknowledged to have been one of the half-dozen key figures in jazz, if not indeed, as he sometimes pretended, its only one.

Clarence Williams

Clarence Williams, another extraordinary personality, was rarely spoken of by his contemporaries as a musician, but only because of his better-known achievements as a promoter and music publisher in New Orleans and elsewhere (in New Orleans, he was the "Williams" of the Williams & Piron Music Publishing Company). Most of his greatest contributions to music were made outside Storyville and will not be dealt with here. In the District, he was less well known as a pianist than as night club or cabaret manager and as producer of some very special "nights." In charge variously of a saloon on Rampart Street and, at times, of the Big 25 and Pete Lala's, he is still remembered as originator of the "Ham Kick." This was a kind of athletic contest in which a ham was suspended from the ceiling and any young lady present was privileged to try to kick it. If she succeeded in doing so the ham was hers, so long as she had "qualified" by demonstrating, as she was accomplishing the feat, that she was not wearing underdrawers.

Quoted in *Hear Me Talkin' to Ya*, Williams recalled the days after he left nearby Plaquemine for New Orleans in 1906, when he was fourteen years of age:

I shined some shoes when I got to New Orleans and made good money, enough to get myself a house and some furniture. My first musical job playin' at a spaghetti place, and before that I was goin' around to all the joints, stayin' up all night and playin' for nothin', or for drinks—whatever they'd give me. At that time, piano players would come in from all over the South for the races, and all the local piano players would listen to 'em to catch ideas. I'd stay up all night and go to work the next day. All the while, I kept figurin' ways to get some money where I didn't have to make time. So I went to all the hotels and restaurants and the cabarets where the colored musicians would be workin' and told them, "Want to get your suits cleaned? Just give 'em to me and pay me on payday." They didn't want to be runnin' to the tailor all the time, so I made a lot of money *that* way.

But one day the porter that worked at this spaghetti place came over to my house and said, "Do you know where I can find a good piano player?" "You're talkin' to him," I said. "I'll go down." And that's how I started. You know, I couldn't play but five or six pieces, and when somebody would ask me to play a waltz, I'd just play *Some of These Days*, or one of the other tunes I knew, in three-quarter time.

Pretty soon I was way ahead of all the other piano players—introducing all the new songs. When Sophie Tucker came to New Orleans in about 1910 or 1911, they would have a ballyhoo truck. (There was always a big to-do about shows and dances, and the bands would get on the trucks and wagons and ride all over town.) . . . and I followed them around all day. At that time she was singin' *Some of These Days*, *Alexander's Ragtime Band*, and other new songs, and after hearin' her sing 'em, I'd go home and play them over until I got them under control. Then at night I'd be able to sing and play them and make some real heavy tips. There'd be money all over the top of the piano.

I was also the first to write away to the North for professional copies of all the latest songs, like *Chinatown* and *That's a Plenty*. I made those songs famous in New Orleans . . . I took about eight lessons, all told."

Williams did his turn at some of the District's top sporting houses—Lulu White's, Countess Piazza's and Gipsy Shafer's among them—despite his really stringent technical limitations. Musically, he is best remembered for the fine piano support he gave to blues singers (most notably the great Bessie Smith) on records, and for the many popular compositions that bear his name, including *Baby Won't You Please Come Home* and *Royal Garden Blues*.

The one, the only, the original Clarence Williams—pianist, promoter, music publisher. (Photograph courtesy Edmond Souchon Collection, New Orleans Jazz Museum)

116

Manuel Manetta

"Professor" Manuel Manetta, shown here with New Orleans' own Oscar "Papa" Celestin (in front). Born in the 1880s, the venerable Manetta continued to be active as a "teacher of all instruments" until his death in 1969.

Of all the Storyville professors, Manetta was the only one who learned at first hand the hard lot of nonpianists in the early jazz bands.

It has been established that Manetta functioned as a full fledged professor at several houses in the tenderloin, beginning in about 1907, and very likely at Willie Piazza's (1908). However, most of his Storyville musical career was occupied with such journeyman chores as playing violin in the expanded Buddy Bolden group (of which he sometimes served as leader) or sitting in on trumpet, trombone, clarinet, guitar, or saxophone (just a few of the instruments on which he was professionally competent) with such legendary jazzmen as Edouard Clem, Frankie Duson, Manuel Perez, and Armand J. Piron (the "Piron" of the Williams & Piron Music Publishing Company). Manetta played at the Tuxedo Dance Hall and at Frank Early's prior to World War I. He tried his luck in Chicago in 1913 but soon returned to New Orleans. Chicago left its imprint on his playing, however, and his latter-day piano style was much closer to the Chicago "skiffle" piano of the twenties than to New Orleans. It may be assumed that he played closer to the Crescent City idiom before his trip north.

Widely respected as a music teacher in Algiers, Louisiana, until his death in October, 1969, Manetta was perhaps best known to jazz audiences in the Crescent City for his uncanny ability to play trumpet and trombone simultaneously and in harmony. Manetta's life, music, and teaching techniques were documented on tape by William Russell over a period of years, but according to Russell the interviews add little or nothing concerning Storyville beyond what is set forth in the present work.

Many other fine musicians worked the mansions of Storyville. Little remains of them but their occasionally repeated names and a rare comment from a contemporary, largely because they got lost in the glare of light that shone on the two titans of New Orleans piano—Tony Jackson and Jelly Roll Morton. What little is known about them follows.

Kid Ross, the only white musician to play for pay in Storyville during its twenty-year existence, worked "steady" at Lulu White's and was, by Jelly Roll's testimony, "one of the outstanding hot players of the country."

Buddy Carter was described by Jelly Roll as "a man that could really play those blues and those things we call stomps today."

John the Baptist, probably the first "professor" in Storyville, worked at Willie Piazza's.

Alfred Wilson was recalled by Jelly Roll: "Poor Alfred Wilson, the girls taken to him and showed him a point where he didn't have to work. He finally came to be a dope fiend and smoked so much dope till he died."

"Albert Cahill [Carroll] didn't smoke dope," Jelly Roll remembered, "but he ruined his eyes staying up all night gambling. Albert was known to be the greatest show player in existence as I can remember." According to Clarence Williams, "Jelly was influenced by Albert Carroll." (The mistaken spellings "Carrol" in *They All Played Ragtime*, "Carrell" in *Jazzmen*, and "Cahill" in *Mister Jelly Roll* all refer to this same Carroll; such errors are easy to understand, as they were derived from oral testimony.)

Sammy Davis (no kin to the song-and-dance man Sammy Davis or his son Sammy Davis, Jr.) was, Jelly Roll Morton would later recall, "one of the greatest manipulators of the keyboard I guess I have ever seen in the history of the world." The "trick baby" whose interview appears elsewhere in this volume remembered "many" piano players but the name of only one, Sammy Davis, who played "faster than anybody I ever heard."

Game Kid, a blues specialist, although extremely competent, cared so little for money that he played only occasionally in the bordellos, but frequently turned up at private parties to perform without pay. As Jelly Roll described him, in *Mister Jelly Roll*, he was

a man that really wouldn't work. He was as ragged as a pet pig, wore a big smile on his face, and was a nice looking brown-skin fellow until you got to his lips. He had nice, fat, greasy lips. Game Kid played the piano all day long after he got up, moving around from one girl's house to another—what we called the "good-time" houses—not for any financial purpose at all, but just to have a good time. That was when you could get a half-gallon can of beer for ten cents and a half-pint of whiskey for twenty-five. So a real big sport in the party (not the piano player, of course, it didn't cost *him* nothing) would rush about ten straight cans of beer and get about a quart of whiskey. Tht whole dog-gone thing wouldn't cost him over two dollars and made him a big sport for a whole evening at a good-time house. And there was the Game Kid playing the blues and just swilling all the lush in the world. He was a howler, I'm telling

you, the best there was in the section when it came to playing blues.

Of another bluesman, Jelly said:

Josky Adams would play the blues . . . It seemed like a family there, Josky playing and singing:

"I wanta a gal that works in the white folks' yard,
A pretty gal that works in the white folks yard.
Do you see that fly crawling up the wall,
She's going up there to get her ashes hauled.
I got a woman lives right back of the jail,
She got a sign on her window—Pussy for Sale."

Jelly Roll also remembered Mamie Desdoumes: "Two middle fingers of her right hand had been cut off, so she played the blues with only three fingers on her right hand . . . it was Mamie first really sold me on the blues." Bunk Johnson remembered Mamie, too: "I knew Mamie Desdoumes real well. Played many a concert with her singing those same blues. She was pretty good-looking, quite fair and with a *nice* head of hair. She was a hustlin' woman. A blues singing poor gal. Used to play pretty passable piano around them dance halls on Perdido Street. When Hattie Rogers or Lulu White would put

Frank "Dude" Amacker, an authentic Storyville "professor."

118

it out that Mamie was going to be singing at their place, the white men would turn out in bunches and them whores would clean up."

Steve Lewis was an extraordinary musician who came along at the tail end of the Storyville era, after Jelly Roll and Tony Jackson had left the scene. Later he would achieve some national recognition as pianist with the A. J. Piron Orchestra, of which he was a mainstay from 1918 to 1938. In 1915 he accompanied the celebrated entertainer known as New Orleans Willie Jackson at the Entertainers and played piano at the Arlington, though not under the auspices of Josie Arlington herself, she having gone to her final reward the previous year. The then directress, Anna Casey, known to the District madams as the most efficient administrator in their midst and a veteran of the mansions and parlor houses, described Steve as "a light-colored boy who was as good as anybody I ever paid to play music. And Jelly Roll—even Tony, himself, worked for me when they were in New Orleans." Later on, in the 1930s, Lewis would be the calliope player on the steamers *President* and *Capitol*. In the *Second Line*, Dr. Edmond Souchon wrote of his "real pianistic virtues . . . his harmonies, his ideas, and his fantastic good taste . . ."

Among the other pianists who worked the brothels were George "Goumar" Robertson, whose summer days were occupied pitching for a Negro baseball team (the New Orleans Brooks), Frank Amacker, Ernest Ferrand, Frank Richards, Burke Russell, Oscar Curry, Poree Nolan, Buddy Christian, Trigger Sam Henry, Brocky Johnny, Rosalind Johnson, Jimmy Arcey, Fred Washington, Harrison Ford, Black Pete, and Ollie Sullivan.

Joseph "King" Oliver

Joseph "King" Oliver is one of the hallowed saints in the heavens of jazz. Though he is best known to most jazz enthusiasts as the teacher of Louis Armstrong, some authorities think that Oliver deserves at least as much renown as his more famous pupil. Indeed, some of them believe that Louis' playing represented a falling away from the "classic" style of Oliver.

His professional career began in 1910 when he was a member of the Eagle [brass] Band and worked nights (at a dollar and a quarter per) for Billy Phillips at the latter's 102 Ranch on Franklin Street. In the same year,

Steve Lewis, a top Basin Street "professor" in the later years of Storyville, toured in Billy Mack's vaudeville troupe with clarinetist Johnny Dodds and Thomas "Papa Mutt" Carey before joining Armand J. Piron's orchestra, a favorite in the Crescent City area well into the 1930s. (Photograph courtesy the Edmond Souchon Collection, New Orleans Jazz Museum)

Joseph "King" Oliver

he played with Richard M. Jones' Four Hot Hounds at the Abadie Cabaret, along with the leader on piano, "Big Eye" Louis Nelson on clarinet, and Dee Dee Chandler on drums. This personnel would vary sometimes, with Wooden Joe Nicholas and Ernest Rogers substituting on clarinet and drums, respectively.

In 1911 Oliver replaced the great Freddie Keppard in the band at Pete Lala's Café, where he played alongside clarinetist Sidney Bechet and trombonist Zue Robertson, with a rhythm section including Frank Ahanie on piano, Joe Pierre on drums, and Herb Lindsay on violin. Others who played in this band at one time or another were the clarinetists Lawrence Duhé and Lorenzo Tio, Jr, the pianists Louis Wade, Buddy Christian, and "Annison," and the drummers John Vigne, Happy Bolton, Dave Bailey, and Henry Zeno.

In 1916 Oliver led the band at John T. Lala's cabaret, with Zue Robertson, trombone, and Billy Marrero, bass, as regulars in the group. During an earlier period, 1914–16, he had played at Pete Lala's under the leadership of trombonist Kid Ory, with Johnny Dodds on clarinet, Lorenzo Staulz on guitar, Ed "Montudie" Garland on bass, Henry Zeno on drums, and Emile Bigard as violinist. Drummers Henry Martin and Minor Hall also took turns with this group, as did Wade Whaley on clarinet and Louis Keppard on guitar. Clarence Williams was manager of the place at this time.

It was in Storyville that Joe Oliver earned his "King" crown one dramatic night while he was employed at Abadie's cabaret. On that night, according to Frederic Ramsey's account in *Jazzmen*, Joe Oliver,

> . . . sat quietly listening to the musicians who were praising Keppard and Perez. He was infuriated by their tiresome adulation; didn't they know that Joe Oliver could play cornet, too? So he came forth from his silence, strode to the piano and said, "Jones, beat it out in B-flat." Jones began to beat and Joe began to blow. The notes tore out, clear as a bell, crisp and clean. He played as he never had before, filling the little dance hall with low, throbbing blues. Jones backed him with a slow, steady beat. With this rhythm behind him, Joe walked straight through the hall, out onto the sidewalk. There was no mistaking what he meant when he pointed his cornet, first towards Pete Lala's, where Keppard played, then directly across the street to where Perez was working. A few hot blasts brought crowds out of both joints; they saw Joe Oliver on the sidewalk, playing as if he would blow

down every house on the street. Soon every rathole and crib down the line was deserted by its patrons, who came running up to Joe, bewitched by his cornet. When the last joint had poured out its crew, he turned the crowd into Aberdeen's [sic] where he walked to the stand, breathless, excited, and opened his mouth wide to let out the big, important words that were boiling in his head. But all he could say was, "There! That'll show 'em!! . . . After that night, they never called him anything but "King" Oliver.

This has become classic jazz folklore. Pianist Richard M. Jones' later version of the tale, quoted in *Hear Me Talkin' to Ya*, is briefer and more colorful, and probably more accurate:

> Freddie Keppard was playin' in a spot across the street and was drawin' all the crowds. I was sittin' at the piano, and Joe Oliver came over to me and commanded in a nervous harsh voice, "Get in B-flat." He didn't even mention a tune, just said, "Get in B-flat." I did, and Joe walked out on the sidewalk, lifted his horn to his lips, and blew the most beautiful stuff I have ever heard. People started pouring out of the

Trumpet king Freddie Keppard, seated, and Sidney Bechet, about 1918.

other spots along the street to see who was blowing all that horn. Before long our place was full, and Joe came in, smiling, and said, "Now that son-of-a-bitch won't bother me no more." . . . From then on, our place was full every night.

Louis Armstrong worshipped King Oliver almost as a father and certainly as a teacher. Oliver, he declared in his autobiography, *Satchmo*, "had such range and such wonderful creations in his soul! He created some of the most famous phrases you hear today, and trends to work from. . . . No one in jazz has created as much music as he has. Almost everything important in music today came from him."

Freddie Keppard

Freddie Keppard had a band in the Tuxedo, in 1908, consisting of himself on cornet, with Eddie Vinson, trombone; George Baquet, clarinet; Narcisse "Buddy" Christian, piano; and Dee Dee Chandler, drums. Later he held forth at Pete Lala's, being replaced by Joe Oliver when

Manuel Perez, shown here just before his death in 1946, was one of Storyville's most highly respected band leaders from 1905 to 1910. He played mainly in Rice's Café on Iberville Street. (Photograph by Mrs. John Menville)

Freddie left New Orleans to take to the North. He also had a band in Groshell's, and it was with Keppard that clarinetist Jimmie Noone got his start in the District.

Jelly Roll said of him: ". . . at the period I'm talking about, the great man was Freddie Keppard . . . he became to be the greatest hot trumpeter in existence. . . . He had the best ear, the best tone, and the most marvelous execution I ever heard and there was no end to his ideas; he could play one chorus eight or ten different ways."

Sidney Bechet recalled, in his autobiography, *Treat It Gentle:* ". . . And After Buddy [Bolden] died Freddie Keppard was King. Freddie kind of took Buddy's way some; he played practically the same way as Buddy, but he *played*, he *really* played."

"He had plenny stren'th—plenny pep," Alphonse Picou declared, ". . . an' damme he mus' had plenny more if he di'n leave it in Vill're Street every night." More than one source remembers the maestro as the scourge of the cribs, a prodigious drinker and ladies' man, prouder of his exploits in these pursuits than of the art that would make his name famous. But for a time, between 1907 and 1910, he was the dominant musical figure in Storyville.

Manuel Perez

A favorite cornetist of the downtown colored "Creoles," a relatively well-educated group, was the handsome, dignified Manuel Perez, whom they much preferred to the likes of Buddy Bolden or, later, Chris Kelly, another idol of the uptown fieldhands and day laborers.

"He played much better cornet than Buddy [Bolden]," the Creole Sidney Bechet insisted in his autobiography. "Perez, he was a musicianer [sic]; he was sincere. He stuck to his instrument. You hear a record, you know—you don't see all that stamping and facemaking; you just hear the music. . . . Manuel Perez—there wasn't none of that in him. He was really sincere. He really played his cornet."

His Storyville colleagues remember that when Perez finished a job he went straight home without stopping for even one drink. In some circles this eccentric behavior was attributed to his having a high moral sense, but a clarinet player with whom he worked a great deal in the District, George Baquet, gave the author a different and more persuasive explanation:

Manuel Perez is so tight [Perez was then still alive] his shoes squeak. A doll, one of the most beautiful in the District, she went crazy for Perez. He wouldn't pay no attention to her. I say to him, "Perez," I say, "Boy, I wish something like that make eyes at me." He don't say nothing. She ask me to fix up something for her wit' Perez. Perez don't say nothing. Then she leave town, this girl. I tell Perez lots of fellows pay twenty dollar a night to go wit' dis girl. I tell him he's too stupid to recognize something good, worth twenty dollar, he can get it for free, an' he let her go like that.

"For free?," he say. "What you mean, for free?"

I tell him, "Sure, for free. She like you, man! . . ."

"Where she's at?" he ask me.

"She lef' town," I tell him.

He don't talk to me no more for week.

According to Danny Barker: ". . . he could hit those high notes. . . . He always had a stomach full of food while . . . most of those fellows . . . were full of whiskey."

Perez had his longest stand in Storyville at Joe Rice's Café, where he played frequently between 1910 and 1913, usually as leader. Lawrence Duhé, a favorite clarinetist of Perez, generally filled that chair, though Baquet often played in his place—and sometimes, but infrequently, Sidney Bechet. According to Alphonse Picou, "Manuel Perez, a cigarmaker by trade, was our leader—a tough cornet, a man that never fail." Thus the pick of Creole New Orleans clarinet players saw service with Perez, and all admired him.

The Imperial Orchestra, organized by Perez, played many engagements in Storyville in the years from 1900 to 1915. Besides clarinetist Baquet, it included George Filhe on trombone (replaced by Buddy Johnson in 1910); René Baptiste on guitar; Jean Vigne and John Mac-Murray on drums at different times; Jimmy Palao on violin; and Billy Marrero on the bass.

Perez is not so well-known to students of jazz history as he might have been had he made phonograph recordings and been less hostile toward interviewers who tried in later years to get his story.

The foregoing were of course only a few of the musicians who worked in Storyville at one time or another. They were the ones whose impact on the District was powerful enough to make them important in determining the very character of Storyville's music. Such other great jazzmen of the period as Buddy Bolden, Frankie Duson, and Buddy Petit made their reputations mainly outside the District, and their occasional appearances in Storyville passed with little notice.

It was largely the piano players, with their access to the "mansions," and the strong cornet-playing bandleaders—Oliver, Keppard, and Perez—active in the dance halls, who were, for a time, Storyville stand-bys. But there were others who functioned from time to time as band leaders, such as the ubiquitous, multifaceted Manuel Manetta (also a "professor," as already mentioned) and the piccolo player Bab Frank and his violinist brother Alcide Frank. There was the accordionist Henry Peyton and the drummer Arnold Depass, who frequently turned up heading a group. The great trombonist Kid Ory's stint as a band leader in the District (principally at Pete Lala's) was authoritative. He left New Orleans in 1919 and did not return until late in life, and then only briefly. He died in Hawaii in 1973.

A point that must be made with some emphasis is that many of the generally acknowledged jazz greats were simply too young ever to have played in the District, though some did have the opportunity to "hang around" as kids and have some of the influence of Storyville and its music rub off on them. Among these are Louis Armstrong, Albert Nicholas, Danny Barker, Preston Jackson, Natty Dominique, and the entire generation of great white Dixieland stars, including the groups that became the New Orleans Rhythm Kings (Paul Mares, Leon Roppolo, Santo Pecora, Steve Brown, Chink Martin, George Brunies), the Original Dixieland Jazz Band's regulars and irregulars (Nick LaRocca, Larry Shields, Yellow Nunez, Eddie Edwards, Emile Christian, Henry Ragas, Anton Lada, and Tony Spargo [Sparbaro], and the Halfway House "pool" (Abbie and Merritt Brunies, Charlie Cordella, the Loyacanos [Bud, "Deacon," and Joe], Bill Eastwood, Red Long, Mickey Marcour, et al.) The cornetists Johnny Hyman (Wiggs), Sharkey, and Johnny Bayersdorfer; the clarinetists Sidney Arodin, Raymond Burke, Tony Parenti, and Irving Fazola; the pianists Norman Brownlee, Armand Hug, Joe Verges, and Irwin LeClere, the drummers Monk Hazel, Leo Adde, Ray Bauduc; the saxophonists Lester Bouchon and Eddie Miller—all these were also singed, to one degree or another, by the fire of Storyville's sounds. Certain "families" active in jazz were also touched with the flame: the Papalias, the Pecoras, the Scagliones all had something of the flavor of Storyville in their horns, something of its rhythms in their hearts.

Raymond Burke, considered by some the most creative jazzman currently active in the city at this writing (1973), remembers:

> I was about eight or nine years old. Me and Leo [Adde] used to go around on Basin Street and play on the banquette [sidewalk] in front of Mahogany Hall or someplace. Leo played a cigar box and I had one of them bobbins, one of them spools they wind cotton thread on. I put tissue paper or butcher paper over it and play it for a horn. People'd throw us pennies, nickles— anything. We'd sometimes take in a dollar."

Louis Armstrong, in the *True* magazine article quoted earlier, recalled his childhood:

> I would delight delivering an order of stone coal to the prostitute who used to hustle in her crib next to Pete Lala's cabaret . . . Just so's I could hear King Oliver play . . . I was too young to go into Pete Lala's at the time . . . And I'd just stand there in that lady's crib listening to King Oliver . . . That was the only way we kids could go into the District—I mean Storyville. . . . All of a sudden it would dawn on that lady that I was still in her crib very silent while she hustle those tricks and she'd say—"What's the matter with you, boy? . . . Why are you still standing so quiet? . . . this is no place to daydream. . . . I've got my work to do" . . .

Child prodigy Tony Parenti, at twelve already the clarinet star of Professor Taverno's Italian Band and known for his precocious solo renditions of *Mr. Dooley, Too Much Mustard,* and *Everybody's Doing It,* confessed many years later for an article in the *Second Line:*

> Also, about once a week, two others from the band and myself used to take instruments over to Storyville and play. The little boys of the sidewalk band naturally appealed to the passers-by, as well as the occupants of the cribs, who used to pass out a little change to us. Sometimes a madame [sic] would ask those in the parlor if they would like a little music while waiting, and if there was no objection, we would sometimes be invited in. We would collect small tips from the people in the parlor, but I must say that no one ever tried to corrupt us because of our obvious young age. Mahogany Hall was one of these.

Louis Armstrong was moved to say: "As many bands as you heard, that's how many bands you heard playing right. I thought I was in heaven. . . ."

Danny Barker remembers that

> . . . in the days before they closed the District . . . the most exciting form of musical entertainment was not the jazz bands but the brass bands. . . . Characters like Bunk Johnson, Buddy Petit, Kid Rena, Frankie Duson, Chris Kelly (who rarely got around to working in Storyville) would be in the nearest barroom drinking— jiving some sporting women and drinking to everybody's health and ruining his own. The bandmen who didn't indulge would be corralled by groups of admirers. . . . It was the greatest thrill of a kid to hold and watch a musician's instrument whom he idolized.

Thus there was indeed an older, bigger, healthier "hall" for jazz than the whorehouse environment could provide. True, Storyville gave many a musician a livelihood—and a better than average livelihood, by the standards of the time, as we shall see later in this chapter. But jazz was not born in Storyville, nor was it even reared there. Storyville was just one part of the passing scene in which this great art form happened to thrive.

The last word on this point may well have been said by Johnny St. Cyr, as quoted in *Mister Jelly Roll:*

> Jazz musicians have to be a working class of man, out in the open all the time, healthy and strong. That's what's wrong today; these new guys haven't got the force. They don't *like* to play all night; they don't think they *can* play unless they're loaded. But a working man have the *power* to play hot, whiskey or no whiskey. You see, the average working man is very musical. Playing music for him is just relaxing. He gets as much kick out of playing as other folks get out of dancing. The more enthusiastic his audience is, why, the more spirit the working man's got to play. And with your natural feeling that way, you never make the same thing twice. Every time you play a tune, new ideas come to mind and you slip that on in.

The Economics of Music in Storyville

On an average night, during its nearly twenty years of legal history, Storyville employed about fifty musicians, including the solo piano players working the mansions and parlor houses. During Carnival season the number might be as many as seventy-five. So far as the proprietors were concerned, whether of saloons or bordellos, the music was free, as we have seen, since the performers were satisfied to work for the gratuities provided by the customers. A few proprietors committed themselves to small minimum guarantees, but the matter was purely academic, since even on poor nights the musicians' take would usually exceed the minimum.

The system worked out very well indeed for the "professors," whose take ranged from ninety to a thousand dollars a week—the latter being realized, of course, only in exceptionally good weeks by the very top performers.

The band musicians knew such levels of prosperity only by hearsay. Among the top band leaders—Oliver, Ory, Keppard—a seventy-five dollar take for the week was considered extraordinarily good. Top sidemen might clear as much as fifty dollars with "private" or "silent" tips. They also got most of their whiskey free from admirers, but whiskey was cheap in those days. The run-of-the-mill band man cleared something less than thirty dollars a week—and this for steady work.

It must be remembered, however, that the purchasing power of the dollar was far greater then than it is now. Furthermore, employment opportunities for blacks in other than menial capacities were rare in those days in New Orleans (and everywhere else). Most musicians who played in the District looked back on their Storyville days as a time of prosperity. As Albert Glenny, the bass player, put it: "Twenny dol' a week wit' no worry is mill'naire pay!"

Piano player Frank Amacker supplied the author with these details:

See, we say I got a fifty-cent piece—and they's four musicians and we all four is gonna eat off this fifty-cent piece. Well, man, I goes into the grocery store and I say to the man, "Gimme a nickel o' red beans" and he puts down a two pound bag o' beans. Then I say "Gimme a nickel o' rice" and he puts down a bag of rice. Now I spent ten cents. Then I tell him, "Now, gimme a lagniappe onion!" That means free. He gives me a free onion because I bought the rice and beans off him. Then I go into another store and I say, "Gimme a nickel salt pork" and he puts it down. Then I tell him, "Gimme a half o' lard and a half o' bread." [Half a nickel's worth, sometimes called a "quartee."] Then I say, gimme some lagniappe salt and pepper. You see, if I buy everything in one store, I only get one lagniappe. Now I spent twenty cents.

Anyway, now I got my rice, I got my beans, I got my meat. I got my bread, my onions and my seasonin'. I take it to my little room, where I'm payin' fifty cents a *week*, and we cook up the red beans and rice with the salt pork and onion.

We get ready to eat. I give one of the men a dime and I say, "Go 'cross the street and get a pitcher o' beer. He goes over with a pitcher that holds a little more than two quarts—and they fill it for him.

Now we eat them red beans and rice and we drink that beer—and after supper I send one of the other boys with another dime and he gets more beer. So now we're all done supper, we got meat and beans and rice left over. We got all the beer we can drink, and I still got ten cents left over from my fifty-cent piece.

Money was money in them days, man.

Alphonse Picou recalled: "Those were happy days, man, happy days. Buy a keg of beer for one dollar and a bag full of food for another and have a *cowein*. These boys don't have fun nowadays. Talking 'bout wild and woolly! There were two thousand registered girls and must have been ten thousand unregistered. And all crazy about clarinet blowers!"

The total pool of musicians employed in the tenderloin for the twenty-year span that Story's ordinance was in effect was barely two hundred. This figure represents about ten percent of the number who have claimed to have worked in the District. As a case in point, the number of musicians who claim to have been in the band at the Tuxedo Dance Hall on the night that Billy Phillips was shot to death exceeds the number of musicians in the New York Philharmonic! In point of fact, one musician was present, and he was not playing an engagement there at the time.

The glamorization of Storyville by the communications media in recent decades has led many a musician to try to identify with what was actually, after all, a not especially admirable phenomenon of American culture. Belatedly awakened to the fact that they are artists, jazzmen grasp for the remnants of the recognition they feel should have been theirs all along. But surely it detracts not at all from the greatness of a Louis Armstrong, an Edmond Hall, or an Albert Nicholas that they were born too late to play in Storyville. It is time to deglamorize Storyville, so far as jazz is concerned. Jelly Roll Morton, who *did* achieve greatness in Storyville, did not identify it with the origin of jazz. His assertion was: "Jazz started in *New Orleans*"— and there was far more to New Orleans than its red-light district!

EIGHT

The Press
of Storyville

The New Orleans daily newspapers, by and large, gave meager coverage to events in Storyville, partly out of a sense, on the part of editors, that such events were not all that important, but largely out of a sense that it ill-served the community to shine the light of publicity on the seamy side of Crescent City life—this despite the fact that the sex business was big business and was making fortunes for a number of the city's leading citizens. (An exception to the rule was the *Daily Picayune's* coverage of the Parker/Phillips imbroglio. See Appendix H.)

There were two weekly newspapers, however, the *Mascot* and the *Sunday Sun,* both of which began publication in pre-Storyville days, that made a point of chronicling the doings of the demimonde before and during the early years of Storyville's legal existence. In addition, several guidebooks, published privately to advertise Storyville's attractions, served much the same function as the entertainment section of the typical big-city newspaper of today. These guidebooks, of which the most important was the famous *Blue Book,* were sold in saloons and barber shops or were sold or given away to incoming passengers at the railway depot. Most of them were financed at least in part by Tom Anderson and featured houses, restaurants, and saloons in which he had some interest. One advertising booklet was prepared for Lulu White's Mahogany Hall and restricted its comments to it alone.

The *Mascot* was originally conceived as a generally muckraking sheet featuring sensational revelations of political corruption. The shock-proof citizens of the Crescent City were in no way astonished by the paper's exposés but relished its gossipy quality and its occasional behind-the-scenes peeks at municipal graft and vice.

Victoria Hall.

A member of Miss White's Club, as accomplished as she is beautiful, a form equal to Venus, a voice not unlike Patti. How could a more accurate description be printed, and what more could be said.

The beautiful
Estelle Russell,

now a member of high standing in Miss White's famous Octoroon Club, a few years ago one of the leading stars in Sam T. Jack's Créole Show, which assertion alone should test the capacity of Miss Lulu's commodious quarters every night.

Gentlemen, don't fail, when visiting Miss White's, to ask for Miss Estelle, for you miss a treat if you do not.

Sadie Levy.

Miss White's Octoroon Club would certainly be incomplete without Sadie. Accomplished, beautiful, and charming. We are not given to flattery, so invite you to call and convince yourself that, while there are others there is only one Sadie Levy. Born and bred right here in this city and a girl which any city should feel proud of.

Clara Miller.

Demure everybody's friend, can sit up all night if necessary, and handicap to put a friend on to a good thing. Why? Because it is her disposition, and who don't want to meet such a young lady? Not one with real blood in his veins. She has been in the principal cities of Europe and the Continent, and can certainly interest you as she has a host of others. When we add that the famous octoroon was born near Baton Rouge we trust you will call on her.

Emma Sears.

This clever girl has been justly termed the colored Carmencita, and the name has certainly not been misplaced. As a tamborine dancer she has no superior and very few equals. Tall, graceful, winning. What more can be said? Let me add: Gentlemen, a visit to New Orleans is incomplete if you fail to visit Lulu White's and ask to see Miss Sears dance, sing or play some of her own compositions on a Steinway Grand.

"Prettie Sadie Reed."

Such is the soubriquet Miss Sadie has gained, and properly—as pretty a form and as accomplished as could be asked for. We cannot possibly do the lady justice by the writing of her accomplishments, so gently request you to personally attend to her by a call at the famous Octoroon Club, presided over by Miss Lulu White.

These are pages from Lulu White's brochure advertising Mahogany Hall. The booklet also included a photograph (not shown) that has been widely reproduced as a portrait of Lulu, but which was actually another portrait of Victoria Hall, shown here.

During its early years, beginning in February, 1882, it attacked those in high places in both state and city government and in the police force, and took passing note of the existence of prostitution in the city, waxing indignant over the apparent willingness of the authorities to permit the "social evil" to continue unchecked, and yet at times sympathizing with the poor "fallen women" who would have no place to go if they were driven out of their bordellos and cribs. Founded by Joseph Livesy and Billy Mack, the nickel weekly came out each Saturday to play its gadfly role. As time went on its political exposures did begin to have an astringent effect on the public, and there is no doubt that certain beneficial social changes were attributable, at least in part, to the influence of the paper.

Livesy, however, died in the winter of 1884, and Mack died just four years later. After 1888, control of the *Mascot* was unstable, and it showed a growing tendency to concentrate on the red-light scene, since this seemed to be productive of the most revenue.

During its first ten years of publication the *Mascot* went to press regularly and missed not a single issue in its first five hundred. After 1891, however, it began to appear with less regularity and in time was missing more publication dates than it met. The last issue of which we have evidence, number 767, is that of October 31, 1896. Thus the paper predated Storyville. However, the social and moral "tone" of the District was anticipated in the *Mascot's* pages. Before ceasing publication, it abandoned its successful tabloid format and appeared as a six-column, eight-page sheet dedicated entirely to prostitution, domestic scandal, and the less savory elements of police reporting. By October, 1896, the column "Lorenzo Says," a long-time feature of the old *Mascot*, had been reduced in title to "Lorenzo" and reduced in substance, as well. What had been a column of pointed jibes at the misdeeds of the city fathers, was now devoted to horse race information (and of a poor quality at that) and crude double-entendre copy such as the following, quoted from the last issue extant, number 767:

Mrs. W——, a mother of the exempt soldier who drilled the married woman is very indignant at the idea that her son should be written up. She is surprised that he should attempt to drill any strange woman. One would think that this old soldier would be tied to his mammy's apron strings. However, though W—— may be only a feather bed exempt and is tied to his mammy's apron strings, still he knows his duty as a gunner and can ram home, elevate and prick the vent with any soldier in the union.

The "Society" column in the same issue provides an illuminating view of what the paper had become. It is cited in its entirety, lest it be supposed that the whole was less ludicrous than any selected excerpts might seem to be. If much that "Bas Bleu" had to say is obscure to us today, it may be supposed that much was also obscure to the author's contemporaries. They, it is true, must have had a better grasp of the slang of the period, but the column abounded in "inside" references whose meaning could have been known only to the relatively few persons involved in the events alluded to. Several items in the column suggest that the writer may have included them because one or more of the parties involved had failed to pay him *not* to include them. But at its worst Bas Bleu's blackmail must have been of the pettiest nature.

Society
The Doings of the Week As Gathered By Bas Bleu

———

MISSES KATE ARCHER AND LILLIAN BLODGETT WILL RUN THE MAISON DE BANANA

———

Kate Soaked the Sloan Diamonds to Raise the Needful—Florrie Davis Will Help the Partners to Raise More Glue.

Bas Bleu has been requested to publish the words of the old and favorite song "The Gipsy's Warning." If the "Gipsy's Warning" was heeded there would not be so much Society news to chronicle. For an initial letter to the song a faithful dog is placed. A dog may prevent thieves from breaking in and stealing, but he cannot prevent a rascally seducer getting in his work. [Though promised, the words of the song were not published.]

"Oh! her name is O'Brien, they've christened her
  Kate,
  "And many's the beauty has shared the same
  fate,
"But Sorra a beauty as beauteous as she,
  "From Ballynacrazy to Donaghadee."

That's what the old song says that Kitty Archer is so fond of singing; just because she thinks she is one of the many beauties who shared the fate of Miss O'Brien. Kittie Archer, the Ancient Hibernian and president of the roasting club, was very mad last Friday when she read what Bas Bleu

In 1886, Charles Dudley Warner, editor of Harper's, *published a travel article on New Orleans. The* Mascot *couldn't agree with his view of the city as a patio paradise, all magnolias and Creole belles. These are, they insist, the "sights . . . the Harpers did not see— the gambling hells of Franklin Street." Note the band on the stand in the center diamond.*

said about her youthful attributes. Kittie declares that she is no "Old Curiosity Shop," but that she is a walking encyclopedia. Kittie is so Kittenish that she has determined to appear at the Carnival Balls as "Alice in Wonderland." If Kittie would take my advice she would appear as "The Modern Sairey Gamp," for she merrily relieves the gents when she feels so "disposed." A lovely lady is Kittie, but there are nothing but features on her face. Kittie is proud of posing as a blue stocking in New Orleans. In New York and other large cities, she is a mere footprint on the sands of time; she is a lady with a past who is looking out for a future. It is to be hoped that some gentleman with a reputation to lose may prove so indiscreet as to write Kittie a few letters, and by so doing give the dear girl the right to make another five hundred, for she is in need of coin just at present. There is a prominent man in New York who often curses the time he learned how to write. I understand Kittie bought a pair of earrings with the five hundred, but the diamond's brilliancy is well nigh surpassed by their owner's natural brilliant face of burnished g——, oh! no, I mean brass.

"Only a woman's hair," that was the inscription Swift wrote on an envelope that contained a tress of Stella's hair. Two locks of hair, one an upper cut, the other a lower cut will form racy pieces of evidence in that damage suit filed by Florence. Dear Girl, you have got yourself in a box that Sid cannot get you out of.

The chappies are wondering who is the beautiful girl who is seen with Miss Gertrude Livingston. She has curly, raven hued tresses, gazelllike eyes and a form that would cause an artist to sigh. She is an angel of beauty and grace. Who is she? Will we be permitted to bask in the sunshine of her smile? Such are the questions the chappies are asking. Bas Bleu now tells that the lady's name is Agnes.

Miss Gertrude Livingston is a wonderful woman; she is one you read about but seldom meet. Just fancy; she recently was presented with a set of furniture that cost a small fortune, and she refused the homage of a lover she could not smile upon. Oh ye traducers of your queen, see what it is to be flattered, petted, exalted far above ordinary mortals and still not to fall from grace, but retain a sense of honor to the last. Her most gracious majesty is like George Elliott, who though not bound by any tie, but that of love, remained faithful to the end to the one she had given her affections. Gertie loves one, and she has placed a seal on the fountain of her heart to keep its waters pure for him.

Bas Bleu sauntered into a cafe one day last week and was the involuntary listener to a conversation between two gentlemen. One said, "We are about to have an eclipse here; the city for a time will wear a funeral aspect. We are about to be deprived of the presence of dear Josephine Icebox and Lillian Blodgett, who will leave for

San Francisco in December. The girls are the most popular and successful members of the demimonde that have ever been here. We have one glimpse of brightness in the horizons; the darlings have announced their intention of returning to this city for Mardi Gras." The other fellow said, "What will Annie do without them?"

An admirer of Miss Alma Ellis has written a letter to Bas Bleu sounding that young lady's praises. The letter tells that Alma is not only the most beautiful, but also the most popular of Miss Annie Camor's doves. That when she goes to the theaters she is the admired of all admirers. Also that Alma is green, but not so green as not to have her eye on the long green. She has several Hebrew friends, but she only tolerates them for the sake of their stuff. To prove that Alma is a real swell, her admirers tell that at times she roosts at the Grunewald and Cosmopolitan Hotels and goes to the City Park on Sundays with her thin friend.

Those two very tender spring chickens, Misses Kittie Archer and Lillian Blodgett, have embarked in business on their own account. The chickens have taken Nelly Haley's house. Lillian soaked her Sloan sparklers to start the venture. The ladies will not have very far to go when they desire to meet their French friend, Marcelle. Of course, Lillian will not go to San Francisco with Josephine Icebox.

People are wondering how Miss Alice Schwartz liked the bilk Nettie Griffin gave her. Alice laughed when she heard that Nettie had bilked Miss Camors. Turn about is fair play, dear Alice. Nettie went to Miss Cleo Mitchell but left her to go back to Miss Camors. Did she pay Annie what she owed her?

Miss Pauline Avery, the Leviathan boss of the Mansion House, has given Bas Bleu a riddle to solve, and that is to guess her name. It is not Aberdeen, but it is might near it. Next week I will guess the name of a great physician.

It is learned that Miss Clara Harper will not visit the Crescent City this year, as no first class house would care to receive her on account of the Simms episode.

Miss Esther Pixley, or the little German Gretchen, has left No. 12 Burgundy Street, and is now located with Dottie Barnett, alias St. Louis Minnie, over the drugstore on Customhouse and Dauphine Street. Gretchen declares that at No. 12 she was willy nilly a virtuous lady for three weeks.

Miss Nosey Fagin has been appointed special correspondent to the Society column of this paper. What Nosey does not know is not worth knowing.

A well known gentleman took Madge Leonard around town one night last week and introduced her as the prima donna of the Rob Roy Opera Company. The bluff did not work for a cent with

GOOD GOD!
The Crimes of Sodom and Gomorrah Discounted.

1893 was a bit early to be bringing lesbianism out in the open, but the Mascot *was less inhibited than most newspapers of the period.*

Lulu White, who said, "Jack, what are you giving us?"

Miss June Clifton wished to go to the theater, but she had not the needful. She sent a message to Henry ———, asking him to lend her $3. Henry wrote her a polite note, informing her that he had too much experience with her in financial matters to trust her again. The inference is that Leon must be deuced hard up, or else that he does not approve of falling hair.

Miss Florence Meeker is at home to her friends (when Joe is not about) on North Rampart Street above the tailor's.

It is said that Daisy Poyner has created a new debt; this time in a fast house. Hubby was with her at the time.

Miss Alty of 139 Customhouse Street, really ought to give up making herself so ridiculous by running after an ice water gambler, known to the police as Kid Carpenter.

The Shay family has returned to this city and are located at the family mansion, No. 26 Marais Street.

Furnished rooms, comfort, cleanliness and privacy assured at The Cottage, 1559 Customhouse Street near Robertson.

Red Top (not the celebrated brand of champagne, but Miss Henrietta Frey who is for free silver) says: "16 to 1 is my motto." She would rather be visited by 16 men than one.

Miss Maggie Porter, of 168 Bienville Street, should leave "Coon Hollow" if she desires her story that she is white to be believed. Does Mack believe you, Maggie, dear?

The attention of Society people is directed to No. 1538 Customhouse Street, near Villere, where they can procure well furnished rooms and an unexcelled table.

The Ponds sisters are now quartered at Nellie Garwright's No. 134 Customhouse Street.

Miss May Cannance has returned to the city from Nashville, Tennessee, whither she had gone on a collection tour.

Dora Sherman was hardly cold before her friend supplied himself with another friend in the person of Rainbow Ray. The lady earned the sobriquet from the fact that she has given her hair as many colors (at different times) as there are colors in the rainbow. Ray adapts her hair to the neighborhood she locates in. When on Marais street she was a blonde, when she moved on to Rampart Street she turned out as a strawberry blonde (white horse). Ray is now residing on Dauphine Street and her hair is assuming the brunette shade, the reason for this is that times are hard and Ray has decided to let nature take its course and by so doing save the

expense of visiting Durel. At one time Ray was the very particular friend of a member of the late council who was indicted. (He is not Crutchy Kane.)

"My lord and some ladies" hoisted "a milk white flag" on which was a "fleur de lis," then headed by a "little trooper" the party marched to 10 and 12 North Rampart street, and then commenced "sowing the wind." Tom Anderson appeared on the balcony; many thought he was about to rehearse the scene from "Romeo and Juliet," but that was not his intention, for he appeared more like "Spartacus, the gladiator" as he addressed the crowd of "lords and ladies." Tom said: "My house, the Arlington, enjoys a most enviable reputation; I care not whether you be lords and ladies or hoodlums and "Bowery girls," it is all the same to me as long as you conduct yourselves. This is a house for public entertainment, and I am so Democratic in my ideas that I consider all men and women equal as long as they behave themselves. However, there are some persons who are supposed to be respectable who can change to hoodlums as quick as the great Fregoli can change from one character to another. Who ever comes here to enjoy, the best stuff in the city must behave or get out."

BAS BLEU

Other items of "Society" news from late issues of the *Mascot*:

"What has become of the sylph-like Miss Freeman?" is a question that has been asked by many of late. Some say that Carrie has found religion, others that she has been trying a newly discovered hair restorer, while others will have it that the gentle Carrie has been carrying too many glasses to her sweet lips.

Mrs. Madeline Theurer (Barracks and Rampart Streets) can brag of more innocent girls having been ruined in her house than . . . in any other six houses in the city.

Mr. E. E. L———, a gentleman who comes here every year with the ponies—Last year he had Millie here and made her go out and hustle to earn money for him.

The swarthy beauty, Miss Lulu White, is taking lessons in singing.

Mme. Dean's dog is suffering from constipation.

Miss Julia Dean . . . is quite annoyed that a rumor should have been spread that a rivalry exists between her house and that of Madame Haley's. Miss Dean is too conservative, and is willing to stick by the good Old American Fashion and to eschew all things savoring of La Belle France.

Her most gracious majesty Gertie Livingston

recently had her picture taken in her most royal robes (robes de nuit) and has sent a copy to "Baby Lou."

Nanon, the Western Beauty, has prepared an admirable article for publication entitled, "What is A Professional?." Nanon handles her subject admirably and points out the injustice so-styled amateurs are bringing to the profession. She argues that gentlemen riders in races who are known to accept fees for riding are disbarred from riding as Corinthians, and she thinks the same rule should apply to amateurs who rob the ladies professional. The article is intended for the Sunday edition of one of the dailies.

A letter from Pensacola, Florida, announces the Countess de Kuneman (Abbie Reed) has ceased her spiritualistic seances and now poses as a religious convert.

Miss Bessie LaMothe has issued cards of invitation to the housewarming of her new domicile, No. 9 South Franklin Street.

Miss Eliza Ridley says, "Biz is bad." Eliza has thoughts of joining the Salvation Army.

Miss Mamie Christine, or as she should be called Mrs. Rev. Christian, for her husband was or is a clergyman and a white one, at that, is preparing for a grand season.

Madame Julia Dean has received a draft of recruits and the fair Julia is bragging loudly of her importation. She seems to forget that the ladies played a star engagement here last winter at Mme. Haley's and they all carry their diplomas with them. No doubt Julia was aware of the fact. She had the intention of sending those stock hands of hers to france [sic] to get initiated, but the arrival of the dames from Chicago will save her the expense. It is said that the Basin Street castle will run in opposition to Mme. Haley's well-known house of bliss.

Even more given to sensationalism than the *Mascot* was the *Sunday Sun,* with offices at 631 Poydras Street, which appeared more or less weekly from 1888 until 1892 but only irregularly thereafter, almost on a special edition basis, until its demise in 1906, by which time it had become virtually a house organ for the red-light district. From time to time, the paper would agitate for some "reform" or carry a report of some colorful domestic scandal of New Orleans without mentioning names. However, by contrast with the *Mascot,* which had honorable intentions (at least in its early years), the *Sunday Sun* was a cynical blackmail sheet of the lowest kind. Even so, for the student of Storyville, it is an invaluable source of gossip that helps us to trace the activities of some of the colorful

denizens and habitués of the Storyville harems. Typical excerpts from the *Sunday Sun* follow, and a complete issue of the paper is reproduced, for the reader's amazement and edification, in Appendix G.

From the *Sunday Sun's* classified listings:

Young man would like to meet young girl about 18. Object fun and enjoyment. George Davis, General Delivery.

A young woman financially embarrassed desires assistance from an elderly gentleman. Corinne, this office.

Will lady with dark complexion and black hair, wearing a black skirt and red waist who noticed gent on a bike near Canal Street car station last Sunday, make appointment. Address Biker, this office.

From the paper's "society" column, "The Scarlet World," which was perused with avid interest by the inhabitants of the District and by "sporting" people visiting from out of town:

Minnie Rosenthal is now living with Miss Jessie Brown, 1542 Customhouse Street. Boys, she is the goods.

Romey Young from Galveston, Tex. is expected in a few days, and has engaged rooms with Miss Margaret Bradford.

Nettie Garbright, who for a number of years kept a sporting house at No. 139 Customhouse Street, and retired to private life, is back on the turf again, comfortably situated at No. 1537 Customhouse Street.

Miss Josie Arlington is suffering with a bad cold, but she is on deck all the same attending to business.

Wm. M. Levy's Sure Cure for Gonnorhea [sic] and Gleet. Cures in 1 to 3 days. Price 75 cents.

Among the landladies who have become very popular is Miss Vivian who keeps a modern establishment at No. 325 Basin Avenue. In this place of joy there can be found a bevy of girls who are not only fine lookers but entertainers in the art. Boys visit this house for a good time.

Abby Reed, better known as the Countess Kuneman, is in Fanny Lambert's. Her friends will be glad to hear she is getting along nicely.

Among the swell houses in the district there is none more popular or attractive than the one which is operated by Miss Antonia Gonzales, on Customhouse Street corner of Villere. All summer this resort has done good business notwithstanding the prevailing dull times. This place is filled with beautiful young women all the time, and a

"IT SHINES·FOR ALL."

The Sunday Sun

☞Devoted to giving all the News of the day.

Price, - Five Cents.

visit to the tenderloin is incomplete without enjoying a good time here. This place is what we might properly term a modern music casino.

Belle Boyd the charming blonde of Mahogany Hall is looking more like a two year old now than ever. Belle is a peacherino.

Tillie Thurman or Carlisle, who keeps a joint on Basin Street near the corner of Conti next to Pelican Four's truck house, is certainly a Pelican of the first water. Boys if you are out looking for a good time and wish to save a doctor's bill we severely advise you to give the above establishment all the room possible. When it comes down to the real thing in the way of low-down tarts, then this is the house you are looking for.

Lou Raymond, better known as Kacklin' Lou, ought to attend to her own business and stop putting her nose into her neighbor's affairs. The way Kacklin' Lou has put the devil in a couple of young girls who were doing nicely with a neighbor of hers, was a caution. Such conduct on the part of a woman as old as Kacklin' Lou is most mortifying. Now will you be good, you naughty old girl, and attend to your own business?

One of the pretty petite brunette queens who has many new surprises for the boys during the holidays and at all times is sweet little Ellie Decorevont known as "Gold Tooth" Washington D.C. belle. This charming little woman can be found at the French Studio at No. 331 No. Basin Avenue.

There is a drugstore at the corner of Customhouse and Marais streets that is selling certain drugs which are prohibited by law except when ordered by a physician. It is not lawful to sell cocaine, but it is sold here just the same.

Miss Nellie Condon the proprietress of 1414 Conti Street is enjoying every blessing of life these days. Nellie is one of those creatures whose irresistible fascinations never fail to captivate the

admirations of everyone, and it goes without saying that Nellie is one of the best of good fellows at all times. She has living with her Edna Woods and other girls who never fail to please.

Nina Jackson who keeps the swell mansion, 1559 Customhouse Street, and who is, herself, one of the jolliest girls in the bunch, has gotten rid of those two tid-bits, May and Mamie, and in their stead she has two of the finest and most charming ladies to be found anywhere. Queen Emmette, known as the Diamond Tooth, is one of the girls and Etta Rose is the other.

Aida Dugant, one of Lulu White's finest, has a good one on her staff. Aida is now wearing a pair of $800 earrings. Aida, they are very becoming.

Last Tuesday George S. Roddy, advance agent of "King Dodo," which is now playing at the Tulane Theater, was out in the Tenderloin acting anything but a gentleman. He went into Maestri's row of low prostitutes, bilking them. One of the women grabbed his hat, and had it not been for the officer on the beat Mr. Roddy would have fared badly. This is the recognized 50 cents colony. George, that is below the standard; did you want it cheaper?

On occasion, the *Sunday Sun* published somewhat more substantial fare. This is from the issue for November 1, 1896:

It has become quite a fad among the gilded youth of New Orleans to keep mistresses. Years ago fast young men about town contented themselves by making rounds of the Tenderloin resorts, have a high old time and then go home. But time has changed. In the first place, rounders of this character cost money. With wine at $5 a bottle and beer at $1 a fast young man and his roll can be quickly parted with at this rate, especially if he has a large thirst and overwhelming affection for some fair creature. Consequently the young men came to the conclusion that life in the Tenderloin was not what it was cracked up to be. While they did not want to give up the society of the young woman, who measures her kisses and her favors by the quantity of coin that is dumped into her lap, they objected to paying such high prices for this pleasure, and therefore reached the conclusion that it would be cheaper and far preferable to take the dainty little darling out of her loud and animated surroundings and install her in a neat, comfortably furnished little cottage, where he could enjoy her companionship without being compelled to sneak in the house or show the landlady that he was a good fellow by paying ten or fifteen dollars for wine every time he called. This is the reason why the fad became so fashionable, and it is now a craze among the young men of New Orleans.

Most of these young fellows who indulge in these luxuries are all well known. Some of them are in business for themselves, while others earn good salaries, and therefore able to meet the not too economic expenses of the house where his loved one presides as mistress. The majority of the gay youths do not desire the rest of the city to know just exactly what they are doing and how they spend the lonesome evenings and consequently they search for very quiet neighborhoods to place their mistresses. Neighborhoods where people go to bed with the chickens and mind no one's business but their own are the neighborhoods for the young fellows and that is why Canal Street shelters so many of the lovely creatures.

It has only been within the last two years that men who owned lots back of Canal street conceived the idea that it would be a paying investment to erect handsome little cottages for rent. Plenty of people were anxious to get away from the noise and excitement of the city and would be glad to rent a cottage so far away, but still considered a part of the city. The result was lovely little cottages sprang up like magic, and soon the rear portion of Canal Street was fairly alive with houses. The gilded young man with a mistress soon spotted these cottages and concluded that they were just the things. . . .

Another article, in the same issue of the *Sun*, alludes to pre-Storyville efforts to segregate vice by police measures, essentially, backed by "resolutions" and the like. The Alderman Story referred to at the start of the piece was of course the same man who would later introduce an enforceable ordinance and give his name, albeit unwillingly, to the District:

THE SUNDAY SUN
Nov. 1, 1896
Cleansing Rampart Street

By Mr. Story—A motion requesting the mayor to call attention to the chief of police to the unlawful use of Rampart Street, between Canal and Esplanade Streets, by lewd and abandoned women, and that the ordinance prohibiting such a condition of things be rigidly enforced.

The above resolution was introduced in the council last Tuesday night and was adopted without a dissenting voice. It is an excellent measure and will doubtless be carried out immediately. For several years women of ill-repute have been moving to North Rampart Street until finally so many of them located on the street that the thoroughfare has become quite as notorious as Customhouse, Burgundy and other streets given over to the Tenderloin females. The women on Rampart Street are not conducting open houses by any means. They conduct houses of assignation under the guise of boarding houses, which are far more dangerous than known houses of prostitution. It is in just such houses that so

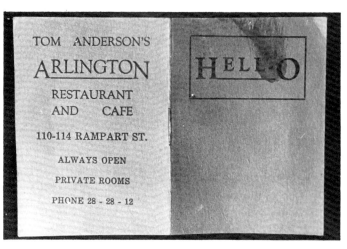

TOM ANDERSON'S
ARLINGTON
RESTAURANT
AND CAFE

110-114 RAMPART ST.

ALWAYS OPEN

PRIVATE ROOMS

PHONE 28 - 28 - 12

HELL-O

TOM
ANDERSON'S
ANNEX

BASIN and CUSTOM-
HOUSE STREETS
PHONE:
3109   2253-22

To keep my friends from
saying mean things while
trying to get a connection
with their girls—that is to
say a Telephone one, I have
compiled this little book entitled "HELL-O" — please
don't misconstrue the name
and read it backwards.
Thanking you for your pa-
tience, I remain,
Yours,
"LITTLE SALTY"

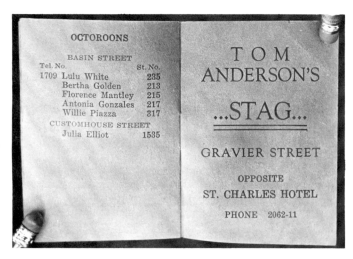

OCTOROONS

BASIN STREET

Tel. No.		St. No.
1709	Lulu White	235
	Bertha Golden	213
	Florence Mantley	215
	Antonia Gonzales	217
	Willie Piazza	317

CUSTOMHOUSE STREET

| | Julia Elliot | 1535 |

TOM
ANDERSON'S
...STAG...

GRAVIER STREET

OPPOSITE
ST. CHARLES HOTEL

PHONE 2062-11

*An urchin would hand you a Hell-o book when you got
off the train at the station in Basin Street. The ubiquitous Tom Anderson obviously had an interest in the
enterprise.*

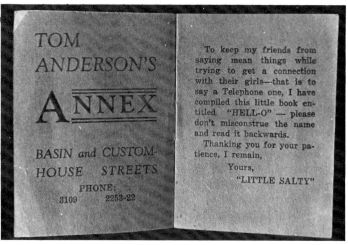

BASIN STREET				BIENVILLE STREET	
Tel. No.		St. No.	Tel. No.		St. No.
211	Flo Meeker	1424	766	Lou Prout	1551
1663	Ollie Nicholls	221	1558	Maud David	1632
788	Grace Simpson	223		N. ROBERTSON STREET	
1888	Josie Arlington	227	2913-22	Cora Isaacs	328
167	Pauline Avery	311		CUSTOMHOUSE STREET	
3554	Dorothy Denning	313	1024	Camille Lewis	1559
	CONTI STREET		3235	Jessie Brown	1542
1793	Ray Owens	1306	1973	Jennie Hope	1540
1114	Mrs. Barron	1320		May Smith	1538
	Nina Jackson & Co.	1418	3427	Fanny Lambert	1547
	Gypsy Shaeffer	1414	1715	May O'Brien	1549
1406	Maud Livingston	1550		Alice Heard	1535
1786	Alice Thompson	1558		ST. LOUIS STREET	
1810	Garnet Runiart	1548	1944	Mai Tuckerman	1424
	VILLERE STREET			HOWARD STREET	
	The Firm	223	1670	Lizzie Curtis	420

many young girls meet their ruin, and if the police would only follow out the new ordinance the street can once more be made inhabitable. There has been a crying complaint from various portions of the city of women of ill repute encroaching on respectable neighborhoods. The police seem to wink their eyes to the evil, for very seldom is any action taken against the proprietresses. Certain limits in the city have been set apart for women of ill repute, and it is a mystery why they are not compelled to vacate respectable neighborhoods and so avoid any contact with the law.

Aside from the *Blue Book*, there were several attempts to produce guidebooks to the tenderloin in the early history of the District. In 1936 a bibliography of these guidebooks was published under the pseudonym "Semper Idem." This work contains much fascinating information but some obvious inaccuracies, as well. However, it is the only work ever published on the subject and frequent reference must be made to it (especially to correct some of the errors).

The *Lid* was an eight-page (unnumbered) publication, 2⅛″ x 2¾″ in size, published in 1905, and carrying two full-page advertisements for Tom Anderson's restaurants. (Semper Idem, incidentally, lists the *Lid* as having been published before 1900, but the Anderson Annex at Customhouse and Basin streets, which is advertised in it, did not open until 1901. The date 1905 is established by comparison of the addresses listed in the *Lid* and those in *Soard's City Directory* for the years involved.) The *Lid* was published as a supplement to the *Blue Book*. Owing to its small size, compared to that of the *Blue Book*, it could readily be given away free without serious loss to the distributor, and issues were usually handed out in the railway station to single men. It contains the addresses of sixty houses of prostitution and the names of the madams. The introduction on page three states:

> No doubt you have read all about the "lid" so it will be useless for one to further descrit it. [sic]
> This little booklet is gotten up expressly for those who belong to that order of "lid destroyers" who believe in making life as strenuous as one possibly can without injury to himself or pocket.
> The names in this booklet are the "class women" as defined in the famous Blue Book and are Billy News' "one best bet" so no matter which one you choose to ring up by phone you can rest assured that you will be well answered.
> THE JUDGE

The *Hell-o* book, probably published after the *Lid*, was almost identical in size and format and contains many of the same names and addresses and the same Tom Anderson ads. However, it was printed in a dark red color, whereas the *Lid* is dark grey.

The *Sporting Guide*, sometimes called the *Red Book*, which first appeared at the end of 1901, was probably predated only by the very first number of the *Blue Book*. Its color was dark red, it was approximately 3″ x 4″ in size, and had twenty-four pages, a third of them left blank to permit the visiting "sport" to write in his own selection of favorite addresses. The introduction states: "This volume is published for the benefit of the upper 'Four Hundred' who desire to visit the Tenderloin District with safety and obtain the desired pleasure accruing from beauty and pleasure, which can be accomplished by following this guide." Its advertisements are similar to those in the *Blue Book*.

The *Red Book*, slightly larger (3″ x 5″), subtitled "A Directory of the Tenderloin," was "a comprehensive and accurate record of the addresses of the sporting ladies in that portion of the town commonly known as Storyville. . . . Give them a call, boys. You'll get treated right." The volume includes a portrait captioned: "The Famous Lulu White, Queen of the Octoroons." The portrait, however, is not of Lulu White but of one of the octoroons over whom she reigned, a Miss Vicki Hall, who is described in Lulu's own promotional piece as "a member of Miss White's Club, as accomplished as she is beautiful, a form equal to Venus, a voice not unlike Patti. How could more accurate description be printed, and what more could be said."

The dating of such items as the *Red Book* is a deductive process. For example, the name of Customhouse Street was changed to Iberville Street in 1904. Since Customhouse Street addresses are used in the *Red Book* and no Iberville Street addresses appear in it, the booklet almost certainly came out prior to 1904. Since the booklet refers to Storyville, it must have been published after 1897. By a comparison of the addresses of better-known prostitutes as listed and their addresses as given in other sources *(Soard's City Directory*, among others) it is possible to determine the probable year of issue.

An 1895 issue of the *Mascot* mentions a guidebook called the *Green Book, or Gentlemen's Guide to New Orleans*. The *Mascot* also states that the book has been "freely distributed" and gives the price as twenty-five cents. Semper Idem, up to the time of the compilation of his excellent bibliography, had found no trace of a copy, and the present author, despite an exhaustive search, has also failed to find such a booklet. It is quite possible, of course, that the story of a *Green Book* was simply invented by the paper.

The *Blue Book*, so far as can be demonstrated, was the earliest Storyville guidebook. The first edition, forty-two pages in length, made its appearance in 1900 and was still close enough to the recent past to list addresses far from the legal red-light area.

It is doubtful that any red-light district other than Storyville ever boasted its own press, but the *Blue Book* was underwritten by Tom Anderson and edited by his right-hand man, Billy Struve. Though formerly a reporter on the New Orleans *Item*, Struve had at best an uncertain command of the rules of grammar, orthography, and rhetoric, but his style was presumably adequate to the demands put upon it. As to that the reader will be the best judge, beginning with the fact that Struve misspelled the very first word in the very first *Blue Book*.

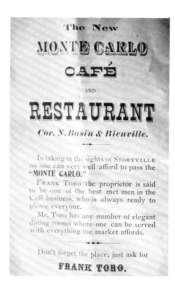

"Stalebread" and his "spasm band" played on the banquette in front of Toro's. Sarah Bernhardt threw them fifty cents for playing a half-dozen of her favorite tunes during dinner.

From the first Blue Book.

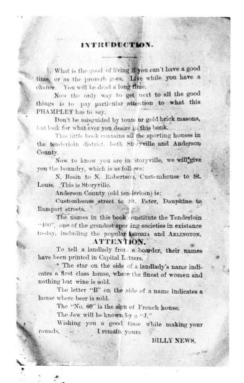

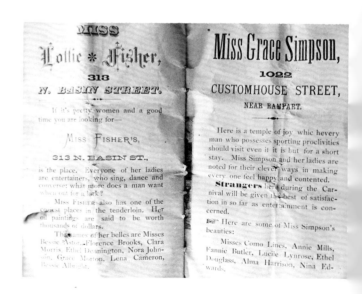

Miss Trilby O'Ferrell of 936 Customhouse Street was *"noted for fun and cleverness the country over." Miss Ella Schwartz' place at 331 Basin Street would soon gain greater notoriety under the aegis of the sinister Emma Johnson. Ella moved up the street to No. 311 about 1906.*

La Schwartz dealt with a higher class of trade in the Mansion.

Owners of the Waldorf Café property on Customhouse Street would soon find the space too valuable for dispensing mere food and drink. By 1900 the property had profitably been converted to cribs.

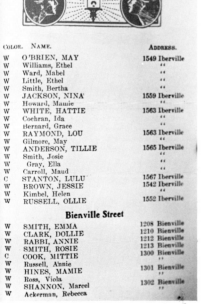

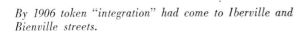

By 1906 token "integration" had come to Iberville and Bienville streets.

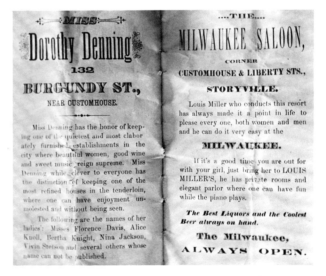

Left: Dorothy Denning was tardy in finding a place in the legal District and was allowed several months to make her move. Right: The Milwaukee Saloon changed hands and names many times in its twenty years. This is the only Blue Book advertisement ever to mention a piano player in all of Storyville, and very few ads mentioned music of any kind.

Miss Eunice Deering

CORNER BASIN AND XX CONTI STREETS

Who is known as the "Idol" of the society and club boys, needs but little introduction, as she is known by the elite's from New York to California.

Her mansion is handsomely furnished, everything being the best that money could procure.

Aside from the grandeur of her establishment, she has a score of beautiful women.

PHONE 4576.

Miss Deering moved out in favor of May Tuckerman because she was afraid of ghosts from the cemetery in view from the parlor window.

Countess Willie Piazza

IS ONE place in the Tenderloin District you can't very well afford to miss. The Countess Piazza has made it a study to try and make everyone jovial who visits her house. If you have the "blues", the Countess and her girls can cure them. She has, without doubt, the most handsome and intelligent octoroons in the United States. You should see them; they are all entertainers.

If there is anything new in the singing and dancing line that you would like to see while in Storyville, Piazza's is the place to visit, especially when one is out hopping with friends—the women in particular.

The Countess wishes it to be known that while her mansion is peerless in every respect, she only serves the "amber fluid."

"Just ask for Willie Piazza."

PHONE 4832 MAIN.

317 N. Basin

Miss Bertha Golden

BERTHA has always been a head-liner among those who keep first-class Octoroons. She also has the distinction of being the only classical Singer and Salome dancer in the Southern States. She has had offers after offers to leave her present vocation and take to the stage, but her vast business has kept her among her friends.

Any person out for fun among a lot of pretty Octoroon damsels, here is the place to have it. For rag-time singing and clever dancing, and fun generally, Bertha stands in a class all alone.

Remember the Number.

PHONE 1535 MAIN

1504 Iberville

Left: Of the madams, Countess Willie V. Piazza was the most musically discriminating. She always had the cream of the "professors" and couldn't stand an out-of-tune piano. Right: Bertha Golden was a one-woman show. Given her five-by-five figure, the "Salome dance" must have been a sight to see.

Mme. Lulu White

COR. BASIN AND XX BIENVILLE STREETS

Nowhere in this country will you find a more popular personage than Madame White, who is noted as being the handsomest octoroon in America, and aside from her beauty, she has the distinction of possessing the largest collection of diamonds, pearls, and other rare gems in this part of the country.

To see her at night, is like witnessing the late electrical display on the Cascade, at the late St. Louis Exposition.

Aside from her handsome women, her mansion possesses some of the most costly oil paintings in the Southern country. Her mirror-parlor is also a dream.

There's always something new at Lulu White's that will interest you. "Good time" is her motto.

There are always ten entertainers who get paid to do nothing but sing and dance.

PHONES: MAIN 1102 AND MAIN 1331

There was only one Lulu—and no need for more than one.

This Book--Not Mailable

To know a thing or two, and know it direct, go through this little book and read it carefully, and then when you go on a "lark" you'll know "who is who" and the best place to spend your time and money.

Read all the "Ads," as all the best houses are advertised here, and are known as the "Cream of Society."

Names in capitals are Landladies. "W" in front of name means White; "C" stands for colored, and "Oct." for octoroon.

The contents of this book are facts, and not dreams from a "hop joint."

You will now find the boundary of the Tenderloin District, commonly called Anderson County or Storyville: North side Customhouse Street to South side St. Louis, and East side North Basin to West side North Robertson Streets.

This is the boundary in which the lewd women are compelled to live according to law.

Yours,
BILLY NEWS.
Sixth Edition.

A word from Honest Billy.

Miss Lillian Irwin

313 BASIN STREET XXX

Miss Irwin has the distinction of conducting about one of the best establishments in the Tenderloin District, where swell men can be socially entertained by an array of swell ladies. As for beauty, her home has been pronounced extremely gorgeous by people who are in a position to know costly finery, cut glass and oil paintings, foreign draperies, etc.

Miss Irwin, while very young, is very charming, and, above all things, a favorite with the boys—what one might say, those of the clubs.

Lillian, as the club boys commonly call her, has never less than fifteen beautiful ladies—from all parts of this great and glorious country. Here are a few of her ladies: Misses Stella Morris, Claudie Sparks, Frankie Wynne, Amber Shepherd, Mollie Gardiner, Essie Carey, Margaret Miller, Ada Beaumont, Ethel Gilbert.

PHONE 3554.

". . . where swell men can be socially entertained by an array of swell ladies."

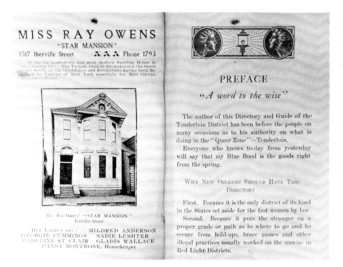

MISS RAY OWENS
"STAR MANSION"
1517 Iberville Street XXX Phone 1793

By far the handsomest and most modern Sporting House in the Crescent City. The Turkish room in this mansion is the finest in the South, all the furnishings and decorations having been imported by Vantine of New York especially for Miss Owens, regardless of cost.

Miss Ray Owens' "STAR MANSION" Iberville Street

HER LADIES ARE: MILDRED ANDERSON GEORGIE CUMMINGS SADIE LUSHTER MADELINE ST. CLAIR GLADIS WALLACE PANSY MONTROSE, Housekeeper.

PREFACE
"A word to the wise"

The author of this Directory and Guide of the Tenderloin District has been before the people on many occasions as to his authority on what is doing in the "Queer Zone"—Tenderloin.

Everyone who knows to-day from yesterday will say that my Blue Book is the goods right from the spring.

WHY NEW ORLEANS SHOULD HAVE THIS DIRECTORY

First. Because it is the only district of its kind in the States set aside for the fast women by law.

Second. Because it puts the stranger on a proper grade or path as to where to go and be secure from hold-ups, brace games and other illegal practices usually worked on the unwise in Red Light Districts.

Lest you go astray.

Miss Antonia P. Gonzales

CORNER VILLERE AND XX IBERVILLE STREETS

CORNETIST SONGSTRESS DANCER

The above party has always been a head-liner among those who keep first-class Octoroons. She also has the distinction of being the only Singer of Opera and Female Cornetist in the Tenderloin. She has had offers after offers to leave her present vocation and take to the stage, but her vast business has kept her among her friends. Any person out for fun among a lot of pretty Creole damsels, here is the place to have it. For rag-time singing and clever dancing, and fun generally, Antonia stands in a class all alone.

Remember the Number.

PHONE 1974.

Mme. Antonia played "Poet and Peasant," too.

Color.	NAME.	ADDRESS.
Oct.	Rinol, Jennie	"
Oct.	Smith, Solo	"
Oct.	Seeker, Thelma	"
Oct.	Brown, Willie	"
W	MOREAU, STELLA	305 Basin
W	LEFEBRE, JEANETTE	307 Basin
W	Brunet, Lizzie	
W	SCHWARTZ, ELLA	311 Basin
W	Devon, May	
W	Jenkins, Alice	
W	Davenport, Mabel	
W	Harris, Gladys	
W	Goldstein, Elizabeth	
W	IRWIN, LILLIAN	313 Basin
W	Beaumont, Ada	
W	Wynne, Frankie	
W	Sparks, Claudie	
W	Miller, Margaret	
W	Carey, Essie	
W	Gardner, Mollie	
W	Gilbert, Ethel	
W	Shepherd, Amber	
W	PIAZZA, WILLIE	317 Basin
Oct.	Hoskins, Goldie	"
Oct.	Richardson, Lottie	"
Oct.	Hart, Margaret	"
Oct.	Day, Earl	"
Oct.	Nerman, Masserine	"
Oct.	Thompson, Rosie	"
Oct.	Harrison, Mamie	"
Oct.	Jackson, Marcel	"

Integrated on the page, segregated on the block.

138

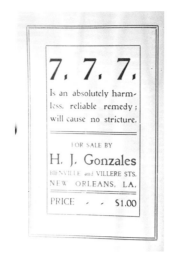

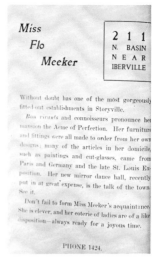

Will we ever know for sure what the author meant by "Queen of Simile"? "Smiles"?

Penicillin, it wasn't.

Miss Flo was also referred to as Flo Mix.

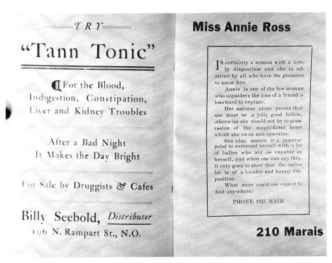

Gipsy Shafer's name was spelled variously in different editions of the Blue Book.

A "Bad Night" meant, of course, a night that had been all too "good"—perhaps at Miss Ross' place. Miss Ross, like My Gal Sal, *was a "jolly good fellow"—short-hand in Victorian America for a girl who was "easy."*

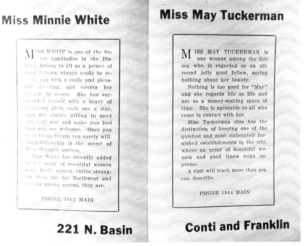

May Tuckerman was another "jolly good fellow," but Minnie White was a "prince of good fellows," surrounded by "queens among queens."

Hilma Burt was indeed, as the advertisement claimed, one of the most popular of Storyville's madams, but she was at 209 Basin Street, not 205.

139

Josie Arlington's advertisement in the first Blue Book.

In such decors as the Arlington provided, how could anyone keep his mind on the business at hand.

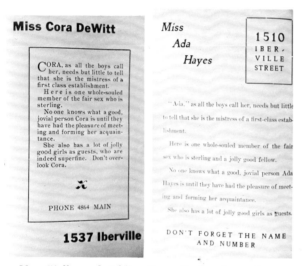

More "jolly good girls" as "guests" of madams who were "jolly good fellows." Miss Hayes' premises were occupied by Sapho [sic] in about 1912.

Lesbian tableaux for the delectation of sports out for something a bit "different."

So refreshing in its simple directness, Mary Smith's advertisement was one of the Blue Book's *more appealing.*

One of the rare Blue Book *blurbs to mention music.*

Miss Brown's premises had formerly been occupied by Grace Simpson, the first president of the so-called Madam's Benevolent Society.

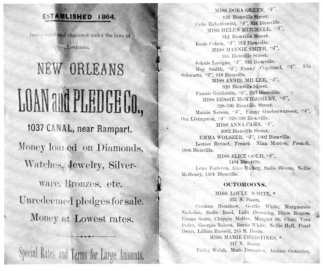

Billy Struve, not noted for his subtlety, juxtaposed a pawnbroker's advertisement and listings for members of Storyville's "Jew Colony," marked "J." in the first Blue Book.

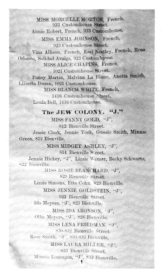

Nobody ever reported the first Blue Book to the Anti-Defamation League, but such labels as "The JEW COLONY" were dropped from later editions—but only because they proved to be bad for business.

Another refreshingly unpretentious advertisement, this one from the second edition of the Blue Book.

Editor Billy Struve didn't have to be able to spell "assignation" to know what it was. Visitors to Storyville from the "Bible Belt"—a major portion of the District's customers—must have been taken aback by the reminder on the left that "the wages of sin is death."

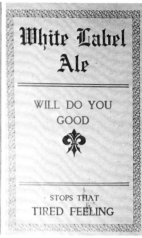

Herbert Asbury, in *The French Quarter*, writes of a great number of editions of the *Blue Book*, but most of these were merely reprints of preceding numbers. There were actually only five different editions, each identifiable by its cover design.

The second edition of the *Blue Book*, forty pages long, had a green cover—not a serious blemish, considering the tenderloin connotations of the word *blue*. Its introduction told the reader:

HOW to be WISE
A man who wants to be a thoroughbred rounder these days has to carry a certain amount of hot air and be a wise guy, no matter how painful.
Now if you are in the A.B.C. class you want to get a move on yourself and "23," and to do it proper is to read what this little booklet has to say and if you don't get to be a 2 to 1 shot it ain't the author's fault.
There is more than one way to spend your coin besides going against brace games and if you pay particular attention to this guide you will never be led astray by touts or gold brick advisors.
The contents of this book are facts and not dreams from a "hop joint."
You will find the boundary of the Tenderloin District commonly known as Anderson County or Storyville: North side Customhouse St. to South side St. Louis and East side N. Basin to West side N. Robertson streets.
This is the boundary in which the lewd women are compelled to live according to law.
THIS BOOK NOT MAILABLE

Semper Idem suggests a date of 1895 for this edition, but its use of the term Storyville stamps it as having come out at least three or more likely four years later. Other details make a date of 1902/03 seem still more likely.

The third edition, which appeared in 1906

and went through several printings during the next two years, ran to ninety-six pages. Tom Anderson had by this time three places to promote in its pages: the Stag, at 712–714 Gravier Street, the Arlington, at 110–114 North Rampart Street, and the Arlington Annex, at the corner of Basin and Iberville streets.

In a preface headed "a word to the wise,"

Many editions of the Blue Book *were published during the legal existence of Storyville, but only five different covers were ever used. The earliest (1898) showed a lady with a fan and conjured up the concept of a "Tenderloin '400'." The latest (1915) is the one with the lyre. Not shown is the edition on which the lyre is upside down, presumably because the printer couldn't identify it.*

142

BLUE BOOK

TENDERLOIN 400.

Struve, identifying himself only as "the author of this directory and guide of the tenderloin district," wrote:

Why New Orleans Should Have This Directory
First. Because it is the only district of its kind in the States set aside for the fast women by *law*. Second. Because it puts the stranger on a proper grade or path as to where to go and be secure from hold-ups, brace games and other illegal practices usually worked on the unwise in Red Light Districts. . . . To know a thing or two, and know it direct, go through this little book and read it carefully, and then when you go on a "lark" you'll know "who is who" and the best place to spend your time and money. Read all the "Ads," as all the best houses are advertised, and are known as the "Cream of Society" . . .
Names in capitals are Landladies. "W" in front of name means White; "C" stands for colored, and "Oct." for octoroon.

Miss Josie Arlington. 225 Basin Street. Phone 1888.
Nowhere in this country will you find a more complete and thorough sporting establishment than the Arlington.
Absolutely and unquestionably the most decorative and costly fitted out sporting palace ever placed before the American public.
The wonderful originality of everything that goes to fit out a mansion makes it the most attractive ever seen in this and the old country.
Miss Arlington recently went to an expense of nearly $5,000 in having her mansion renovated and replenished.

Within the great walls of the Arlington will be found the work of great artists from Europe and America. Many articles from the Louisiana Purchase Exposition will also be seen.

Miss Antonia P. Gonzales. Corner Villere and Iberville streets. Cornetist. Songstress. Dancer.
The above party has always been a head-liner among those who keep first-class Octoroons. She also has the distinction of being the only Singer of Opera and Female Cornetist in the Tenderloin. She has had offers to leave her present vocation and take to the stage, but her vast business has kept her among her friends. Any person out for fun among a lot of pretty Creole damsels, here is the place to have it. For ragtime singing and clever dancing, and fun generally, Antonia stands in a class all alone. Remember the number. Phone 1974.

Miss Ella Schwartz. 311 Basin Street.
Nowhere will you find a more complete and

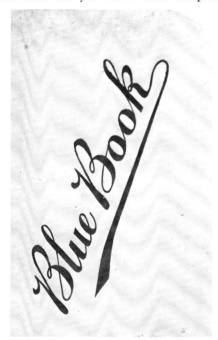

better conducted "Palace of Sport" than the "Mansion."
Miss Ella Schwartz, who is at the head of this famous establishment, is known far and near for being what the "boys" of the hour call a "jolly" good fellow. Ella has let nothing pass her that goes to make life worth living for; so when out for a "gay" time you want to give her place a call, if it be only to form her acquaintance—which, I'll assure you will please you in your meanest mood.
Aside from the magnificence of her home, she has always a score of most handsome ladies, who are a "jolly" good crowd to be amongst.
Remember the name—MANSION.
PHONE 1324

Miss Lillian Irwin. 313 Basin Street.
Miss Irwin has the distinction of conducting

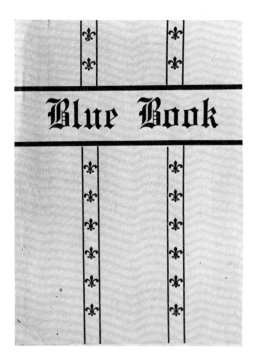

about one of the best establishments in the Tenderloin District, where swell men can be socially entertained by an array of swell ladies. As for beauty, her home has been pronounced extremely gorgeous by people who are in a position to know costly finery, cut glass and oil paintings, foreign draperies, etc.

Miss Irwin, while very young, is very charming, and, above all things, a favorite with the boys—what one might say, those of the clubs.

Lillian, as the club boys commonly call her, has never less than fifteen beautiful ladies—from all parts of this great and glorious country. Here are a few of her ladies: Misses Stella Morris, Claudie Sparks, Frankie Wynne, Amber Shepherd, Mollie Gardiner, Essie Carey, Margaret Miller, Ada Beaumont, Ethel Gilbert.

Phone 3554.

Miss Grace Simpson. 223 North Basin Street.

There are few women in this country who are better known than Grace. To operate an establishment, where everyone is to be treated exact, is not an easy task, and Grace deserves great credit for the manner in which she conducts her house. Grace has always made it a mark in life to treat everyone alike and to see that they enjoy themselves while in her midst. There are few women who stand better with the swell people than Grace, who has always kept one of the best and most refined houses, in which a private man may be entertained by lots of handsome and well-cultivated ladies. A visit once will mean a long remembrance and friendship.

Phone 788.

Miss Eunice Deering. Corner Basin and Conti streets.

Who is known as the "Idol" of the society and club boys, needs but little introduction, as she is known by the elite's from New York to California.

Her mansion is handsomely furnished, everything being the best that money could procure.

Aside from the grandeur of her establishment, she has a score of beautiful women.

Phone 4576.

Countess Willie V. Piazza. 315 Basin Street.

Is the one place in the Tenderloin District you can't very well afford to "pass up." The Countess Piazza has made it a study to try and make every one jovial who visits her house. If you have the "blues," the Countess and her girls can cure 'em. She has, without doubt, the most handsome and intelligent Octoroons in the United States. You should see them; they are all cultivated entertainers.

If there is anything new in the singing and dancing line that you'd like to see while in Storyville, Countess Piazza's is the place to visit, especially when "one" is out hopping with friends—the women in particular.

The Countess wishes it to be known that while her maison joie is peerless in every respect, she only serves the "amber fluid."

Mme. Lulu White. Corner Basin and Bienville streets.

Nowhere in this country will you find a more popular personage than Madame White, who is noted as being the handsomest octoroon in America, and aside from her beauty, she has the distinction of possessing the largest collection of diamonds, pearls, and other rare gems in this part of the country.

To see her at night, is like witnessing the late electrical display on the Cascade, at the late St. Louis Exposition.

Aside from her handsome women, her mansion possesses some of the most costly oil paintings in the Southern country. Her mirror-parlor is also a dream.

There's always something new at Lulu White's that will interest you. "Good Time" is her motto.

There are always ten entertainers who get paid to do nothing but sing and dance.

Phones: Main 1102 and Main 1331.

Miss Margaret Bradford. 1559 Iberville Street.

If there was ever an affiable person, it is certainly portrayed in full when the name "Bradford" is mentioned.

If it was within my power to name Kings and Queens, I would certainly go out of my way to bestow the title of "Queen of Simile" on Miss Margaret.

Miss Bradford is one of the few women who can say she has friends, who are friends indeed, and who are with her in all her adventures.

Her "Chateau" is grandly equipped, and is lacking of nothing.

Pretty women, good time and sociability has been adopted as the counter sign of Miss Bradford's new and costly home.

Miss Flo Meeker. 211 N. Basin near Iberville.

Without doubt has one of the most gorgeously

fitted-out establishments in Storyville.

Bon vivants and connoisseurs pronounce her mansion the Acme of Perfection. Her furniture and fittings were all made to order from her own designs; many of the articles in her domicile, such as paintings and cut-glasses, came from Paris and Germany and the late St. Louis Exposition. Her new mirror dance hall, recently put in at great expense, is the talk of the town. See it.

Don't fail to form Miss Meeker's acquaintance. She is clever, and her coterie of ladies are of a like disposition—always ready for a joyous time.

Phone 1424.

The Firm. 224 North Villere Street.

The "Firm" is one of the few gorgeously furnished places in the Storyville District, so located that the most particular persons in the world can reach it without being seen by anyone.

The "Firm" is under the sole direction of Miss Leslie, who is a princess, and her ladies are of like type.

The "Firm's" success is due to its quiet location, as well as to its able management by Miss Florence Leslie, who has not overlooked anything that goes to make a place famous. The "Firm" is also noted for its selectness.

You make no mistake in visiting the "Firm." Everybody must be of some importance, otherwise he cannot gain admittance.

Mme. Emma Johnson. 331 and 333 Basin Street.

Better known as the "Parisian Queen of America," needs little introduction in this country.

Emma's "House of all Nations," as it is commonly called, is one place of amusement you can't very well afford to miss while in the Tenderloin District. Everything goes here. Fun is the watchword.

Business has been on such an increase at the above place of late that Mdme. Johnson had to occupy an "Annex." Emma never has less than twenty pretty women of all nations, who are clever entertainers.

Remember the name, EMMA JOHNSON. 331 and 333 Basin Street.

Rarely did our guide compose copy with more obscure motives than in his tribute to the delights housed in the 221 Basin Street salon of Miss Ollie Nichols, which were said to include "an array of beautiful women who know how to cleverly entertain the most tedious gentleman."

The advertisement for Miss Ray Owens' Star Mansion, at 1517 Iberville, also deserves special comment, for it reveals that this young lady had advanced in the world in the years since the first edition, in which she was listed among the *filles de joie* entertaining at Josie Arlington's. By the time this third edition went to press, she was able to boast that all the furnishings and decorations had been "imported by Vantine of

New York especially for Miss Owens, regardless of cost."

The fourth edition of the *Blue Book*, a hundred four pages in length, first appeared in about 1908 and continued in circulation until 1912. Its preface displayed the slogan "*Honi Soit qui Mal y pense*" ("Evil to him who thinks evil") and continued to expand on that seemingly unending question: "Why New Orleans Should Have This Directory?" A third reason was proposed rather tardily, considering the fact that it was the one most commonly discussed in pre-Storyville times: "It regulates the women so that they may live in one district to themselves instead of being scattered over the city."

There were further changes under the continuing admonition that "This Book Must Not Be Mailed":

To know the right from the wrong, to be sure of yourself, go through this little book and read it carefully, and then when you visit Storyville you will know the best places to spend your money and time, as all the BEST houses are advertised. Read all the "ads."

The book contains nothing but Facts, and is of the greatest value to strangers when in this part of the city. The Directory will be found alphabetically, under the heading "White" and "Colored," from Alpha to Omega. The names in capitals are landladies only.

You will find the Tenderloin District or Storyville; North side Iberville Street to South side St. Louis, and East side North Basin to West side North Robertson streets.

This is the boundry in which the women are compelled to live according to law.

No outright venereal disease "cures" were touted in this edition, but many patent medicine peddlers continued to use the *Blue Book* as an effective advertising medium. Profusely illustrated with photos of the interiors of many of the bagnios, this *Blue Book* was the most elaborate effort to which Struve had yet dedicated himself.

It may be noticed that some reshuffling of locations now was in evidence. Ella Schwartz, for instance, had taken up at 311 North Basin, leaving her famed Studio at No. 331 to the proprietorship of Emma Johnson.

Our editor continued his assault on the language with such usages as "a bevy of charming girls" and "she serves only the amber fluid."

The fifth and final edition, a hundred two pages plus covers, and the most sophisticated of Struve's promotional efforts, first appeared in 1912 and was reprinted for the last time in 1915.

Tackling once again the thorny question of "Why New Orleans Should Have This Directory," Struve added yet another reason: "It also gives the names of women entertainers employed in the Dance Halls and cabarets in the District"—a highly significant addendum, reflecting as it did the increasing importance of these places in the economy of the District. The cabarets covered were the Casino Cabaret, 1400 Iberville Street; the Abadie Cabaret, 1501 Bienville Street; the My Place Cabaret, 1216 Bienville Street, the Union Cabaret, 135 North Basin Street; the Rice Café and Cabaret, 1501 Iberville Street; the Villa Cabaret, 221 N. Franklin Street; the 102 Ranch Cabaret, 206–208 N. Franklin Street; the Lala Cabaret, 135 N. Franklin Street, and the New Manhattan Cabaret, 1500 Iberville Street.

The advertisement for Tom Anderson's Annex acknowledged, for the first time, "Billy Struve, Manager" (in red letters) and also mentioned music, again for the first time: "All the latest musical selections nightly, rendered by a typical Southern darky orchestra."

The directory listed a total of seven hundred seventy-three women: four hundred twenty-five White, two hundred fifty-one Negro, nine octoroon, seventy-two White "cabaret" entertainers, and sixteen Colored "cabaret" entertainers.

By the time the fifth edition went to press, many of the houses had achieved virtually institutional status. The Cairo, "Snooks" Randella's place at 320 North Franklin, was advertising "oriental Dancers." Miss Martha Clark billed her-self as "one of the few types of pure Roman Beauties hailing from the sunny shores of Italy."

At 327 Franklin, Maud Hartman was presiding over the Club, which was "always open to visitors." The reader was invited to "Come and join 'The Club' and meet the members [sic]."

At Diana and Norma's ". . . everything goes . . . and those that cannot be satisfied there must surely be of a queer nature."

"Miss [Gertrude] Dix has an orchestra in her ballroom that should be heard—all talented singers and dancers." (Presumably they also performed on musical instruments.)

Miss Edna Hamilton's women "are all of high class and culture."

At Emma Johnson's, not only *"Aqui si hable Espanola"* [sic] but also *"Ici on parle francais"* [sic]. Struve also pointed out that "business has been on such an increase . . . that Mme. Johnson had to occupy an 'annex'."

Grace Lloyd, captured in a philosophic humor, "regards life as life and not as a money-making space of time."

In a tour de force of dictional destruction, our reporter's final paragraph on behalf of Miss Olga Lodi's pleasure palace concluded: "Aside from the magnificance [sic] of her home, she has a score of most handsome ladies who are a 'jolly' crowd to be among."

As for Frances Morris' bagnio at 1320 Conti Street: "Everybody must be of some importance, otherwise he cannot gain admittance."

Editor Struve managed to spell Willie Piazza's name two different ways in one advertisement (correctly once) while assuring his readers that "the Countess Piazza has made it a study to try and make everyone jovial who visits her house."

Bertha Weinthal took an extra full-page to promote the appearance on her premises at 311 North Basin Street, of one Mademoiselle Rita Walker, whom Bertha characterized as "the Oriental Danseuse . . . one of the first women in America to dance in her bare feet."

The *Blue Book*, for all its editorial failings (some of them perhaps more the result of errancy on the part of the printer than on the part of the editor), remains a fascinating and unique document. Each edition, printed by the tens of thousands and distributed free by barkeeps to favored customers or sold for a quarter by the newsboys who hawked the *Picayune* and *Item* at every tenderloin corner, is now a rare collector's item.

NINE

Some Anonymous Survivors of Storyville

The following reminiscences, seven in all, have been selected from a total of twenty-six tape-recorded interviews and are thought to be fairly representative of the rest. Of the three men represented, only one made his living from Storyville; the other two were customers. Of the women, one was a madam of a grade-A, mansion-type house (though not one on Basin Street); one was a long-term inmate of a "name" house on Basin Street; one was a black who worked a crib in the poorest section of the tenderloin; and one was an underage performer in an Emma Johnson "circus."

If some of the substance of these interviews offends the sensibilities of some readers of this volume, the author can only say, by way of apology, that the most lurid material has been omitted—not out of a desire to "draw the line" somewhere, but because the omitted interviews represented individual deviations and thus were not representative of the majority of Storyville's denizens.

In only one significant respect must these seven people be considered not quite representative. By their accounts, life in the District was not really all that damaging to individuals and the price of dissoluteness was not all that high. All seven were in good health when interviewed (in the early 1960s), were living to ripe old ages, and were, with one exception, moderately to highly prosperous. The fate of many of Storyville's inhabitants, and even many of its patrons, was not always so happy. These seven are survivors, individuals who managed somehow to live through it all. For each of them, there were many others who died horribly from the effects of venereal disease, narcotics overdosage, alcoholism, and the like.

In the course of the interviewing, nineteen complete testimonies were taken that are not represented in this work. Of these persons, two were bartenders in the District who were quite willing to cooperate but possessed surprisingly little information of consequence (although some of the routine facts they reported have been used elsewhere in this volume). The other seventeen were women. Some proved to be senile or otherwise intellectually damaged to the point that meaningful communication with them was hardly possible. Others were so self-centered that even during the days of their optimum activity they had failed to observe much of what was going on around them. The extent to which they could remember the fine points of their dress and costume was remarkable, and yet they could not remember where or how they ate or the men in their lives (except as escorts). They could recall all their illnesses and infirmities and could catalog the names of those who came to see them in their most trying crises, but they could not remember such elementary details as whether or not they had ever been in the hospital. These women were completely "authentic," but their reports could add nothing of significance to our knowledge of Storyville. A few of them, misunderstanding the author's motives and, being relatively uninhibited, merely pro-

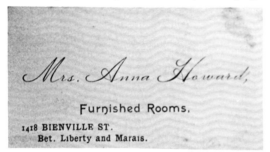

Mrs. Anna Howard,

Furnished Rooms.

1418 BIENVILLE ST.
Bet. Liberty and Marais.

ceeded to relate, with some gusto, the most obscene things they could remember. While the author had no reason to disbelieve them, it did not appear that their stories helped to clarify the image of the District.

In transferring the interviews from tape to paper, the author has chosen to present them as monologues. That is, his many questions have been deleted, as have inconclusive or unilluminating remarks and repetitions that did not add to understanding or supply needed emphasis.

A "Trick Baby"

"Violet," as she will be called here, was not yet sixty years old when interviewed, and yet she had been active as a prostitute in the Dis-

trict prior to its closing in 1917. She has been married since 1921 and has three grown daughters and one son. Two of the daughters are college educated; the third preferred to marry young. The other children are also married and all have children of their own. Violet's husband knows of her former activity and was, indeed, her customer on a couple of occasions. She is a plump housewife who speaks in distinctively New Orleans accents (which no attempt will be made to duplicate). She understood the serious purposes of the inquiry and, although sensitive to the possibility that her recollections might appeal to the prurient interest of some, she showed no tendency to exploit the fact by revelling in her past. She displayed neither shyness nor false modesty but, rather, a refreshing matter-of-factness.

"I was born in 1904 in the wintertime. I was a 'trick' baby. That means my father was just one of them johns that paid my mother for a fuck. I was born upstairs, like in the attic of Hilma Burt's house on Basin Street. A lot of kids was born in that attic and in the Arlington attic and other places like that. There was a midwife used to come . . . for all the girls who got caught. Why do people think whores can't have kids?

"I read in a book one time about one of the houses that was selling a mother and daughter combination for fifty dollars a night. The man that wrote the book acted like that was some kind of a freak act or something. Well, you can write the truth is that I remember fifty combinations like that and I was one myself, and I know two girl friends, both still living, that were in the same kind of an act. I ain't ashamed of what I did, because I didn't have much to do with it. I don't blame my mother much, either. I ain't no more ashamed of that, anyway, than I am to be a member of the human race. The johns can't help it either, you know. It ain't their fault. Just seems like the good Lord ain't got good sense.

"Nobody never stopped me from seeing my mother and the rest of the girls turn tricks. I don't remember anytime when I didn't know what they did, or what a man's prick looked like. Sometimes I'd watch through them portiers like they had then, and other times I'd walk right in the room and nobody said nothing.

"I got to know what a yen pok [part of the preparation process for the smoking of opium] smells like cookin' and knew it put people to sleep before I was five years old. I don't remember Hilma Burt. By the time I got old enough to know what was going on, Gertrude Dix was in charge.

"We moved into a smaller house on Conti Street. The madam was Edna Hamilton. She had three girls and then my mother and me. There was one big parlor and a piano. I only remember the name of one piano player, Sammy Davis. He was colored and he played the piano faster than anybody I ever heard. All the piano players was colored fellows . . .

"One night when I was ten years old I walked into the bedroom where my mother turned her tricks. The john was in there with her and he had his pants off. She was, you know, washing off his prick with a wash cloth. She said this is my kid. He said don't I think a good little girl ought to help her mother. They both laughed. My mother asked me if I wanted to help and she held up the wash cloth. I didn't think nothin' of it. You know, like I said, I seen so much of this from the time I was born. So I took the wash cloth and washed him off, and they both laughed and he give me a dollar. Well, that routine went over so big, pretty soon all the other girls were laughing about it, and then my mother used to get me to do the wash-up act everytime she turned a trick. I'd get one and two dollar tips nearly every time, and then the other girls started gettin' me to wash off *their* tricks, too, before and after, and Edna got the word around and it sure helped business. I was takin' in maybe a hundred dollars a week myself, and the other girls was gettin' more johns.

"The johns never bothered me. I didn't have nothin' even to feel yet. But they liked to have me around in the room while they fucked. One time Cora one of the girls had a john and she was sucking him off. It was nothing new to me. I seen it plenty of times before but only lately I'd be in the room while they were doing it. I said 'I can do that.' So we took turns . . . Then he fucked her while I felt his balls . . . I made five dollars for my end of that one, and then I started turning tricks myself just by blowing. I was still only ten years old and not very big so I didn't fuck. It was two years more before I did that. So I was a virgin for two years.

"But after I found out what the johns would pay for, I started all kinds of stunts with 'em except fuckin'. One time Edna called me down to the parlor. There was four johns sitting there about half-juiced. I had on a white party dress to make me look about four years younger than

I was. That was Edna's idea. She said to blow all of them. One of them was feeling my cunt while I did this. None of them seemed to want to come. Everybody just laughed. Then one of them, a thin, bald one, asked me how I'd like to go upstairs with him and I did. In the bedroom he asked me whether I ever had my cunt sucked, and I said no, because that was the truth. So he went ahead and did it to me and it felt real nice, you know—but nothing happened because I was too young. Anyway I made fifty that night by myself, which was pretty good for a ten-year-old kid.

" . . . The first time I ever got fucked wasn't at Edna's but at Emma Johnson's—you know,

they called it the Studio on Basin Street next to the firehouse. I was twelve and Edna had been sendin' me over there nights to be in the circus. I don't need to explain what that is do I? Well, I was in the circus two or three nights a week. There was another kid my age . . . Liz . . . she's still alive. Oh, yes! That's right. She's the one. Well, when you talk to *her* you can check this. We used to work together. By this time we were getting a little figure and looked pretty good . . . and neither one of us was afraid to do them things the johns liked, so we'd get a hundred a night to be in the circus. My mother was in the circus, too. She's the one who used to fuck the pony. Emma kept a stable in the yard and a colored man, Wash, used to take care of the two ponies and the horse. In the daytime me and Liz *rode* the ponies around the yard [. . .]. Ain't *that* somethin'?

"So this one night, Emma had some live ones in the house and she says to me she thinks I'm ready to fuck, and will I do it for half of what she gets for me. Usually I never talked anything over with my mother anymore, but this time I did. She said that since I was getting hair on my cunt, I might as well go ahead. So, Emma she had a big mouth—a loud voice, made a speech about me and Liz and how everybody in the District knew we was virgins, even though we did all these other things and that if the price was right, tonight was the night and she'd have an auction. Some snotty kid bid a dollar and Emma had one of the floor men slug him and throw him out in the street. One man bid the both of us in, honest to God, for seven hundred and seventy-five dollars *each*! A lot of johns bid, and he wasn't gonna be satisfied with just one. He bought us both. Well, we went upstairs with him. He wanted us both together, and you know how it is, we thought he ought to be entitled to *somethin'* for all that money, so we came on with everything we could think of, includin' the dyke act which we been doin' anyway in the circus and we got to like it so much we'd lots of times do it when we was by ourselves. We did a dance we had worked out where we jerked ourselves and each other off and we started to play with him but I didn't hardly *touch* him when he came. Well right away he went to sleep with us on the bed with him and in a little while, maybe an hour, he woke up, and the three of us fooled around until he got in shape to do something and we managed to get him into Liz. I could tell it hurt her and she bled pretty good too, but afterwards she said it wasn't so bad and she was glad it was over. But the john didn't have enough left to do nothin' with me so he arranged with me and Emma to hold me over to the next night.

"The next night he came around to Edna Hamilton's and that's when I got broke in. It wasn't bad, and he really thought, all around, he had his money's worth.

"He looked to be about thirty-five or forty. A nice lookin' fellow—I don't know who he was, but I could tell the way he talked he was from New Orleans.

"The next year the district closed down. I had money saved and I got a job. I was always high priced. Not because, you know, I was so pretty or nothin', but because I was a novelty, and I didn't hang around long enough to get wore out. I got a job as a waitress. Yes, I still turned a few tricks, but after I started goin' with my husband, I cut all that out. My mother moved into a crib in the French Quarter and kept on until she got too old. No. I was lucky, I never got the clap and, so far as I know, neither did my mother. You know what! *She's* still livin'! It won't do you no good to talk to her. Her head don't work right no more. But she gets around. She lives in her own place and does her own cookin'.

"I don't know if it was a good life or a bad life. I know I got a good life *now*, and I know how to appreciate it. But I don't know how I'd feel about it if I went through the whole life, you know, with pimps and dope and turning tricks till I was fifty.

"All my three girls is older now than I was when I quit the business, and I don't see that they're much better off than I was at their age. I

know it'd be good if I could say how awful it was and like crime don't pay—but to me it seems just like anything else—like a kid who's father owns a grocery store. He helps him in the store. Well, my mother didn't sell groceries."

Throughout the interview "Violet" was composed and was never suggestive in her manner or tone. Later, the author had an opportunity to speak at great length with "Liz" (who by then was working as a cashier in a working class barroom) but her recollections were too hazy to be of much value. She did, however, remember the defloration episode, and as she heard Violet describe the scene on tape she nodded along with the narrative.

A Pimp

"Marc" hasn't been in New Orleans for many years, although the bar he owns is in a town not too many miles from the Crescent City. He hasn't stayed away for fear of being recognized and scorned, or because of any transportation inconvenience.

"Everything's so *high* in New Orleans. The town is closed down tight, and I'm too old, anyway for fuckin'. I can do all the drinkin' I want right here in my own place, but I never was too much for the bottle. Or dope an' things like that. No, I never married. What the hell for? I always got all the cunt I wanted, *free*. In fact ain't that why you want to talk to me? —because *I* got paid for it? Ha, ha!

"I was born in 1888. Yeah, in New Orleans. That makes me seventy-three now, don't it? So naturally, I remember before there *was* no Storyville. I never heard nobody call it that till lately. My ol' lady—it wasn't no secret—was a whore in Dauphine Street, and that's where I was born—in a little house on Dauphine Street in the French Quarter. It's still there. I remember when the law set up the district, because that's when we moved over to Liberty Street. It was in 1898. I don't know who my ol' man was. Just another trick, *you* know. Anyway, the ol' lady died in 1903 from the clap. One day I come back to the place from school. . . . You surprised? You *had* to go to school. It was the law . . . and she was missin'. The woman who lived next door tol' me she just went to the 'ice house' (popular term for the isolation hospital) for medicine. I never seen her again. I didn't try to see her at the hospital, because I always been afraid of them places—and anyhow, I didn't 'specially *feel* like seein' her.

"Well, in them days, you know, anytime a kid had to get out an' hustle a livin', he'd go sell newspapers. I went around by Tom Anderson's and I told him I had to start sellin' papers, because the ol' lady didn't come back from the hospital and he give me a dollar an' tol' me I could sell papers on the banquette in front of his place for a while . . . You know you couldn't just sell papers *any* place. You had to have your own corner—and he had to get the kid whose corner it was to go someplace else for a couple of weeks. Anyway this kid never come back. I suppose he found some better way . . . Well, I kept the corner. Yes . . . I remember them piano players . . . Tony Jackson? . . . Yeah, I remember him. He was a fruit. No, I never did hear him play, but I'd see him gettin' out of a hired hack in front of Hilma's . . . Most everybody knew Jelly Roll. I knew he played piano, but to me he was the champion pool player around there. Flashy dressed boy. He used to wear a sharp cap all the time. Like now

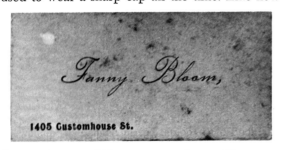

Fanny Bloom,

1405 Customhouse St.

those sports car kids wear, you know. He was a pimp, too.

"When I was fifteen years old, I started think-

in' I better think about doin' somethin' else, because I couldn't be sellin' papers all my life. But I was makin' pretty good, maybe seven dollars a week off papers and another couple of bucks in tips for 'steerin'.' You know, like recommendin' places. I was gettin' to be a pretty good-lookin' boy, too. Then this broad stopped on the corner one day an' she says to me, 'Sonny, you an' me could do a little business.' And she gives me a pack of little cards with her name an' address on 'em an says every time a trick comes in with one of these cards, she'll pay me twenty-five cents each for 'em. So I tell her yes, and I'm supposed to put my initials on the back of the card so she'll know who she owes. She was on Iberville Street. Not exactly a crib. It was like a two-room place she had with another broad, but they had a kitchen and a real inside toilet.

"So every week she'd stop by the corner and give me maybe a dollar-an'-a-half, two dollars. Every time she'd leave me more cards. So one

Miss Julia Dean,

341 N. Basin St.
Corner Conti.   New Orleans.

week she didn't show up and I went around by her place, because I figure I gave out just as many cards as usual the business couldn't go down to nothin'. So I passed by her place. In the day, I remember. It was still bright sunshine. I says I come by because you never stopped to give me my money this week. She smiles at me and says she was busy and asks me to sit down and then she comes and sits in my lap and asks me if I ever got fucked. I tell her sure. I tell her a fellow can't be spending all his time in the District without getting fucked. But I'll tell *you* the truth. I never had none in my life to that time. I guess I was a little late, you know, growin' up. Besides, I seen so much of it by the ol' lady, you know, it didn't seem like so much . . .

"Well, anyway, she started unbuttonin' my pants and before I knew it we was rockin' on the bed and I bet the whole thing didn't take more than thirty seconds. So we get finished an' she

151

washes me off an' I put on my pants an' she says to come around any time. I says where's my money—an' she tells me I had a dollar seventy-five comin' but she charges two dollars a trick an' didn' I think I had a bargain. So you know, I punched her in the mouth. Then I knocked her down and took the roll out of her stockin'. It was eight dollars. She started in cryin' an' sayin' she wouldn't have nothin' to eat, and why couldn' I take my dollar seventy-five and give her back the rest. I threw her a dollar and tol' her no whore was gonna hold out my money on me an' get away with it. She says she's sorry an' I tell her to go to hell an' I leave. After all, fuckin' is one thing, but money is money.

"I didn't think I'd see *her* no more, but I didn't understand then that a lot of them whores *like* to get hit. Next day she comes around with more cards. I tell her I don't want to bother with her no more, and she says she'll give me *fifty* cents a trick. So I says OK. Well, then, I used to go around every couple of days to collect, and if I felt like it, to get some fuckin' and the girl she was livin' with who had the other room started gettin' real friendly and before you knew it they was *both* payin' me off. And gettin' real jealous of each other.

"Well, I didn't have much education, but I wasn't stupid. And I see how these broads was with money and I begin to understand how all these big-shot pimps got all those broads workin' for 'em and them guys buy theirselves diamonds and sharp clothes and like that. So one day them broads have a real fight over me. I forget what about, but I was right there. So I slug 'em both until they both cryin' and I tell 'em they better do like I say or I'll go away and leave 'em both. By that time I understood that nothin' had to make sense no more. Just you had to know how these broads *are*.

"I figured out that I would do better if instead of takin' my percentage off the broads like I was doin', I'd be better off if *I* paid the rent and took *all* the money. Then I could give 'em back what they needed to get along on. They never said a word.

"Well, y*ou* know, by the time I was seventeen I had eight broads turnin' tricks for me. I wasn't sellin' no more papers, because I was makin' about three hundred a week clear. I'd have to lay each one of 'em once or twice a month.

"I was payin' off a few key bartenders and drivers to 'steer' for me and buyin' them fancy clothes and hard hats. By eighteen I had two big diamonds. Cost me twelve hundred. [He exhibited his left hand showing two rings set with very large, yellowish diamonds.] I bought diamonds, but I never sold one. They cost plenty money.

"Later on, I opened up a whorehouse of my own . . . I didn't *open* it, it was already runnin' —but I bought it an' spent some money fixin' the inside. I found out you have to spend some money to make any. In 1902, I must have had a average of thirty women all the time. I guess from 1902 to 1917 I did a half a million dollars. You understand not all for myself—but still it was big money.

"I used to hang out in Billy Phillips' place around on Franklin Street. That's before he got killed, you know. All them gamblers was always in there, and other pimps. You know in them days all pimps was gamblers. Except me, I mean. I just didn' see no percentage in gamblin'. I used to *watch* 'em and figure to myself they didn't know how to handle their money. The truth is, money got to be what you call a hobby with me. I just got so I liked money, a lot of times better than them things you could buy with it. You know I seen so many of them half-assed big shots with two or three broads on the turf all dressed up with fake diamonds—I know they was fake, because they used to try to sell 'em to me when they got broke. [He extracted a jeweler's loupe from his pocket.] But you can't fool me with no fake diamond. Ha, ha. So when them guys start actin' big, with gamblin' an' all, I figure I got say thirty thousand in the bank and I can buy an' sell 'em all.

"Me an' Tom Anderson got to be *good* friends. I help him get elected to the state legislature. After all, he come up jus' like me—an' he give me my first dollar to get started. *He* used to hang around by Billy Phillips' some times too, you know—to get away from the tourists who come by his own place to shake his hand. He was a *real* big man. Even today people don't realize how much power he had in the city— even the state. He had a picture of himself shakin' hands with President Roosevelt—the first Roosevelt. You can't get no bigger than that.

"Me an' Tom Anderson used to sit together by Phillips'. He used to say spend money. Spend a *lot* of money—but save a little more than you spend. Mostly he didn't have much to say, Tom. There was plenty money spent in Phillips' place. It was just a low-down hole-in-the-wall. This [indicating his own modern premises with a sweeping gesture] is a palace along by Phillips'. But he *had* a location. He had music, you know —live music all the time. Colored bands they played ragtime. Them broads of mine, the biggest thing I could do for one of them was to take her to Phillips' to dance. Sometimes I'd take one by Phillips' during the time of the month when she couldn't work anyway and buy her a drink or two, and maybe dance with her once. She wouldn't bother me for weeks afterwards. Them broads! You have to understand them. Money don't really mean *nothin'* to them like people think.

"I don't need to tell you I saved my money. I got plenty good real estate. I got this bar. I got a fine home with a big yard . . . What am I gonna do with it when I die? Ha, ha. I ain't dyin' so fast. I don't think about things like that.

"I don't care that I made mine pimpin'. How I was gonna make it, sellin' papers? I was in business like anybody else, and I run it good. Better than the rest of 'em. I wasn't no lush. I didn't take dope an' I didn't gamble. What's wrong with that? The rest of 'em is all gone. Some just got broke and disappeared. Some let whiskey an' dope get 'em. I know three what killed their*selves* and two that got knifed to death by their broads. A lot of 'em got put in jail for different things. Mostly for tryin' to stay in the same business after it become illegal in 1917. You know, like when prohibition come in they got in gangs and one thing and another. Some got killed, even, in gang fights.

"But I saved my money an' I'm still here. The rest of them guys is gone—but I'm still here."

A Man About Town

This well mannered and gracious gentleman, "René," was a world traveler who had a first-hand knowledge of the world's most celebrated tenderloin districts in their heydays. His customer's point of view on Storyville is thus of all the more interest.

The scion of an old and prosperous New Orleans family, "René" also made a large fortune on his own. In his middle seventies when interviewed (he is now deceased), he remained to the very end a *bon vivant* and an expert in the delights of the senses.

In his early years, "René" was notorious as a ringleader of Mardi Gras pranksters and many of his exploits have become legendary. It is said that his personality and "style" inspired the elder Douglas Fairbanks' interpretation of the role of D'Artagnan in *The Three Musketeers*, and that he also influenced the elegant "manners" on display in the original film version of *La Bohème*. It is certain that "René" was acquainted with Fairbanks and also with John Gilbert, who played in the silent screen version of the Puccini opera.

It is said, also, that "René" was a combatant in the last duel fought in City Park "under the oaks," and one of his seconds still lives to corroborate the tale.

The interview took place in the luxurious surroundings of "René's" New Orleans home.

"America is a wonderful, a magnificent nation—but its people know nothing about the enjoyment of pleasant things. This goes for food,

wine, music, the dance, the theater, the exhilaration of art . . . and most of all for sex and its infinity of forms.

"As purveyed by Storyville, sex took its most disgusting, least attractive, and least satisfying form. We are not children and we know that prostitution is engaged in by women purely for profit. We expect its rules to be governed by the laws of supply and demand. I consider the quality of sex in Storyville to constitute an indictment against the American man's taste and degree of civilization. That he would spend his money for so shoddy a product as the District provided makes one hesitate to put quality into the manufacture of bread, shoes, or cars. You would have thought that the prostitutes of Storyville might have, in their own interests, been more artful—made some moves to disguise the fundamentally predatory nature of the profession, thereby building and holding stable clientele and increasing prices to accommodate the need for the greater expenditure of time per customer. That they did not points to no weakness of imagination or talent, but only to the lack of discrimination or appreciation among the patrons. Experience taught these women that American men 'don't know the difference.'

153

"Well, what you want to know about is the time when I 'didn't know the difference,' isn't it? There *was* such a time. My father took me. I'm sure he had the tacit approval of my mother, since in those days, at least in our group, people were always worried about the effects on the brain of masturbation and seemed to think it was safer to expend semen in some rented woman. They were also afraid of venereal diseases, but had the superstitious belief that this could be avoided by a process they described as 'being careful.' Well, I learned all my father could teach me about 'being careful' and I later spent a fortune with doctors to control the ravages of both gonorrhea and syphilis—and so did he. My father really died from the effects of syphilis—although that's not what it said in his lengthy obituary in the *Picayune*.

"I remember hearing a piano playing *In The Good Old Summertime*. This must have been, I guess, 1903 or 1904. My father filled my billfold with money and we drove to the corner of Basin and Bienville in our own carriage, driven by our own Negro coachman. My father said we would go to Lulu White's place. He also called it 'The Hall of Mirrors,' but not 'Mahogany Hall.' I didn't hear people call it 'Mahogany Hall' until several years later.

"By the way, they have the curbstone from Lulu's down at the Jazz Museum—but of course you'd know that. Well. I alighted on that very curbstone with my father, and in we went. The instant we stepped inside that door, it became apparent that, though ornate, the taste reflected in the furnishings and decor was just miserable. There was just too much of everything. In the foyer were two oversized pieces of poor sculpture showing semidraped female forms, certainly not aphrodisiac in character. Imitation Renaissance tapestries and wall hangings of particularly muddy color hung everywhere. The oriental rugs, possibly actually *from* the Orient, were thick but shoddy imitations of the luxurious pile and color for which the East is famous.

"Lulu White, herself, greeted us after we'd been announced by a Negro doorman. I don't know what you may have heard about Lulu, but take my word for it, she was a monstrosity . . . laden with diamonds worn not selectively but just put on any place there seemed to be an inch to accommodate them. She wore a red wig that hardly pretended to be natural in color. She smelled overpoweringly of perfume. Lulu was obviously Negro. She, in her way, acted the

grande dame to the hilt, although she gave the impression that she'd never seen a real *grande dame*. Her efforts to appear cultured were quite ludicrous. Her quick smile was as faked as the color of her wig. She had one of those masculine type voices that ring with authority and remove all traces of femininity.

"We were invited into the main parlor, a melange of parquet flooring and rugs, overstuffed and overcarved furniture and more ill-selected 'art' and sculpture. The girls, though, were something else again. They lounged on sofas and chairs, and were dressed in extremely revealing evening clothes. I guess there were a dozen or so. I confess to having been a little nervous. Lulu called one of the girls over and said, 'Rita, this is M'sieu René————. You take him and see that he has a *real good time*.'

"Rita was a very beautiful girl whom I knew to be an octoroon only from the fact that she was one of Lulu's girls. Her fair skin and light, brown eyes, which I remember well, should have made it possible for her to enter into white society without question. I suppose she couldn't have been more than nineteen, but I assumed then, from the vantage point of my sixteen years, that she was an 'older woman.'

"Of course, my father assumed that I was about to have my very first sexual experience with a female, but he was just as wrong as he could be—although I had never been with a prostitute or even seen the District before.

"We had champagne, Mumm's Extra Dry of a very inferior year. The man playing the piano was white, I'm sure, even though I have been led to believe that only Negro musicians performed in this capacity in the District. I thought his playing very impressive and said so. The girl suggested that I tip the 'professor,' which I did. Five dollars. I asked him to play *Every Little Movement Has a Meaning All Its Own*, which I had heard in New York the previous winter, and was astonished to find that he knew it and could play it. As I say, I was nervous—not because of the fact that I was about to have a sex experience, but because I expected something quite sensationally evil and was conscious of being a guest in a world-renowned den of iniquity.

"The young lady, apart from certain studied theatricality, was just as ill-informed and gauche as she could be. She led me upstairs to a bedroom of medium size, dominated by a fourposter bed, quite dusty looking—the drapes, I mean. She got out of her clothes and invited me to do the same. She approached me and seized my genital organ in one hand, wringing it in such a way as to determine whether or not I had the gonorrhea. She did this particular operation with more knowledge and skill than she did anything else before or after. I was not taken aback, because I had already heard about this part of the procedure from many people, including my father. She washed me with some foul-smelling disinfectant and lay down on the bed, inviting me to mount her. This I proceeded to do, and the mechanical procedure that followed endured for perhaps a minute. She then washed me and herself again, politely asked me if there would be anything else, and when I thanked her and said no, she asked for ten dollars. I apologized, telling her I didn't know whether the money was paid to the girl or to some sort of cashier at the close of the evening. Back in the parlor, I found my father still conversing with Lulu. He was astonished that I had finished so quickly. Not a half-hour had gone by since our entrance. Lulu said to be sure and look her up next time I was downtown.

"Outside, I asked my father how it happened that he, too, hadn't availed himself of Lulu's facilities while we were there, and he replied that he had! It was my turn to be astonished.

"'Lulu White,' he said, 'is a fascinating woman.' I didn't agree, but I didn't say anything about it. Today, after about sixty years, I still don't agree.

"I've been in whorehouses all over this globe. I've been in the cheap brothels of Montmartre and in the House of Seven Stories in Tokyo. I've been fucked in Singapore, Kimberly, San Juan, Buenos Aires, and Calgary, and I can report with authority that no house on Basin Street was in it with the cheapest places in these other countries. The foreign whores, somehow, manage to feign an attitude that leads you to believe, at least for the moment of intercourse, that you have their attention and that they are interested in seeing that you have a pleasant time. While they never do it free, they always seem just a little surprised when you hand them the money— as though they'd forgotten about this crass detail. They have, how shall I describe it, pride in their workmanship. Some, at times, show a certain art consciousness, as though in recognition of the possibilities of the development of substantial aesthetic qualities in sexual congress. Storyville whores, no matter how well-dressed or how gaudily expensive the whorehouse, were

avaricious, greedy, and uncouth. Really low-class people, despite the *Blue Book* ads.

"Since the customers demanded no better, I guess they got what they deserved. No house in the District could, with their practices, survive for a month in Paris, even if they cut prices below the poorest-class brothels in Europe. But then you can't buy a decent loaf of bread here, or a really well-engineered car made in America —and even one of our famed old French restaurants in the Quarter served me oleomargarine! It's never a matter of price. Americans, knowing no better, accept shoddy merchandise and produce it, too. There's no art—no satisfaction—in it.

"Off and on, I patronized those District houses for about twelve years. Only, however, because it was convenient. It took much time and trouble to seduce the young ladies of our social circle, though I sometimes *took* the time and trouble. These experiences, few and far between, were much more satisfying—but it was difficult to make the effort with the District so near.

"Asbury, in his book, quoted Willie Piazza as complaining that the 'country-club' girls were

ruining her business. There weren't enough country-club girls ready to put out to materially affect Willie's business.

"What ruined Willie Piazza's business is that Willie Piazza never learned her business, and her competitors were just as slipshod, incompetent, and worst of all, obviously greedy, as she. They took more and more for less and less until by the time the District was closed down there were scarcely four hundred girls left working in it."

A Madam

"Madam J——" operated one of the large mansions in the District. The circumstances of the interview were such that the author himself knew neither the lady's professional name nor which house was hers. Certain facts lead him to believe he might be able to identify her, but not with certainty, and the effort would be wasted, in any case, since she would have to remain anonymous for the purposes of this work. Her statements have been checked against other information in the author's possession, leaving no doubt as to her authenticity and general truthfulness.

"Madam J——" speaks with a distinctly midwestern accent. She is obviously well-educated and her diction is excellent. At the time of the interview, in 1961, she said that she was eighty-one years old. She was very slim and tall, wore horn-rimmed glasses, and still used make-up in noticeably large quantities. Twice a widow, she is obviously in excellent financial circumstances. The interview took place in a large Southern city (not New Orleans), where she was active in civic goodworks, especially those related to the arts, until the death of her second husband, at which time she retired from public life. Here is her tale.

"When I was sixteen years old I became involved in a public scandal of a sexual character. I had not been 'ruined,' as they say—as a matter of fact, the whole affair was childish—but back in 1896 families had pretty rigid ideas. As the Jezebel of the family, I was shown the door. My mother handed me a thousand dollars in cash with a note from my father telling me he'd send

PHONE 766.

Furnished Rooms,

FOR GENTLEMEN ONLY.

LOU PROUT,
1551 BIENVILLE ST.   Bet. Villere & Robertson.

fifty dollars a month wherever I wanted it and instructing me never to darken his door again. Neither my mother nor my two sisters, brother nor father, said a single word to me. Not even 'Good-bye.'

"There was no possibility of my becoming established in any kind of business or work of a legitimate nature in my home city, and I went to New Orleans, since I always dreamed of living in a warm climate. I checked into the St. Charles Hotel immediately upon my arrival and was almost immediately recognized by a fellow

townsman who knew of my 'shame.' This beast made advances to me at once, and threatened to expose me should I refuse his attentions. Of course, I repulsed him indignantly and not another hour passed before everyone in the hotel knew my story. In a very short time, the same day, I received a note from a Miss Lottie Fischer, including her calling card. She said she had heard of my difficulties and could help me if I cared to avail myself of her aid.

"Now, I had never heard of Miss Fischer, and I was comparatively innocent, but not so innocent as not to suspect what Miss Fischer had on her mind and what kind of 'aid' she was offering. Nevertheless, low in spirits as I was following my encounter with that awful man, it flashed through my mind that if I was to have the reputation of a scarlet woman, I might as well become one, since that seemed to be the only direction in which society permitted a 'ruined' young girl to go. I remind you that I remained a virgin.

"I answered Miss Fischer's note by messenger, inviting her to call, I believe, at 11 A.M. the following day, which was to be a Sunday. I recall this because I planned to meet her on my return from church. She arrived looking quite the great lady in the Floradora outfit which was then in vogue. She had jet black hair, big, light gray eyes, and was, altogether, I think, the most beautiful, charming woman I had ever seen. I invited her to be seated on the delightful settee—the St. Charles had such gorgeous, beautifully furnished big rooms in those days—and she looked for all the world like a live Fragonard. I remember almost every word she had to say.

"'My child,' she said, 'this is, for all its size, a very small town. I have heard about you from people in the hotel whom I pay for such information, I tell you frankly—because it is my business to find such girls as you. I know you have been cast out as ruined by your family, and as the world is made, the ruined girl must live as a ruined girl unless she is to take the veil. However, it is a life which has its compensations, especially in the mansion of Lottie Fischer, which is, as everyone knows, the most exclusive and fashionable in town.'

"She was so straightforward and pleasant about it that I might have forgotten she was offering me a career of prostitution. Nevertheless, I could see that it was perfectly logical that she should have come to see me. That's how things were in those days. Just as she described them. I agreed to go and see her house, then—and to meet her girls, with whom she said I should get on very well. However, I was careful to tell her it was unlikely I should consider her offer favorably. She gave me her address and I promised to call that same afternoon.

"I found the house ornate, but not without taste—I'd love to *have* some of those pieces now —and was introduced to the four girls who constituted Miss Fischer's 'staff.' I found them pretty but common, and I told Miss Fischer later that I appreciated her interest, but had decided to get on as best I could otherwise. She was disappointed, I thought, but remained cordial and pleasant, making no attempt to convince me with salesmanship to remain at her house. We parted quite friendly. She told me that if I should, in the future, change my mind, she would be pleased to see me. I thanked her quite sincerely and departed.

"Once outside, I was shocked at myself for even considering such an offer, but I confess I felt a little devilish about having been inside a house of ill-repute, especially discussing employment.

"The next day, I took modest rooms in the French Quarter and spent the day reading want-ads and considering how I might best plan for my future. I observed that the requirement for references was uniform in most advertisements, and I had no references. Neither did I have experience at any kind of work. I was fortunate, however, in securing employment as tutor to three children whose French speaking mother desired them to lose their Creole accents when speaking English. In our interview, she was delighted to hear my accent, since it was obviously not even southern. I taught these children for a year, and by the time they were through, they sounded as American as I do. The lady was kind enough to find me other pupils. But it was boring.

"It was in the winter of 1898 that I again met Lottie Fischer, this time in Krauss' Department Store. I told her what I'd been doing, and she appeared to be genuinely pleased to hear that I'd been able to make my way. I invited her to luncheon, but she considerately pointed out that it would do me no good to be seen in public with her. Then, almost as an afterthought, she said, 'It seems that each time I see you I have a business proposition to offer. But it occurs to me that you might be just the one to be inter-

ested. Could I come to visit you and discuss it?' I said yes and gave her my address.

"I wish you could have seen her when she arrived at my place later in the week! My Lord, she wasn't wearing a disguise, but I never would have recognized her. She was wearing [long report of a nondescript outfit]. And this is what she told me. She said she was investing money in this new mansion on Basin Street but that she still had a property on Iberville that was too good to let go. She said she wanted a partner who could invest a little money, take care of the place, and supervise the girls. She made it sound like running a nursery. I wouldn't have to get involved with the men at all. By this time, identification with the District didn't sound so bad anymore. In the first place, it had become legal and many people thought of district property as investment just like any other business. I confess I was swayed by the apathetic attitude the public seemed to have about it. Nevertheless, I didn't think I had enough [capital] to go into it. Including the money I had originally gotten from my father and what I had been able to save from my income and earnings—you'd be amazed how far money went in those days—I had almost twelve hundred dollars. My investment in Lottie's enterprise was only seven fifty. So here I was in business for myself, and only eighteen years old. The way the arrangement was in those days, I could just collect rent from the girls—fifteen dollars a week, each. There were four of them, so I collected sixty dollars a week. Because I had the responsibility, I kept two thirds and paid Lottie one third; so I could make over two thousand dollars a year for *myself* just collecting rents! The next year she let me buy her part out for seven hundred fifty dollars.

"Meanwhile, Lottie and I became quite good friends. By now, I thought nothing at all about dropping in on her at her place on Basin Street in the morning for a cup of tea. I hadn't had a thing to do with men, in or out of the District. It may sound odd to you, but I spent a lot of time reading and taking piano lessons and practicing. I might have welcomed proper suitors, but my strange position in society made those I could have had undesirable and I had little opportunity to meet others.

"Then Lottie told me of a man she thought I'd enjoy meeting. She said he was a real gentleman, very powerful in politics and that he had seen me before, going into Lottie's. Lottie had told him all about me, and I agreed to go driving with him on a Sunday.

"We became very good friends, and eventually became partners in an excellent property which I managed and which continued right up until 1917 when we were closed by the law."

"Yes, I remember Lulu White. She was short and inclined to excessive plumpness. She dressed in atrocious taste and missed no opportunity to display her diamonds. She wore a bright red wig.

". . . Willie Piazza was an elegant lady. Did you know she wore a monocle? She wasn't pretty —in fact she had a kind of horsie look. *She* could have passed. Lulu and Piazza were the only Negro owners on Basin Street.

"Josie Arlington was a horror. She was an ugly, scarred, loudmouthed, low-class woman, but pretentious. Most of us had nothing to do with her when we could help it. I can't believe as fine a gentleman as Mr. Anderson ever had anything to do with her except in business matters.

"Both Hilma [Burt] and Gertrude [Dix] were fine ladies. We all liked Gipsy Shafer, too, although she tended to be uncouth. She was good natured. I don't know why she always picked on May Tuckerman—maybe because May seemed so ineffectual and got so furious.

"One time she found out that May was having an evening gown and two street dresses made and Gipsy got to the dressmaker and paid her quite a lot of money to make the dresses quite a bit smaller than they were supposed to be. Then she saw May on Basin Street and said, 'My, you're putting on weight, May! Better watch it!' She put some other girls up to it, too, and quite a few people were telling May she was getting too plump. Well, after the dresses were delivered, we didn't see May for nearly a month. When she did put in an appearance, she was haggard from loss of weight. Nothing but skin and bones, you know. When May found out what Gipsy had done, she tried to get her man to go and beat Gipsy up, but he thought it was the funniest thing he'd ever heard of and couldn't stop laughing. After that, we'd always tell May she'd better watch her weight and she would call us some very un-ladylike names. She eventually made up with Gipsy.

"Florence [Snooks] Randella spent more time gambling than tending to business, and it eventually ruined her. Lizzie [Lizette] Smith was really a favorite of Mr. Anderson's. She enter-

tained some of the biggest of the movie people when they came to New Orleans. I remember seeing her with Mr. Tyrone Power, Sr., Bill Farnum, and with Enrico Caruso, the opera star.

"There used to be a lot of real royalty that visited the district incognito—but King Carol

of Rumania attended one of those lewd shows of Emma Johnson's. I'm not sure whether he had become king yet at that time.

"After the District closed, I left and was married in 1919. My husband knew nothing of my previous career. He died in 1931 and I remarried in 1934. I maintained no contact with the colleagues of my Storyville days, except Gertrude Anderson [Dix]. I visit her whenever I find myself in New Orleans. I've been back frequently, especially for Carnival, which I dearly love.

"I *do* understand why there's been so much interest in Storyville in recent years. I honestly can't give you too much on the lurid side of the district."

A Crib Woman

Among the seven interviewees represented here, Carrie was the only one who had to be paid to cooperate, but only because it proved impossible to convince her that she would remain anonymous. To the very end she was convinced that her correct name and address would be given and her picture taken for publication. She felt she should be entitled to ten dollars for this. The author would have offered her at least this much in any case, her personal circumstances being such as to make such an offer logical.

Carrie is of medium build and of very dark brown pigmentation. She doesn't know her exact age but in 1961, at the time of the interview, she guessed she was about sixty-eight or nine. She took a perverse pride in the fact that both her parents had been born slaves. Her last name is French, but she does not speak the patois, though she does know some Creole words and expressions; she says that her father and mother did speak it. So far as she knows (or knew in 1961), her father is still alive, though he left home in 1928 and hasn't been heard from. Her mother still lived in New Orleans and may have been a prostitute at one time; Carrie didn't know for sure, but she couldn't see any reason why the old lady *shouldn't* have been, since times were always hard. Both parents were of the lowest economic class and worked as domestic and field laborers.

Carrie is completely illiterate. She grew up in a poor neighborhood near Perdido Street on the uptown side of Canal Street, within a block of Louis Armstrong's birthplace. Her speech is almost an unbroken stream of obscenity, scatology, and blasphemy, and she does not seem to know which terms constitute "decent" usage and which do not. Her dialect is so thick that it is difficult to follow and the author had, many times, to ask her to repeat words and sentences. In transcribing the tapes, an attempt has been made to convey something of the sound of her way of speaking, but a thoroughgoing phonetic transcription would be virtually unreadable. The following discourse is, as might be supposed, quite primitive, but is not without its poetry.

"Shit! Somebody come to Carrie to fin' out somethin'? Shit! Whut ya wanna know, mistuh? Ya wanna know was I a who'? Shit! You knowed dat befo' ya come heah! Whut d' shit you gonna put *Carrie* in a book fo'? So she can be the onliest son of a bitch dat cain't read it? Shit! I don' know when I stahted. I been fucking f'om befo' I kin remembuh! Shit, yes! Wit' my ol' man, wit' my brothas, wit' d' kids in da street. I done it fo' pennies, I done it fo' nothin' . . . An' you know whut, mistuh? I got a quatah fo' sucking off a ol' niggah yes*tiddy!* [Raucous laughter] Whut d' shit do I caiah!

"I took up livin' in d' Dist'ict in d' same day Marie Laveau die. [This reference is no doubt to the notorious Widow Paris who died in 1901. If this is the case—and it seems to be—Carrie is three or four years older than she thinks she is.] I remembuh dat, because d' day I tooken to stayin' in d' room on Rob'ts'n Street, all dem cunts was talkin' about Marie Laveau was daid. Den, d' very fustest prick dat come into dat room—a white fella, wanted to get blowed—he

says to me 'I din' expec' t' see none a youse nigguhs wuhkin' d' day Marie Laveau die.' Marie Laveau, you know—she was d' queen of d' voodoos. Sho' I b'lieve d' voodoo! Shit! You *bettah* b'leeve it! Marie Laveau! Fuck! She had some *powah!*

"I ain't *nevuh* stopped toinin' tricks, mistuh! Dey ain't many no mo'—but shit! Dem pricks givin' away money, Carrie'l take it.

"In dem days all on Rob'ts'n Street was watcha call cribs, see! Oh, you *knows* whut dey is. Well I had me one a *dem.* When I staht out in d' beginnin' I paid twenny cents a day rent. Latuh on it go up to thutty-fi' cent, and den t' fifty cent. I stayed deah on Rob'ts'n Street fo' yeahs an' yeahs . . . an' den d' law run us out. You unnastan' we wuzn' doin' nothin' agains' d' law, you know. But d' fuckin', sonabitchin' bastidd cops dey run us all out. D' fuckin' bastidds!

"Well, I use' t' get whutever I could. But mos'ly d' prices wuz d' same on d' street. Depen' was it a weekday or a Sat'dy or Sundy or a holiday—daytime, nightime, you know . . .

"Mos'ly, fo' plain fuckin' on a weekday night, I use' t' get twenny-fi' cent. Ten cents in d' daytime. We chawged fifty cent, mos' always fo' suckin' off an' seven'y-fi' cent fo' lettin' d' prick come in our ass. We didn' hawdly get no call fo' nothin' else. Good weeks I could take fo'ty dolluh. Big money dem days. All dem prices was double fo' Sat'dy an Sundy—an' they wuzn't no limit come Cawnival time.

"On Rob'ts'n Street most all dem mens what come wuz nigguhs. Dey come fo' fuckin'. Dat's all dey hawdly done.

"White boys? . . . Shit! Dey come fo' every-t'in' else. Mos'ly dey come fo' suckin' off. Sometime' dey come fo', fi', six at one time, all jam in dat po' li'l crib an' pay me a dime to let 'em watch me suck 'em. Shit! Carrie don' caiah!

"One time on d' Fo'th of July, a bunch o' white pricks grab me outten ma crib and ca'y me t' d' cohnuh. Dey taken off all ma clo'es an dey tie ma han's an' feet t' d' light pole. Den one of 'em stick a big salute [firecracker] up my cunt an' anothan one up ma ass an' he light both a dem! Shit! I *done* some holla'in'! A fuckin' police, he standin' right deah an' he laughin'. Motherfuckin' son of a bitch! Shit! Dem t'ings din' go off . . . but dey sho scaiahed d' shit outta me! Dey wuzn' loaded. It was jus' one a dem jokes, *you* know! Dey laughin' and laughin'.

"Dey ca'y me back to d' crib. Shit! I tell you

d' troof! I tell you d' troof! I was laughin' ma-self, an' cryin', shit! I din' know whut d' fuck I was doin'. Den dey tells me to blow 'em all an' dey says dey ain't gon' gimme a cent an' dey tells me lucky dey din' blow up ma cunt. So, *you* know! I done what dey said, man! I din' caiah about no money. I jus' wann see 'em get d' fuck outto ma crib. So I shet up and sucked 'em all off. When I got done, one of d' mens gimme twenny dolluh an' say Carrie is a good spo't. Den dey all sings dat song. 'Fo' She a Jolly Good Fella,' *you* knows dat song. Me, I'm thinkin' 'Jolly Good Fella'—Shit! but I taken dat twenny dolluh. Dat waz d' bigges' pay I evah got at one time—but, shit! I don' wanna make no mo' *dat* way!

"I use' t' stay aroun' by d'Frenchmans when I wuzn' in d' crib. Mosly like t'ree, fo' 'clock in d' mawnin'. Shit! I use t' *drink* some a dat Rollyrye! [Raleigh Rye whiskey was the most popular brand in the District.] Listen to dem dicty nigguhs playin' an' singin' an' ca'yin on. Bud Cawtah [Buddy Carter], dat was ma man! fo' playin' *you* know. He played dem blues *all* d' time, nuthin' but dem blues. *Low* blues, I mean, f'um *way* back-o'-town! He *played* some blues! He wuzn' hincty . . . All dem dicty people use t' hang by d' Frenchmans like t' heah dat fruit Tony Jackson bes' of anybody. But I tell ya d' troof, mistuh, dem t'ings he sing, I don' unnastan. Lotta time I din' know whut dem woids *mean*. He play pretty, I give 'm dat—but ma man was Bud Cawtah.

"Aft' awhile, ah got a stiddy man. A dawk skin woikin' man. A cawpentah. Well, shit, you know how 'tis wid dese heah who's. Evvy one a dem got a man she give all her money! I ain' no diffen' I give *mah* man mah money. One time I buy him a box back suit, an' you know what he do? He punch me in d' head an' tell me he don' need no suit, he need money. Aft' dat I jes' give him mah money. Ah doan know why. Ah jes' give him ma money.

"But, shit! Dat man wa'n't lak d' res' o' dem mens. You know whut he done? He took dat money an' he put it in d' postal savin's—like a bank dat was. Well, it wa'n't long aft' dat, de fuckin' son of a bitch *police* run us out'n d' Dist'ict. An' it look lak Carrie is in real trouble. Den dat man come an tel' me he done kep' dat money in d' postal savin's an he done tooken an' bought a barroom uptown. An' he tooken me to live in d' upstaiahs flat wit' 'm, like ma'ied folks. Co'se we din' get ma'ied.

"Lot o' us nigguhs don' get ma'ied but jus' lives like dat. Well, at dat time, me an him bot' had d' clap. He paid fo' medicine an' d' doctuh an' got us bot' cu'hed fum d' clap. At dat time, I stahted woikin' downstaiahs tendin' d' bah an' fum dat time I on'y toined tricks special times lak if us had payments t' make on d' bah an' like dat. He jus' kep' on woikin' an' I do believe he woik hisself to det'. Come d' depression, I jus' nachelly los' evvat'ing lak evvybuddy else.

"Shit! —You awright, man! You mus' be some kin' a p'fessuh—ha ha—I don' mean dem piana playin' kin' a p'fessuh—but how come you knows all 'bout d' Dist'ict? You *cain't* be ol' enuf to rec'lect d' Dist'ict. Shit! You ain't gonna take mah pitcha? You ain' gonna put mah real *name* in yo' book? Shit, man! How dem people who reads yo' book gon' know you ain't make up all whut I tol' ya? Carrie don' caiah!"

In the course of the above interview with "Carrie," *this* subject never came up, but later, though she hadn't mentioned it, the author found that in the course of her bawdy career "Carrie" had given birth to nine children, six girls and three boys, all of whom lived at least to maturity. One of the boys was killed in World War II. The rest are all alive at this writing. How she managed to survive, herself, let alone to provide for this fatherless brood, would undoubtedly make a gripping novel.

A Working Stiff

Prostitutes, pimps, madams, musicians and barkeeps made up most of the permanent population of Storyville, but on any given evening, the majority of the folk to be seen on its streets were ordinary workingmen, the backbone of the District's trade. Even as late as the 1960s, when these interviews were being conducted, it was not too difficult, in New Orleans, to find and talk to members of this giant fraternity. It soon became clear to the author that, while there might not have been such a thing as an "average" customer, the treatment that each received at the hands of the whores was almost identical. A mass service that developed mass techniques, Storyville came to be an impersonal, callous sex-mill.

In our interview with "René," we had the opportunity to glimpse the relationship between the top economic level of New Orleans society and the Basin Street mansion. "Lew," by contrast, was an "ordinary" workingman. He is a retired railword worker, now living modestly in the French Quarter. Actually, he's not "average" at all. His intellectual attainments are considerable: although his formal education did not extend into the first year of high school, he has a good working knowledge of four languages and reads assiduously in all of them. He is a mild old gentleman, slight of build, one of many to be seen almost any morning in New Orleans, sitting in rocking chairs on the banquettes in front of their houses, reading books or newspapers. He recalls the past:

"I'd probably be better off today if I'd never heard of it [Storyville] . . .

"Naturally, as a wage laborer, I couldn't afford those luxury palaces on Basin Street—but there were little parlor houses on Iberville Street. . . . I've heard the cost of sex in the days of the District discussed with no agreement reached on the facts by many who had and had not had experience in the tenderloin. Some say the cribs went from twenty-five cents to a dollar, the parlor houses a dollar to two and the mansions from five to fifty dollars. . . . The real truth is, though, that an evening in *any* house, no matter what the going rate was reported to be, always cost you just as much as you had in your pocket.

"Those places were organized to take *all* your money. Let's say you went into a so-called two-dollar house. Well, you couldn't very well sit down in the parlor without buying a little wine

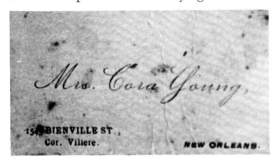

or at least putting some change in the player piano. It would cost you usually a couple of dollars before you even got around to the business you came for. Clever girls, once they got you in a boudoir, would always offer little 'extra' services, for 'extra' prices, naturally—and you'd *pay!* Things are not easy to resist at such times. Of course, they never tried to sell you anything *afterwards*. They were smart enough to know that the man leaving is not the same man

as the man entering. I heard that Grace Hayes had a pet raccoon that was trained to pick the pockets of her customers. If that isn't true it's the only story I know about ways to take your money in the District that wasn't.

"I remember when the train used to pull into the sheds at the old station, I'd look out from the cab—we'd come in *real* slow—and there'd be the girls standing at the windows, all dressed up in fancy clothes—just posing, you know. My god they looked pretty from that distance. I couldn't wait to get out of the engine cab, get my card punched out and run right over to the District—and I mean *run!* I was only nineteen or twenty then—and at that age a young fellow *will* run for something like that. I had a locker to change clothes, you know—and I'd leave most of my money in it, but I'd take along five dollars. I'd get it changed so as to have a two-dollar bill to pay the woman; then I'd have a one dollar bill to pay for the bottle of wine. Then I'd get four quarters to drop in the mechanical piano for music and dancing. Then two fifty-cent pieces to do for 'extras'. You had to do it this way, because you couldn't ever get change for anything. Once you'd hand over any kind of a bill or coin, that was it. That would be the last you'd see of it. After all, you'd figure, that's the business they're in. That was part of the game . . . really the *main* part . . .

"Then when you first went *in* the house, why there'd be the girls, maybe three or four—dressed up to kill—in ball gowns and things like that. They were young girls, mostly—and usually good-looking ones. The player piano only had *fast* tunes. I used to *like* to dance—but I like waltzes and slow things. But it seemed like everything they did was fast, especially take all your money and get you out of there so they could take on more customers. Well, the girls would dance with you as long as you kept on feeding the box. Of course, the minute you got in the door you'd find the maid there, a colored girl, wearing one of those maid's uniforms, with a maid's cap and an apron and asked you what you wanted to drink. You'd get a quart of wine and see that all the girls had a drink.

"Well, after a couple of dances—maybe you'd dance with each one of the girls—they'd rub up against you and tell you in your ear what they could do for you, until you made up your mind which one you wanted and then you'd take her—or *she'd* take *you* upstairs to a small 'boudoir'. They all called 'em 'boudoir's in those houses. You wouldn't believe how fast those girls could get their clothes off. Usually, they'd leave on their stockings and earrings, things like that. A man usually took off his trousers and shoes. New girls didn't give you a second to catch your breath before they'd be all over you, trying to get you to heat up and go off as soon as possible. The more experienced ones knew that if they'd give a fellow a minute to relax first they could get the business over with sooner . . . When it came down to the actual act, though, the routine was standard.

"She'd take hold of your prick and milk it to see if you had the clap. I think the girls could diagnose clap better than the doctors at that time. She'd have a way of squeezing it that, if there was anything in there, she'd find it. Then she'd wash it off with a clean wash cloth. They had little washstands. There'd be a pile of wash cloths and a pile of clean towels on the washstand. Then she'd fill the basin with water and put in a few drops of purple stuff—permanganate of potash, it was—they didn't have Lysol in those days—then she'd wash you with it. She'd lay on her back and get you to top of her so fast, you wouldn't even know you'd come up there on your own power. She'd grind so that you almost felt like you had nothing to do with it. Well, after that, she had you. She could make it go off as quickly as she wanted to—and she didn't waste any time, I'll tell you . . . I'd say that the whole thing, from the time you got in the room until the time you came didn't take three minutes.

"She'd wash you off again, and herself. Then she'd get dressed, without even looking at you —you could see she was already thinking about nothing but getting downstairs. But she'd be smiling, though, as if everything was just fine and she'd had a good time. You'd give her your two-dollar bill and get your trousers and shoes on. I'll tell you, five minutes was a long time to spend in one of those rooms. In fact, from the time you'd come in the front door of the house until you'd be back out on the banquette hardly ever took more than fifteen minutes! And there you'd be, standing on the banquette without a cent in your pocket, and no place to go but maybe home. And that would be the last place in the world you'd want to go.

"I'd go back over to the station and get a few more dollars out of my locker, and go back to the District. I guess my favorite spot to go to was Frank Early's saloon. I'd just sit around there and have a few drinks—maybe hang around until three o'clock in the morning. There'd be fellows I knew and we'd talk. Oh, yes—the whorehouses would give you a little lagniappe when you left. Sometimes a flower for your buttonhole or a feather they'd stick in your hatband. Those days, everybody wore a hat. When I first started going around to these places, I thought they were just being nice, but I found out later that they had something like a trade association among themselves and that they'd pass these things out to mark you, so that the hustlers in the bars and night clubs would know you'd already had it for that night and not to waste time hustling you for *that*.

"In the saloons they had these girls, too, mostly a lot tougher. They'd be what you call today, 'B-girls.' If you weren't *marked* (with a flower or feather) one of these girls would come up to the bar and ask you if you'd like to go sit in a booth with her and buy her a drink. If you did, she'd have her drink with you, probably hers would have hardly any alcohol in it, and she'd try to get you to take her either to a house or sometimes upstairs in the cabaret. And when I say *try*, I mean she'd put her hand in your pants or anything else to get you excited enough to take her up on it. You know there were 'rooming' houses there where you could just take your own girl and rent a room by the hour or half-hour. You'd get a room with a bed in it and a towel, a wash cloth or sponge and a little bar of soap for fifty cents. Strong smelling soap that looked and smelled like Octagon soap they used to use to do the laundry.

"How did I feel about it all? That's a sensible question. I wish I could give you a straight answer. One thing, though, I was never satisfied. I don't mean that I thought that the girls or the district had cheated me—but I always had the feeling afterwards that *life* had cheated me. I always had the feeling that there must be something more—more *fun*, you know . . . Of course, they'd drain me off. I'd be depleted and enervated—but I never had the feeling of satisfaction that I was always looking for. The truth is that a man wants something more from a woman than that—and it's not easy to find even outside a district. Most all the married women you run across are just a different kind of whore. But a man keeps looking for somebody he can just feel—well, like he isn't always *alone*. That's why I had a hard time deciding to get married, and that was a mistake. I'd have been better off to take one of those girls out of a parlor house and make her respectable. My marriage didn't last very long.

"When they closed the District down, I kept on going to whorehouses. It wasn't so convenient anymore, because they were all over town. It helped that the prices went down on account of

Miss Flossie Smith,

1407 Customhouse st.   New Orleans.

the increased competition—but if anything, you felt like you were getting even less for your money than ever before.

"Yes, I did get hooked with venereal disease. It wasn't cured, but it was well-controlled by the doctors so that I never thought I felt any serious ill-effects from it. Then, about twenty or twenty-five years ago—whenever penicillin came out—I got cured.

"I guess I'm pretty lucky that by the time the reformers drove the price of whoring up to where a working man can't buy it, I didn't need it any more.

"No, I can't say I have happy memories of the District. If I hadn't had it to fall back on, I might have made more of myself. But then, I can't blame what my life turned out to be on the District. I just had a weakness for those whores —and they were so easy to get. But I think the young men today—and the young girls, too— would be better off if they had a regular district going, instead of the way things are now."

A Working Girl

Lola was born in the Dominican Republic, but to most of May Spencer's Storyville patrons (and no doubt to May, herself) the geographic and ethnic status of such a place was vague and uncertain and so Lola was represented as being Cuban—and she still so represents herself. It matters not that neither Lola nor her parents ever saw Cuba.

In 1961, when these interviews were conducted, Lola had been in the United States for fifty years. Married in Santo Domingo at the age of sixteen, she was brought to New Orleans by her husband in 1911 and abandoned within the year. She still speaks English with a very strong Latin-American accent, and her command of the language is extremely limited. Most of the author's questions had to be asked in Spanish. Her own Spanish, colloquial in the extreme, was even less intelligible than her English, so she told her story, as best she could, in the latter language. An attempt has been made to convey something of the phonetic flavor of her English (an exact phonetic transliteration would be virtually unreadable). Omitted passages, indicated by dots, represent false starts caused by language difficulties.

The subject was selected as representative of the few surviving regular working girls of one of the better Basin Street mansions for five years or more. She never aspired to go into business for herself. She now has a share in a small barroom and spends almost all of her time sitting there, sipping a drink, though she actually consumes relatively little alcohol in an average day. Once she must have been quite beautiful, one of those Latin "spitfire" types who might have been billed, had she gone into pictures, as "The Cuban Bombshell" or some like title.

"... May Spencer, she's right nex' door Weelie Piazza on Basin Street, hah? You know thees place? Oh, no. You too young. May Spencer, she's Dago, you know. She's speak espanish, too. She's take me in her house 1911— I coo'n't speak no Eenglish. She's treat me better than my mawther, May Spencer. People says she rooeen't me, May Spencer. She din' rooeen't me! I was *puta* [whore] at home befor' I come dees country.

"... Home, I din' have fine clothes, I din' have mawney, I din' have nawthing but goo-for-nawting hawsban' mak' me work for heem.

"I start to work for May Spencer when I'm seexteen years. You wanna know what I *do* dare? You *know* what I do, no? ... But ees not de same all over de worl' de ... bueno, you wanna know—de *routine?* Como se dice— how you say *routine* een Espanish? Ah! Si ... de details of de life ... bueno ... I get up each day, t'ree, faw in de afternoon ... We eat downstair—ees no dining room, ess keetchen weet' roun' table—we eat. Seex, sometime seven, eight muchachas. Si, coffee, French bread—not very much we hongry in de mawning ... To us, mawning, si ... Everybody talk, talk, like young girl she talk, hah? ... Yes, I am de younges', but de oldes' maybe twenny-wan, two.

163

May Spencer may be thirty-fi'—but she talk, too, like young girl. We do nawthing till maybe seven o'clock. We take bath. May Spencer have *two* bathtubs. *Piazza* don' have two bathtubs . . . Everything very clean by May Spencer. We dress always party clothes. I hav' nine party dress, two street dress. Den, pues, we seet! No. Upstairs we seet een our room. Later, maybe eight o'clock, downstair de bell she's ring. We go, *all* de girls, we go downstairs, because when de bell she's ring, ees because a man you know —a cawstomer hees cawm een. Eef ees *beeg*, tall man, de leetle girls go by heem, talk to heem . . . Eef ees *leetle* man, de *beeg* girls talk with heem . . . Quien sabe? . . . May Spencer, she unnerstan' t'ings like dees, she make plenny mawney. What I say to man? I say, you know, 'Hello, hawney!' I say 'My, you so han'some, why you no come before?'. I say 'You jus' my type!' T'ings like dat dey don' mean nawthing, but de man like dees, hah?

"We drink wine weet' heem. Een May Spencer house she have only good wine. De piano player he play . . . yes, si! I remember some dem song. I learn Eenglish from song. He play, 'My Wife She's Gone to de Country, Hooray! Hooray!' Very funny! He's play 'O, You Byooteefool Doll' . . . My favoreet ees 'Meet Me Tonight Een Dreamlan'. Ees very preety dees song. We try to dance weet' man. Mos' man, he don' wan' dance, he always geev more mawney to piano player den man who *like* dance. I don' know why. Ees always dees way.

"Aft' while, de man he peek out wheech girl he gon' take, you know, for upstairs—an' dey go. Eef ees me, we go to nex' floor, I have room weet all kin' Mexican t'ings. Ees sombreros, you know, mantillas, serapes, all dees t'ings. I nevair see such t'ings at home, but May Spencer, she teenk good idea for my room, she teenk eet look very Cuban. You know wan t'ing. I teenk

dey don' have t'ings like dees een Cuba, too, hah? She call me 'la Cubana' an' she geev me Mexican t'ings! Ha ha!

"I take off my party dress . . . I exameen hees, heem, you know, to see he has not de clap. I wash heem weet' dat medeecene stoff. I lay on de bed, an' he do what he want. Ees nawthing, you know—maybe wan, two minute. Si! I can make heem do eet queecker, but mos' all de time eet ees not necessary. He ees queeck by heemself.

"I take de mawney, at lees fi' dollair an I go downstair . . . Ah, Si! I get dress again firs', ha, ha! De mawney I geev to de maid. She hol's all de mawney. Den I wait for one more man.

"Mos' I take t'ree, faw men upstair every night. Saturday, Sawnday, fi', seex, seven. Mardi gras, I don' know . . . Si, we work every night—well, dose time, once a mont' like you say, we go on 'Old Country Time' May Spencer call eet. Dat mean we tak' care awv cawstomer deeferent way, you know . . . Si, like dey cawl 'French.' Some dem houses on Basin Street don' do hardly nawthing else *bot* dat—bawt een May Spencer house only each girl once a mont'.

"Maybe t'ree o'clock in de mawning, we eat. Ees good comida in May Spencer house. Ees always bes' meat, fuit, vegetables—all you wan'. Plenny bawtter; plenny meelk. Some time we get hongry before dat, we sen' street boy to Toro for po'-boy sanweech. Ees always lee'l boy in street, dey run faw you. He breeng po'-boy sanweech, I pay heem. You don' *teep* heem because Toro geev heem, how you say, commeession, bawt *I* always geev heem fi' cent. He, Toro, he make special po-boy jus' faw *putas*, no awnions—you know because de mens dey don' like smell awnions.

"Sawmtime we get up early, go by Canal Street an' look in de staws. Ees manny t'ings een de staws an' we got plenny mawney you know for buy annyt'ing; but clothes, mos' de time we buy from salesmens dey come from Nort'. De salesmen, you know, dey got t'ings, more how you say up-to-date.

"May Spencer she's tell us salesman he gon' be dere Sawnday ten o'clock in de mawning we get up early we get dress to see clothes. One girl, a blonde hair girl, she *marry* wan dees salesmens she go leev een Cheecago. De salesman he tak' orders he write een hees book. May Spencer she pay faw everyt'ing, and den she tak' back a leetle every week unteel ees enough mawney. All de womens dey see us een Canal Street dey look on our dresses an' dey know dey deen come from no staws een New Orleans, so dey know we all *puta*—but we don' care. *Dey* all *putas,* too!

"W'en de District she close, May Spencer she say she gon' open new house someplace else. She geev me mawney an' [I] promeese I gon' go work for her some maw—bot dey poot her een jail two, t'ree day, an' she go 'way an' I don' see her no maw. I get two letters from her she sen' from Pheeladelphia about nineteen twenny. Nineteen twenny I get marry. Wan maw time nineteen t'irty tree.

"May Spencer treat me real good. Like maw-ther. Better."

So ends our brief excursion into the lives of a handful of the survivors of the rigors of life in Storyville. One wonders where was the glamor in which legend has wrapped the District.

(Photograph by Ernest Bellocq)

165

TEN

The Triumph of Virtue

Hesitation Blues

"Legislature voted the District down . . .
Legislature voted the District down . . .
Damn good way to spread the hookers over town.
Tell me how long will I have to wait?
Can I have it now—
Or must I hesitate?"

This song parody, sung by the New Orleans musicians right after the District was closed down, expressed the feelings of most Orleanians. Its third line proved to be prophetic.

※※※

Like everything else about Storyville, its disestablishment has been romanticized and sentimentalized by film and television producers, by some self-anointed jazz "experts," and by certain writers of popular social history. We have been asked to imagine the likes of a Mr. Tom Anderson and Mmes. Lulu White, Countess Willie V. Piazza, and Josie Arlington sitting around a table in the Arlington Annex drinking bittersweet toasts to past glories as they await the first strokes of the clock signaling the precipitous closing of their gay, colorful amusement park, while outside a pitiful parade of tearful hearts-of-gold harlots in carriages and platoons or whores on the hoof (with mattresses on their backs) move down Basin Street to the accompaniment of such old blues standards as *Stormy Weather, Moanin' Low,* and *Blues in the Night,* as played and sung by a horde of ragged jazz musicians and the Hall Johnson Choir.

Such imaginings, epitomized in the late-1940s film *New Orleans,* to which the likes of Louis Armstrong and Billie Holiday lent their names and reputations, are as close to the reality of Storyville's last days as the tunes just named are to the blues—light-years away.

To confine matters to what *actually* occurred in Storyville in these days, we offer the following chronology of events as they happened:

August 1917: Open prostitution is banned within five miles of any United States army installation, by order of Secretary of War Newton D. Baker, and Secretary of the Navy Josephus Daniels follows suit with respect to United States naval installations.

August 27–31: Mr. Bascom Johnson representing the War and Navy departments, makes a personal tour of Storyville and interviews Tom Anderson and other leaders of New Orleans "Society." He declares that the area falls within the definition of Secretary Daniels' decree on the subject of prostitution and instructs Mayor Martin Behrman to comply forthwith.

September 10: Mayor Behrman travels to Washington to protest the Navy Department's high-handed actions but fails even to secure an appointment with either Daniels or President Wilson. Thus the top brass of the American democracy evince no interest in even hearing the merits of the case discussed.

September 24: Mayor Behrman receives the following incredible—and some would say illegal—threat from Secretary Daniels: "You close the red-light district or the armed forces will."

October 1: A "last warning" is issued.

October 2: Mayor Behrman presents to the City Council an ordinance providing for the disestablishment of Storyville.

October 9: The ordinance, to take effect at midnight, November 12, 1917, is passed under protest by the City Council.

October 13: The New Orleans *Times-Picayune* publishes the rumor that owners of Basin Street houses and others plan to burn their brothels down in order to collect on the fire insurance. The state fire marshal promises an investigation but turns up no evidence of such a plot.

October 15: Leading insurance firms cancel fire insurance in Storyville properties.

November 10: The bulk of the New Orleans police force is assigned to the District to put down riots and demonstrations but there are none. Many of the houses have already closed and the occupants have vacated the premises and resumed business elsewhere in the city.

November 11: Civil Court Judge F. D. King refuses Gertrude Dix' request for an injunction to prevent the city from legally enforcing the ordinance to close Storyville.

A 1940s sign of the times, when what was left of Storyville was being torn down to make way for a housing project. (Photograph by Dave Scherman)

In 1938 much of Basin Street was still standing, but it had not been "open for business" since 1917. The vice it had once harbored and kept within bounds was now to be found in every part of town. The two-story place in the right foreground (No. 317), was Countess Willie V. Piazza's. The Great Depression was reflected in the sign on the side of No. 301, formerly Frank Toro's Monte Carlo Cabaret: "All Day Parking—5 Cents." The four vacant sites making up the parking lot once boasted the establishments of May Spencer (No. 315), Lillian Irwin (No. 313), Bertha Weinthal (No. 311), and Frances Gilbert (No. 307). The two-story brick place on the corner (No. 239), was Lulu White's saloon, on the second floor of which Billy Struve maintained his offices. The larger building visible directly behind it is Mahogany Hall, minus its cupola.

167

The uptown lake corner of Franklin and Conti streets before demolition. Maud Hartmann's brothel, the Club, is at the left (with little girl on step). Sophie Fielure occupied the place in the center, and Edna Hamilton received guests in the building on the corner. (Photograph by Dave Scherman)

November 11: The Supreme Court of Louisiana rejects Miss Dix' petition for a writ of mandamus requiring the city court to issue an injunction.

November 12: All remaining madams and houses are personally informed by policemen that they can continue to live where they are but cannot continue to do business without facing arrest and prosecution.

Midnight, November 12: Most inhabitants are long gone from Storyville, but some stay on and continue to do business, with police protection.

Beginning on October 9, 1917, when the ordinance to close the District was adopted, most of its denizens prepared to leave. They viewed the close-down as politically motivated and planned to move to other parts of town and to continue operation on an illegal basis. This they did.

During the next thirty days, moving vans were to be seen hauling furniture, some to these new addresses, others to the warehouses of the secondhand dealers, who took advantage of the plight of the madams by paying picayune amounts for expensive items. Willie Piazza's celebrated white piano, for example, which she had kept in tune for the likes of Tony Jackson and Jelly Roll Morton, was knocked down for an incredible dollar and a quarter. Gradually and quietly the District closed up shop, and by deadline time the streets were virtually unoccupied. What had until very lately been America's only legal red-light district had faded into history. On June 20 of the following year, Gertrude Dix was sentenced to five days in jail for operating a house of ill-repute (at her old address), as were a number of other madams rounded up in various raids.

Purely from a practical viewpoint, Storyville had demonstrably provided the best practical solution to the problem of controlling prostitution that the nation had yet seen—or has seen to this day. In the first place, the fact of a legal district emboldened the citizenry to demand strict enforcement of the law, so that no house could long operate in a "respectable" neighborhood without experiencing a great deal of trouble from police. It is a fact that almost immediately upon establishment of Storyville, and throughout its twenty years, there just were no functioning houses of ill-fame in New Orleans

The downtown river corner of Iberville and Franklin streets in 1942, as the demolition of Storyville continued. Only the front of the Entertainers was still standing (behind automobiles); this structure, in which many famous jazzmen once played, was also known as the 101 Ranch, the 102 Ranch, and Phillips' Café. Behind it, Mahogany Hall is visible, its famous cupola already gone. The name "Lala's" was imbedded in the banquette of the corner building.

outside the District and the small Negro section around Perdido and Gravier streets (which was formally legalized early in 1917, on a racially segregated basis, before the federal intervention). More striking still was the undeniable fact that legalization actually brought about a statistical reduction in the incidence of prostitution in the city.

Instituted by ordinance in 1897, Storyville began legal operation on January 1, 1898. In 1899 the city fathers, in a report signed by Mayor Walter C. Flower and Chief of Police D. S. Gaster, counted some two thousand prostitutes in Storyville, occupying two hundred and thirty houses, cabarets, houses of assignation, and cribs. A decade later, the United States census report for 1910 showed a decline of fifty-five houses and cribs, and a decline in the number of prostitutes to eight hundred, of whom two hundred fifty were black, four hundred fifty white. Lulu White, who had flaunted thirty-one octoroons in 1900, now employed only three on a regular basis. These declines took place in the face of an increase of some fifty thousand in the city's population—and a river- and seaport city, at that.

By 1917, then, precious few tarnished ladies remained to evacuate Storyville. There were only sixteen houses worthy of the term, and about seventy-five one-girl cribs. The total number of women involved was about four hundred, about half of whom were working only on a part-time basis. Crib rentals had dropped from the 1904 peak of three dollars fifty cents a night to half a dollar.

Throughout the Storyville period reformers had quivered with righteous frustration and cried for abolition of the District. They made much of the "blot" on the city and pointed to Basin Street as the "cradle of crime" and the "destruction of Southern womanhood," never facing the fact that year by year the city was witnessing an undeniable decline of the "social evil" for the first time in the history of New Orleans or, for that matter, in the history of any large American city. It is heartening to recall that the demise of Storyville was not accomplished through the efforts of these loud-mouthed, self-righteous know-nothings but came about by order of the federal government, which ignored the city's needs and history against the will and good judgment of the majority of its citizens. But the reformers were happy, anyway.

It is instructive to take note of what they were happy about.

To begin with, the town began at once to fester with vice. North Rampart Street, Julia Street, and Tulane Avenue began to sprout passion blooms. Within a year there were streetwalkers and houses of assignation throughout New Orleans. Police books again were loaded down with ineffectual arrests and ineffectual sentences. The French Quarter became a pesthole of prostitution once more. Bienville, Conti, Dauphine, St. Louis, Burgundy, and Toulouse streets, redeemed for two decades from the blight of prostitution, were once more overpopulated with vulgar whores each striving to outdo the others in snatching unwary males from the street by fair means or foul.

Cab drivers and bellboys found that the real money in their jobs came through procuring and pimping, and by the end of 1918 bellboys in the leading hotels were actually *paying* a thousand dollars a year for their jobs. Payoffs to politicians and police again assumed major proportions and the taint of vice spread into every district of the city, uptown to the elaborate Garden District residential section, and all the way out to Carrollton. Wherever there were people there was vice.

Control became a futile aspiration when both police and public could see that the only truly effective control policies in their history had been outlawed by federal intervention. The city surrendered to uncontrolled vice and saw itself devaluated and corrupted beyond its worst fears.

As Louis Armstrong recalled, in his *True* magazine article (November, 1947):

The river side of Marais Street from Conti to St. Louis. These higher class cribs actually had inside plumbing. The three identical buildings kept two dozen women employed in 1904.

. . . that's when the United States Navy commenced to getting warm . . . and that meant trouble and more trouble. Not only for the vice displayers but for all the poor working people who made their living in Storyville such as dishwashers—and lots of people whom were in different vocations. . . . I'm telling you it was a sad situation for anybody to witness. . . . I was only fifteen years old . . . but at that age —being around from a real young age delivering stone coal in those cribs—hanging around the pimps, Cotch players, etc., I really knew what it was all about. . . . So I had to feel sorry just like the rest of them. . . . The law commenced to arrest all the prostitutes they caught standing in the doors. . . . And send them over to Isolation Hospital to be examined. . . . And if they had the least thing wrong with them—or they're blood bad—they'd be sent away for a long time. . . . And believe me, they were lots of prostitutes who had to be sent away for treatment. . . . And of course reports from those cases help the Navy to have a strong alibi to close her down. . . .

After Storyville closed down—the people of that section spreaded out all over the city. . . . So we turned out nice and reformed. Some went into other neighborhoods kind'a bootlegging the same thing. . . . Especially the neighborhoods which was lively and jumped just a wee bit. . . . In the Third Ward where I was raised there were always a lot of honky-tonks, gambling, prostitutes, pimps going on. . . . But all on a small scale. Very small at that. . . . Where it would cost you from three to five dollars to see a woman in Storyville—it didn't cost but fifty to seventy-five cents to see and be with a woman in the Third Ward. . . . There were no whites up this way at all. They were all colored. Right *amongst* all this vice—I still went to Fisk School, right in the heart of it all. At Franklin and Perdido Streets . . . every corner had a saloon and honky-tonk in the rear. . . . They call them lounges up North. Of course, those honky-tonks weren't as elaborate either. . . . But I'm just trying to give a fast picture of how a lounge would look in the rough without all of that swell ta doo stuff they put in nowadays. Decorately speaking. . . .

They weren't any standing in the doors, either. . . . Because after Storyville closed—that one situation wasn't supposed to ever happen in New Orleans again. . . . And it didn't. Now after Storyville shut down, the girls couldn't just call out the doors for beer. But the wrinkle was— they could catch a "john" [a customer] and call down to whatever saloon they'd like to trade with and say these words "Oh Bell Boy Oh Bell Boy" and when the bell boy from that particular saloon answers this chick will say to him "Bring me half a can." . . . Which means a nickel of beer. . . . And he'll say O.K. and into the saloon and repeat the same thing—and less than a few minutes he'll be on his way over to this

The uptown river corner of St. Louis and Marais streets in the District. (Photograph by Scoop Kennedy)

small-time whore's house with this half a can (nickel of beer). . . . She meets him at the door with her bucket or pitcher—he pours it in and collects the "Tack" (I mean the nickel) and returns to the saloon and sits outside on a beer barrel and waits for another order. . . . He gets a salary just delivering drinks. . . .

The scene a few years later, during the 1920s, was well described by Robert Tallant in his book *Romantic New Orleanians:*

There were many cheap bars and after Prohibition many speak-easies—several to a block in some places, which did not bother to conceal their existence. There were one or two of these latter that became almost smart—such as the old Press Club—but most were shoddy, forbidding and the frequent scene of brawls, sometimes of murder.

But none of this was what the uptown ladies meant when they shook their heads and whispered about "Frenchtown." What they were thinking about were the prostitutes and the open sexual immorality then operating in the section. For along certain streets, such as Bienville, Conti, Dauphine and St. Louis, there were lines of houses of prostitution, most of them cheap cribs, the remains of what had once been one of the most gilded and rococo red-light districts in the United States. When Basin Street closed and prostitution became "illegal," many of the women had simply moved a little closer to the river, into the Creoles' city, and others of the more unappetizing sort had hurried to New Orleans to join them.

Prostitution in the French Quarter after World War I was devoid of the faintest hint of glamour. Competition was keen, so labor was cheap; there were hundreds of women who were glad to let a man into their houses for two dollars, many who would accept a dollar, and some who would even take fifty cents when business was bad or on a rainy Monday night. Strangers in the city compared it all with the worst districts of Marseilles, of Honolulu, of Singapore. Women stood naked in doorways, behind drawn blinds, or sat in windows, calling out to passing men. Some of them stood on sidewalks in kimonos, which they would flash open now and then to display their bodies. A few would even seize a man as he went by and try to argue him into doing business. There were cheap dance halls here and there, too, which later became taxi-dance halls that featured loud jazz bands. There were other shows, also—the "circuses" or "Freak shows," as displays of eccentric forms of eroticism were called.

The "action" available to the visitor to New Orleans nowadays is tawdry and sordid enough to cause oldtimers—some of them, at least—to remember Storyville with affection.

Bourbon Street, which replaced Basin Street

as the Crescent City's sin-image, is a welter of unattractive and usually dirty saloons (the washrooms, especially, must be seen to be believed), most of which feature platoons of stripteasers billed as "exotic" dancers. They are, by and large, harridans in varying stages of physical decomposition (some are in their fifties) whose dancing consists largely of making the copulatory movements known in their trade as "bumps" and "grinds." These they embellish with vulgar hand gestures that they hope will be effective as a come-on to men at the bar or passing by on the street. As the doorman—often the most talented entertainer in the place—delivers his carny pitch on the erotic delights allegedly to be found within, opening and closing the front doors so as to allow his sidewalk audience to see some of the action on stage (but not so much as to be turned off by it), the women on-stage inside divest themselves of their scanty costumes to display bodies scrawny, bloated, wrinkled, or flabby—and naked except for the legally required "pasties" concealing the nipples of the breasts and very, very brief panties, called a "patch," designed to cover the pudendum while leaving the buttocks exposed and free to wiggle—a garment that frequently has the effect of emphasizing the flaccidity of the wearer's belly.

When they are not on stage, the prime role of these women is to mix with the customers in an effort to persuade them to buy more drinks at unlikely prices. They are of course less interested in the customers' drinks than in their own far more expensive "B-drinks," which they surreptitiously spit into a chaser glass. (After all, who wants to swallow a gallon of weak tea or watered sauterne in the course of a night's work!) The "persuasion" is accomplished by means ranging from crude flattery to groping the patron under the table. Most of these women are available for sexual games at prices as inflated for value offered as the highly dilute beverages dispensed by the management.

In more recent years, in the late 1960s and early 1970s, first "topless" and lately "topless and bottomless" go-go dancing, sometimes on table tops in a few establishments, have been added to Bourbon Street's offerings, but even in these places voyeurs out for raw meat are usually cheated: the inevitable pasties are kept carefully in place all the time (being a considerable bother to put on and take off, according to the women who have to wear them), and the patch, almost never removed for the audience, is pulled aside rarely if at all, and then only for a special customer known not to be "fuzz" and willing to pay big for a brief peek (a "flash") at what it conceals.

In still other establishments female impersonators do their grotesque parodies of strippers and go-go girls—but not "bottomless," as this would destroy the illusion. There are "gay" bars galore, and troupes of male hustlers looking for "new friends" along the several Bourbon Street blocks from St. Peter Street up to the Jean Lafitte hotel and in Jackson Square. On some nights there seem to be more male streetwalkers than female, though there are so many of both sexes that keeping count would be impossible. Other homosexuals linger in the men's rooms of a half-dozen pornographic movie theaters and peep shows, on the apparent theory that some of the male patrons, especially those in their thirties or older, will be susceptible to their wiles. For "straight" patrons not interested in so "changing their luck," as the saying goes, "massage parlors" in the immediate vicinity of some of the theaters offer "physical therapy" to those in need—masturbation usually, fellatio if the man has the price, but almost never copulation, at least not on the premises, since that would require the girl to divest herself of her pasties and patch!

Adjoining Jefferson Parish has its houses of prostitution, which employ New Orleans cab drivers, on commission, to "steer" suckers into them. Here, too, the going rate varies but is always too much for value received, and cab fare alone may run to twenty or thirty dollars. Moreover, the "mark" is also encouraged to lose his money in various gambling games. Most of these resorts are "bust-out" places, which means woe betide the hired help if the sucker leaves with more than his return cab fare. It is no secret that a large number of cabbies supplement their own incomes, too, by "rolling," or taking the money from the pockets of, intoxicated customers. These cabbies solicit openly on the streets. It is not unusual for the driver to have a prostitute right in the cab with him, in the front seat, and to offer her back-seat favors for whatever price he thinks the traffic will bear.

Besides these civic attractions, there is available a horde of younger and much more attractive call girls who may be brought to the guest's hotel room by the enterprising bellhop. Their fees range from fifty to a hundred dollars and are out of reach of the average Orleanian and even most visitors not on expense accounts. Rarely has the author walked alone in the area of Bourbon Street without being solicited for such services. He has made it his business to

Condemned in 1939, these Robertson Street cribs, in the "Negro" section of the District, rented for twenty cents a night in 1899, three or three and a half dollars a night in 1913, and less than a dollar a night by the end of 1915, as the District's fortunes fluctuated. (Photograph by John W. "Knocky" Parker)

establish the fact that prostitutes may be had for the asking in most of the city's hotels.

It is not to be assumed that the authorities have made no effort to establish effective controls. For one thing, they insist on those pasties and patches. And not too many years ago exception was taken to the posters outside of the upholstered sewers of Bourbon Street showing naked (and inexcusably homely) females. The proprietors were required to cover all exposed navels in those photographs, which they did—with tiny bows of silk ribbon. Let no one say that the Crescent City isn't on its toes in the suppression of vice!

The most effective symbol of the effects of social hypocrisy on the city may be cited in the revolting spectacle of a saloon that prospers just off Bourbon Street. Here, no prostitution occurs or is encouraged; there are no B-girls employed by the management. Instead it has made itself the headquarters for hordes of exhibitionistic and immature "collegiate" elements. During holiday periods, these well-to-do young hoodlums, the scum of the South's colleges and universities, make the street an impassable thoroughfare heaped with empty beer cans, vomit, and unbelievable quantities of broken glass that the "high-spirited" young gentlemen and Southern belles hurl to the pavement.

The late Tom Anderson once stormed out of his place brandishing a baseball bat to disperse a small group of Tulane lads who were serenading in front of the brothel of his lady love, Gertrude Dix, with their own version of "I Wish I Was in Dixie." Such pranks, considered scandalous even by the bawds of Basin Street, were harmless in contrast with the sometimes wanton and vicious acts perpetrated in today's French Quarter by the latter-day "college crowd," including the many self-styled "revolutionaries" whose actual "cause," with few exceptions, is hedonistic self-indulgence. Force of numbers makes them feel free to insult escorted women of all ages, to mangle the radio antennae and slash the tires of parked automobiles, and occasionally to enjoy a fun-killing. A few years back, for example, "students" cold-bloodedly murdered a homosexual in Père Antoine's Alley without reprisal from the law—all in the name of good clean fun.

By comparison, the "action" still to be found in the vicinity of the old Negro red-light district, to which allusion has been made several times

The uptown corner of Marais and Conti streets before demolition in 1939. The parlor house on the left, behind the boy, was Alice Perry's place of business. (Photograph by Dave Scherman)

A row of cribs, barred and marked for demolition, on the downtown side of Conti Street, as seen through the characteristic wrought iron of a brothel gallery on the uptown lake corner of Marais and Conti streets. (Photograph by Dave Scherman)

Above left: Mahogany Hall, its famed cupola long-gone, just before its demolition. On the right, Lulu White's saloon, with Billy Struve's offices on the second floor. Above right: Up these steps climbed many an affluent "sport," eager to rent one of Lulu White's bevy of delectable octoroons. Bottom: Inside Mahogany Hall in later years. (Bottom photograph by Dave Scherman)

in these pages, seems almost benign in its honest depravity.

As noted elsewhere in this work, the original Storyville ordinances specified the limits of an uptown restricted district but its actual establishment was postponed. As matters turned out, this district was not established until early 1917, and thus enjoyed legal status for only a few months before being closed down, supposedly, by the federal government.

Oddly enough, the same ordinance, reproduced elsewhere in this volume, provided that Storyville would henceforth be all white—a provision that posed a serious problem for the likes of the Countess Willie Piazza and Lulu White, both of whom would have been required to move their brothels to the uptown district, had not both districts been disestablished later in the year.

At all events, the uptown district had been operating right along, illegally but with legal status promised for the future. Because it had been illegal in the eyes of the city authorities during most of its existence, this uptown district was not greatly disturbed when the federal authorities also declared it to be illegal, along with Storyville. Indeed, many of the uptown bawds hardly noticed the change. Certainly the federal order was ignored by the rugged "Baby Dolls" and their rivals, the "Gold Diggers," bands of uninhibited girls given to every kind of bawdiness from as early as 1912, and continuously thereafter, into the late 1960s, especially around Mardi Gras time.

Though their activities had little to do with Storyville as such, their continued existence (with new recruits continually being added, of course) and their manner of living, from a time preceding World War I to the present, fittingly illustrate the facts of urban vice to which Alderman Story's ordinance addressed itself so effectively, and with which the political and law enforcement authorities of today are seemingly unable to cope. The definitive account of the "Baby Dolls" is found in the book *Gumbo Ya Ya,* researched and written by the Louisiana Writers Project of the Work Projects Administration, under the direction of Lyle Saxon. This excellent work deserves extensive citation here:

> . . . the night before Mardi Gras blazed to a new height. In one dimly lighted place couples milled about the floor, hugging each other tightly, going through sensuous motions to the music. Drug addicts, prostitutes, beggars and workingmen, they were having themselves a time . . . Young black women tried to interest men, who sagged over the bar, their eyelids heavy from liquor and "reefers." One woman screamed above the din: "I'll do it for twenty cents, Hot Papa . . ."

> A small girl shoved her way through the crowd . . . "Wait'll you see us Baby Dolls tomorrow," she promised. "Is we gonna wiggle our tails!"

There follows a colorful description of matters attending to the Zulu Parade.

> A crowd of Baby Dolls came along, all dressed up in tight, scanty trunks, silk blouses and poke bonnets with ribbons tied under dusky chins. False curls framed faces that were heavily powdered and rouged over black and chocolate skins. The costumes were in every color of the rainbow and some that are not. They joined the crowd, dancing and shaking themselves.

> "Sure, they call me Baby Doll," said one of them, who was over six feet tall and weighed more than 200 pounds. "That's my name."

> "I'm a Baby Doll today and every day. I bin a Baby Doll for twenty years. Since I always dressed like a Baby Doll on Mardi-Gras, the other girls said they would dress like me; they would wear tight skirts and bloomers and a rimmed hat. They always say you get more business on Mardi Gras than any other day, so I had a hard time making them gals close up and hit the streets. See, mens have fun on Carnival. They come into the houses masked and want everything and will do anything. They say, "I'm a masker, fix me up." Well, them gals had a time on Mardi Gras, havin' their kicks.

> "The way we used to kick 'em up on that day was a damn shame. Some of the gals didn't wear much clothes and used to show themselves out loud. Fellows used to run 'em down with dollar bills in their hands, and you didn't catch none of them gals refusing dollar bills. That's why all the women back Perdido Street wanted to be Baby Dolls.

> "We sure did shine. We used to sing, clap our hands, and you know what 'raddy' is? Well, that's the way we used to walk down the street. People used to say, 'Here comes the babies, but where's the dolls?'

> "I'm the oldest livin' Baby Doll, and I am one bitch who is glad she knows right from wrong, because I figures wrong makes you as happy as right, don't it?

> "Say what you like, it's my business. I'll tell anybody I sells myself enough on Mardi Gras to do myself some good the whole year round. There ain't no sense in being a Baby Doll for one day only. Me, I'm a Baby Doll all the time.

> "Just follow a Baby Doll on Mardi Gras and see where you land. You know, if you follow her once you'll be following her all the time. That's the truth."

She discusses her man, a retired burglar.

"He is all right. Me and him done plenty lemons together." [A lemon is a method of extracting a man's roll while he is busy with a woman.] "He got the peelin' an' I got the juice.

"Dago Tony got me into a business once that was too hot to keep up, but man, was it solid! He'd give the drunks a big hooker with knockout drops in their glass, and when they passed out, I was on 'em. The trouble was I had to hit too many of them niggers over their heads. They'd wake up too quick. I seen so much blood drippin' from people's heads I got scared and cut that stuff out."

Present considerations occupy the narrator.

"You're holdin' me up. I got to hit the streets. There's more money for me in the streets than there is here. Maybe I'm missin' a few tricks." And she was off through the crowd around the floats, walking "raddy" to attract attention.

"*I* was the first Baby Doll," Beatrice Hill asserted firmly. "Liberty and Perdido was red hot back in 1912 when that idea started. Women danced on bars with green money in their stockings, and sometimes they danced naked. They used to lie down on the floor and shake their bellies while the mens fed them candies. You didn't need no system to work uptown. It wasn't like the downtown red light district, where they made more money but paid more graft. You had to put on the ritz downtown, which some of the girls didn't like that. You did what you wanted uptown."

The author describes Beatrice as "fifty-two and about beat out now" (this was written in

Mahogany Hall in its death throes, 1949.

1945) and notes that "her arms and legs are thickly spotted with black needle holes. She still uses drugs and admits it. Also she goes to Charity Hospital and takes treatment for syphilis. Back in 1912 she made fifty to seventy-five dollars a day for hustling and stealing . . . She's been to jail for murder, shooting, stealing and prostitution."

"Them downtown [Storyville] bitches thought their behinds was solid silver," she recalls contemptuously, "but they didn't never have any more money than we did. We was just as good lookers and had just as much money. Me, I was workin' right there on Gravier and Franklin Streets.

"We gals around my house got along fine. Them downtown gals tried to get the police to up our graft, but they wouldn't do it. Does you remember Clara Clay, who had all them houses downtown? Well, we was makin' good money and used to buy up some fun. All of us uptown had nothin' but good-lookin' men. We used to send them downtown 'round them whores and make 'em get all their money until they found out and had 'em beat up. Then we stopped. I'm tellin' you that was a worse war than the Civil War. All the time we was tryin' to outdo them downtown gals.

"I knew a lady, name was Peggy Bry; she used to live at 231 Basin Street. Well, anyhow, Miss Bry gave a ball for the nigger bitches in the downtown district at the Entertainers Café, and she said she didn't want no uptown whore there. All them gals was dressed up to kill in silks and satins and they had all their mens dressed up, too. So, we figures and figures how we could go and show them whores up with our frocks. I told all my friends to get their clothes ready and to dress up their mens, 'cause we was goin' to that ball.

"Everybody got to gettin' ready, buying up some clothes. Sam Bonart was askin' the mens what was the matter and Canal Street was lookin' up at us niggers like we was the moon. We was ready, I'm tellin' you. . . . I got hold of a captain, the baddest dick on the force, and I tells him what was what. I tells him a white whore is givin' a ball for niggers and didn't want us to come. He says, 'Is it a public ball?' And I says it is. He tells us to get ready to do our stuff and go to that ball. You see, the captain knows we is in war with them downtown bitches. Me, I figures he was kiddin', so I went to him and told him if he'd come downtown with us I'd give him a hundred dollars. He says, sure he would.

"Child, we got the news around for the gals to get ready. And was they ready! Is the sun shinin'? It was a Monday night and Louis Armstrong and his Hot Five [not chronologically possible and, moreover, this group was strictly a recording group, out of Chicago, and never

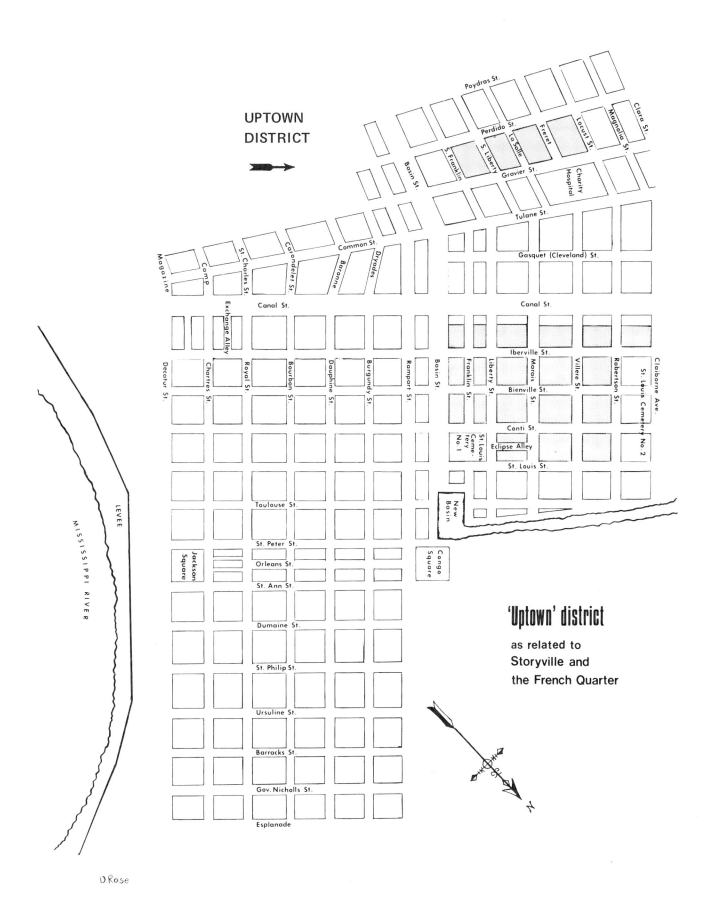

UPTOWN
DISTRICT

➡

Poydras St.

Perdido St.

Gravier St.

Tulane St.

Clara St.

Magnolia St.

Locust St.

Freret

La Salle

S. Liberty

S. Franklin

Basin St.

Charity Hospital

Gasquet (Cleveland) St.

Common St.

Dryades

Baronne

Canal St.

Canal St.

Magazine

Camp

St. Charles St.

Carondelet St.

Exchange Alley

Iberville St.

Decatur St.

Chartres St.

Royal St.

Bourbon St.

Dauphine St.

Burgundy St.

Rampart St.

Basin St.

Franklin St.

Liberty St.

Marais St.

Villere St.

Robertson St.

St. Louis Cemetery No. 2

Claiborne Ave.

Bienville St.

Conti St.

St. Louis Ceme- tery No. 1

Eclipse Alley

St. Louis St.

New Basin

Toulouse St.

St. Peter St.

Jackson Square

Orleans St.

St. Ann St.

Congo Square

Dumaine St.

St. Philip St.

Ursuline St.

Barracks St.

Gov. Nicholls St.

Esplanade

LEVEE

MISSISSIPPI RIVER

Exchange Alley

'Uptown' district

as related to
Storyville and
the French Quarter

N

D. Rose

179

played publicly] and Buddy Petit was gonna be playin' at that ball. We called up Geddes and Moss [funeral directors] and hired black limousines. You know them whores was livin' their lives! All the houses was shut down, and the Captain was out there in front. I'm tellin' you when that uptown brigade rode up to the Entertainers Café, all the bitches came runnin' out. Then they saw the Captain and they all started runnin' back inside. We just strutted up and filed in and filled the joint. I'm tellin' you, that was somethin'.

"The first thing I did was to order one hundred and four dollars worth of champagne, and the house couldn't fill the order. The Bartender says, 'You got me.' I took all the place had, and the band starts playin' 'Shake That Thing,' and dedicates it to me. This white bitch, Miss Bry, comes runnin' up to me and says, 'Look here, this is my party for my friends.' I says, 'Miss Bry, I'm the one who showed you how to put silk teddies on your tail. Who is you? What's your racket?' Then the Captain walks up, lookin' hard and he says: 'Miss Bry, you ain't got no right in this public dance. If you don't shut your trap, I'll pull you in.' Man, would you keep quiet? Well, that's what she did.

"One of my gals—I think it was Julia Ford—got up on a table and started shakin' it on down. We took off all her clothes, and the owner of the place started chargin' admission to come into the dance. Miss Bry raised particular hell about this, then went on home. We broke up that joint for true. The Entertainers ain't never seen a party like that.

"Let me tell you, and this ain't no lie: Every

girl with me had no less than one hundred dollars on her. We called that the hundred dollar party. Say, niggers was under the tables tryin' to find the money we was wastin' on the floor. I remembers one nigger trying to tear my stockings open to get at my money till my man hit him over the head with a chair, and that nigger went to the hospital. 'Course it all ended in a big fight and we all went to jail.

"It wasn't long after that when a downtown gal names Susie Brown come to see me. She says she wants to work uptown, so we give her a chance. She got to makin' money and soon she was the best dressed gal in Gravier Street. I didn't mind, me. She was workin' in my house and her bed percentage was fine. I done seen time when I made fifty dollars in a day just waitin' for Susie to get done turnin' tricks.

"Shux, that wasn't nothing. When them ships come in, that's when I made money. All them sailors wanted a brownie. High yellows fared poorly then, unless they got in them freakish shows. When I took in fifty dollars in them days it was a bad day. I was rentin' rooms payin' me a dollar every time a gal turned a trick. Then I had two gals stealin' for me, and I was turnin' tricks myself.

"Lights was low around my house and some awful things was done right in the streets. The police? Shux, does you know what we was payin' the law? Every gal paid three bucks a day and the landlady paid three and a half, but we didn't mind at all, cause we made that with a smile.

"Everywhere we went like the Silver Platter, the Elite, the Black and Tan and so on, people used to say 'Look at them whores!' We was always dressed down and carried our money in our stockings. See like around Mardi Gras Day? We used to break up the Zulu Ball with money, used to buy the King champagne by the case. That's another thing, we had the Zulus with us. Shux, we took Mardi Gras by storm. No we wasn't the Baby Dolls then; I'm talkin' about before that.

"In 1912, Ida Jackson, Millie Barnes and Sallie Gail and a few other gals downtown was makin' up to mask on Mardi Gras Day. No, I don't know how they was goin' to mask, but they was goin' to mask. We was all sittin' around about three o'clock in the morning in my house. A gal named Althea Brown jumps up and says, 'Let's be ourselves. Let's be Baby Dolls. That's what the pimps always called us.' We started comin' up with the money, but Leola says: 'Hold your horses. Let every tub stand on its own bottom.' That suited everybody fine and the tubs stood.

"Everybody agreed to have fifty dollars in her stocking, and that we could see who had the most money. Somebody says, 'What's the name of this here organization?' And we decided to call ourselves the Million Dollar Baby Dolls, and be red hot. Johnny Metoyer wanted us to come along with the Zulus but we said nothin' doin'.

The downtown river corner of Conti and 400 N. Robertson (the station wagon is on Robertson) in later years before all but a few last traces of what had been Storyville was turned over to the wreckers.

We told Johnny we was out to get some fun in our own way and we was not stoppin' at nothin'.

"Some of us made our own dresses and some had 'em made. We was all lookin' sharp. There was thirty of us—the best whores in town. We was all good-lookin' and had our stuff with us. Man, I'm tellin' you, we had money all over us, even in our bloomers, and they didn't have no zippers.

"And that Mardi Gras Day came and we hit the streets. I'm tellin' you, we hit the streets lookin' forty, fine and mellow. We got out about ten o'clock. We had stacks of dollars in our stockings and in our hands. We went to the Sam Bonart playground on Poydras Street and bucked each other to see who had the most money. Leola had the most—she had one hundred and two dollars. I had ninety-six dollars and I was second, but I had more home in case I ran out. There wasn't a woman in the bunch who had less than fifty dollars. We had all the niggers from everywhere followin' us. They liked the way we shook our behinds and we shook 'em like we wanted to.

"Know what? We went on downtown, and talk about puttin' on the ritz! We showed them whores how to put it on. Boy, we was smokin' cigars and flingin' ten and twenty dollars through the air. Sho, we used to sing, and boy did we shake it on down. We sang 'When the Sun Goes Down' and 'When the Saints Come Marchin' Through I Want to Be In That Number.' We wore them wide hats, but they was seldom worn, 'cause when we got to heatin' we pulled 'em off. When them Baby Dolls strutted, they strutted. We showed our linen that day, I'm tellin' you.

"When we hit downtown all them gals had to admit we was the stuff. Man, when we started pitchin' dollars around, we had their mens fallin' on their faces tryin' to get that money. And there you have the startin' of the Baby Dolls. Yeah, peace was made. All them gals got together."

The "Baby Dolls" and their ilk are still to be seen in New Orleans, at times, in the neighborhood of Claiborne Avenue and St. Philip Street.

It may readily be seen, then, to what extent vice was controlled by the expedient of closing Storyville and making an end, once and for all, to legalized prostitution in a restricted area. To the credit of ordinary citizens of the Crescent City, one hears little boasting around town concerning its current high level of morality. In 1908, a prominent clergyman had this to say in a sermon: "What a virtuous and godly city, now that sin has a place of its own. If we have need to conquer our errant neighbor, we may do so merely by cleansing ourselves." No such conquest has since been accomplished in New Orleans or in any other large city in America.

A workman disassembles the staircase of Mahogany Hall in 1949. The visible balustrade was really solid mahogany. Collectors bought each piece.

181

Coda

"*Honi Soit Qui Mal y Pense*"

In 1949, John Wigginton Hyman, a great New Orleans cornet player in whose horn one can still hear echoes of the lip slurs and intonations of King Oliver, strolled idly through the rubble of what had once been Lulu White's fabulous Mahogany Hall.

The demolition experts were putting the final cosmetic touches on their bad work—sweeping up the rubble. Earlier, members of the National Jazz Foundation had auctioned off the last of the building's relics—fine mirrors, ornately carved woodwork, and such—to collectors of New Orleansiana.

Hyman, known to the jazz faithful as Johnny Wiggs, stooped to pick up some gaudy strips of wallpaper that the workmen had torn off and tossed aside. He stacked them carefully in the back of his car and took them home, the last scraps of the sin empire that had been bawdy enough to shock the world. He felt no strong sentimental attachment to Storyville, even though it had been an uncle of his, Thomas McCaleb Hyman, who had drafted the Story ordinances that established the District. The vices that Storyville dispensed would have had little appeal for a man of Johnny's temperament, and though a jazz musician, and a thoughtful, historically oriented one, he knew very well that jazz and Storyville had been associated only fortuitously and only briefly. But he also knew, as most New Orleanians knew, that not all change is for the better, and that Mayor Martin Behrman had been right when he delivered himself of his deathless comment: "You can make it illegal, but you can't make it unpopular."

For Johnny Wiggs, the scraps of wallpaper symbolized, it may be supposed, the passing of an era, the very end of a part of his beloved New Orleans and of America itself. He had some of the pieces neatly framed and sent them to friends as mementoes of Storyville's end.

Then, one day a housemaid, mistaking the remaining scraps for ordinary trash, threw them out.

As do all Crescent City dwellers, Johnny knew that the United States Navy killed the District to no good effect whatsoever, so far as controlling or reducing prostitution was concerned. As a life-long resident and property owner, he knew that after 1917, just as before the District was established in 1897, prostitution spread throughout New Orleans, and that nowadays, when you make an investment in a residential or business structure, you can't really be sure that today's "nice neighborhood" will be the same tomorrow—the pretensions of zoning laws notwithstanding. In short, he knew, as most New Orleanians do, that the legal District, garish, bawdy, unkempt, and greedy as it had been, reduced the amount of prostitution and associated crime in New Orleans, and that it reduced the cost of policing the city and, even more markedly, the extent of police corruption. He knew that it contributed to stabilization of property values, that it made for a safer and more livable municipal environment even for those who chose voluntarily to linger in the small area comprising Storyville or in the even smaller segregated uptown district that was legalized early in 1917.

Johnny Wiggs is not one to be taken in by fake glamor, and Lulu White's shrieking wallpaper certainly did not symbolize for him a humane, gracious way of life. And yet somehow he felt, one senses, that the tinsel splendor of a Mahogany Hall bespoke a better way than does today's leering cabdriver, who greets lone males on French Quarter streets with "Hey, Papa, wanna meet a nice young girl?"

"Vice," Johnny's uncle had declared, more than half a century before, "is a product of a culture, not of sinners."

In March, 1890, the *Mascot* congratulated this earlier Hyman, then a New Orleans city attorney, for his zeal "in the Recorder's Courts prosecuting the cases of notorious lewd characters against whom affidavits have been made for occupying rooms in one story houses and on the ground floor of other houses devoted to such purposes."

Even then, however, Hyman recognized that a better way of controlling vice was an urgent necessity, and he was already at work on the proposals that would, seven years later, provide a workable administrative solution. At first, the *Mascot* misconstrued his statements on the subject. The paper thought he was "waging war on that class of females in the hope that they will be forced to keep themselves somewhat within the limits of decency and that the people will be saved from the revolting spectacles of immorality on the part of such females, as so frequently meets one's gaze while travelling in the street cars and on many respectable streets where these females have located. Mr. Hyman certainly has the wish of all good citizens for his success in the prosecutions." Eventually, however, like most responsible Orleanians, the *Mascot* came around to Mr. Hyman's point of view and campaigned vigorously for the passage of the Story ordinances.

Unregulated vice had created untenable problems for the city of New Orleans. Storyville was instituted to cope with these problems. That it was successful in so doing is doubted by no one familiar with the facts. Its end came not because it had outlived its usefulness but because a higher legal authority, the federal government, ordained it (illegally, by the way, in the judgment of some Constitutionalists). On October 2, 1917, Martin Behrman, in presenting the ordinance that would turn the lights out in Basin Street, summed it up nicely:

> Pretermitting the pros and cons of legislative recognition of prostitution as a necessary evil in a seaport the size of New Orleans, our city government has believed that the situation could be administered more easily and satisfactorily by confining it within a prescribed area. Our experience has taught us that the reasons for this are unanswerable, but the Navy Department of the Federal government has decided otherwise.

That the city had been right and the Navy Department wrong was demonstrated conclusively by subsequent events, just as the futility of the Prohibition Amendment to the Constitution was demonstrated by events—and just as the futility of laws against possession or use of certain drugs is now being demonstrated by events. The practical corollary to Mayor Behrman's observation, "You can make it illegal, but you can't make it unpopular," an observation whose truth is not limited to prostitution, is that when something that is genuinely popular is declared to be illegal, it is no longer effectively subject to any administrative regulation and the "problem," whatever it is, is almost certain to be aggravated.

On November 12 the mayor might have added, paraphrasing Lord Tennyson: "The old order changeth, giving place to worse; . . . Lest one good custom should corrupt the world."

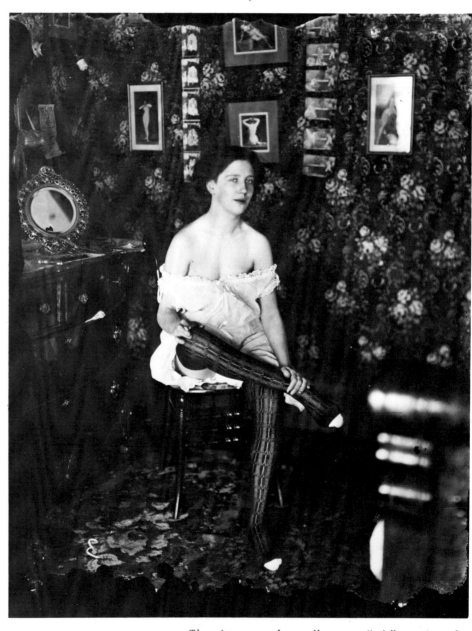

The pictures on her wall were a "mix": erotic nudes and "action" photos, plus infant children shown with a goose. (Photograph by Ernest Bellocq)

Appendices

APPENDIX A: A city of New Orleans brief in the George L'Hote suit to prevent establishment of the district known as Storyville

APPENDIX A: A city of New Orleans brief in the George L'Hote suit to prevent establishment of the district known as Storyville

SUPREME COURT OF THE UNITED STATES
October Term, 1899

No. 204.

GEORGE L'HOTE AND THE CHURCH EXTENSION
SOCIETY OF THE METHODIST EPISCOPAL CHURCH,
Plaintiff in Error,

versus

THE CITY OF NEW ORLEANS, ET AL.,
Defendants in Error.

In Error to the Supreme Court of the State of Louisiana.

BRIEF FOR DEFENDANTS IN ERROR

This case comes to this Court by a writ of error to the Supreme Court of the State of Louisiana. The facts of the case are as follows: —

STATEMENT OF THE CASE.

In the year 1857 the Common Council of the City of New Orleans passed Ordinance No. 3267, O.S., and Ordinance No. [. . .].

BRIEF FOR DEFENDANTS IN ERROR

This case comes to this Court by a writ of error to the Supreme Court of the State of Louisiana. The facts of the case are as follows: —

STATEMENT OF THE CASE.

In the year 1857 the Common Council of the City of New Orleans passed Ordinance No. 3267, O.S., and Ordinance No. 3428, O.S., fixing the limits outside of which it was illegal for lewd women to live. Subsequent amendments were made by Ordinance No. 6302, O.S. The limits or districts, defined by these ordinances are marked upon the maps in the transcript, pages 114 and 122. [The complete text of the 1857 ordinance, No. 3267, O.S., will be found in Appendix B.]

These ordinances remained in force until the year 1890, when Ordinance 4434, C.S., was passed, changing the limits, but otherwise being substantially the same as the ordinances enacted thirty-three years before.

This ordinance is printed at the end of this brief. It was not copied in the transcript, because of agreement between counsel (see page 16, transcript).

In January, 1897, the Council passed Ordinance

13,032, C.S., (printed on pages 6 and 7 of the transcript), by which a large portion of the district covered by Ordinance 4434 was excluded from the limits. [The complete text of Ordinance 13,032, C.S., of January 29, 1897, will be found in Appendix C.]

In July, 1897, Ordinance No. 13,485, C.S. (printed on page 5 of the transcript), was passed, which extended the limits, authorized by Ordinance 13,032, C.S., so as to include St. Louis street within the territory outside of which lewd women were excluded. [Ordinance No. 13,485, C.S., of July, 1897, will be found in Appendix D.]

It will be noted that none of these ordinances compelled or authorized lewd women to live *within* certain limits of the city; they simply prohibited them from living *outside of* certain limits.

In order that the Court may more clearly understand the question, we ask your Honors' attention to the maps printed in the transcript on pages 114 and 122. From this you see that, in 1857, a very large portion of the City of New Orleans was within limits outside of which lewd women could not live.

As the City grew, it became necessary to change the boundaries of the district, and in 1890, Ordinance 4434 was adopted. This ordinance excluded such women from all that part of the City outside of a district bounded by Poydras, St. Louis, Claiborne and the river; excluding, however, Canal, Rampart, St. Louis and Conti streets.

Under this state of affairs these women frequented a very large part of the city, extending, as the map shows, from the river to Claiborne street and from Poydras to St. Louis street. By the year 1897, because of the growth and progress of the city, it happened that this included a very valuable and populous section; it included a neighborhood filled with stores, churches, public schools, etc. The City Council, considering these facts, in 1897, passed Ordinance 13,032, C.S., which curtailed these limits by excluding all that part of the city in the old limits, which was between Basin street and the river.

In other words, they simply took the limits defined by the old ordinances and declared that hereafter lewd women should not live within that part of the old limits bounded by Basin street, the river, Poydras and St. Louis streets.

A short time afterward, finding that St. Louis street was practically abandoned to this class of people, and had been for some years past (which we may consider the evidence in the transcript proves conclusively), they passed Ordinance 13,485, C.S., by which the limits were changed so as to include St. Louis street. Ordinance 13,485 was promulgated July 7, 1897.

On September 22, 1897, George L'Hote, a respectable and well known citizen, representing himself to be a property owner on Treme (or No. Liberty, as printed on the maps) street, near St. Louis street, but outside of the limits included by the ordinance, presented a petition to the Court, stating that he lived near St. Louis street, and that his neighborhood was a virtuous one, and that the

city had adopted an Ordinance 13,485, amendatory of Ordinance 13,032, whose natural result would be to allow lewd women to live within a half square of his house; and further, that such neighbors would annoy him and would depreciate the value of his property, and would force him and his virtuous neighbors to leave the locality, where they had lived for so many years.

Further, Mr. L'Hote states that the Common Council of the city, having previously designated the limits within which such women should live, had thereby exhausted whatever power the Council had in the matter and were without legal right to change, alter or modify the same; he further says that there was no good and sufficient reason for the enactment of said ordinance, or for the changing of the limits previously existing and established; and he asks that this Ordinance 13,032, as amended by 13,485, be declared null and void—the prayer of his petition being as follows: [. . .]

'Wherefore petitioner prays, the annexed bond and affidavit considered, that a writ of injunction do issue herein, directed to the city of New Orleans, through its Mayor and D. S. Gaster, Superintendent of Police, enjoining, restraining and prohibiting said city, its officers, agents, representatives and employees, and the said Superintendent of Police, and each of them, from in any manner enforcing or attempting to enforce said Ordinance No. 13,032, C.S., as amended by Sec. 1 of Ordinance No. 13,485, C.S. That said city of New Orleans, through its Mayor and D. S. Gaster, Superintendent of Police, be severally cited to appear and answer this petition, and that after due proceedings said injunction be maintained and perpetuated, and said ordinance be declared unconstitutional, illegal, unreasonable, and as such null and void and without any legal force, validity or effect whatsoever.'

On his petition an injunction issued *ex parte*, enjoining the Mayor and Chief of Police 'from in any manner enforcing or attempting to enforce Ordinance No. 13,032, C.S., as amended by Sec. 1 of Ordinance No. 13,485, C.S.'

The Supreme Court of Louisiana gave judgment in favor of the city of New Orleans, against both plaintiffs, L'Hote and the Methodist Church Extension Society, on the grounds stated in the opinion which is found at page 125 of the transcript:

'The regulation of houses of prostitution would seem to be so clearly connected with public order and decency, the policy announced by the ordinance has been so long exerted in all large cities of our country, and the power has had such frequent recognition in the charters of this city that it would seem the power itself cannot be successfully controverted.'

ARGUMENT.

The assignments of error filed by the plaintiffs are found on pages 133 and 134 of the transcript, and are eight in number.

I.

The first assignment of error is, 'that the Court erred in holding that Ordinances Nos. 13,032 and

13,485, C.S., do not deprive plaintiff and intervenor of the equal protection of the law.'

Where the equal protection of the law comes in here, we are at a loss to see. These ordinances simply say that lewd and abandoned women shall not live outside of certain parts of the city of New Orleans. One of the plaintiffs in error lives outside of these 'limits', and the other plaintiff in error is a Methodist Church Society, domiciled in Philadelphia, which has a Chapel located within those 'limits'. Where on earth these plaintiffs can find any reason for concluding that an ordinance prohibiting lewd women from living beyond certain 'limits' deprives these plaintiffs of the full protection of the law we fail to see. This point was not argued in the Court below, and counsel for defendants in error are unable to understand the application of this so called error in this case.

II.

The second error assigned is 'that the Court erred in refusing to hold that the said ordinances and the power conferred upon the Mayor of the city of New Orleans thereby were not due process of law'. The ordinances named, which are found on pages 5 and 6 of the transcript, speak for themselves. The power that they confer upon the Mayor is simply a power of supervision. This power of supervision consists in this; that whenever the Mayor finds any house to be dangerous to morals of the city of New Orleans, he can order the occupant to move therefrom within five days, and if such occupant fails to remove within the prescribed time, then an affidavit is made before a magistrate, and the question decided whether or not said occupant is violating the ordinance, and whether or not the house is dangerous to public morals; and if the Recorder finds these facts to be true, he inflicts a punishment upon the occupant. This finding of the Recorder is subject to an appeal to the Criminal District Court for the Parish of Orleans.

Louisiana Constitution of 1898, Article 139: —

'The Criminal District Court shall have appellate 'jurisdiction in all cases tried * * * before the Recorders' Courts 'of New Orleans.'

This method is surely 'due process of law', giving the violator a trial in two different Courts, where witnesses can be heard, and a decision had whether or not the Mayor wisely or legally exercised his power.

III, IV and VI.

The third, fourth and sixth errors assigned are, respectively, that the ordinances deprive plaintiffs of property without due process of law, that they are not a valid exercise of the police power, and that they violate rights guaranteed or secured by the Federal Constitution.

The plaintiffs in error evidently mean by the third assignment of error, that if the city of New Orleans, in fixing the 'limits' outside of which lewd and abandoned women shall not live, should happen to fix the lines in some places where property owned by the plaintiffs is situated, that the proximity of that class of people would lessen the value of the property of plaintiffs, and that this deterioration would amount to a taking of property without due process of law.

In this connection we call the attention of the Court to the inconsistency of plaintiffs' demands.

The Methodist Church is situated on Bienville street in square No. 159 (see map, page 122). This particular square whereon this church is built has formed from time immemorial a portion of the district where lewd and abandoned women have been allowed to dwell. Before the church was built, these women were allowed to live in this section. See map, page 114 of the transcript.

It comes with ill-grace now from the Church Society to complain that an ordinance adopted in 1897, which is really a reiteration of an ordinance adopted in 1857, is null and void and to their prejudice, when they had moved in that neighborhood at a period when that particular spot was dedicated to the vicious element. In fact, their Chapel was evidently originally erected for missionary work amongst the class in whose midst it was established, and their existence is its only *raison d'etre*.

As to Mr. L'Hote, the other plaintiff, who joined this Church in the assignments of error, he lives outside of the 'limits', at No. 522 Treme street (Treme being called N. Liberty street on the map in evidence), which is in square 153 of the map on page 122.

For 40 years Mr. L'Hote's residence has been just as close to the limits allotted to lewd women, but in 1894 the Council adopted Ordinance 4434, C.S., which changed the limits outside of which lewd women might dwell. By agreement of counsel the map found on page 115 of the transcript, correctly delineates the boundaries of the so called limits, and there your Honors will see that the lines of 4434, C.S., ran straight along St. Louis street from the river to N. Claiborne street, coming within one-half of a square of Mr. L'Hote's residence. It also comes with bad-grace from Mr. L'Hote, he having lived for so many years in a neighborhood whose characteristics are fully set forth in the transcript, and which section is no different under the contested ordinance from what it was under the ordinances which prevailed for fifty years, to come into Court and question the ordinance of 1897. For even if he succeeds in wiping out the ordinance of 1897 and under the same principle the ordinance of 1890, he will find that his residence will be similarly situated, with reference to this class of people.

But apart from this question of inconsistency, and apart from that fact that for many years the surroundings of Mr. L'Hote's residence and of the Church Chapel have been of the lowest describably in point of reputation, his house being one of the few respectable houses in the neighborhood, we must not say that if a city government should name a district within which lewd women can or cannot live, that such an act deprives people of their property without due process of law.

These poor creatures must live somewhere, and it surely lies within the discretion of the City Council to set apart certain districts for their occupancy, and having legally and honestly exercised that discretion the Court should hesitate to revise the Council's decision.

It is of course very probable that some one must suffer in the injury to his feelings, etc., but that is *damnum absque injuria,* to which some must submit in order that the whole population may benefit.

The police power of the city granted to her by the State in her various charters, gives her the right to regulate its lewd women.

Act 20 of 1882, Louisiana Legislature, Sec. 8, Clause 11:

'The Council shall have the power to regulate the police of theatres, * * * houses of prostitution and assignation, and to exclude such houses from certain limits, and shall have power to close the same, * * * and to authorize the Mayor and police to close such places.'

The existing city charter is the Act of Louisiana Legislature Act 45 of 1896. Section 15, Clause 11 of that Act provides: —

'The Council shall have power, * * * to regulate the police of theatres, * * * houses of prostitution and assignation, and to close such houses in certain limits, and shall have power to exclude the same, * * * and to authorize the Mayor and police to close such places.'

The regulation of such houses and such women is essentially a police power of the city, and when the City Council, in the exercise of its discretion, enacts an ordinance, declaring that such people shall not live outside of certain limits, they have acted wisely in their discretion, and the courts will not interfere with them, as that would be substituting the discretion of the courts for the discretion of the Council, and that is certainly something that this Court will not sanction.

The City Council represents the entire body of citizens; they have at heart the best interests of the city; when they exercise this discretion legally, and set aside a portion of the city, outside of which lewd and abandoned women may not live, we think that such discretion should not be interfered with by the Court, unless it should be shown that it was done with unreasonableness or prejudice.

Now, what does the evidence in this case disclose? We find that in the district formerly set apart for such people, by Ordinance 4434, C.S., there are to-day nine churches, two schools and ten public buildings. That in the territory covered by Ordinance 13,485, there are only one church, one school and not one public building. The discretion of the City Council surely was correctly exercised, and on this comparative statement concerning the two districts, the new one is certainly the one where less harm can result.

Right here let us call to the attention of the Court that this district, which is called the 'new district', is not now, for the first time, set apart for such purposes. It has always been a part of the district set aside for such purposes since 1890, when Ordinance 4434, C.S., was adopted.

Consequently, it does not follow that because a portion of the territory set apart in 1890 for lewd women is hereafter to be devoted exclusively to respectable people, that such action on the part of the City Council is to be considered as devoting for the first time the rest of that district to other uses.

Again, when we examine the testimony in the case we find witness after witness saying that the objection to such people leaving the front of the old district and moving into the back of the old district springs not from any yearning to improve the moral tone of the city, but rather from a selfish desire to keep rented to these characters the houses in the front of the old district, which the new ordinance forces them to abandon.

v.

The fifth assignment of error is, that the Court erred in not holding that that ordinances attacked make arbitrary and unjust discrimination against the Church Society, which, plaintiffs say, belongs to the colored race. This is another remarkable claim. How on earth an ordinance, which on its face simply prohibits prostitutes and lewd women from living outside of certain limits, can be considered a discrimination against a religious corporation that found a field of missionary labor in a portion of the city set aside for abandoned and lewd women, we cannot perceive.

There is no mention made in the ordinance of colored people or of churches for colored people. As we have said before, in our answer to the third, fourth and sixth errors assigned, it will be seen from the maps that the district which is set apart in the recent ordinance, has been embraced for years and years back by the district wherein lewd and abandoned women were confined. That church is the only church in the district, there being only one public school (and that on the outskirts of the district)—and not a single public building within its limits.

In fact, if that class of people must live somewhere, no section of the city can be found, where they can be placed with less danger to the morals of the city, than the district described on page six of the transcript.

There can be no discrimination against the colored church by an ordinance prohibiting prostitutes from living in certain sections of the city of New Orleans. Mr. L'Hote, the other plaintiff, is a white man. How can a white man and a Philadelphia corporation combine in a plea that this same ordinance discriminates against the colored race? There is no question of race, color or previous condition in this case. It is simply and purely a reasonable exercise of the police power of the city of New Orleans.

vii.

The seventh assignment of error is, that this ordinance violates the fourteenth amendment to the Constitution of the United States. We presume by this is meant, a violation of section one of that 14th amendment, being that part of it which reads: —

'No State shall make or enforce any law which shall abridge the privileges or immunities of citizens of the United States, nor deprive any person of life, liberty, or property, without due process of law.'

The preservation of the public morals, is one of the duties of a municipal corporation, which call for the exercise of the police power, and where, as in this case, the police power of the State is used for the purpose of suppressing vice, and of excluding bawdy houses from certain limits, and confining houses of prostitution and ill-fame to certain parts of a city, such exercises will never be construed as a violation of the Fourteenth Amendment.

'Every citizen holds his property subject to the proper exercise of the police power, exercised either by the Legislature or some subordinate political corporation.

'It is settled that police laws and regulations are not unconstitutional, even though they may disturb the enjoyment of individual rights. If the individual suffers any injury, it is deemed *damnus absque injuria*, or, in the theory of the law, the injury to the owner is deemed compensated by the public benefit the regulation is designed to subserve.'

1st Dillon on Municipal Corporations, p. 93.
1st Dillon, Section 310.
Black's Constitutional Law, page 310.
Dwarris on Statutes, p. 455.

That the adoption of ordinances regulating bawdy-houses is within the undoubted police power of a municipality is well settled by the weight of authority can, in no respect, be considered as open to discussion.

The Federal Constitution, broad and comprehensive as it is, was not designed in any respect to interfere with the power of a State, sometimes termed its police power, to prescribe regulations to promote the health, peace, morals, education, and good order of the people.

Barbier vs. Connolly, 113 U.S., 31.

Ordinances to regulate and confine the prosecution of business, even lawful and not immoral in character, within certain definite territorial limits have been held by this Court as being purely police regulations, within the competency of a municipality possessed of ordinary powers.

Barvier vs. Connolly, 113 U.S., 27.

Soon Hing vs. Crowley, 113 U.S., 797.

In a matter so closely connected with the public morals as the regulation of houses of prostitution, it would hardly seem necessary to adduce reasons or cite authority to maintain that their confinement to certain prescribed limits, in the judgment of the municipal authorities best calculated to mitigate their evil effects, is obviously included within the ordinary powers of a municipal corporation.

State vs. Karstendeik (La.), 39 Lawyers' Reports Annotated, 521.

In Louisiana the power to suppress such establishments has been held free from constitutional objection.

City vs. Roos, 35 La. An. Rep., 1011.

There can be no merit in the seventh assignment of error, for the ordinances in question are surely a legitimate exercise of the police power for the protection of the public health and morals, and as such do not violate the Federal Constitution.

VIII.

The eighth assignment of error, that the Court erred in rendering judgment in favor of defendants, is fully disposed of by the consideration of the arguments relative to the other errors assigned.

We respectfully submit that the opinion and decree of the Supreme Court of the State of Louisiana are correct and should be affirmed.

Respectfully submitted,
JAMES J. McLoughlin,
Assistant City Attorney,
Sam'l L. Gilmore,
City Attorney.
For Defendants in Error.

APPENDIX.

Ordinance 4434, Council Series, Adopted April 15th, 1890.

Be it ordained by the Common Council of the city of New Orleans, Sec. 1:

Section 1. That public prostitutes or notoriously lewd and abandoned women are forbidden to stand upon the sidewalks in front of or near the premises they may occupy, door or gate of such premises, or to occupy the steps thereof, or to accost, call or stop any person passing by, or to walk up and down sidewalks, or to stroll about the city streets indecently attired, or in other respects so to behave in public as to occasion scandal or disturb and offend the peace and good morals of the people.

Section 2. That it shall not be lawful for any lewd woman to frequent any cabaret or coffee house or to drink therein.

Section 3. That all houses, buildings or rooms occupied or inhabited by lewd women, and all houses of prostitution and of assignation, shall at all times be subject to the visitation of the police, and it shall be the duty of the police, while strictly enforcing the provisions of this ordinance, to extend to such lewd and abandoned women the same protection given to other inhabitants of this city.

Section 4. That it shall not be lawful for any public prostitute or woman notoriously abandoned to lewdness to occupy, inhabit, live or sleep in any house, room or closet situated without the following limits, and that said women are excluded from any other portion of the city outside of the limits now specified, viz.: South side of Poydras street from the Mississippi river to Claiborne street, west side of Claiborne street from Poydras to St. Louis street, north side of St. Louis street from Claiborne street to the river, and along the river bank from St. Louis to Poydras street; provided, that nothing herein shall be so construed as to give the right to any lewd women to occupy a house, etc., as herein provided, in any particular portion of the city.

Section 5. That it shall not be lawful for any public prostitute notoriously abandoned to lewdness to occupy, inhabit, live or sleep in any one story house, or a room or closet of the first or lower story of any house in the city of New Orleans outside of the limits specified in section 4 of this ordinance.

Section 6. That it shall not be lawful to establish or carry on a house of prostitution or assignation within the limits specified in section 4 of this ordinance.

Section 7. That any person, whether agent or owner, who shall knowingly rent or hire, or continue to rent or hire, after being notified by the Mayor that he or she is acting in contravention of this ordinance, any house, building or room to any woman or girl notoriously abandoned to lewdness, shall be brought before the Recorder of the District in which the offence is committed and punished as provided in section 10 of this ordinance.

Section 8. That wherever a house of prostitution or assignation, within or without the limits established by this ordinance, may become dangerous to the public morals, either from the manner in which it is conducted or the character of the neighborhood in which it is situated, the Mayor may, on such facts coming to his knowledge, order the occupant of such house, building or room, to remove therefrom within a delay of five days, by service of notice on such occupants in person, or by posting the notice on the door of the house, building or room, to remove therefrom, within a delay of five days, and upon such occupants failing to do so, each shall be punished as provided in section 10 of this ordinance.

Section 9. That in the event that the occupants of such house, building, or room, referred to in section 8, do not remove therefrom after the infliction of the penalty, the Mayor is authorized to close the same and to place a policeman at the door of such premises to ward away all such parties who shall undertake to enter.

Section 10. That any person or persons who shall violate the provisions of this ordinance or who shall disturb the tranquility of the neighborhood, or commit a breach of the peace, shall be subject to a fine not exceeding $25, to be imposed by the Recorder of the District in which the offence shall be committed, and in default of payment of the fine, to imprisonment in the Parish Prison for a term not exceeding thirty days.

Section 11. That each day any person shall continue to violate the provisions of this ordinance shall constitute a separate offence.

Section 12. That Ordinances 3267, O.S.; 3428, O.S.; 7141, A.S.; 7325, A.S.; and 2051, C.S., on the same subject as this ordinance be repealed.

Section 13. That nothing in this ordinance shall be taken to affect or repeal Ordinance 4101, C.S., relative to prostitutes on Canal street, or Ordinance 3430, C.S., relative to prostitutes in the Fifth District, nor to allow prostitutes to occupy, inhabit, live or sleep in any house, room or closet, situated on the following streets, viz.: Rampart, St. Louis and Conti streets.

An Ordinance concerning Lewd and Abandoned Women.

To Live within certain portion of the city.

No. 1084. (1) That it shall not be lawful for any woman or girl, notoriously abandoned to lewdness, to occupy, inhabit, live or sleep in any one-story house or building, or the lower floor of any house or building situated within the following limits, voz.:

In the first district—Between the river and Hercules, Circus and Rampart streets, Felicity road and Canal Street.

In the second district—Between the river and Basin street, Canal and Toulouse streets, and between the river, the bayou St. John, Toulouse street, and Esplanade street.

Amended by No. 1098

In the third district—Between Esplanade street, Elysian Fields, the river and Broad street.

In the fourth district—The river, the Carrollton railroad, the upper line of said district and Felicity road, under the penalty of not less than twenty-five dollars for each and every contravention thereof, and the further penalty of twenty-five dollars for each and every day such woman or girl shall occupy, inhabit, live, or sleep in any one-story house or building, or the lower floor of any house or building, or any room or closet on the lower floor of any house or building within the limits aforesaid, after the notice from the recorder of the district wherein such woman shall be found contravening thereto; and in default of payment of such penalty aforesaid, such woman or girl shall be imprisoned not less than thirty days.

Duty of police and recorders.

No. 1085. (2) That it shall be the duty of all police officers, policemen and watchmen to arrest any woman or girl found in contravention to the foregoing section, and take her before the recorder of the district where-in she be found in contravention, who shall impose upon her the penalty set forth in said section, and in default of payment thereof, shall condemn her to not less than thirty days' imprisonment; and said recorder shall further notify such woman or girl to remove from and quit the premises so occupied or inhabited by her within three days from such notification, under the penalties imposed by said section.

To pay tax and obtain license

No. 1086. (3) That it shall not be lawful for any woman or girl, notoriously abandoned to lewdness, to occupy, inhabit, or live in any house, building or room situate within the limits described in the first section of this ordinance, and not in violation of, or prohibited by the said section, without first paying in to the city treasurer the tax imposed by this ordinance, and procuring from the mayor of this city a license to inhabit or live in or occupy a house, building or room within said limits as aforesaid—nor shall it be lawful for any person to open or keep any house, building, dwelling or room within the limits of this city for the purpose of boarding or lodging lewd and abandoned women, or of renting rooms to such women, without first paying the tax hereinafter levied, and procuring from the mayor a license so to open and keep a house, etc., as aforesaid. Every person failing to comply with the provisions of this section, shall pay a fine of one hundred dollars for each and every contravention, and in default of payment shall be imprisoned not less than thirty days. One half of the fine shall be for the benefit of the informer. Provided, that nothing herein contained shall be so construed as to authorize the issuing of licenses to occupy or inhabit any one story house or building or the lower floor of any house or building situate within the limits described in the first section of this ordinance.

Annual tax, etc.

No. 1087. (4) That an annual license tax of one hundred dollars be and the same is hereby levied upon each and every woman or girl notoriously abandoned to lewdness, occupying, inhabiting, or living in any house, building or room within the limits prescribed in the first section of this ordinance, but not in contravention thereof— and an annual tax of two hundred and fifty dollars upon each and every person keeping any house, room, or dwelling for the purpose of renting rooms to or boarding lewd and abandoned women, which said tax shall be payable in advance on the first day of February of each and every year.

Amended by No. 1100.

Mayor's duty as to licenses.

No. 1088. (5) That the mayor of this city be, and is hereby authorized, upon the production of the receipt of the treasurer of this city, showing the payment of the tax levied by section fourth of this ordinance, to grant the license required by the third section of this ordinance. Which license shall be recorded in a book to be kept for that purpose in the mayor's office, and shall set forth the name of the party to whom granted, the number of the house or building which she intends to inhabit, occupy or live in, the name of the street, where the same is situated, and the number corresponding with that of the record in the aforesaid book. And for which license and recording, the party to whom it is granted shall pay one dollar and fifty cents. Said license shall expire on the thirty-first day of January.

Disturbing the peace—penalty.

No. 1089. (6) Any woman or girl notoriously abandoned to lewdness, who shall occasion scandal or disturb the tranquility of the neighborhood, or

commit a breach of the peace, shall be fined not less than ten dollars, nor more than twenty-five dollars for the first offense, and for the second offense shall be fined not less than twenty-five dollars, and for the third offense, shall forfeit her license, and shall be dealt with as provided by the act concerning vagrants, etc.

Not to frequent cabarets.

No. 1090. (7) That is shall not be lawful for any lewd woman to frequent any cabaret, or coffee-house, or to drink therein, under the penalty of not less than five dollars for each and every contravention, or of being dealt with as provided by the act concerning vagrants, at the discretion of the recorder before whom she may be brought.

White women and free women of color not to live together, etc.

No. 1091. (8) That it shall not be lawful for white women and free women of color, notoriously abandoned to lewdness, to occupy, inhabit, or live in the same room, house or building; nor for any free person of color to poen or keep any house, building or room, for the purpose of boarding or lodging any white woman or girl notoriously abandoned to lewdness, under the penalty of not less than twenty-five dollars for each and every contravention; in default of payment, the person so contravening shall be imprisoned not less than thirty days. One half of the fine shall be for the benefit of the informer.

Hiring rooms and houses, etc.

No. 1092. (9) That each and every person who shall rent or hire any house, building or room, to any woman or girl notoriously abandoned to lewdness, in contravention of this ordinance, shall pay a penalty of fifty dollars for each and every girl or woman such person shall rent or hire to as aforesaid.

Mayor, in certain cases, to order their removal.

No. 1093. (10) That whenever a petition signed by three respectable citizens residing within the vicinity of any house, building or room occupied or inhabited, or frequented by one or more lewd women, shall be presented to the mayor, stating, under oath, that such house, building or room is a nuisance, and that the occupants thereof are in the habit of committing indecencies by the public exposure of their persons, etc., it shall be the duty of the mayor immediately to notify the owner or lessee of such house, building or room, that such report has been made, and to order him or her to eject from the premises so occupied the persons in possession at the time of the complaint. And any person refusing or neglecting to comply therewith, shall be fined not less than twenty-five dollars, nor more than one hundred dollars for each and every month during the continuance of the nuisance complained of. And the mayor is hereby further authorized to order the occupants of the house, building or room to remove therefrom within a delay of five days, and upon said occupants failing to do so, each shall be fined not less than ten dollars a day for each and every day such occupants shall remain in violation of said order, and in case of failure or refusal to pay said fine, each occupant shall be imprisoned for a time not exceeding thirty days.

Police powers, etc.

No. 1094. (11) That all houses, buildings, dwellings, or rooms occupied or inhabited by lewd women, shall at all times be subject to the visitation of the police of this city.

Forbidden to stand in front of their houses or sit on the steps, etc.

No. 1095. (12) That it shall not be lawful for any woman or girl notoriously abandoned to lewdness, to stand upon the sidewalk in front of the premises occupied by her, ot at the alleyway, door or gate of such premises, nor sit upon the steps thereof in an indecent posture, nor accost, call, nor stop any person passing by, nor to walk up and down the sidewalk or banquette, nor stroll about the streets of the city indecently attired, under the penalty of not less than ten (10) dollars for each and every contravention; and in default of payment, such woman or girl shall be imprisoned not less than fifteen days.

Opposing police.

No. 1096. (13) That any person who shall interfere with, obstruct, or prevent any of the police of this city from enforcing the provisions of this ordinance, shall be fined not less than twenty-five dollars, and in default of payment, shall be imprisoned not less than thirty days.

Police to enforce this ordinance.

No. 1097. (14) That it shall be the duty of the police of this city, strictly to enforce the provisions of this ordinance, and to arrest all persons contravening against the same, under the penalty of dismissal.

When to go into effect.

No. 1098. (15) That this ordinance shall go into effect, and be in full force from and after the first day of February next.

Amended by No. 1101

Repealing clause.

No. 1099. (16) That all ordinances, or parts of ordinances, contrary to the provisions of this ordinance, be, and the same are hereby repealed.

City Ordinance, No. 3267. Approved March 10th, 1857.

APPENDIX C: The original ordinance of Alderman Story, Ordinance No. 13,032, C.S., establishing restricted district.

Mayorality of New Orleans
City Hall, January 29th, 1897.
NO. 13,032, COUNCIL SERIES.

Section 1. Be it ordained by the Common Council of the City of New Orleans, That from the first of October, 1897 it shall be unlawful for any public prostitute or woman notoriously abandoned to lewdness to occupy, inhabit, live or sleep in any house, room or closet situated without the following limits: South side of Customhouse street from Basin to Robertson street, east side of Robertson street from Customhouse to Saint Louis street, from Robertson to Basin street.

Provided that no lewd women shall be permitted to occupy a house, room or closet on St. Louis street. Provided further, That nothing herein shall be so construed as to authorize any lewd women to occupy a house, room or closet in any portion of the city.

Section 2. That it shall be unlawful for any person or persons, whether agent or owner to rent, lease or hire any house, building or room to any woman or girl notoriously abandoned to lewdness or for immoral purposes outside the limits specified in section 1 of this ordinance.

Section 3. That public prostitutes or notoriously lewd and abandoned women are forbidden to stand upon the sidewalks in front of or near the premises they may occupy, or at the alleyway, door or gate of such premises or to occupy the steps thereof, or to accost, call or stop any person passing by or to walk up and down the side walks, or to stroll about the city streets indecently attired, or in other respects so as to behave in public as to occasion scandal, or disturb and offend the peace and good morals of the people.

Section 4. That it shall not be lawful for any lewd women to frequent any cabaret or coffee house or barroom and to drink therein.

Section 5. That it shall be unlawful for any party or parties to establish or carry on a house of prostitution, or assignation without the limits specified in section 1 of this ordinance.

Section 6. That wherever a house of prostitution or assignation within or without the limits established by this ordinance, may become dangerous to public morals, either from the manner in which it is conducted or the character of the neighborhood in which it is situated, the Mayor may, on such facts coming to his knowledge, order the occupant of such house, building or room, to remove therefrom within a delay of five days, by service of notice on such occupants in person, or by posting the notice on the door of the house, building or room, to remove therefrom within a delay of five days, and upon such occupants failing to do so each shall be punished as provided in section—of this ordinance.

Section 7. That in the event that the occupants of such house, building or room referred to in section 6, do not remove therefrom after the infliction of the penalty the Mayor is authorized to close the same and to place a policeman at the door of such premises to warn away all such parties who shall undertake to enter.

Section 8. That any person or persons who shall violate the provisions of this ordinance, or who shall disturb the tranquility of the neighborhood or commit a breach of the peace, shall be punished by the Recorder having jurisdiction, for the first offense by a fine not exceeding $5.00, and in default of payment by imprisonment not exceeding 10 days, for the second offense by a fine not exceeding $10.00 and in default of payment by imprisonment not exceeding 20 days and for any subsequent offense by a fine not exceeding $25 and in default of payment by imprisonment not exceeding 30 days.

Section 9. That each day any person or persons shall continue to violate the provisions of this ordinance shall constitute a separate offense.

Section 10. That on and from the day this ordinance takes effect all ordinances in conflict therewith be and the same are hereby repealed —provided that nothing herein contained shall affect ordinance 12,456, C.S., relative to prostitutes in the Fifth District.

Adopted by the Council of the City of New Orleans, January 26th, 1897.

W.R. BRASHEAR,
Clerk of Council.
Approved Jany 29th, 1897.
W.C. FLOWER,
Mayor.

A true copy:
T. H. THORPE,
  Secretary to the Mayor.

APPENDIX D: Ordinance establishing district known as Storyville as amended July 6, 1897 (Ordinance No. 13,485, C.S.), with September 1, 1897, supplement.

Ordinance No. 13,485 (July 6, 1897)

BE IT ORDAINED by the Common Council of the City of New Orleans, That Section 1, of Ordinance 13,032 C.S., Be and the same is hereby amended as follows: From and after the first of October, 1897, it shall be unlawful for any prostitute or woman notoriously abandoned to lewdness, to occupy, inhabit, live or sleep in any house, room or closet, situated without the following limits, viz: From the South side of Customhouse Street [name later changed to Iberville Street] to the North side of St. Louis Street, and from the lower or wood side of North Basin Street to the lower or wood side of Robertson Street; 2nd: —And from the upper side of Perdido Street to the lower side of Gravier Street, and from the river side of Franklin Street to the lower or wood side of Locust Street, provided that nothing herein shall be so construed as to authorize any lewd woman to occupy a house, room or closet in any portion of the city. [Note that the second area, from the upper side of Perdido Street, etc., was held in abeyance until passage of Ordinance 4118 in 1917. See Appendix E.]

[September 1, 1897, addendum]

It shall be unlawful to open, operate or carry on any cabaret, concert-saloon or place where cancan, clodoche or similar female dancing or sensational performances are shown, without the following limits, viz: from the lower side of N. Basin Street to the lower side of N. Robertson Street, and from the South side of Customhouse Street [later Iberville] to the North side of St. Louis Street.

APPENDIX E: Ordinance 4118, C.C.S., passed on February 7, 1917, and incorporated in the legal decision reproduced here, recognized two "restricted districts" and stipulated (1) that the old downtown district (Storyville) would henceforth be for white prostitutes only and (2) that the newly legal uptown district would be for black prostitutes only. Under the ordinance, which is included in the definitive court decision reproduced here, even such powerful Basin Street madams as Lulu White and Willie V. Piazza would presumably have had to move to the uptown district, had the federal Navy Department not forced the disestablishment of both districts later in the year.

NO. 22,624.

SUPREME COURT of LOUISIANA

CITY OF NEW ORLEANS,

Appellee,

versus

WILLIE V. PIAZZA,

Appellant.

Appeal from Second Recorder's Court of New Orleans.

ORIGINAL BRIEF ON BEHALF OF PLAINTIFF AND APPELLEE.

SYLLABUS.

1. "No person can have a right to engage in the business of gambling, prostitution, or any other avocation which is contra bonos mores. So also, the legislature may lawfully forbid the prosecution of any business which, though not inherently vicious, or immoral, is regarded as contrary to public policy, or amounts to a depredation upon the rights of others."

Black, Const. Law, p. 352.

2. "The City of New Orleans has the power to assign the limits beyond which houses of prostitution shall not be permitted; an ordinance of that character merely asserts the municipal functions to secure public order, decency and morals, and violates none of the guarantees or the rights of persons and property contained in the Federal and State Constitutions."

L'Hote vs. City of New Orleans, 51 An. 93.

L'Hote vs. City of New Orleans, 177 U. S. 587.

City Charter, 1870, Section 12; of 1882, Sec. 8; of 1896, Sec. 15; of 1912, Sec. 1, Paragraph e; Sec. 6, Art. 1, and Art. 2, Paragraph d; Section 8, Articles 10 and 13.

3. Any house or any room or any part of a building used for the purposes of prostitution outside the limits fixed by municipal ordinance for houses of that character, is a disorderly house.

Act 199 of 1912.

4. "The regulations which are induced by the general sentiment of the community for which they are made and upon whom they operate cannot be said to be unreasonable."

Chiles vs. Ches. & O. Ry. Co., 218 U. S. 71; Plessy vs. Ferguson, 163 U. S. 537; Roberts vs.

City of Boston, 5 Cush. 198; Westchester R. R. Co. vs. Miles, 55 Pa. St. 213-214.

5. In Barbier vs. Conolly, 113 U. S. 27-31, it was said: "But neither the amendment (Fourteenth)—broad and comprehensive as it is—nor any other amendment, were designed to interfere with the powers of the State, sometimes termed its police power, to prescribe regulations to promote the health, peace, morals, education and good order of the people."

L'Hote vs. City of New Orleans, 177 U. S. 596.

6. An ordinance of the City of New Orleans (No. 4118, Commission Council Series), which segregates colored prostitutes in one district where prostitution is tolerated, and segregates white prostitutes in another district where prostitution is tolerated, and provides a penalty for violation of its provisions, is valid, and violates no provision of State or Federal Constitutions.

STATEMENT.

Willie V. Piazza, a negress, appeals from judgments and sentences rendered against her by the Recorder of the Second Recorder's Court of the City of New Orleans for conducting a colored house of prostitution at No. 317 N. Basin Street, in violation of Section One of Ordinance No. 4118, Commission Council Series of the City of New Orleans, as charged in Affidavit No. 53863, and for using said house, 317 N. Basin Street, as its owner, in violation of Section Three of said ordinance, as charged in Affidavit No. 53885. These cases were tried together at the hearing, under agrement that the demurrers filed and bills of exception taken to overruling of demurrers should apply to both cases as though they were being tried separately, the judgments to be rendered on each affidavit, which was done (Tr., pp. 2 and 3); and the cases come up to this Court in same transcript.

The accused withdrew her plea of not guilty in each case, and read in open court a demurrer, to which counsel for City excepted (Tr., p. 4). The demurrer (demurrers) was overruled and the case ordered to be proceeded with; the accused excepted; the Court overruled the exceptions, ordering, however, that certified copies of the ordinance and affidavits be filed, which order was complied with (Tr., pp. 5, 6, 7, et seq.); the sentences of $25.00, or thirty days' imprisonment in the parish prison in default of payment of fine, being imposed, as before said, in each case (Tr., pp. 2 and 3).

The appeal involves the constitutionality of the above-mentioned ordinance, and, therefore, we transcribe it in full, giving Sections 1 and 3 thereof in black letter as follows:

Mayoralty of New Orleans,
City Hall, Feb. 7, 1917.
Calendar No. 4224.

No. 4118, Commission Council Series.

Be it ordained by the Commission Council of the City of New Orleans, the following to-wit:

Section 1. From and after the 1st day of March, 1917, it shall be unlawful for any prostitute, or woman notoriously abandoned to lewdness, of the colored or black race, to occupy, inhabit, live or

sleep in any house, room or closet situated outside of the following limits, viz: from the upper side of Perdido Street to the lower side of Gravier Street, and from the river side of Franklin Street to the lower or wood side of Locust Street.

Section 2. From and after the 1st day of March, 1917, it shall be unlawful for any prostitute, or woman notoriously abandoned to lewdness, of the Caucasian or white race, to occupy, inhabit, live or sleep in any house, room or closet situated outside of the following limits, viz: from the south side of Customhouse (now Iberville) Street to the north side of St. Louis Street, and from the lower or wood side of North Basin Street to the lower or wood side of Robertson Street.

Section 3. From and after the 1st day of March, 1917, it shall be unlawful for any person or persons, whether the agent or owner, to rent, lease or hire any house, building or room to any woman or girl notoriously abandoned to lewdness, of the colored or black race, or for immoral purposes, outside the limits specified in Section 1 of this ordinance.

Section 4. From and after the 1st day of March, 1917, it shall be unlawful for any person or persons, whether agent or owner, to rent, lease or hire any house, building or room to any woman or girl notoriously abandoned to lewdness, of the Caucasian or white race, or for immoral purposes, outside the limits specified in Section 2 of this ordinance.

Section 5. Nothing herein shall be construed to authorize any lewd woman to occupy a house, room or closet in any portion of the city; nor shall anything herein be construed to repeal Ordinance No. 6701, New Council Series, nor to modify or amend said ordinance except so far as relates to the segregation and separation of persons of the colored, or black race from persons of the Caucasian or white race, and the renting, leasing or hiring of houses, buildings or rooms, within the limits specified in Section 1 of said Ordinance No. 6701, New Council Series.

Section 6. Any person or persons who shall violate any of the provisions of this ordinance shall be punished by the Recorder having jurisdiction, for the first offense by a fine of not less than twenty-five dollars ($25.00), and in default of payment, by imprisonment not exceeding thirty days; and for the second offense, by a fine of not less than twenty-five dollars ($25.00) and imprisonment for thirty days.

Section 7. Each day any person or persons shall continue to violate the provisions of this ordinance shall constitute a separate offense.

Adopted by the Commission Council of the City of New Orleans, February 6th, 1917.

GEORGE FERRIER, JR.,
Clerk of Commission Council.

Approved February 7th, 1917:
MARTIN BEHRMAN, Mayor.

A true copy:
JOHN P. COLEMAN,
Secretary to the Mayor.

We do not copy the demurrers, which are identical except as to the numbers thereof, nor the exceptions of the accused to the over-ruling of the demurrers; they are set forth in **extenso** in the transcript.

We note, however, that the exceptions as set forth in appellant's brief, claiming to incorporate the demurrer, give correctly neither the exceptions as taken down at the trial, nor the demurrer; Articles 11 and 12 of the demurrer, incorporated in the exceptions, as printed in the brief, are totally different from Articles XI and XII of the demurrer of record.

Nevertheless, passing that by, inasmuch as the appellant seems to pitch her case largely upon a quibble, which she raises in Article II of her demurrer, incorporated in Article I of the printed exceptions, and as said article concisely sets forth most of her other grounds of complaint, we quote it at length, as follows:

"That this segregation ordinance passed by the Commission Council of the City of New Orleans, and known as Ordinance No. 4118, Commission Council Series, is not sufficient in law to warrant the charge made in affidavit number fifty-three thousand eight hundred and sixty-three and the charge made in affidavit number fifty-three thousand eight hundred and eighty-five against this defendant, by the City of New Orleans through the Hon. Martin Behrman, Mayor of the City of New Orleans; Harold Newman, Commissioner of Public Safety; James Reynolds, Inspector of Police, and Corporal E. J. Smith, said officers acting for the City of New Orleans in their respective capacity, and that said ordinance is void **because it does not in fact prohibit prostitution** in respondent's premises, No. 317 N. Basin Street, **but does in fact prohibit defendant** from living in her said property from and after March 17, 1917. That the enforcement of said unlawful ordinance would deprive defendant of her personal liberty and property without due process of law and in derogation of her common rights; that same is oppressive, unjust and impolitic, and that said law is **ultra vires** of the municipal corporation of the City of New Orleans, unconstitutional and void."

In succeeding articles petitioner claims that the ordinance is in violation of Article II of the Constitution of the State of Louisiana, and of Article XIII of the Constitution of the United States; of Articles 166 and 167 of the Constitution of this State, and of Article XIV and Article I, Section 10, of the Constitution of the United States, and that the ordinance is an unreasonable, unlawful and unnecessary abuse of the police power, etc., etc.

To the demurrer is appended a copy of a petition, or of part of a petition, filed by the accused in the Civil District Court for the Parish of Orleans, wherein petitioner alleges herself to be of the colored or negro race, conducting a house of prostitution at No. 317 N. Basin Street, which she claims to own, and prays for an injunction restraining the city from evicting her or her tenants from the said property, from interfering with or embarrassing her in the conduct of her said "business," or otherwise enforcing the provisions of said Ordinance No. 4118, C. C. S.; also copy of order of the Court granting a preliminary injunction, limited to restraining the city from evicting petitioner or her tenants from said premises.

The testimony in the record shows that the accused is a negro prostitute, conducting a house of prostitution within the limits set apart by said ordinance exclusively for white prostitution.

ARGUMENT.

It may be said, on ample authority, that the use to which appellant puts her premises, and that her occupation and that of her inmates, roomers, or tenants—the operation of a house of prostitution and prostitution—are contra bonos mores, one in which no one can claim a right to engage, and which is subject to rigorous regulation and even extirpation by either legislative statute or municipal ordinance, so that the appellant is without right or standing in the Courts to sue to prevent, or to oppose in any way, regulation of her said occupation or "business," or to resist legislative or municipal suppression of it:

"Many statutes have been enacted in the various States for the promotion and preservation of the public morality. And they have almost without exception been sustained by the Courts as valid police regulations. Among these should be mentioned ° ° ° those designed for the extirpation of brothels," etc.

Black, Const. Law, p. 345.

"In the exercise of the police power, the State may limit the right of employment. Trades and kinds of business which are essentially noxious may be altogether prohibited by the legislature, if it shall deem such action conducive to the public welfare. No person can have a right to engage in the business of gambling, prostitution, or any other avocation which is contra bonos mores."

Black, Const. Law, p. 352.

It was with such well-founded view of appellant's plight in mind that counsel for the city replied to the demurrer, saying, in part:

"That the existence of what is known as Storyville is the result of a city ordinance, which creates and defines same; that the defendant herein owes whatever right she now possesses primarily to the existence of this ordinance, and that the power of the Municipal Government to **create** necessarily carries with it the power to **destroy**, and, therefore, includes the middle ground of creating limitations instead of destroying; that instead of the ordinance now complained against by way of demurrer, the City of New Orleans could have deprived defendant of any right to have a house of that character at all, and that, therefore, a complaint by way of demurrer against the present ordinance should have no force or effect before this Court, a conclusion which counsel for the city prays will be reached by this Court in passing upon this demurrer."

Let us, nevertheless, see what powers the legislature has granted to the City of New Orleans, which it may exercise in the regulation or suppression of the "social evil."

In the first place, there is the **GENERAL POWER**, adequate to the occasion, found in paragraph (e) of Section 1 of the Charter, Act 159 of 1912, which reads:

"The city shall also have all powers, privileges and functions which, by or pursuant to the Constitution of this State, have been, or could be, granted to or exercised by any city."

That this power alone is ample for the purpose of the ordinance in question is demonstrated by the application made of it and scope given to it in LeBlanc vs. City, 139 La. 113, and in City vs. Shuler, 140 La. —; 73 So. Rep., p. 715.

Then there is Article I of Section 6 of the Charter, whereby the city has the power, and whereunder it is its duty

"To preserve the peace and good order of the city."

And there is paragraph (d) of Article 2 of Section 6, whereby and whereunder the city has the power and duty

"To suppress all nuisances."

Then there is the very pertinent provision of Article 10 of Section 8 of the Charter, giving to the city the discretionary power

"To regulate the police of theaters, public balls, dance houses, concert saloons, taverns, hotels, houses of public entertainment, shops for retailing alcoholic liquors, **houses of prostitution and assignation, and to close such houses from certain limits, and shall have power to exclude the same,** and to close houses and places for the sale of intoxicating liquors when the public safety may require it, and to authorize the Mayor and police to close such places." (Black letter ours.)

The Charter, granted by Act 45 of 1896, contained similar provision. See Section 15 of Article IV, No. 11.

Finally, by Article 13 of said Section 8 of the Charter, the Commission Council has the plenary grant

"To exercise general police power in the City of New Orleans."

In affirmation of these various grants of power, with particular application to Article 10 of Section 8 of the Charter, we have Act 199 of 1912, making it a misdemeanor to operate a "disorderly house," and defining a **disorderly house** by Section 1, thus:

"That a disorderly house is hereby defined as any house of public entertainment or of public resort, or open to the public, conducted in such a manner as to disturb the peace and quiet of the neighborhood; also any place in which lewd dancing is permitted, or in which lewd pictures are accessible to view, **or any house used for the purpose of prostitution outside the limits fixed by Municipal Ordinance for houses of that character;** provided, that the use of any room, or any part of a building, for any of the purposes, or in any of the ways hereinabove enumerated shall constitute such room or such part a disorderly house." (Black letter ours.)

The record contains copies of restricted district Ordinance No. 13,032, Council Series of the City of New Orleans, approved January 26th, 1897; amendatory Ordinance No. 13,485, C. S., approved July

7th, 1897, changing the boundaries of the district below Canal Street created by Ordinance No. 13,032, C. S., and creating a second restricted district above Canal Street, identical with the district to which colored prostitution and colored prostitutes are limited or confined by Section 1 of Ordinance No. 4118, C. C. S., in question here; also of Ordinance No. 6701, N. C. S., approved August 2d, 1910, amending Ordinance No. 13,032 as amended by 13,485, C. S., in particulars not pertinent at the moment.

The validity of these ordinances as proper exercise of the police and other powers of the city was upheld in the case of L'Hote vs. City of New Orleans, 51 An. 93, where the change of the limits of the restricted district below Canal Street affected by Ordinance No. 13,485, amending 13,032, was contested on various grounds as unconstitutional, oppressive, unreasonable, etc.:

"The regulation of houses of prostitution would seem so closely connected with public order and decency; the policy announced by the ordinance has been so long exerted in all large cities of our country, and the power has had such frequent recognition in the charters of this city, that it would seem the power itself cannot be successfully controverted. City Charter of 1870, S. 12; of 1882, S. 8; of 1896, S. 15."

L'Hote vs. City of New Orleans, 51 An. 96.

"The City of New Orleans has the power to assign the limits beyond which houses of prostitution shall not be permitted; an ordinance of that character merely asserts the municipal functions to secure public order, decency and morals, and violates none of the guarantees of the rights of persons and property contained in the Federal and State Constitutions."

L'Hote vs. City of New Orleans, 51 An. 93.

The above quoted case was affirmed by the Supreme Court of the United States in 177 U. S., p. 587, which quotes those portions of Ordinances Nos. 13,032, and the amendatory Ordinance 13,485, which recite the boundaries of the restricted districts and the changes made:

"Obviously, the regulation of houses of ill-fame legislation in respect to women of lewd character, may involve one of three possibilities: First: absolute prohibition; second: full freedom in respect to place, coupled with rules or conduct; or, third: a restriction of the location of such houses to certain defined limits. Whatever course of conduct the legislature may adopt is in a general way conclusive upon all courts, State or Federal. It is no part of the judicial function to determine the wisdom or folly of a regulation by the legislative body in respect to matters of a police nature.

"Now, this ordinance neither prohibits absolutely nor gives entire freedom to the vocation of these women. It attempts to confine their domicile, their lives, to certain territorial limits. Upon what ground shall it be adjudged that such restriction is unjustifiable; that it is an unwarranted exercise of the police power? Is the power to control and regulate limited only as to the matter of territory? May that not be one of the wisest and safest methods of dealing with the problem? At any rate, can the power to so regulate be denied? But given the power to limit the vocation of these persons to certain localities, and no one can question the legality of the location. The power to prescribe a limitation carries with it the power to discriminate against one citizen and in favor of another."

L'Hote vs. City of New Orleans, 177 U. S. 587.

The Ordinance No. 4118, Commission Council Series, recognizes two "restricted districts," created by prior ordinances mentioned; two districts in which alone prostitution is tolerated.

By this ordinance, however, one of these districts, viz: "From the upper side of Perdido Street to the lower side of Gravier Street, and from the river side of Franklin Street to the lower or wood side of Locust Street," is now designated as the district within which prostitution by women of the colored or negro race, and the renting, and so forth, of houses or rooms to prostitutes of the colored or negro race, or for immoral purposes of women of the colored or negro race, are absolutely restricted. See Sections 1 and 3 of the ordinance.

The other district, viz: "From the south side of Customhouse (now Iberville) Street to the north side of St. Louis Street, and from the lower or wood side of North Basin Street to the lower or wood side of Robertson Street," is now made the district to which prostitution by women of the Caucasian or white race, and the renting, and so forth, of houses or rooms to prostitutes of the Caucasian or white race, or for immoral purposes of women of the Caucasian or white race, are absolutely and exclusively restricted. See Sections 2 and 4 of the ordinance.

Thus, prostitution by the colored or negro race is confined solely to the one district, and prostitution by the white or Caucasian race is confined solely to the other district. And, as heretofore, outside of these districts prostitution or prostitutes are barred from the city. See also Section 5 of the ordinance.

Now, we have the owner of a building within the limits to which are restricted prostitution by, and prostitutes of, the white race, and from which are prohibited prostitution by, and prostitutes of, the colored race, in which building she, a negro prostitute, conducts a negro house of prostitution and lodges the negro prostitutes, her roomers or tenants, demurring to the ordinance, on the ground that "it does not in fact prohibit prostitution in respondent's premises, No. 317 N. Basin Street, but does in fact prohibit the defendant from living in the said property from and after March 17th, 1917."

This is quibbling with the language of the ordinance.

The contention being, that when Section 1 declares that "it shall be unlawful for any prostitute, or woman notoriously abandoned to lewdness, of the colored or black race, to occupy, inhabit, live or sleep in any house, room or closet situated outside of the following limits," etc., and that when Section 3 of said ordinance declares "it shall be unlawful for any person or persons, whether agent or owner, to rent, lease or hire any house, building or room to any woman or girl, notoriously abandoned to lewdness, of the colored or black race, or for immoral purposes," etc., that prostitution by and prostitutes of the colored race are not prohibited in the district in which is situated appellant's property, and so in her premises; and that, although she confessedly and provedly conducts in said premises a colored house of prostitution, is herself a negro prostitute, as also her roomers or tenants, the ordinance does not cover her case.

The contention is wholly without merit. A prostitute is one who practices prostitution, and prostitutes of the colored race are barred from this particular district, and may not occupy any house or room in it under the terms of the ordinance; but a colored girl or woman who does not practice prostitution, who is not a prostitute, may rent or occupy a house or room in such district if she pleases. It is not colored girls or women, all colored girls or women, but only those who are prostitutes, or are notoriously abandoned to lewdness, who may not hire, occupy or live in houses or rooms outside the district to which the ordinance in sufferance of their vocation assigns them. The ordinance, therefore, does not affect colored women taken or considered as such simply, but only those engaged in prostitution.

There is no denial to colored women as such, simply, to live in their own property, or to make any other use of it than prostitution or the harboring of prostitutes, if their property is situated in the district assigned to white prostitution. There is a denial to colored women of the right or privilege, to use these terms, to live in their own property as prostitutes, i. e., to practice prostitution in their own property, or to permit its use for purposes of prostitution except their property be situated in a specified district, from which, in turn, white prostitutes in like manner are absolutely barred.

Let us note, again, the provisions of Act 199 of 1912, which make "any house used for the purposes of prostitution outside the limits fixed by municipal ordinance for houses of that character" a **disorderly house,** and by which also "the use of any room, or any part of a building, for any of the purposes hereinabove enumerated, shall constitute such rooms or such parts a disorderly house."

"Is the power to control and regulate limited only to the matter of territory? May that not be one of the wisest and safest methods of dealing with the problem? At any rate, can the power so to regulate be denied? But given the power to limit the vocation of these persons to certain localities, and no one can question the legality of the location."

L'Hote vs. New Orleans, 177 U. S., p. 597.

"The truth is, that the exercise of the police power often works pecuniary injury, but the set rule of this Court is, that the mere fact of pecuniary injury does not warrant the overthrow of legislation of a police character."

L'Hote vs. New Orleans, 177 U. S. 598.

In a civilized community, no one is free to conduct himself or herself wholly as he or she may please, and without regard to the ordinary usages of society, and the regulations which the governing authorities of such communities have established as rules of conduct for the members of the community to protect the public health, comfort, safety and morals.

So, the right of the owner to use his property, for himself immediately, or for what he may esteem to be the benefit of others, is important; but it is not so absolute that he may at all times, and under all circumstances, and in every way, use it as he pleases, regardless of the public morals, safety or welfare.

The maxim of the civil law, **sic utere tuo ut alienum non laedas,** is quite as well established as the common law doctrine that a man may do as he pleases with his own. All rights—certainly all rights of property—are relative:

"The police power of the State over private property and rights of property is based upon the principle that all property is held subject to the supervision of the government, in order that it may prevent the use of property to the injury or prejudice of others * * *. For example, the use of property for the carrying on of noxious, offensive, or dangerous trades may be prohibited or regulated."

Black, Const. Law, p. 359.

"No person can have a right to engage in the business of gambling, prostitution, or any other avocation which is contra bonos mores. So also the legislature may lawfully forbid the prosecution of any business which, though not inherently vicious, or immoral, is regarded as contrary to public policy, or amounts to a depredation upon the rights of others."

Black, Const. Law, p. 352.

By way of parenthesis, it may be here noticed that any one engaging in the occupation of prostitution in person, or by keeping a bawdy house, whether in her own or another's property, and even in a "restricted district" where it is tolerated, engages in a "business" universally denominated and generally denounced as an **evil** or a **vice,** in which she can legally claim no right of ownership, possession, or other rights, which the lawmaker may not regulate, still further abridge, or altogether abolish. And one who acquires property situated in a restricted district, which she uses for lewd and immoral purposes, voluntarily and knowingly assumes and takes the risk that that district may be made larger or smaller, changed to another locality, or abolished altogether, as the lawmaker may determine to better serve the interests of the community, its morals, peace, order, safety, or welfare.

It is clear that the ordinance does not deprive the respondent of her personal liberty by compelling her to live in certain specified limits, in violation of Article II of the Constitution of Louisiana, and Article XIII of the Constitution of the United States; nor impair the obligations of any contract she has made, nor divest any vested right in her, in violation of Article 166 of the Constitution of Louisiana; nor take and damage her private property without just and adequate compensation being first paid, in violation of Article 167 of the Constitution of Louisiana, or without due process of law against her consent and without compensation, in violation of the Fourteenth Article of the Constitution of the United States; nor does it run counter to Article XIV of the Constitution of the United States, providing that no State shall deprive any person of life, liberty or property without due process of law, nor deny to any person within its jurisdiction the equal protection of the laws, or otherwise offend against the State or Federal Constitutions.

It is settled that police laws and regulations are not unconstitutional, even though they may disturb the enjoyment of individual rights. If the individual suffers any injury, it is deemed **damnum absque injuria,** or in the theory of the law, the injury to the owner is deemed compensated by the public benefit the regulation is designed to subserve.

> 1 Dill. Mun. Corp., p. 93; 1 Dillon, p. 310; Black, Const. Law., p. 310; Dwarris, Statutes, p. 455.

The Federal Constitution, broad and comprehensive as it is, was not designed in any respect to interfere with the power of a State, sometimes termed its police power, to prescribe regulations to promote the health, peace, morals, education, and good order of the people.

> Barbier vs. Connolly, 113 U. S. 31.

"Ordinances to regulate and confine the prosecution of business, even lawful and not immoral in character, within certain definite limits, have been held by this Court as being purely police regulations within the competency of a municipality possessed of ordinary powers."

> Barbier vs. Connolly, 113 U. S. 27; Soon Hing vs. Crowley, 113 U. S. 707.

"In this respect we may premise by saying that one of the difficult social problems of the day is what shall be done in respect to those vocations which minister to and feed upon human weaknesses, appetites and passions. The management of these vocations comes directly within the scope of what is known as the police power. They affect directly the public health and morals. Their management becomes a matter of growing importance, especially in our larger cities, where, from the very density of population, the things which minister to vice tend to increase and multiply. It has been often said that the police power was not by the 'Federal Constitution' transferred to the nation, but was reserved to the States, and that upon them rests the duty of so exercising it as to protect the public health and morals. While, of course, that power cannot be exercised by the States in any way to infringe upon the powers expressly granted to Congress, yet until there is some invasion of congressional powers or of private rights secured by the Constitution of the States, in this respect is beyond question in the courts of the nation.

In **Barbier vs. Connolly, 113 U. S. 27, 31,** it was said:

> "But neither the amendment—broad and comprehensive as it is—nor any other amendment, were designed to interfere with the power of the State, sometimes termed its police power, to prescribe regulations to promote the health, peace,

morals, education, and good order of the people."

> **L'Hote vs. City of New Orleans, 177 U. S., p. 596.**

It is clear that the ordinance is not an **ex post facto** law aimed at the liberty and property of colored prostitutes in any illegal or hostile sense, "attempting to punish this class for their past conduct, by compelling them to live in the narrow limits designated by the city in Section 1 of this ordinance," etc., as glibly asserted in appellant's brief.

> "That there are limitations to the power asserted by this ordinance may be conceded. It does not, however, readily occur to the mind that confining houses of this character within certain limits by the appropriate ordinance is violative of any of the constitutional guarantees invoked in this discussion before us. The ordinance neither sanctions nor undertakes to punish vice. The power to punish vice not in the form of an offense, denied by the argument and enforced by the authorities we find in the briefs, is, in our view, entirely distinct from the function the ordinance asserts as belonging to municipal government by the express terms of the City Charter. It is urged, too, the ordinance is a license for vice, and, hence, illegal. Tiedeman on Police Power, p. 291. Undoubtedly, the Court should refuse its aid to any ordinance, if of the character asserted by the argument. **The vice, the subject of this ordinance, beyond the reach of penal statute, is simply subjected by this ordinance to that restraint demanded by the public interest. The unfortunate class dealt with by the ordinance must live; they are not denied shelter, but assigned that portion of the city beyond which they are not permitted to establish their houses. Thus viewed, the ordinance cannot be deemed open to the objections that it either punishes or grants a license to vice beyond the competency of the Council."** (Black letter ours.)

> **L'Hote vs. City of New Orleans, 51 Ann. 93.**

Were it true that the limits allotted in sufferance of colored prostitution are narrow, as claimed in the brief for the first time, it would be a question which, in matters of this sort, as the Supreme Court of the United States said in L'Hote vs. City of New Orleans, addresses itself to the discretion of the local legitlature, the wisdom or folly of which does not concern the Court. So said this Court in the same case in these words:

> "If the ordinance is lawful, this question of space is, in our opinion, confided to the Council, and not the courts."

> **51 Ann., p. 97.**

It is also argued in the brief that it is unreasonable and oppressive to allocate the colored prostitutes to a section of the city largely inhabited by colored people, and confine them to a district already inhabited by colored prostitutes. We should suppose that such distribution of the district would be quite appropriate, as there is everywhere manifest the exceedingly strong tendency of the members of each race to separately congregate. **The truth of the matter, the real reason for the opposition and objection, is the fear of the loss of trade of those debased white** men on whose indulgence of their appetites in sexual intercourse with colored prostitutes the keepers of negro bawdy-houses hope to thrive and prosper.

We do not believe that the courts will lend aid and comfort to the conservation of such a state of things, which, in the interest of public decency, health, morals, good order and welfare, and in response to the general sentiment of the community, this ordinance will abate in a very great measure, if not wholly suppress.

The crux of the argument for appellant is in the contention of the right of the colored prostitute to ply her vocation, not in **as good a locality** as her white sister in shame, but in the **same locality.**

It is not an **equality** of rights and privileges (if we can use such terms in this case) that are demanded, but **identity.** So appellant argues that she is "punished" because colored prostitutes are prohibited from plying their trade in the white district.

"It is to be carefully borne in mind that it is not identity of rights and privileges which this amendment (Fourteenth) guarantees, but equality. Hence, for example, while it would not be competent for the legislature of a State, in establishing and prescribing regulations for the public schools, to exclude negro children from the benefits of the public school system on account of their color only, yet the State may establish separate public schools for colored children, and require them to attend those schools or none, provided the accommodations, advantages, and opportunities, and the relative appropriation of the public funds for their support are in all respects equal to those provided for white children."

"It is lawful for a railroad company, or other common carrier, to provide separate carriages, or other separate accommodation, for different classes of patrons, where the distinction is founded on some reasonable ground and there is no invidious discrimination against any, and there are equally desirable accommodations for all who pay at the same rate. Thus, a distinction may be made, in railroad cars and waiting rooms, between men and women, or between negroes and white people."

"A statute declaring intermarriage of a negro and a white person illegal, or a nullity, or a felony, is not inconsistent with, or repugnant to, the provisions of the Fourteenth Amendment. Such a law cannot be said to deny to any person the equal protection of the laws. And the same is true of an act providing a greater punishment for adultery between a white person and a negro than for adultery between those of the same race. This is not a discrimination against any particular race, but simply provides a penalty for an offense which could only exist when the parties were of different races."

Black, Const. Law, p. 469, with numerous authorities.

The objections that are advanced in support of what is claimed to be discrimination in this ordinance have already been advanced in the many cases, State and Federal, regarding segregation of the races in schools, trains, coaches, waiting rooms, and the like.

Appellant brushes these cases aside, by arguing that in the coach or car cases no property rights were involved, as if, forsooth, there could be a property right to engage in prostitution, or that the cessation on the part of the lawmaker or governing authority of the sufferance of prostitution in any locality deprives the owner of property in such locality of any vested property rights—a most unwarranted contention, as we have heretofore shown; and in the case of schools, putting the admitted reasonableness of the segregation upon a plea similar to that of **de minimis,** that children only attend school for a few hours a day.

The truth of the matter is, that in laws and ordinances establishing segregation the legislating authority recognizes racial distinctions, and the sentiment of the community respecting these distinctions; and in determining the question of reasonableness of statutes and ordinances affecting segregation of the races, enjoys a large discretion "to act with reference to the established usages, customs, and traditions of the people, and with a view to the promotion of their comfort, and the preservation of public peace and good order, and, as said, having in view also the sentiment prevailing among the people where the law is to operate.

We shall now call the Court's attention to some of the cases which hold valid and constitutional statutes and ordinances affecting segregation of the races, and we beg to note that many of these cases were adjudicated by courts sitting north of Mason and Dixon's line, where, if anywhere, the civil rights of the colored race have received full recognition, showing that the feeling against close contact of the races is not confined to the South.

We especially call the Court's attention to the case of Chiles vs. Chesapeake & Ohio Railroad Company, 218 U. S. 71, where it was held, that since Congress had failed to act with respect to the separation of colored and white passengers, on interstate trains, an interstate colored passenger, under the rules and regulations of a railroad company, could be compelled to occupy a separate compartment on a train. If such a regulation by a mere railroad company can be held not an unreasonable discrimination against the colored race, then, a **fortiori,** such must be the decision in the case of the ordinance of a great and congested metropolis, passed under ample grant of power, implied and expressed, in the interest of peace, order, safety, health and morals, and carrying into effect the prevailing sentiment of the community, based upon racial dissimilarities and antipathies, shunning social amalgamation naturally, and **revolting against the very closest of physical contacts.**

"It may be said, in a general way, that the police power extends to all the great public needs. Camfield vs. United States, 167 U. S. 518. It may be put forth in aid of what is sanctioned by usage, or held by the prevailing morality, or strong and preponderant opinion to be greatly and immediately necessary to the public welfare."

Noble Bank vs. Haskell, 219 U. S. 104.

It cannot be denied that the separation of colored prostitutes from white prostitutes is in the interest of the peace, good order and morality of this great city of the South, and that the Commission Council of the city is the proper judge of the preponderating opinion of the community as to the necessity of the ordinance; nor will this Court fail to recognize the prevailing sentiment of the community against social intermixture, miscegenation by illicit intercourse or intermarriage, and other forms of close contact of the races.

The earliest and leading case on the subject was written by Chief Justice Shaw, of Massachusetts, in the case of **Roberts vs. City of Boston, 5 Cushing 198,** decided in 1849. This case is notable, not only as the decision of a great Northern judge in the State where, and rendered at a time when, the movement for the emancipation of the colored people was active, but also because the alleged right of the negroes to sit side by side with the whites in the schools of Boston was championed in that case by no less a person than the celebrated Charles Sumner. Answering the contention of Mr. Sumner, the Court, through Chief Justice Shaw, said (5 Cushing 148):

"It is urged that this maintenance of separate schools tends to deepen and perpetuate the odious distinction of caste, founded in a deep-rooted prejudice in public opinion. This prejudice, if it exists, is not created by law, and probably cannot be changed by law. Whether this distinction and prejudice, existing in the opinion and feelings of the community, would not be as effectually fostered by compelling the colored and white children to associate together in the same schools may well be doubted; at all events, it is a fair and proper question for the committee to consider and decide upon, having in view the best interests of both classes of children placed under their superintendence. We cannot say that their decision upon it is not founded on just grounds of reason and experience, and in the results of a discriminating and sound judgment."

This Massachusetts case is quoted, with approval, in the case of **Plessy vs. Ferguson, 163 U.S. 544.** In **Westchester R. R. Co. vs. Miles, 55 Pa. St. 213-214,** the Supreme Court of Pennsylvania say:

"The right to separate being clear in proper cases, and it being the subject of sound regulation, the question remaining to be considered is whether there is such a difference between the white and black races within this State, resulting from nature, law and custom, as makes it a reasonable ground of separation.

"The question is one of difference, not of superiority or inferiority. Why the Creator made one black and the other white we know not; but the fact is apparent, and the races distinct, each producing its own kind and following the peculiar law of its constitution.

"Conceding equality, with natures as perfect and rights as sacred, yet God has made them dissimilar, with those natural instincts and feelings which He always imparts to His creatures when He intends that they shall not overstep the nat-

ural boundaries He has assigned to them. The natural law, which forbids their intermarriage and that social amalgamation which leads to a corruption of races, is as clearly divine as that which imparted to them different natures. The tendency of intimate social intermixture is to amalgamation, contrary to the law of races. The separation of the white and black races upon the surface of the globe is a fact equally apparent. Why this is so, it is not necessary to speculate; but the fact of a distribution of men by race and color is as visible in the providential arrangement of the earth as that of heat and cold. The natural separation of the races is, therefore, an undeniable fact, and all social organizations which lead to their amalgamation are repugnant to the law of nature. **From social amalgamation it is but a step to illicit intercourse, and but another to intermarriage.** But to assert separateness is not to declare inferiority in either. It is not to declare one a slave and the other a freeman; that would be to draw the illogical sequence of inferiority from difference only. It is simply to say that, following the order of Divine Providence, human authority ought not to compel these widely separated races to intermix. The right of each to be free from social contact is as clear as to be free from intermarriage. The former may be less repulsive as a condition, but not less entitled to protection as a right. When, therefore, we declare a right to maintain separate relations, as far as is reasonably practicable, but in a spirit of kindness and charity, and with due regard to equality of rights, it is not prejudice, nor caste, nor injustice of any kind, but simply to suffer men to follow the law of races established by the Creator Himself, and not to compel them to intermix contrary to their instincts."

It is worthy of note that this philosophical discussion of the status of the two races, and the fundamental principles upon which separation of the black and white races may be justified, came from a Pennsylvania Court at the very time when people were voting upon the Fourteenth Amendment, and when the subject was one of bitter feeling between the North and South, and of heated political discussions throughout the country.

The right of the Legislature to enact such laws as shall give the children of the white and colored races equal educational advantages, but in separate schools, has been recognized and declared in Pratt vs. Commissioners, 94 N. C. 709, and in McMillan vs. Committee, 107 N. C. 609.

In the latter case the Court quotes with approval Gaines vs. McCann, 21 O. 210, saying:

"In the case of Gaines vs. McCanna, 21 Ohio, 210, Judge Day, delivering the opinion of the Court, says: 'Equality of rights does not involve the necessity of educating white and colored persons in the same school any more than it does that of educating children of both sexes in the same school, or that different grades of scholars must be kept in the same school; any classification which preserves substantially equal school advantages is not prohibited by either the State or

Federal Constitution, nor would it contravene the provisions of either.' "

McMillan vs. Committee, 107 N. C. 609.

The same North Carolina Court also refers to a New York case to the same effect, as follows:

"Where the statute of New York allowed the Board of Education to adopt regulations for the admission of pupils, so that they assigned all to schools affording equal advantages, and a colored man sought by **mandamus** to compel the admission of his children to a school where white children were taught instead of that for colored children, to which they were assigned by the board, the two schools affording equal advantages, the Supreme Court of New York refused the **mandamus**, among other reasons, because a citizen was not allowed to select a school which his children should attend, in the face of a reasonable regulation made by the board by authority of law."

Dietz vs. Eaton, 113 Abott's Pr. R. 164 and 165.
McMillan vs. School Committee, 107 N. C. 609.

In Louisville & Nashville Railway Co. vs. Mississippi, 133 U. S. 587, a statute requiring railroads to furnish separate but equal accommodations was upheld, but the Court did not consider that the question whether such accommodation shall be a matter of choice or compulsion on the part of passengers to enter into the case.

In Ex Parte Plessy, 40 An. 80, was considered a similar statute of Louisiana, providing that the officers of passenger trains in this State were required under penalty to assign each passenger to the coach or apartment used for the race to which such passenger belongs; that any passenger insisting on going into a coach or compartment to which by race he does not belong shall be liable to a named penalty; and that the officer of such railway shall have power to refuse to carry any passenger refusing to occupy the coach or compartment to which he is assigned.

The statute was held to violate neither the thirteenth nor fourteenth amendment of the United States Constitution. We quote two of the syllabi:

3. In such matters equality, and not identity or community, of accommodations is the extreme test of conformity to the requirements of the amendment. (14th).

"4. The regulation of domestic commerce is as exclusively a State function as the regulation of interstate commerce is a Federal function. This statute is an exercise of the police power and expresses the legislative conviction that the separation of the races in railway conveyances, with proper sanctions for substantial equality of accommodation, is in the interest of the public order, peace and comfort. It is a matter of legislative power and discretion with which courts cannot interfere."

The decision of this Court was affirmed in Plessy vs. Ferguson, 163 U. S. 537, from the opinion rendered in which case we quote the following pertinent passage:

"So far, then, as a conflict with the fourteenth amendment is concerned, the case reduces itself to the question whether the statute of Louisiana is a reasonable regulation, and with respect to this there must necessarily be a large discretion on the part of the Legislature. In determining the question of reasonableness it is at liberty to act with reference to the established usages, customs and traditions of the people, and with a view to the promotion of their comfort, and the preservation of the public peace and good order. Guaged by this standard, we cannot say that a law which authorizes or even requires a separation of the two races in public conveyances is unreasonable, or more obnoxious to the fourteenth amendment than the acts of Congress requiring separate schools for colored children in the District of Columbia, the constitutionality does not seem to have been questioned, or the corresponding acts of State legislatures."

In Chiles vs. Chesapeake & Ohio Railway Co., 218 U. S. 71, it was held that, under the rules and regulations of that railroad company an interstate colored passenger could be compelled to occupy a separate apartment on a train, Congress having passed no regulations with respect to the separation of colored and white passengers on interstate trains. The syllabus reads as follows:

"As held by the Court of Appeals of Kentucky, a railroad company has the right, in that State, to establish rules and regulations which require white and colored passengers, even though they be interstate, to occupy separate apartments upon the train provided there is no discrimination in the accommodations.

"In this case **held**: That an interstate colored passenger was not compelled to occupy a separate apartment on a train in Kentucky from that occupied by white passengers under a State statute, but **under rules and regulations of the railroad company.**

"Whether interstate passengers of different races must have different apartments or share the same apartment is a question of interstate commerce to be determined by Congress alone. **Louisville & Nashville Railroad Co. vs. Mississippi**, 133 U. S. 587, and the inaction of Congress in that regard is equivalent to the declaration that carries can by reasonable regulations separate colored and white passengers.

"The regulations which are induced by the general sentiment of the community for whom they are made and upon whom they operate cannot be said to be unreasonable."

After discussing the case of Hall vs. DeCuir, 95 U. S. 485, wherein the Court held an act of the State of Louisiana, which required those engaged in the transportation of passengers among the States to give all passengers traveling within that State, upon vessels employed in such business, equal rights and privileges in all parts of the vessel, without distinction of race or color, and subjected to an action for damages the owner of such vessel who excluded colored passengers on account of their color from the cabin set apart for whites during the passage, which was held to be a regulation of interstate commerce, and, therefore, void, and distinguishing between that case and the case before it, the Court went on to say:

"In Plessy vs. Ferguson, 163 U. S. 540, a statute of Louisiana which required railroad companies to provide separate accommodations for the white and colored races was considered. The statute was attacked on the ground that it violated the thirteenth and fourteenth amendments of the Constitution of the United States. The opinion of the Court, which was by Mr. Justice Brown, reviewed prior cases, and not only sustained the law, but justified as reasonable the distinction between the races on account of which the statute was passed and enforced. It is true the power of a legislature to recognize a racial distinction was the subject considered, but if the test of reasonableness in legislation be, as it was decided to be, 'the established usages, customs and traditions of the people' and the 'promotion of their comfort and preservation of the public peace and good order,' this must also be the test of the reasonableness of the regulations of a carrier, made for like purpose and to secure like results. Regulations which are induced by the general sentiment of the community for whom they are made and upon whom they operate cannot be said to be unreasonable. **See,** also, Ches. & O. Ry. Co. vs. Kent, 179 U. S. 388."

The contention of counsel for the appellant, made in the conclusion of their brief, that if this Court should hold this ordinance valid, then perhaps at some time the City of New Orleans might pass an ordinance segregating all colored men who have been saloonkeepers to one small section, and make it unlawful for them to live or sleep elsewhere, and similarly segregate white men who have been saloonkeepers to another section, shoots wide of the mark of the evident intent of the ordinance in question. Some such inept arguments have been advanced before in similar cases. In Plessy vs. Ferguson, 163 U. S. 549-550, the Court dealt with such a one, as follows:

"In this connection it is also suggested by the learned counsel for the plaintiff in error that the same argument that will justify the State Legislature in requiring railways to provide separate accommodations for the two races will also authorize them to require separate cars to be provided for people whose hair is of a certain color, or who are aliens, or who belong to certain nationalities, or to enact laws requiring colored people to walk upon one side of the street and white people upon the other, or requiring white men's houses to be painted white and colored men's black, or their vehicles or business signs to be of different colors, upon the theory that one side of the street is as good as the other, or that a house or vehicle of one color is as good as one of another color. The reply to all this is that every exercise of the police power .must be reasonable and extend only to such laws as are enacted in good faith for the promotion of the public good and not for the annoyance or oppression of a particular class."

We pass lightly over the cases concerning laws and ordinances enacted in various States to segregate colored and white races in a measure by prohibiting the establishment of residence in the future upon given streets or blocks by white or colored people, except where a majority of residents of such street or block are white or colored, which counsel for appellant discusses at large.

These enactments are not germane to the ordinance in question. Nevertheless, ordinances of such character have been adjudged a reasonable exercise of the police power, and, therefore, valid, by the decisions of the highest courts of three States, passing directly upon them, viz:

State vs. Gurry, 121 Md., 534;

Hopkins vs. Richmond, 117 Va. 692;

Buchanan vs. Warley, 165 Ky. 559.

In two others—**State vs. Darnell, 51 L. R. A. (N. S.) 332,** and **Carey vs. Atlanta, 81 S. E. Rep. 456**—ordinances of a similar nature to the first three cited, were held invalid, in the Darnell, or North Carolina case, mainly because the town of Winston had no grant of police power; and, in the Georgia case, the Chief Justice was absent, and Judge Lumpkin, concurring in the result, dissented from the reasons of the Court.

The Kentucky case is now before the Supreme Court of the United States. With the solution which that Court may give of the problem before it we have little or no concern; ours is a vastly different question, which we thought had been long since definitely determined.

We have given this case, perhaps, more consideration than it deserves, and are confident that this Court will maintain the validity of the ordinance and affirm the judgment of the lower court accordingly.

Respectfully submitted.

I. D. MOORE,
City Attorney.
JOHN F. C. WALDO,
Assistant City Attorney.
GEO. F. BARTLEY,
Assistant City Attorney.

APPENDIX F: A directory of jazz musicians who performed in the legally constituted tenderloin district known as Storyville between January 1, 1898, and November 17, 1917

t=trumpet, c=cornet, tb=trombone, cl=clarinet, m=mellophone, vt=valve trombone, g=guitar, bj=banjo, b=bass, d=drums, p=piano, v=violin, tu=tuba, acc=accordion, pc=piccolo ° =frequently leader.

Ahanie, Frank - p
°Albert, Tom - t
°Allen, Henry, Sr. - t
Amacker, Frank - p
Annison, ——— - p
Atkins, Eddie - tb
Avery, Joseph "Kid" - tb

Bailey, Dave - d
Baptiste, René - g
Baquet, George - cl
Barbarin, Paul - d
Barnes, Emile - cl
Barnes, Harrison - tb
Barthe, Wilhelmina - p
Bechet, Sidney - cl
Ben, Paul - tb
Benoit, John - d
Benson, Hamilton "Hamp" - tr
Benton, Tom - g
Bertrand, Buddy - p
Bigard, Emile - v
°Bocage, Peter - v, t, c
°Bolden, Charles "Buddy" - c
Bolton, "Red Happy" - d
Bontemps, Willie - b
Boyd, George - cl
Braud, Wellman - b
Brooks, Joe - g, bj
Broussard, Theo - b
Brown, Jimmy - b
Brown, Johnny - cl
Brown, Octave - tb
Brown, Tom - mandolin
Brundy, Walter - d
Butler, Joseph - b

Campbell, Arthur - p
°Carey, Thomas "Mutt" - c, t
Carroll, Albert - p
Carter, Buddy - p
Carter, Willie - d
°Celestin, Oscar - t
°Chambers, Tig - c
Chandler, Dede "Dee Dee" - d
Charles, Hippolyte - c
Christian, Narcisse J. "Buddy" - p
°Clem, Edouard - t
Coborn, Tom - b
Cornish, Willie - tb
Cottrell, Louis - d
Coycault, Ernest "Nenny" - c
Coycault, Phil "Pill" - cl

Davis, Sammy - p
Dawson, Eddie - b
Decou, Walter - p
Delisle, Baptiste - tb

Delisle, Louis. See Nelson.
°Depass, Arnold - d
°Desvigne, Sidney - c
Dodds, Johnny - cl
Dodds, Warren "Baby" - d
Dominguez, Paul, Sr. - v
DuConge, Oscar - c
Duhé, Lawrence - cl
Dutrey, Honore - tb
Dutrey, Sam, Sr. - cl
°Duson, Frank - tb

Elgar, Charlie - v
Evans, Roy - d

Fernandez, Albert - cl
Filhe, George - tb
Ford, Henry - b
Foster, Abby "Chinee" - d
Foster, George "Pops" - b
°Foster, Willie - bj, v
°Frank, Alcide - v
°Frank, Bab - pc
French, Maurice - tb

Gabriel, Albert - cl
Galloway, Charley - g
Garland, Ed "Montudi" - b
Gaspard, Tom "Oak" - b
Glapion, Raymond - bj
Glenny, Albert - b
Goldston, "Black Happy" - d
Gorman, Israel - cl
Gould, Johnny - v

Hall, Minor - d
Henry, Oscar "Chicken" - p
Henry, Sonny - tb
°Hightower, Willie - c
Howard, Joe - c, tu

Jackson, Eddie - b
Jackson, Frank - c, tu
Jackson, Jessie - bj
Jackson, Tony - p
Jackson, Ulysses - tb
James, Louis - cl
°Johnson, Bill - b
Johnson, Buddy - tb
°Johnson, Bunk - c
Johnson, Jimmy - b
Johnson, Lonnie - g
Johnson, Yank - tb
Jones, David - s
Jones, George - b
°Jones, Richard M. - p
Joseph, John - b
Joseph, Willie - cl

Kelly, Ernest - tb
°Keppard, Freddie - t

Keppard, Louis - g, tu
Kimball, Andrew - c
Kimball, Henry - b
King, Wiley - b

°Lacoume, Emile
   "Stalebread" - g, bj, p
Landry, Tom - vt
Lenares, Zeb - cl
°Lewis, Dandy - b
Lewis, Foster - d
Lewis, Steve - p
Lindsay, Herb - v
Lindsay, John - tb, b
Lindsay, Papa - g
Love, Charlie - c
Lyons, Bob - b

MacCurdy, Charles - cl
MacMurray, John - d
MacNeil, James - c
MacNeil, Wendell - v
Manaday, Buddy - bj
°Manetta, Manuel - p, v, c, tb, g
Marrero, Billy - b
Marrero, John - bj
Marrero, Simon - b
Martin, Coochie - g
Martin, Henry - d
Matthews, Bill - d, tb
Matthews, Ramos - d
°Metoyer, Arnold - c
Mitchell, Albert - bj
Mitchell, Bebe - d
Moore, Charles - g
Morton, Jelly Roll - p
Mumford, Brock - g

°Nelson, "Big Eye"
Louis Delisle - cl
Newton, Willie - b
°Nicholas, Joseph
"Wooden Joe" - cl, t
Nickerson, Phil - g
Nolan, Poree - p
Noone, Jimmie - cl

°Oliver, Joseph "King" - c
Olivier, Adam - v
°Ory, Edward "Kid" - tb

°Palao, James A. - v
Palmer, Roy - tb
Parker, Willie - cl
Payne, Richard - g
°Perez, Manuel - t
°Petit, Buddy - t
°Petit, Joe - vt
°Peyton, Henry - acc
Philip, Joseph "One-Eye
Babe" - b

Picou, Alphonse - cl
Pierre, Joe - d
°Piron, Armand J. - v
Predonce, Johnny - b
Preston, Walter - bj

Rankin, Hugh - b
Raphael, Bernard - tb
Rapp, Butler "Guyé" - bj
°Rena, Henry "Kid" - t
°Ridgely, William "Bebé" - tb,
Robertson, Zue - tb
Robinson, Oscar - b
Rogers, Ernest - d
Ross, Kid - p
Rubean, Lutzie - b

St. Cyr, Johnny - bj, g
Santiago, Willie - g, bj
Sayles, George - g
Scott, Alex - b
Scott, Arthur "Bud" - g
Small, Freddie - cl
Smith, John "Sugar Johnny" - c
Staulz, Lorenzo - g

Thomas, Bob - tb
Thomas, George W. - p
Tilman, Cornelius - d
Tio, Lorenzo, Jr. - cl
Tio, Luis "Papa" - cl
Trepagnier, Ernest "Ninesse" -

Valentin, Bouboul - vt
Vigne, Jean - d
Vigne, John - p
Vigne, John "Ratty" - d
Vigne, Sidney - cl
Vinson, Eddie - tb

Wade, Louis - p
Warner, Albert - tb
Warner, Willie - cl
Warneke, Louis - sax
Washington, Fred - p
Washington, George - tb
Welch, Joe - d
Welch, Joe - v
Whaley, Wade - cl
Williams, "Black Benny" - d
Williams, Clarence - p
Williams, George - g
Willigan, Bill - d
Wilson, Alfred - p
Wilson, Udell - p
Wood, Eddie - d

Zeno, Henry - d

APPENDIX G: A typical issue of the Sunday Sun

CARNIVAL EDITION.

The Sun.

Established 1888. NEW ORLEANS, SUNDAY, FERUARY 25, 1906.

PRICE FIVE CENTS
Newsdealers and Carriers 3 cents

Another Carrie Nation.

Alice Thompson of 1022 Conti as alleged to have gone in search of her friend and what she done was a plenty.

One good thing follows another but it is not often the case that one rough house rather fol-low another so close in its wake, but such is the case how-ever. We had occasion very re-cently to report the cases of two rough houses, and it has since al-so come to pass that the old max-im of the fatal three is again veri-fied. The two previous cases we refer to were read with interest by the society set many our dear girls found themselves, endeavor-ing to feret out how girls who claimed to be ladies could won-tonly commit themselves in such ways. The third case to come un-der our notice lately is that of a well known girl Alice Thompson of 1022 Conti street who is charg-ed in the Second City Criminal Court before Judge A. M. Aucoin by Louise Blass of 1018 Bienville street with malicious mischief. The alleged misconduct on the part of this lady is said to have transpired on February 19, about dusk when it claimed Alice visit-

The French Balls.

And the probable candidates for the Queen Title.

The event of the Mardi Gras season in the four-hundred social circles of which our dear girls re-present a large percentage will be those warm french balls given at Odd Fellows Hall on Saturday and Tuesday nights respectively. These strictly local affairs, which have long since become famous will exceed all former balls, and a grand time at high revelry will be given those attending. These great events will be conducted as in the past by the two well known gentlemen which means a whole bit. The topic of conversation among the landladies and leading girls of the district during the week has been relative to the queenship and much speculation has been rife among them. Among those spoken of are the Misses Josie Arlington, Margaret Brad-ford, Hilda Burt, Margaret Miller, Jessie Brown, Kay Owens, Flor-ence Lesslie, Flora Meeker, and following all star boarders Myrtle Burke, Eva Standford, Daisy Mer-rit and many others too numerous to mention.

ed the home of Louise in search of a friend and while there wrecked some portions of the household effects said to be valued at thirty dollars. Miss Cora Turner a resi-dent of the latters home is said to have witnessed the Carrie Nation act and will be used as a witness.

Loe Letters.

Endeing and Sweet Figure in a prominent Society Scandal.

Miss Rosa Lish who formely re-sided in this City at No 1213 St Charles Ave is now in New York, according to the Journal taking a prominent part being the pro-secutrix in a rich breach of prom-ice suit to the tune of $2000 damages During the action of the trial new love letters breathing affection exposed in the hands of the parties have been brought to light. The suit is directed against H B Sauss, of No 317 East Nine-teenth Street, by Miss Rose Lish, of No 533 Madison Avenue, who is a tall brunette, 28 years old, she says the defendant earns a large salary as a traveling salesman. The money is not asked as a balm to wounded affections, but as a re-compense for humiliation, and for the trouble of preparing a trous-seau In all the letters it was ap-parent that the first name of the young woman, Rose, furnished in-spiration, or rather, was a basis for "flowery" language. Mr Strauss was away from Miss Lish conside-rably, as he traveled, but in all letters the writer expressed feve-rish desire to find the Rose bloom-ing fragrant and sweet upon his return,

Judge Ford.

Girls and others when in trouble should consult Judge Tom Ford the well known practicing attorney at law, who takes cases before all Courts. He is a good one, and one of the most popular lawyers in town.

The Cosmopolitan.

The really first class swell french house No 1510 Customhouse St, conducted by Miss ... good time. See Sapho the little mascot, sweet Marrie the girl who knows how to entertain and many other good things too numerous to mention. Every language is spoken here and all the new fancy dances given nightly.

Wm. M Levy's sure Cure for Gonorrhea and Gleet, Cures in 1 to 3 days. Price 75 cents.

Keep posted. Read and ad-vertise in the Sun.

"I ask damages for my humilia-tion and for the trouble that I had taken to prepare my wedding—not for my wounded affections." said Miss Lish.

205

SUNDAY SUN.

ISSUED BY

Sun Publishing Company.

Devoted to Sporting and Social
Events of the Day.

Office : 508 Caronde'et 3d Floor.

Published Every Saturday.

SUBSCRIPTION PRICE:

One Year, in Advance..............$2.00
Six Months, " 1.00
i ngle Copy, " 5

Advertising Rates furnished on application at this Office.

The Sun is Non-Mailable.
Use Express.

This Week

Tulane—McIntyre and Heath
Grand Opera House—Old
Heidelberg
Orpheum—Modern Vaudeville.
Greenwall — Manchester's
Cracker Jack.
Crescent—Maid and the Mum-
my.
Lyric—How Baxter butted in.
Elysium —Ten nights in a bar-
room.
French Opera—Opera.
Knights of Momus— Ball and
Pageant, February 22nd,
Arrival of Rex. King of the
Carnival, Monday afternoon,
February 26th.
Knights of Proteus, Ball and
Pageant, Monday, February 26
Rex Parade, Mardi Gras, Feb-
ruary 27th.
French Ball at Odd Fellows
Hall, Saturday, February 24th.
Two Well-Known Gentlemen
Ball at Odd Fellows Hall,
Mardi Gras night.

SCARLET
WORD.

The Arlington Saloon, No.12 N.
Rampart street, presided oer by
Tom Anderson, is the prinipil and
most popular resort for allsporting
men. Everything you get here is
first-class.

The Arlington over Anderson's
Annex has been doing a fine Carnival business during the week.
Miss Arlington was in hopeof oc
cupying a portion of her Mnsion
ere this, as was stated in thipaper,
but it now transpires that it will be
fully fifteen days before th Contractor can turn over the Mnsion.

Miss Hilda Burt the lovig proprietress of the Star Mansi. who
took a flying trip to St Luis, returned last Sunday.

There are several dive along
Basin which we advise te boys
to steer clear off by readig the
Sun, and keep posted on atters
pertaining to your future health
and well fare.

Read Block's advertisemnt else
where in this paper. It is nteres-
ting to you all, girls.

Little Grace of Basin near
Bienville street who tried suicide
Tuesday night is now sorry she
tried it for her idiot act has cost
her the loss of a very dear
producing friend.

One of the pretty petite brunette queens who has many new
surprises for the boys during
the holidays and at all times is
sweet little Ellie DeCorevont
known as "Gold Tooth" Washington D C belle. This charm
ing little woman can be be found
at the French Studio No 331 N
Basin avenue.

The establishments kept by
Miss Ivy Abronds of Bienville
and Robertson streets are filled
up with a bunch of swell little
ones, for Mardi Gras. Boys this
is the place to go when out for a
good time. New surprises all
the time.

Mardi Gras is now upon us
and everybody will lay aside
business cares for a few days
and give way to fun, frolic and
sport, and don't forget the two
french balls Saturday and Tuesday night

There was a big rumpus in
one of the leading establishments
on Basin ave last Wednesday
night when the bell boy tried to
kiss a chambermaid She would
not have it and thus, consterna
tion.

A well known local landlady is
now dickering for the upper
floors of Anderson's Palaial Annex now occupied by Miss Josie
Arlington, and it is rumored
when Miss Josie shall have moved into her new home her present temporary quarters will be
turned into a permanent sport
ing establishment and operated
on the swellest plans. The lady
now after the place is well known

LULU WHITE

The above cut is the swell Lulu
White who is known by reputation
the World over. Lulu is without
a doubt one of the swellest landladies in the country and also bears
the reputation of being the Queen
of Diamonds, as she wears a young
fortune in the precious stones,
nightly. The Magogany Ha'l the
name of her establishment contains
at the present time 40 of the swellest Octoroons in the World. This
mansion is situated on Basin Avenue and Bienville street.

Mary Smith does not expect
much this Mardi Gras. No wonder
she needs new material and faces.

Maggie Wilson a buxom and
pretty little woman who lives at
1314 Customhouse street, informs
the Carnival visitors who are out
for a good time to call on her, and
she will give them a run for their
money. And that's no dream.

Read the Sun.

The Arlington.

This gilded palace has a national reputation and is know the World over. In this mansion are to be found a fine contingent of fascinating girls. The Arlington has broken records for a number of lovely queens; and it has now in its mansion eighteen of the creme de la creme of female lovliness to be found. Popular Annie Casey is still the efficient and well liked housekeeper. Strangers here during the carnival will be royally entertained, and a sweller or more elegant mansion does not exist. Until Miss Arlington's Mansion is finished she is to be found over Anderson's Annex corner Basin avenue and Customhouse street.

----o----

Miss Hilda Burt

Star Mansion.

Miss Burt a young woman of great popularity and one who has been in our city but a short time, has become one of our most popular landladies, and her Mansion, "The Star" which is situated at No. 1442 Customhouse street has become the rendezvous of the bon tons. Miss Burt has made great preparations for the Carnival, and those visiting this famous establishment will be assured of a most enjoyable time. Her ladies are truly dreams.

----o----

Miss Jessie Brown.

Maison De Joie.

Miss Brown has the honor of keeping one of the finest and most elaborately furnished establishments in the city, where beautiful women, good wine and sweet music reign supreme. Jessie is clever to every one and keeps one of the most refined houses in the Tenderloin. Miss Brown's number is 1542 Customhouse street. A royal time will be accorded all those visiting this up-to-date establishment, Jessie is a good fellow, full of fun, intelligent and as pretty as a doll. It is no wonder she is making so many friends,

MISS FANNIE LAMBERT.

- -

The Phoenix.

Among the landladies who are doing fine and dandy is Miss Fanny Lambert who keeps that elegant mansion No 1547 Customhouse streets. Miss Fanny is a recognized good fellow and enjoys a very prosperous business in the village. She is surrounded by a number of swell entertainers and good lookers who can please the most fastidious.

MISS FLORA MEEKER'S

Palace of Mirth.

Everybody in the sporting world knows Miss Flora Meeker and she knows everybody worth knowing. So it is unnecessary at this time to make any introductory remarks about Miss Meeker, suffice to say she is still at her same old place where she has been for a number of years past, doing a boss business which she deserves, Miss Flora is well thought of by all and her house is patronized by the best element. Carnival visitors should not overlook this swell mansion where the cream of female loveliness will be found which is situated at No. 211 Basin avenue.

----·----

Miss Julia Dean.

Boys if you are looking for a good time, visit the home of Miss Dean at the Corner of Conti and Basin Avenue, and get acquainted with some fine young girls who can cure the worst case of blues on earth. Miss Julia is a fine, good fellow, and has no equal when it gets down to real article.

Miss Dean is the oldest landlady in the district to-day and all through her life she has been known to conduct nothing else but a first class establishment.

----o----

Read the Sun.

Miss May O'Brien.

The Irish Queen.

Miss May O'Brien, proprietress of 1549 Customhouse street, popular with all, has a house full of beautiful young girls and increasing her business daily. May is the Irish Queen, and always has a sweet smile on her face. The many strangers who will come to the city during the Mardi-Gras should not fail to visit this establishment. A royal time will be accorded all those visiting this up-to-date house at any time.

Miss Lou Prout.

Miss Lou Prout whose reputation for keeping a swell furnished room house is second to none, is located at No. 1551 Bienville, between Villere and Robertson streets. Miss Lou, because she continues to do a good business is perhaps the most popular woman in that line of business a fact which is proven by the swell patronage given her establishment. Strangers and others in quest of a good time can find it at this house.

Society Continued.

Jules Kuhn still has his eye on the little Basin street blonde. Say old boy, we give you credit for having a good taste in looks.

Belle Boyd the charming blonde of Mahogany Hall is looking more like a two year old now than ever. Belle is a peacherine

"Its" or jennie men as they are sometimes called are plentiful around Canal and Franklin streets. The police ought to break this bunch of human vampires up.

A certain saleslady in one of the Canal street stores ought to let up meeting the proprietors son-in-law on Carondelet and Lafayette streets before we spring a story on them.

The conductor on the Dauphine line ought to stop making sweet eyes at the negress employed corner North Rampart and Conti street. Shame.

Minnie Rosenthal is now living with Miss Jessie Brown 1542 Customhouse street. Boys, she is the goods.

A grand french ball will be given to night and every night during the week at the French Studio on Basin Avenue, boys this is the house to visit these times for a hot time. Ellie the gold tooth kid is the star and she is a dandy too.

This is the leading french house in the country and every language on the globe is spoken and new attractions are being booked all the time. So boys get in line for Studio.

Read The Sun

Boys and girls when you are hungry and haven't got much money go to the "Little Place Around the Corner," No 1503 Bienville near Marais street, kept by J Dalliano. He has a Mexican cook who is a good one. Short orders, and oysters in every style will be found there.

Harry, why don't you go and see Edith, she is grieving about you, and looks awful bad. Make up Harry, she's a good fellow and loves you.

Miss Marguerite who keeps at Nos 213 and 215 Basin avenue is doing fine and dandy. She has several fine looking girls living with her who are up to date, and ready for any good old time. Visit the place and be convinced.

Say Clara Moore, you better be careful that some one don't make you pay a beer license.

Romey Young from Galveston, Tex is expected in a few days, and has engaged rooms with Miss Margaret Bradford.

Thousands have seen her, and millions have heard of her, such are the expressions of many regarding the extensive popularity of Countess Willie Piazza, who operates a swell house at No 317 Basin avenue. Carnival visitors should visit this establishment if they want a swell time.

There is but one house, and one alone, that can be termed first class on Robertson street, and this place is Miss Ivy Abronds corner Bienville. The others we have our doubt. So boys beware, lest you get caught out that way.

Read the ads elsewhere in these columns of the C, C,C,Club and the "Two Well known Gentlemen." These Clubs give their annual balls on February 24 and 27th Mardi Gras.

Estelle, who occupies the neat cottage 305 Basin ave, near Bienville, has an idea of business, Estelle is a pronounced brunette and a genuine Parisian buxom and very pretty woman. Estelle has many friends who admire her for the many good qualities she possesses. She is an entertainer, speaks several languages, and is a thorough good fellow. A visit to her will not be regretted.

Among the swell houses in the district there is none more popular or attractive than that one which is operated by Miss Antonio Gonzales, on Customhouse street corner of Villere. All summer this resort has done good business notwithstanding the prevailing dull times. This place is filled with beautiful young women all the time, and a visit to the tenderloin is incomplete without enjoying a good time here. This place es what we might property term a modern music casino.

Miss Margaret Miller the sweet and amiable landlady who occupies 337 Basin avenue is making so many friends of late that she cannot entertain half of them. It shows to reason why she is so popular. Miss Marguerite is a good fellow, and a swell entertainer. She has also a house full of pretty girls, and to convince yourselves of this, visit the house. Don't forget the number, 337.

Two sweet girls from Hattiesburg Miss. have come here and have embarked in business at No. 1418 Conti Street, and the firm is styled Douglass and Wells, Vivian the senior partner is a petite and charming person, while her partner Nina is enhancing to say the least. So boys if you want to have a good time visit these girls and they will entertain you in true Mississippi style.

Miss Gypsy Shafer a queen among landladies of 1552 Customhouse Street entertains her patrons in true up-to-date style and those who have visited this swell establishment always return. The lady entertainers now with Miss Gypsy are of the creme de la creme stock, and as Miss Shafer herself is a fine fellow well known through out the city it is no wonder her house is doing so well. Strangers in town for the Carnival should by all means visit this house and enjoy a swell time with the girls.

Miss Mittie Cook who keeps a beautiful double cottage at Nos. 1509 and 1511 Customhouse street, wants her friends and patrons to know that she has increased her staff and she now has a house full of beauties. For a good time visit this establishment, boys, as the motto is good treatment and a run for your money.

Lulu White, the Queen of Diamonds and the proprietress of Mahogany Hall, always gets the cream of business if there is any. She is always surrounded by the finest and prettiest lot of Octoroon beauties to be found in the country. Her house has a national reputation.

Among the landladies who have become very popular, is Miss Vivian who keeps a modern establishment at No. 325 Basin avenue. In this palace of joy there can be found a bevy of girls who are not only fine lookers, but entertainers in the art. Boys visit this house for a good time.

Miss Annie Ross who is known far and wide for a keeping one of the most orderly houses in the city and who is located at No. 210 Marais street has made many additions to her staff and boys when you are out for a good time visit these girls you will find them always ready to give you a good time and a run for your money. Here are their names; Grace Williams, Bertie Williams Nellie Hook, Jessie Herring, Camille Dupre, Mamie Snyder and Josephine Lore.

Miss Nellie Condon the proprietress of 1414 Conti street is enjoying every blessing of life these days. Nellie is one of those creatures whose irresistible fascinations never fail to captivate the admirations of every one, and it goes without saying that Nellie is one of these best of good fellows at all times. She has living with her Edna Woods and other girls who never fail to please.

Boys when you go out looking for a real good time, where you take no chance what so ever. The house you want to visit is that one operated by that princess of good fellows Miss Ivy Abronds situated at the corner of Bienville and Robertson streets (also a very quiet reserved spot in the tenderloin). In this establishment can be found at all times a bunch of beautiful young girls all the time who can please the most fastidious and exacting.

Read the Sun.

HINTS FOR FARMERS

Lameness In Horses.

In a general way wounds on any part of the body may be treated as follows: First remove all dirt or foreign matter. Cold water is good at first, but it must not be continued too long or it will cause cicatrization, and it should be stopped as soon as all fear of inflammation is over. In the fore quarters lameness is generally in in the foot or in the parts below the knee; in the hind quarters it is in the hamstring, fetlock or the foot, these being the most susceptible parts. If the reason for lameness cannot be at once seen, the shoe should be removed and the foot examined carefully; the shoe may be too tight or there may be a tender part on the sole of the foot. If so, relieve pressure or apply poultices. If the coronet, fetlock joint or sinews are tender, apply cold or warm bathing and rest. Strains of the fetlock are very frequent, and cold dressings should be applied, with a moderately tight bandage. Lameness in the shoulder is very rare.—American Cultivator.

Barnyard Manure.

Barnyard manure not only supplies food for plants, but it enables the soil to retain more moisture. This is often a very important quality and is never estimated by the chemist in comparing it with commercial fertilizers. It also seems that, while keeping the surface soil more moist, it also increases the water deeper down, thus making the best possible condition for plant growth. Of course when rough manure is plowed under the first effect is to dry out the surface, but this does not last long. When it is once thoroughly wet and settled this eff—— disappears. The first foot of well manured land may hold eighteen to twenty tons more of water per acre than the same soil unmanured.

... congratulated Mr. Bigelow ... awkwardly on this address, and the learned traveler replied:

"That is a doubtful compliment. It reminds me of a remark that a friend of the groom's made at a New Hampshire wedding.

"This friend, an observant chap, watched the groom closely during the ceremony and at the end bore down on the happy man, shook him warmly by the hand and said:

"'Bill, ye done good. I had an idee ye would be skittish while ye wuz bein' tied up, but, begosh, ye looked as bold as a sheep!'"—Washington Post.

Got Quay's Opinion.

A young Philadelphia lawyer eager to shine in party councils once consulted the late Senator Quay as to ways and means, says the New York Times.

"I've been in politics over a year," he said, "and I find it rather a difficult problem. I can't say I'm getting on very rapidly, and I'm fast losing my individuality, and I'm fast losing my individuality, and I'm fast losing my individuality, is it?"

"Well," answered the senator in a droll, quiet way, "I should say it was the best thing that could happen to you."

The French Studio which is known as one the chief attractions of Storyville is one of the brightest and best place to visit when out for a good one. Miss Emma Johnson the old lady is too well known to need introductions suffice to say is the swellest on the avenue and her girls are the finest to be found anywhere. Every language is spoken here and all other new dances are seen here nightly. So boys when looking for a real first class house go to the French Studio on Basin ave.

THE

Royal Restaurant

AND

Oyster House,

136-38-40 Royal Street,
Corner Iberville

TORTORICH BROS., Proprietors.

Open Day and Night.

Phone Main 281-Y

We make a specialty of our
, Drip Coffee.

JAMES J. BEL,

CARPENTER and BUILDER,

Office and Store Work
a Specialty

"Now, my child," said the anibal mother to her youngest hopeful, "I want you to be on your good behavior and not make a pig of yourself."

"What for?" demanded the young savage.

"Because we're going to have that new minister for dinner."—Exchange.

More Suitable Name, He Thinks.

"Some people insist on referring to flats as 'apartments.'"

"It's wrong," answered the discontented man. "They are compartments."—Washington Star.

Utilizing the Log.

Miss Querie—I understand you had a narrow escape crossing the Atlantic?

Mr. Hard-Port—Yes, indeed. The coal ran out, and the captain had to split up the ship's log to keep the fires going.

Exhausting.

Mrs. Gramercy—Which of your social duties do you find most exacting?

Mrs. Park—To appear interested in the things that don't interest me.

It is the simpleton who doesn't dare to be simple.

Fifteenth Grand Fancy Dress and Masquerade Ball

TO BE GIVEN BY THE......

C. C. C. CLUB,

AT ODD FELLOW'S HALL,

On Saturday Night. Feb. 24, 1906.

Subscription Price, $3.00.

Tickets and Ladies Invitations can be procured by applying at Anderson's Saloon, No. 112 N. Rampart Street, or to Lamothe's Restaurant, No. 137 St. Charles Street.

Grand Fancy Dress and Masquerade

BALL,

——TO BE GIVEN BY THE——

Two Original Well-Known Gentlemen,

AT ODD FELLOWS HALL,

On Tuesday Night, Feb. 27, '06,

Price of Admission, $3.00.

Tickets and Ladies' Invitations can be procured by applying at Anderson's Saloon, No. 112 N Rampart Street, or to Lamothe's Restaurant, No 137 St. Charles Street.

==WEST END==

Hotel and Restaurant

Open Summer and Winter.

T. Tranchina,

Proprietor.

Phone 2292.

THE LITTLE PLACE

AROUND THE CORNER,

JAKE DALLIANO, Prop.

1503 Bienville St., near Marais.

Oysters in all Styles,

Macaroni, and all short orders
a specialty.

Prices Moderate.

MANUEL SALAZAR,
Cook.

Our Leading Brands, "Centennial Rye," "Raleigh Springs," "Southern Cross Rye" and Athletic Club."

GOODMAN BROS..

Importers, Distillers and
Wholesale Liquors,

Memphis, - - Tenn.

D. J. McEVOY,
New Orleans Salesman.

Phone 2614 L Main.

Members of the Real Estate Auction
Exchange
225-227-229 Baronne Street.

J. T. BRADY.　　　T. J. MOULIN,

BRADY & MOULIN,

AUCTIONEERS,

Real Estate and Insurance,

739 Union Street.

Phone Main, 4427.

209

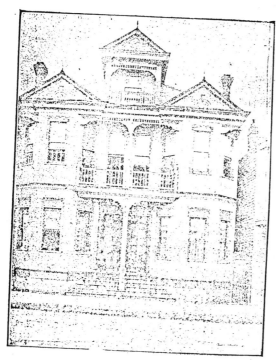

THE FRENCH STUDIO.

The above cut represents the new French Studio of Miss Emma Johnson formerly of 159 Customhouse St.

As originator of the French Studio Miss Johnson has established a line of business envied by most of the French women. Emma was for several years at 159 Customhouse street and moved to her present large and beautiful house, 331 and 333 N Basin Avenue, some three years ago. The French Studio is crowded with girls of all nations and to those who are looking for a genuine circus is the place.

Advertise in the Sun.

210

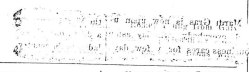

Zimmer a Jockey Trainer.

A. Zimmer, who trains for T. D. Sullivan, has been in racing a comparatively short time, and consequently his success in the development of jockeys is the more remarkable. In three years he has brought out Fuller, Crimmins and Shilling, a record to be proud of. Crimmins and Shilling are riding in such form that they are growing in popularity and give promise of being two of next year's best boys. They have still much to learn before they can be called finished horsemen, but they are apt pupils and are in a good school.

THE UNION SAILOR.
How Organization Has Improved the Condition of Jack Tar.

To show how the trades union has benefited society it is only necessary to point out what it has done for the sailor. Before the seamen were organized Jack enjoyed less consideration than any other representative of skilled labor. When, however, he came into the range of the trade union's activity he was transformed into an entirely different man.

He was made to understand his own rights and powers and to insist upon the one and to exercise properly the other. He was no longer a kind of human driftwood floating from port to port and during on the way all kinds of injustice and bad treatment. Steadily, since he became a trades unionist, the seaman has risen in self respect and the respect of others.

He is now quite universally a man with a local habitation and a name and no longer a roving, reckless tar, to be made the scapegoat of every riotous disturbance on shore. A confirmed spendthrift before, with no thought of the morrow, he is now in the majority of cases a thrifty man. The trades union has brought out his good points, of which he always had a large number, and he now enjoys respect that formerly he could not command.

Temperance has spread among the seamen until now intoxication is the exception and not the rule. Order also is a part of their lives ashore, and the influence of the law abiding sailor dominates every group of which he is one.

The trades union has made citizens of all the sailors that have invoked its fraternity. It has insisted that the members of the Seamen's union should ... out their citizenship papers and ... fostered and in every way has cultivated the self respect of its members. The consequence has been that some of the most skilled labor that we have today is performed by men who formerly were sailors.

The structural iron workers, for instance, have among them more men who have been sailors than any other class, for the structural iron worker requires the peculiar kind of nerve and skill that the sailor learns on board ship in keeping his head at dizzy heights and working swiftly and carefully in perilous and cramped positions.

The personnel of our merchant marine has greatly improved in character since the trades union has been at work among the sailors, and with the growth of the trades union's influence that personnel will continue to improve.—Labor Leader.

Payroll of the Steel Trust.

A booklet just issued gives the number of employees of the United States Steel corporation at present at approximately 50,000 men. Of this number over 10,000 are engaged in various manufacturing properties of the corporation. Last year the total number of all employees in the service of the corporation was 167,709 compared with 168,127 in 1902. The total amount paid in salaries and wages last year was $120,769,826. This year's total is expected to fall much below that because of reductions and dropping from the payroll of a number of high salaried employees "taken over" in consolidations. It is estimated that this year's salary and wage roll will not exceed $1 ...

New York Labor Unions.

The New York Labor Bulletin, published quarterly by the state department of labor, says in the editorial summary of the current issue:

"The industrial depression of the last year is reflected in the check to the growth of labor organizations in certain industries, notably the manufacture of machinery and tools. The decline in the metal trades, about 10 per cent, is fairly general throughout the state. In New York city, however, the principal forces were in the building and the woodworking trades.

"At the end of September the bureau of labor statistics had 2,505 labor unions on its records, a decrease of fifty-one since March 31. The aggregate membership of all unions was 391,681, a decline of 8,051, or 2 per cent, since March."

Champion of Human Rights.

The labor movement is more a question of humanity than a question of the almighty dollar. It has accomplished more in that direction practically than any other society, not even excepting the church. It is the greatest movement in the championship of human rights and human liberty.—Galveston Journal.

Such Is Life.

Pitiless Greed, insatiate to oppress
And grind the faces of the suffering poor!
A lower wage means more of wretchedness,
Of cold and want than toil has felt before,
But Plenty, knowing not the keen distress,
Piles up the burdens Labor has to bear.
Of suffering a little more or less
Will matter not for those long used to care.
While in its lair Want's specter grim doth hide,
...

A Householders' Union.

The flat dwellers and householders of Chicago propose a union the object of which is stated to be the regulation of rents and exposure of rent raising conspiracies, furnish legal advice and defend members in litigation for right, agitate for civic rights, enforce ordinances relating to sanitary conditions, to work for street improvements, compel landlords to live up to their leases, supply heat and make promised improvements and to co-operate with labor unions and other organizations working in the interests of the landless class.

LABOR NOTES.

Union labor continues to thrive in Indianapolis notwithstanding the fact that Parry's "buggy" shop is located within its gates.

Label agitation is being taken up more extensively by many unions. It is a work that is bound to prove valuable. Boom the label and buy union label goods.

The Hatters' union of England is said to be one of the richest unions in the country. It has $100,000 invested.

The Master Painters' association and the Brotherhood of Painters, Decorators and Paper Hangers of Pittsburg have signed another wage scale and agreement for 1905, which is practically a continuation of last year's contract.

Read The Sunday Sun and be wise.

THE DAILY PICAYUNE—NEW ORLEANS, TUESDAY, MARCH 25, 1913.

DANCE HALL FEUD ENDS IN DEATH OF TWO RIVALS

William Phillips and Harry Parker Killed in Early Morning Battle.

GUNMAN HARRISON DANGEROUSLY HURT

Phillips Assassinated by the Others and Charlie Parker, Who Is Also Wounded.

DOUBLE CROSS THEORY

Police Declare Belated War on the Shameful Resorts and Order All Closed.

William Phillips, proprietor of the 102 Ranch Dance Hall; Harry Parker, alias Abraham Sapio, proprietor of the Tuxedo Dance Hall, killed; Charles Harrison, alias "Gyp the Blood," dangerously wounded; Charles Parker, alias Isadore Sapio, wounded, and a colored waiter boy employed in the Tuxedo saloon, on North Franklin Street, slightly wounded in the hand, is the result of a shooting affray which occurred at 4:30 o'clock yesterday morning in the barroom of the Tuxedo Dance Hall.

The shooting was a decidedly mixed-up affair, and while there is no question as to who killed Phillips, who was the first victim, there is doubt as to who killed Harry Parker and wounded his brother, Charles, and "Gyp the Blood." It was a desperate affair throughout, and the interior of the saloon, visited several hours after the shooting, showed this plainly. A glass mirror behind the bar was shattered with a pistol ball. A door communicating with a hallway leading into the dance hall was wrenched from its hinges and a glancing shot plowed a furrow ten inches long in the door and a bullet split the planks in a partition in the rear of the saloon.

WAS AN OLD FEUD.

It was an existing feud between the two dance hall keepers which dated back nearly a year which brought it all about and had led to frequent encounters between the parties during that time. What occurred yesterday morning is told as related by witnesses to the affray, all habitues of or residents in the underworld. The dance halls close up at midnight on Saturday and remain closed until Monday evening, when the saturnalias again begin and are carried on throughout the week as soon as night falls. While there is no dancing or music after midnight Saturday until Monday night, yet the halls themselves cannot be said to be closed, for ranged along the walls on each side of the dancing floors are boxes or booths, in each of which is a table with benches for the accommodation of such as desire to watch the dancers while sipping beer, liquor or wines, as the case may be, and there can always be found women and men in these boxes and booths, even while there are no other attractions. Such was the case yesterday morning when the shooting occurred.

The waiters and bellboys usually have a resting spell during this time and they sometimes pass away time by visiting the various places and indulging in drinks. James Enright, employed by Phillips, with two others entered the rival saloon, the Tuxedo, about 4 o'clock. Enright was under the influence of liquor, and when one of his companions assaulted a cashier of the Tuxedo saloon he remained, while the others fled. Enright was accosted by Harry Parker, who ordered him out of the saloon and grasped him by the collar to eject him. Enright resisted, when Parker commenced beating him and finally forced him outside.

PHILLIPS' NAME MENTIONED.

While struggling with Enright and using strong language, the name of Phillips came up, and Parker is said to have made some uncomplimentary remarks toward him. These words were repeated to Phillips, who was in his place of business diagonally opposite the Tuxedo, and when told of this he went over to see about it. Phillips had had several quarrels and one of two fist fights with Parker, and he went over to Parker's place in his shirtsleeves. He entered the saloon, and, accosting Parker, told him that he ought not to beat up his employees because he had a grudge against him, but if he wanted to take it out to try it on him, who was able to defend himself. After a short wrangle matters seemed to simmer down and Phillips went back to his place of business. With a view to ending the trouble and fixing up differences he returned to the Tuxedo, taking with him two friends, whom he had invited to drink with him. They entered the Tuxedo, and Phillips, laying a dollar down on the counter, invited all hands to join him in a drink. Harry Parker was behind the counter, and his brother, Charles, also, but towards the end nearest the dance hall. Harrison, or "Gyp the Blood," was employed in the Tuxedo as a waiter, but when Phillips entered the second time he hurriedly left the place. While Phillips was leaning over the counter with his hands on the dollar bill, "Gyp the Blood" stepped up be-hind Phillips, and, placing the muzzle of his revolver to Phillips' back, he fired. Then he fired three more shots in rapid succession, one of them grazing Phillips' neck.

FELL IN THE STREET.

Phillips then ran out and across the street towards his place of business, but just as he stepped across the curbing in front of his place he fell, and in a few moments expired. This, however, did not end the shooting, for as soon as he had left other shots were fired. Harry Parker was shot in the back and staggered back into the dance hall. Charles Parker was shot in the left arm and in the back, while "Gyp the Blood" was shot in the back of the head and seriously wounded. The colored boy was somewhere in the sa-

HARRY PARKER.

loon and received a wound in the hand. He claims one of the bullets fired by "Gyp the Blood" in the very beginning of the affair did it. Charles Parker fell behind the counter and "Gyp the Blood", in front of the counter, but a few feet from where he stood when he shot Phillips. Harry Phillips was still alive, and the ambulance, having been sent for to take Phillips to the hospital, took Parker instead, Phillips having expired before the ambulance arrived. "Gyp the Blood" and Charles Harris were also taken to the hospital and "Gyp the Blood" placed under the influence of opiates. Charles Parker would not speak about the affair at all and "Gyp the Blood" could not, and even when he recovered from the influence of the opiates he refused to say anything about the affair.

STATEMENTS OF WITNESSES.

Captain Leroy and his men secured about twenty witnesses to the affair and their statements were taken. Nearly all agreed as to the shooting of Phillips, which appeared to have to the shooting of Parker and the others, the statements were at variance. Among those who were on the scene were Tony Battistina, proprietor of a saloon at the corner of Bienville and North Franklin Streets, and Albert Morris, bartender for Phillips.

213

Morris had a revolver, but Battistina denied that he had any weapon, but he saw "Gyp the Blood" fall and he picked up the revolver which he dropped out of his hands and handed it over to the police. Some of the witnesses, among them Charles Parker, himself, accused Battistina with having shot and killed Harry Parker, and Morris was accused of having shot and wounded Charles Parker, but both these denied the accusation in toto. No one was accused of having shot and wounded "Gyp the Blood," and there were some who believed that he had been shot by Parker from behind the counter. Harry Parker, according to the statements, was standing in front of Phillips at the time he was shot and the bullet struck the mirror just behind him, while one bullet found imbedded in the partition wall must have passed uncomfortably near Charles Parker where he stood at the end of the counter. The bullet which grazed the door was picked up on the floor. The revolver of "Gyp the Blood" had four chambers discharged

WILLIAM PHILLIPS.

and was recovered by the police. Another revolver, a forty-one Colts, was found on the sidewalk in front of the saloon, and a third, a magazine or automatic Colts, was found on a shelf behind the counter, where Harry Parker was standing in front of Phillips.

Two wounds were found on the body of Phillips, one on the back of the neck, which only grazed the neck, and the other passed through the arm and into the body between the fifth and sixth ribs and perforated the left lung and went into the right lung, where it remained imbedded and was extracted by the coroner.

One wound was found on the body of Harry Parker. The bullet entered the back and passing inward and downward perforated the left lung and diaphragm, causing internal hemorrhage and death.

PARKER AND PHILLIPS' FEUD.

The origin of the feud existing between Parker and Phillips dates back about eight months. Phillips purchased Parker's interest in the 102 Ranch Dance Hall about a year ago, and for two or three months after that Parker remained with him. Parker then left and engaging with Harry Brooks and Will Harris he opened the Tuxedo, which is just opposite his place, which he had sold to Phillips. Phillips, when he heard that Parker was about to open up an opposition hall to his after selling out to him and promising not to open up another dance hall in the district, became angry and used every effort to

prevent a license and permit being given to Parker and his partners. He went around among the neighbors to get up a counter petition to that circulated by Parker, and among those who took part with Phillips was Battistina, who kept a saloon at the corner of Bienville Street, just below, and naturally wanted to keep out all competition that he could. Battistina, however, would not sign against the permit, but held aloof, refusing to sign in favor of it. This is what is supposed to have caused ill feeling between Battistina and Parker, but Battistina denies this most emphatically and claims that, while Parker had not been speaking to him for a long time, he had only a few days since commenced speaking to him and visited his place several times and drank with him.

However, this had nothing to do with Parker, and Phillips was unsuccessful in keeping Parker out, and Brooks, one of the partners in the new place, having a lot of money, fitted out a fine dance hall, as dance halls go. After that Phillips and Parker quarreled often and on several occasions came to blows, Phillips usually getting the best of the fistic arguments, and such was the state of affairs between them last Monday morning.

Parker has been in the limelight quite frequently. He came here several years ago from New York and opened a saloon in the Tenderloin District, with an Italian, at the corner of Liberty and Customhouse Streets. Selling out this establishment, he opened up the 102 Ranch Dancehouse. His brother Charlie, while not directly interested in the house, was a frequent, if not a constant, visitor there, and while there met a woman who was the friend of a man named Anstett. Charlie Parker alienated her affections from Anstett and then tried to get the woman to swear out an affidavit against Anstett for violating the white slave law. This brought on trouble between Anstett and Charles Parker, and a shooting affray resulted in which Parker was wounded. This occurred in the saloon of Battistina, and the latter was a witness against Parker and this, too, may account for the ill-feeling existing between Battistina and the Parkers. Some time after this Harry Parker while drunk met Anstett in a saloon at the corner of Bienville and Marais Streets and Parker shot at An-

CHARLES HARRISON.

stett. These several affairs brought the entire crowd before the district attorney and the Criminal Court, and then it developed that Parker was not the name of the two men, but that their real names were Abraham and Isidore Sapiro, and Assistant District Attorney Warren Doyle had them indicted under their real names. After this Parker seems to have become disgusted with the dance hall business and sold out to Phillips about a year ago.

FROM NEW YORK SLUMS.

The Parkers were well known in the

slums in New York and recently when Rosenthal was murdered there and many of the bad men of New York left for the good of the city and country, some of them came here, among them the man known as "Gyp the Blood." The latter name is that of one of the most desperate of the New York gunmen and Harrison, when he came here, adopted the name, probably thinking it would give him prestige. When this influx of former friends arrived Parker sought to obtain employment for them, and employed some of them in his dance hall as waiters. It was customary to pay waiters a dollar a night, and this with the tips they received often ran up the receipts of a waiter to eight or ten dollars per night. Parker discharged some of his men and hired these fellows from New York, cutting out the dollar a night wages and making them depend entirely on tips for their compensation. The other waiters objected to this and Phillips would not adopt the same measures, and neither did the proprietors of the other dance halls. The waiters became angry and fights between them were frequent. One waiter, an ex-prize fighter, was set upon by half a dozen waiters from rival saloons and badly beaten up one night, and since then there has been a regular war between them. When Enright, therefore, came into the Tuxedo Parker was only too anxious to find an excuse to put him out and incidentally to give him a beating, and this is what brought on the fight. As to "Gyp the Blood," but little is known except that he was one of the gang of ruffians who infested New York, but he was by no means a shining light among them, but like many from the metropolis he imagined that the worst there was better than the best here. He was loyal to his employer, and when he found that Phillips was a thorn in the side of Parker he determined to get him out of the way at the first opportunity, and did so. Whether Parker knew of this cannot be said, for he is dead now, and "Gyp the Blood" cannot or will not speak.

The shooting aroused the indignation of Superintendent Reynolds to such an extent that he determined to close up every dance hall in the district, and issued orders to Captain Leroy to at once close up these places. Further than that the superintendent says that he intends to keep them closed up. The body of William Phillips was taken to his residence, 2427 Banks Street, from whence the funeral will take place at 3 o'clock this afternoon. The body of Parker, or Sapiro, was conveyed to Mrs. Lynch's undertaking establishment, and if instructions are not received here before this morning the body will be interred in a temporary grave until later, when it will be exhumed and sent North. It is possible that it may be sent away this forenoon, however.

THE DOUBLE CROSS.

The Underworld's Theory About the Dance Hall Tragedy.

When the Parker brothers died from bullets received in the Tenderloin war, what is believed to be one of the coldest and vilest plots ever perpetrated, even in the eyes of the underworld, according to its constituents, died in their hearts, and only one lingers between life and death who can throw a light on the subject. He is Charles Harrison, alias "Gyp the Blood."

A crime which would leave an everlasting stigma on the instigators, which, even in his low business, would be too obnoxious to be tolerated, was the one attributed to the Parkers. The crime is that of the double cross, or in their own vernacular, "working both ends against the middle." Even in the degradation of the underworld a "man's a man"—to fight and fall, or stand. With one exception fairness in battle is a part of their creed, and that is when dodging the officers of the law.

That through personal animosity and

business competition the Parker brothers and their gang wanted "Billy" Phillips out of the way is known, and a common warfare of personalities for two years—since Phillips opened the 102 Ranch—has been in vogue. However, save for a personal combat between the clans, nothing serious has ever occurred.

In police circles this animosity became manifested in the nature of sureties and collaterals for miscreants. Should a Parker henchman become embroiled in Phillip's place, it was Parker who placed a collateral for his release from jail, or if Phillips' friend was arrested in Parker's place the same was evident. In this way—in personalities and in business—the strained relations gradually grew, with Phillips gaining the upper hand.

Although Phillips was above Parker in his standing, according to the ruling of the little world of degradation, his business was below the standard set by the Tuxedo, Parker's place. Phillips, however, was ahead of Parker in his personal standing and was practically recognized as king of the dance hall men. Although he was known as a good "mixer" in the Tenderloin, he had the happy facility of making lasting friends and acquaintances.

Parker was practically the opposite type. Surly in disposition, with an air of one forced into fellowship, he generally could be seen standing, quietly at the end of his bar, or seated at the table with his mistress and a party of habitues. Fearless to a fault, always ready to fight and with a general carelessness regarding the city or state code, he flourished in his business, owing to the fact that his place was of a more commodious nature than Phillips'.

But, according to Tenderloin experts, Parker longed for the personal power of the apparent gentlemanly proprietor who held forth across the street. The feud started out of the business rivalry, rising to blows and finally culminating in death to both sides, would lapse at times, with a mutual agreement in the nature of a truce. During these times the heads of the factions, surrounded by a large party of male and female admirers, would be seen frequently "spending" freely in the house of their enemy. This was due to Tenderloin ethics.

However, even this show of fellowship on the part of Phillips and Parker only worked toward the fathering of greater animosity on the part of Parker, who sought to have Phillips removed, that he might reign as social and business king of the district which they inhabit. To gain this purpose, Parker—Harry—together with his brother are supposed to have worked the "double-cross."

Receiving "Gyp" in their midst as a "bad gunman from New York," it is alleged the Parkers sought to make a tool of him with a price of his ultimate death to cover their deed. It is believed by the frequenters of the places who knew of the factional feeling, that Parker connived with Gyp to kill Phillips. To keep up his boasted record, and with a possible promise of financial gain, Gyp eagerly agreed.

However, this is believed to have been the simplest portion of the plot. "Squealing" is not an unknown factor in the underworld, and of this Parker, one of the most hardened, knew well. Under pressure the true story of the assassination would be worked from the murderer and he would become implicated.

Fearless of any ordeal under which he may have to go, but with a subconscious abhorrence of the law which he so frequently violated, it is believed that Parker thought to inject himself and brother into the quarrel which must ensue at the killing and in the fusillade kill his hireling, thereby burying the story of the crime. Gyp was seriously wounded in the pistol battle, and this greatly adds to the belief.

According to the negro porter's statement, who was an eyewitness to the shooting, Gyp and the two Parkers were the only ones who were shooting, or had revolvers. Following the dastardly shot, which was fired into Phillips' side, while he was staggering out of the place, one of the Parkers fired at him. Both fired practically at the same time, but one of the bullets is supposed to have sped for the murderer, causing the serious wound in Gyp's shoulder.

Following the first fusillade no other shots were fired, save for the rapid cracking of Gyp's revolver, when he wheeled on his employees. Evidently realizing that he had been "double-crossed," the paramount thought in his brain was to "get even."

It was then, when he wheeled on Parker, that he proved himself a real "gunman," and a good one, too. Wounded, perhaps fatally, he wheeled and dealt out death with a lightning accuracy that has perhaps never before been equaled in New Orleans criminology. In a last dying effort he avenged himself of the "double-cross," and though perhaps steeped in crime, carried with him the grim satisfaction of "getting even."

THE DANCE HALLS

And Their Status in the Tenderloin World and Ways.

All day yesterday and last night a high tension hung over the tenderloin district, where the killing of the two Parker brothers and "Billy" Phillips occurred. Unlike any other section in which a death may occur, the tenderloin has a pulse whose pulsations are erratic and contrary to natural tendencies.

Throughout the streets, in the cabarets and about the dance halls a quiet gossip was carried on fretfully in almost a whisper. Everywhere the sensational pistol battle was food for conversation, but in this, too, the tenderloin ethics were uppermost. Men feared, yet seemingly fearless, refused to take sides in the discussions which naturally followed the shooting.

Instead of hiding in unknown quarters, as is generally the case following a sensation, the eyewitnesses and acquaintances of the dead men flocked the streets and stood in large groups for hours at a time in front of the closed dance halls. Curious sightseers also flocked in hundreds all day yesterday and last night to see the scene of the shooting.

At each place—the Tuxedo and the 102 Ranch—the shades were drawn and both were closed, not even the bars being opened. A dim light showed from behind the curtains, evidently the light of some guard who had been placed on duty in the places. All other lights about the places were extinguished.

The Tuxedo dance hall and bar and the 102 Ranch dance hall and bar and several other similar places in the tenderloin are, according to visitors and tourists, to be found only in this city. In no other city in the country are such places in vogue, run on the principle that they are here. Some similar resorts exist elsewhere, but ethically they are diametrically different.

The Tuxedo, a model of the dance halls which make up a good part of the tenderloin, occupies a berth on North Franklin between Bienville and Iberville. The bar faces the street and opens, without screens, the full width of the part apportioned to it, onto the street. Petitioned off from the bar is a narrow runway leading to the dance hall. This is a large hall, possibly 100 feet in length and about 30 or 40 feet wide.

At the lower end of the hall a stand has been erected for the music, about 12 feet from the dancing floor, and is connected with by a small, narrow stairway. Here a negro band holds forth and from about 8 o'clock at night until 4 o'clock in the morning plays varied rags, conspicuous for being the latest in popular music, interspersed with compositions by the musicians themselves. The band has a leader who grotesquely prompts the various pieces, which generally constitute several brass pieces, a violin, guitar, piccalo and a piano.

The leader of the band at the Tuxedo was the pride of the house. Harry Lauder, Billy Van or George Evans never had anything on him in funny facial expression or funny twists of the legs. When he led the band people stopped to watch his antics. He was probably the only salaried man in the band, the others being supported by tips received from the dancers.

Along the walls of the dance hall were grouped chairs and tables, where the intermission between the dances were spent. White-coated waiters waited the tables, depending on the tips they made for a livelihood. It was such a person as this, the recognized scum of humanity, that Gyp the Blood, Phillips' murderer, was. In these halls also several women worked, it is alleged, for the money that they made on "checks."

The "check" system is one of the universal features of dance halls the country over. The women, sloughed in the depths of degradation, frequent the halls and dance with those who happen to walk in the place. Custom decrees that the man who dances with one of the women must buy a drink during the intermission. For this drink both for himself and the woman he pays 25 cents each. The woman is given a check, redeemable from the proprietor following the night's work at 12 1-2 cents each. The dances are advertised as being free, but it has been estimated that they cost a man on the average of 60 cents—50 cents for drinks, 5 cents tip to the waiter and 5 cents tip to the band.

All the Tenderloin, however, is not ruled in this manner. There are distinct social bodies who whirl in this little world, three in number. They are the dance hall women, the women who inhabit immoral houses and the women who habituate cafes, or cabarets. The last mentioned are the exclusive set, although they mingle freely with the women from the immoral houses. These two sets, however, seemingly abhor the presence of the dance hall women.

Cabarets are practically a new feature in the Tenderloin of New Orleans, having been in existence for about two years. Dance halls have had several years' life in the city. The cabaret idea was first exploited in the rear of a saloon at Basin and Iberville. Formerly little beer gardens occupied the rear portion of the saloons, but an enterprising girl—a castoff of the stage—conceived the idea of making a living by singing in the Tenderloin. The laws prohibited a woman entering the barroom, consequently she gained permission from the owner to sing in the beer garden.

This culminated in the establishment of the miniature restaurants in the rear of the saloons, with a small, raised platform in one corner of the room. On this raised platform, cheap vaudeville actors gather and sing, put on small sketches and generally amuse the throngs which gathers for the tips they receive in the trays passed among the drinkers and diners occasionally. In these places the latest song hits are exploited by energetic entertainers before they are sung on the stage. Many of these entertainers who have permanent positions are in the hire of the various popular music publishing houses.

Here women from houses and women living outside of the Tenderloin restrictions gather and meet in a general Bohemian atmosphere. It is in these places, also, that some chorus girls and soubrettes and some real actors gather following a night's performance to enjoy the evening. During their stay in the places they generally entertain their fellows in art by a rendition of their latest songs, a skit from their sketch, or some clever bit of stage work.

From the cabarets these crowds generally go in bodies to the dance halls and while away an hour among themselves. Although this environment is higher than the dance halls, it constitutes a portion of the Tenderloin, and similar places are run to a good advantage as far away from North Rampart, which is known as the dead line, as Dauphine Street.

Two Held for Murder.

Last night Anthony Battastina, a saloon-keeper, of Bienville and Franklin, who was charged with the murder of Harry Parker, and William Morris, a bartender, who is charged with shooting Charles Parker, were removed to the Parish Prison on the order of Superintendent of Police Reynolds.

PUBLIC DISGUST.

Police Think That Good Reason for Closing Dives.

That the dance hall is a thing of the past as far as New Orleans is concerned was the positive statement made last night by Superintendent James W. Reynolds. "As long as the operators of the places were willing and able to conduct them properly," said Superintendent Reynolds, "the police had no objection and the resorts were tolerated, but now that they have shown a disposition to operate outside of the law, it is evident that the public has become disgusted, and I have determined to close all places where men and women of the underworld congregate in nightly orgies."

The halls were operated under a double license of restaurant and dance hall and were in existence for several years past. Following the disgraceful double murder and the wounding of several frequenters of the places yesterday Superintendent Reynolds immediately issued an edict calling for the prompt closing of all dance halls in the city and revoking all permits thereto. In consequence all such places were closed yesterday morning at 11 o'clock.

Commissioner Newman denounced the disgraceful shooting in no uncertain terms, and was highly in accord with the views expressed by Superintendent Reynolds regarding the closing of the dance halls.

"While I refrained from interfering in the running of the places," said Commissioner Newman, "I have always felt that such resorts are a disgrace to a community, and I heartily approve Superintendent Reynolds in wishing to clear the city of all such places."

Bibliographical Note

Upon publication of this book, most of the documentary material on which it is based will be donated to the Rare Book Division of the Howard-Tilton Memorial Library at Tulane University. This donation will include, it should be added, hundreds and indeed thousands of relevant photographs and other artifacts omitted from the book for one reason or another. Microfilm copies of all known issues of the *Mascot* have been given to this library, to the Louisiana State Museum, and to the New Orleans Public Library. The last named institution is especially rich in contemporary newspaper holdings—the *Sunday Sun*, the New Orleans *Item*, the New Orleans *Picayune*, the New Orleans *Times*, *Figaro*, the *True Delta*, the *Delta*, the *Crescent*, the *Tribune*, the *Courier*, and the *Louisiana Weekly*—all of which were consulted by the author and are available to any serious researcher.

The Storyville researcher can spare himself the trouble of seeking to consult the photo files of the New Orleans daily papers (the *Times-Picayune, et al.*), since they have maintained no such files for the period under consideration. Investigation of the New Orleans plat books, birth records, death certificates, police records, etc. in the appropriate municipal offices will prove to be almost as fruitless: the records, insofar as they concern Storyville and the people connected with it directly or indirectly, have been vandalized.

A law of the State of Louisiana makes it impossible to determine (officially) who owned particular real estate. However, the geographical reconstruction of the District (what was where) and the placing of its inhabitants (who was where, and when) was accomplished by my reading in their entirety, name by name and address by address, the annual volumes of *Soard's City Directory* from 1894 through 1919. This directory, though not exciting reading, is a corrective to such publications as the *Blue Book* and the *Sunday Sun*, with their many misspelled names and incorrect addresses (as even the inattentive reader must have noted in the representative extracts reprinted in this volume). Having said that, I must hasten to add that the red-light journalism of Storyville (and, for the pre-Storyville period, the

Mascot) constitutes an invaluable source of information—if cross checked against *Soard's*.

Much of the present work—perhaps most of it—is based on information supplied by some hundreds of individuals personally familiar with one aspect of the District or another, usually at first-hand. Such oral testimony has to be used with caution, of course. When documentary corroboration was not available, the assertions of the various informants were not accepted as even possibly true unless affirmed by two or more individuals not known to each other. A wealth of material, much of it of great interest, has been omitted for lack of such corroboration.

Among these informants, approximately seventy had what can be termed a close association with Storyville per se—madams, prostitutes, pimps, regular customers. They must remain forever anonymous, but I take this opportunity to thank them, one and all.

Jazzmen Johnny Wiggs and Raymond Burke told me what they knew about the District, as did the late Paul Barbarin, Peter Bocage, Walter Decou, Abby "Chinee" Foster, Charlie Love, Manuel Manetta, Johnny St. Cyr, and Tony Parenti. In addition, I have incorporated material from private conversations with musicians that occurred long before I began to consider research for this work. Some of them—alas, too few—are still among us. Among those who gave me their own slants on Storyville were Louis Armstrong, Joseph "Kid" Avery, George Baquet, Sidney Bechet, Thomas "Mutt" Carey, Oscar "Papa" Celestin, Lee Collins, Warren "Baby" Dodds, George "Pops" Foster, Ed "Montudi" Garland, Albert Glenny, Willie "Bunk" Johnson, John Lindsay, Edward "Kid" Ory, Alphonse Picou, Charles "Sunny" Henry, Oscar "Chicken" Henry, William "Bebe" Ridgley, Luis Russell, Ferdinand "Jelly Roll" Morton, Frank Amacker, Papa John Joseph, Albert Warner, Avery "Kid" Howard, Punch Miller, John Casimir, George Lewis, Spencer Williams, Clarence Williams, George Brunis, Abbie and Merritt Brunies, Jack "Papa" Laine, Larry and Harry Shields, Tony Giardina, Willie Humphrey, *et al.*

The testimony of guitarist Danny Barker, both written and oral, has been of enormous value. His as yet unpublished memoirs—unpublished but widely quoted and, sad to say, plagiarized by some—constitute what must eventually come to be recognized as a major body of jazz poetry. He is generous with his genius, both as a writer and as a musician, and he made his writings freely available to me.

Published works touching on the subject of Storyville and kindred matters vary greatly in quality. Those that I have found to be the most useful are, obviously, the ones from which I have quoted the most liberally: the WPA Writers' Project masterpiece, prepared under the direction of Lyle Saxon, *Gumbo Ya Ya* (New York: Houghton Mifflin Company, 1945, 1973), Alan Lomax's (and Jelly Roll Morton's) *Mister Jelly Roll* (New York: Hawthorn Books, Inc., 1950, 1973), and the invaluable compilation of personal statements from many sources, *Hear Me Talkin' to Ya*, edited by Nat Shapiro and Nat Hentoff (New York: Holt, Rinehart & Winston, 1955).

A number of published books were consulted, among them Walter C. Allen's *King Joe Oliver* (London: Sidgwick & Jackson, Ltd.); Herbert Asbury's *The French Quarter* (New York: Knopf, 1936) and *Sucker's Progress* (New York: Dodd, Mead & Co., 1938); Sidney Bechet's *Treat it Gentle* (New York: Hill & Wang, 1960); Rudi Blesh's *Shining Trumpets* (New York: Knopf, 1946); Rudi Blesh's and Harriet Janis' *They All Played Ragtime* (New York: Grove Press, 1959); Warren "Baby" Dodds' *The Baby Dodds Story* (Los Angeles: Contemporary, 1959); Adolphe W. Roberts' *Lake Pontchartrain* (New York: Bobbs, Merrill, 1946); Charles Edward Smith's and Fred Ramsey's *Jazzmen* (New York: Harcourt, Brace, 1939); Robert Tallant's *Mardi Gras* (New York: Doubleday, 1948), *Voo Doo in New Orleans* (New York: Macmillan, 1946), and *Ready to Hang* (New York: Harper, 1952). The novels *Count Roller Skates* by Thomas Sancton (New York: Doubleday, 1956) and *For Men Only* by Beth Brown (Kendall, 1930), although avowedly fictional, seem to reflect a reasonable sense of responsibility to history—at least in spirit.

Among the periodicals consulted were: *Esquire, The Record Changer, Eureka, Collier's Weekly, Life, Jazzways, The Jazzfinder, The Jazz Record, Jazz Information, True,* and *The Second Line.*

Acknowledgments

My first acknowledgments are to the many musicians and others having personal knowledge of Storyville who provided circumstantial information about the place—its ways, its state of mind. Their names—most of them, at least—have been given elsewhere in these pages. Without their invaluable contribution, this work would lack much, perhaps most, of whatever merit it may have.

Many individuals helped significantly at various stages. I am especially grateful to Bill Russell, who besides starting me on the project (a story in itself, one that should be told someday), made freely available all of his own rare photographs and documents; Larry Borenstein for a multitude of helps; Barbara Reid, who made her collection of old New Orleans city directories available on a take-out basis; Robert W. Greenwood and Dorothy Whittemore of Tulane University's Howard-Tilton Memorial Library for research assistance; Maggie Fisher, whose stenographic talents went far beyond typing and into areas where the exercise of intelligence became a factor in the author's confidence; Jerome Cushman and the staff of the New Orleans Public Library for research assistance; Mary Mitchell Rose for skilled photo processing; Diana Rose for execution of the maps; the photo-magicians at the Charles A. Franck Company; the late Dr. Edmond Souchon for many favors; the late C. E. Frampkin of the Louisiana State Museum; the late Felix Kuntz, whose private collection of Storyville relics and papers was freely placed at my disposal; Dr. E. A. "Pancho" Carner for tedious fact-checking.

I am grateful to the following individuals and institutions for permission to reproduce photographs from their collections: City Archives Department, New Orleans Public Library; the Edmond Souchon and Maurice Dekemel collections, New Orleans Jazz Museum; Duncan Schiedt; Danny Barker; Mrs. John Menville; American Music Records; Dave Scherman of Time, Inc.; Scoop Kennedy; and John W. "Knocky" Parker.

Index

O'Brien, May, 34, 62, 100, 101, 207
O'Conor, Inspector, 67
Octoroon Queen, 80
Odd Fellows Hall, **22**, 23, 62, **142**
O'Deall, Lillie, 102
O'Ferrell, Trilby, **137**
Okey Poke, 55
Oliver, Joseph "King," 87, **88, 94,** 107, 119–121, 122, 123, 124, 204
Olivia, the Oyster Dancer, 85
Olivier, Adam, 111, 204
Olympia Band, 107
One-Eye Sal, 10
O'Neil, Dan, 9, 10
O'Neill, Corporal, 27
One-Legged Duffy, 15, 27
101 Ranch, The, 67, 72, **94,** 95, **169**
102 Ranch, The, 68, 72, **94,** 120, 146, **169,** 213, 214
Onery Bob, 55
Original Creole Serenaders, The, 69
Original Crescent Palace, The, 102
Original Dixieland Band, The, 92
Original Dixieland Jazz Band, The, 69, 122
Original Tuxedo Orchestra, The, 95
Ory, Edward "Kid," 69, 87, **88, 94,** 105, 120, 122, 124, 204, 216
Otero, Richard, 49
Owens, Ray, 62, 72, 87, **89,** 101, 102, **138,** 145, 205
O, You Beautiful Doll, 164

Palao, James A., 69, 204
Palao, Jimmy, 122
Palmer, Roy, 204
Papalia family, 123
Papaloos, Madame, 53
Parenti, Tony, 122, 123, 216
Parker, Charles, 67, 213
Parker, Harry, 67, 68, 213–215
Parker, John W. "Knocky," **173,** 217
Parker, Mrs., and daughters, 19, 102
Parker, Willie, 204
Parker Brothers, 55
Parker/Phillips, 125
Passing Show, 111
Paulding School, 43
Payne, Richard, 204
Peachanno, 55
Pearls, The, 113
Pecora, Santo, 122
Pecora family, 123
Pelican Four, 132
Pensacola Kid, 58, 94
Perdido Street, 177, 178
Perez, Manuel, 107, 117, 120, **121–**122, 204
Perfumed Garden, The, 29
Perry, Alice, **174**
Pete Lala's Cafe, 72, **88,** 90, 115, 120, 121, 122, 123, 146
Peterson, Addie, 19
Petit, Buddy, 122, 123, 178, 204
Petit, Joe, 204
Peyton, Henry, 122, 204
Philbrook, Mary E., 65
Philip, Joseph "One-Eye Babe," 204
Philippa Street, 102
Phillips, Billy, 55, 67, 68, 95, 120, 124, 125, 152, 153, 213–214
Phillips, Philip J., 68
Phillips' Café, 72, **94, 169**

Phoenix, The, 72, 100, 101, **141**
Piazza, "Countess" Willie V., x, xi, 52-53, 59, 62, 63, 71, 72, 82, 84, **85,** 99, 111, 115, 116, 117, **138,** 144, 146, 155, 158, 163, 164, 166, **167,** 168, 177, 193–203, 208
Picayune. See *New Orleans Daily Picayune.*
Picayune House, 102
Pickett, Emma, 8, 9, 102
Picou, Alphonse, 122, 124, 204, 216
Pierre, Joe, 120, 204
Pig Ankle, The, 72, 87
Pigeon, Euphrasine (Lottie), 54, 55
Piggy, 55
Piron, Armand J., 117, 119, 204
Pixley, Esther, 129
Plummer, Sadie, 101
Ponds sisters, 130
Pontchartrain Beach Amusement Park, 85
Poodle Dog Café, The, 72, 92
Porter, Maggie, 130
Power, Tyrone, Sr., 158
Poyner, Daisy, 130
Predonce, Johnny, 204
Press Club, The, 172
Preston, Walter, 204
Pretty Baby, 74, **91,** 111
Prevost, Abbé, 5
Prince Basile, 54, 55
Progressive Union, 64
Protection Oil Company, 44
Prout, Lou, 101, 102, 207
Provenzano's Saloon, 102
Pupsy, 55

Queen Emmette, 133
Queen Gertie, 24, 26, 27
Queen of the Demi-monde, 80
Queen of the Octoroons, 135
Queen of the Voodoos, 54

Ragas, Henry, 92, 122
Rainbow Ray, 130
Raines, Josie, 27
Rainey, Ma, 105
Raleigh Rye, **xii,** 160, 212
Rampart Street, **71,** 102, 133, 135, 170
Ramsey, Frederic, 120, 216
Randella, Florence "Snooks," 95, 102, 146, 158
Rankin, Hugh, 204
Raphael, Bernard, 204
Rapp, Butler "Guyé," 204
Raw Head, 55
Ray, Diana, 77, 98
Raymond, Lou, 132
Razzy Dazzy Spasm Band, **58**
Ready Money, 55, 94
Ready to Hang, 216
Record Changer, The, 53, 111, 216
Record Oil Refining Company, 44
Red Book, The, 135
Red Hot Peppers. See Jelly Roll Morton's Red Hot Peppers.
Red-Light Liz, 9
Red Light Social Club, 22, 23, 24
Redmond, May, 102
Red Top, 130
Reed, Abbie, 102, 131
Reed, Gentle Annie, 101, 102

Reed, Kitty, 27, 101, 102
Reed, Sadie, **126**
Regency Shoes, **76**
Reid, Barbara, 217
Rena, Henry "Kid," 123, 204
Reynolds, James W., 214, 215
Rice, Johnny, 55, 122
Rice's Café, 72, 90, **121,** 122, 146
Rich, Mary, 15
Richards, Frank, 119
Richards, Lillie, 16, 17
Ridgely, William "Bebe," 204, 216
Ridley, Eliza, 131
Ringrose, William B., 34, 35
Ripley, Beulah, 48
Roberts, Adolphe W., 216
Robertson, George "Boar Hog," 58
Robertson, George "Goumar," 119
Robertson, Zue, 120, 204
Robertson Street, 96, 102, 159, **173, 180**
Robinson, Oscar, 204
Robinson's Dime Museum, **104**
Rob Roy Opera Company, 129
Roddy, George S., 133
Rodrigues, Marie, 18
Rogers, Ernest, 92, 120, 204
Rogers, Hattie, 115, 119
Roig, Lola, 101
Romaine, Florence, 101
Romantic New Orleans, 172
Roody Doody, 55
Roosevelt, Theodore, 152
Roppolo, Leon, 122
Rose, Diana, 217
Rose, Etta, 133
Rose, Irma, 19
Rose, Mary Mitchell, 217
Rosenthal, 214
Rosenthal, Minnie, 131, 208
Ross, Annie, 102, **139,** 208
Ross, Kid, 84, 106, 117, 204
Ross, Miss, **139**
Rowe, Bob, 55, 94
Royal Garden Blues, 117
Rubean, Lutzie, 204
Rudabarger, Fanny, 65
Rudy, Fanny, 65
Runiart, Garne, 102
Russell, Burke, 119
Russell, Estelle, **126**
Russell, Luis, **71,** 216
Russell, Ollie, 101
Russell, William, v, 117, 217
Ruth, Babe, 61

Sailing Down the Chesapeake Bay, 74
St. Claire, Lou, 101
St. Cyr, Johnny, 107, 109, 115, 123, 204, 216
St. James Infirmary Blues, 94
St. James Methodist Church, **76**
St. John Street, 102
St. Louis Cemetery No. 1, **76,** 85
St. Louis Cemetery No. 2, **76,** 101
St. Louis Street, 37, **76,** 93, 95, 102, 170, **171,** 172
St. Peter Street, 173
St. Philip Street, 181
Sancton, Thomas, 52, **70,** 216
Sanford, Gertie, 98
Santiago, Willie, **71,** 204

Storyville, New Orleans

was composed in Linotype Caledonia and Bodoni

by Printers Service Company,

printed by Benson Printing Company,

and bound by Nicholstone Book Bindery,

all of Nashville, Tennessee.

Display type was set by the ad shop, New Orleans,

and the jacket was printed by

Commercial Printing Company, Birmingham, Alabama.